50 GREAT CITY WALKS

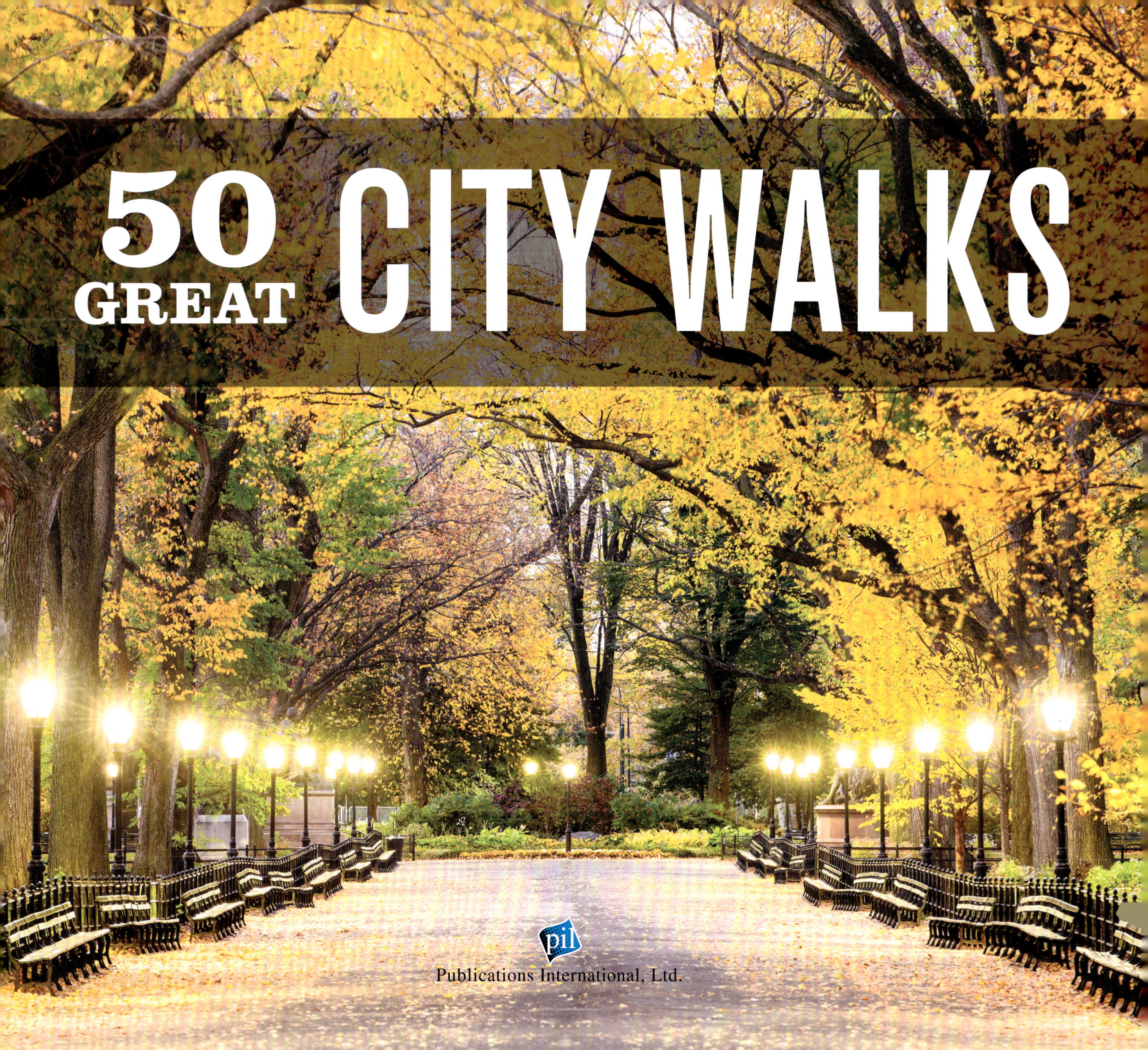

Publications International, Ltd.

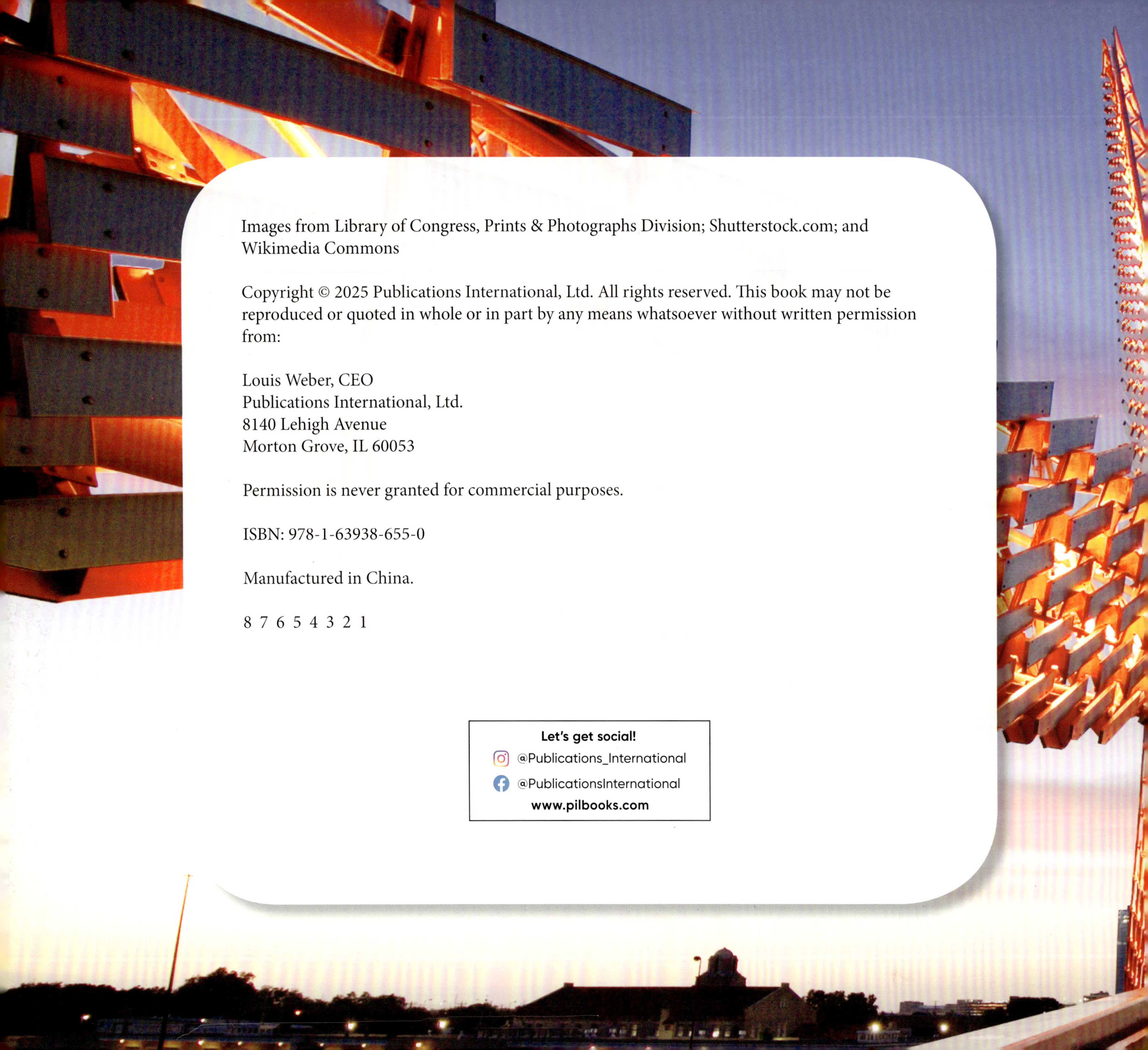

Images from Library of Congress, Prints & Photographs Division; Shutterstock.com; and Wikimedia Commons

Louis Weber, CEO
Publications International, Ltd.
8140 Lehigh Avenue
Morton Grove, IL 60053

ISBN: 978-1-63938-655-0

Manufactured in China.

8 7 6 5 4 3 2 1

Let's get social!

@Publications_International

@PublicationsInternational

www.pilbooks.com

Table of Contents

Northeast

Southeast

South

Midwest and Plains

Mountain States and Southwest

Pacific

Introduction

Our country's cities are full of sights to see and places to explore, from historic architecture to world-class museums to sculpture gardens to shopping districts. *50 Great City Walks* compiles fifty routes and trails in more than forty American cities to give inspiration and information. You'll find a mix of walks: some short and others longer; some family-friendly and others more strenuous hikes; some focused on history and others on modern culture. And though these are urban walks, you'll find a lot of natural beauty in walks along waterways and through botanic gardens and urban parks.

For each walk, we give some basic information such as length and points of interest you might see along the way, so you can decide if the walk would be one you'd like to take. Vivid photographs show the sights and add extra information.

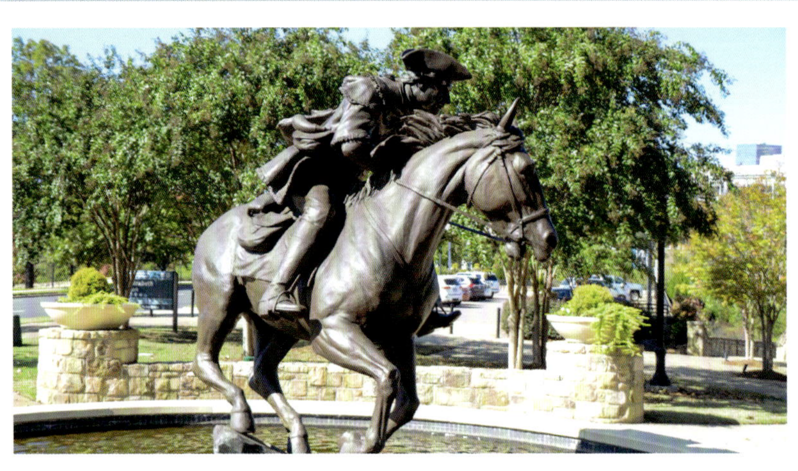

Liberty Walk, Charlotte

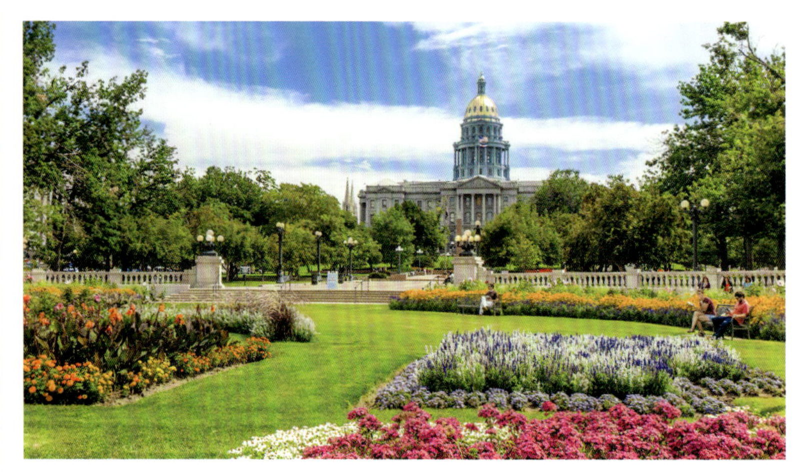

Colorado State Capitol building

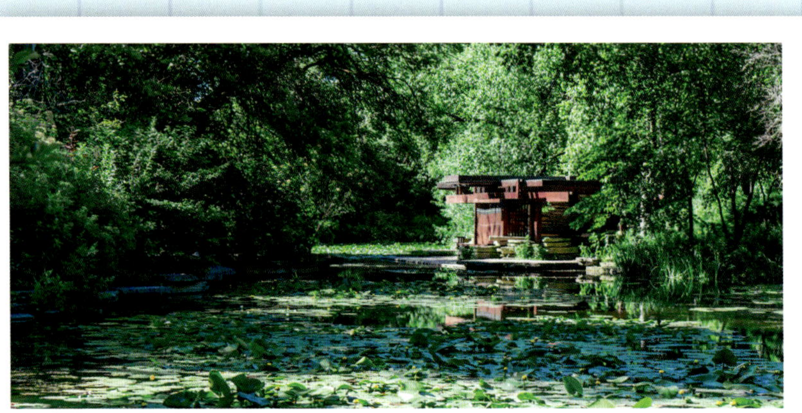

The Alfred Caldwell Lily Pool in Lincoln Park, Chicago

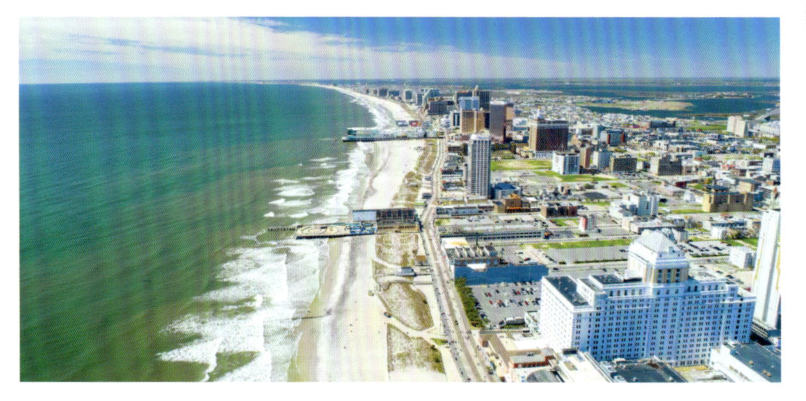

Atlantic City Boardwalk

Some of the routes you'll find include:

- Walks with a focus on local or national history, like Baltimore's Heritage Walk, Boston's Freedom Trail, the Memphis Heritage Trail, and Charlotte's Liberty Walk
- Walks along scenic waterways, like Indianapolis's Canal Walk, Wichita's Arkansas River Path, and Chicago's Riverwalk
- Walks through massive urban parks with gardens, zoos, and museums, like Houston's Hermann Park, San Francisco's Golden Gate Park, and Portland's Washington Park
- Walks along multi-use trails, like the Jack Markell Trail in Delaware and the Ann and Roy Butler Hike and Bike Trail in Texas
- And much more!

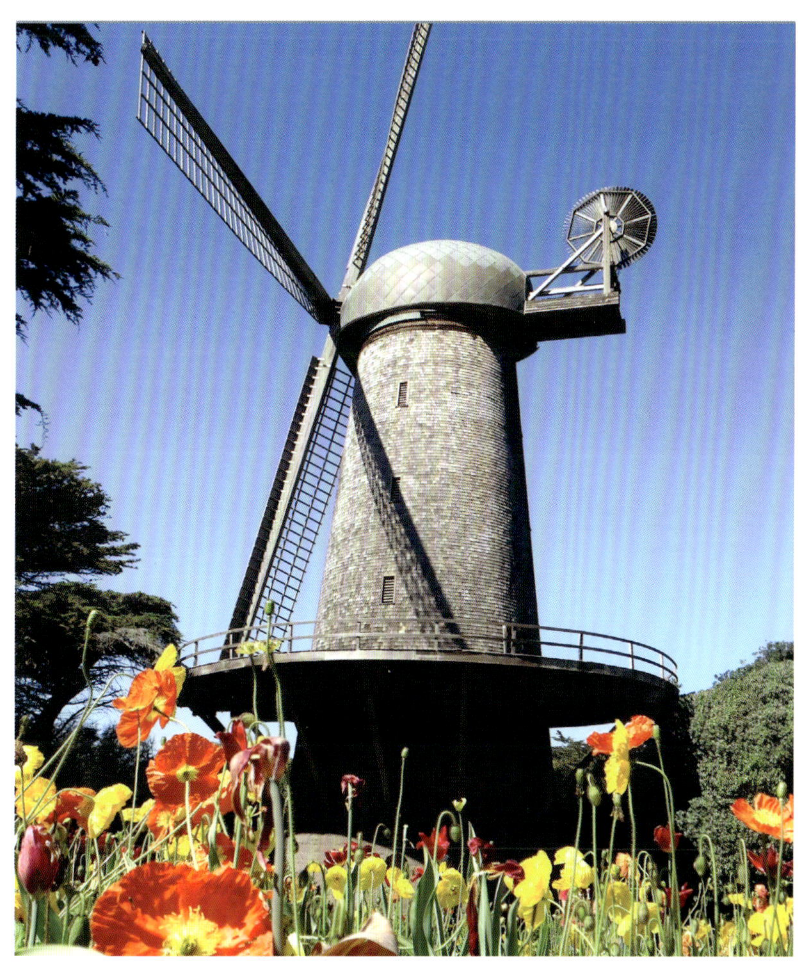

Windmill at Golden Gate Park, San Francisco

If you decide to do one of these walks in person, here are a few things to keep in mind:

- For each walk, we've given several points of interest—places like museums, zoos, and botanical gardens. For walks with many points of interest, we do not expect that you would be able to explore all of them in depth on the same day, but instead select a few of them.
- While we give an approximate length for each walk, it does not account for the time you might spend walking inside a given attraction, like a museum or zoo.
- Smaller attractions like house museums may have limited opening hours, or only be open on certain days of the week. As you plot your walk, check opening hours for any place you'd like to visit. Some sites may also require advance tickets.
- Always be considerate in residential areas. Many historic homes that are architecturally significant, for example, may be private residences. Do not walk on private property without permission.
- For longer walks, carry water with you, and food if needed!

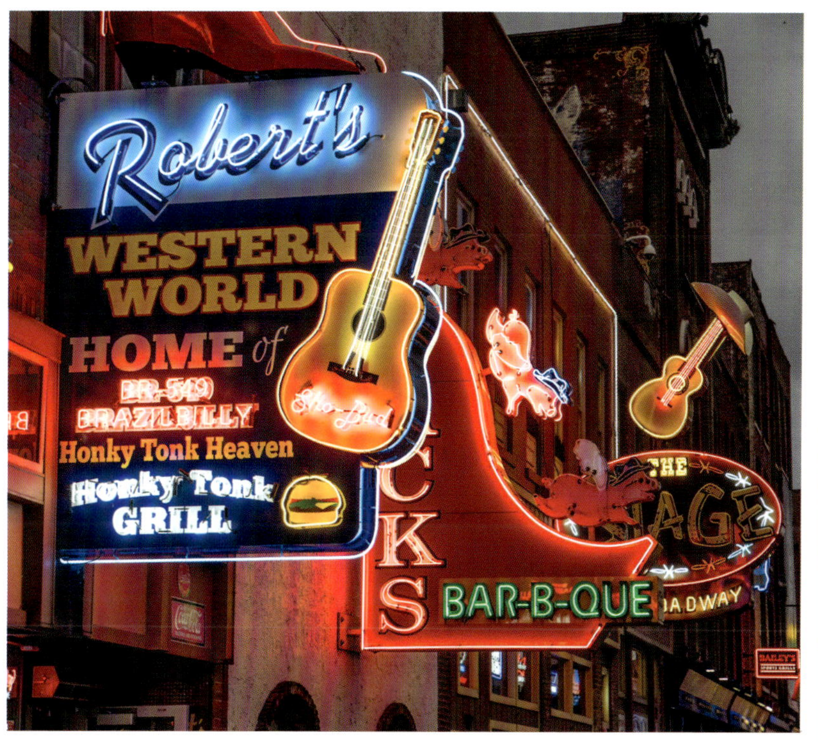

Broadway, Nashville

Freedom Trail

Location: Boston, Massachusetts
Length: 2.5 miles
Start point: Boston Common (Boston)
End point: Bunker Hill Monument (Charleston)

Boston natives and visitors can follow the red brick road that commemorates the deep, rich history of Boston, Massachusetts, and the United States. Boston played a crucial role during the Revolutionary War, and a number of sites on the pedestrian path pay specific tribute to that time, from the Old North Church where two lanterns were hung to signal information to Paul Revere and other midnight riders to the Old South Meeting House where the Boston Tea Party was planned. However, many of the sites also have historical importance from before or after the American Revolution, from Boston Common, the first public city park in the United States, to the Old Corner Bookstore that was once home to the publisher of works by native sons Henry David Thoreau and Nathaniel Hawthorne in the 1800s.

The Freedom Trail was developed in the early 1950s. Journalist William Schofield sparked the idea, while Mayor John Hynes implemented it. Today, tens of thousands of people each year walk the pedestrian trail and learn more about the history of the city, state, and country. Interested parties can take a paid 90-minute tour—led by a guide garbed in historical costumes—offered by the Freedom Trail Foundation, which provides an overview of the exterior grounds of featured sites. Those interested in exploring sites in more depth will want to take a full day, or even two, to wander the Freedom Trail themselves and stop inside each site. The sites are run by an assortment of different entities, and some do charge for entrance. For those looking for a quick bite along the way, Faneuil Hall is home to Quincy Market, a food hall with plenty of tasty options.

Points of Interest

Boston Common
Massachusetts State House
Park Street Church
Granary Burying Ground
King's Chapel and King's Chapel Burying Ground
Boston Latin School Site / Benjamin Franklin Statue
Old Corner Bookstore
Old South Meeting House
Old State House
Boston Massacre Site
Faneuil Hall
Paul Revere House
Old North Church
Copp's Hill Burying Ground
USS *Constitution*
Bunker Hill Monument

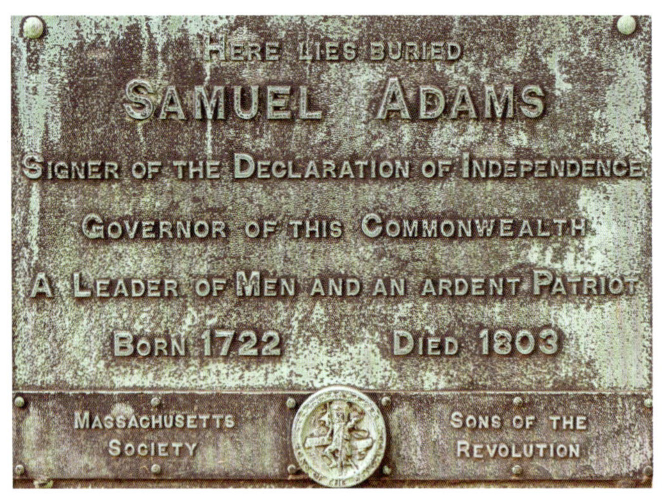

A number of luminaries are buried in Granary Burying Ground next to Park Street Church, including Paul Revere, Samuel Adams, John Hancock, Peter Faneuil, and Crispus Attucks and the other victims of the Boston Massacre.

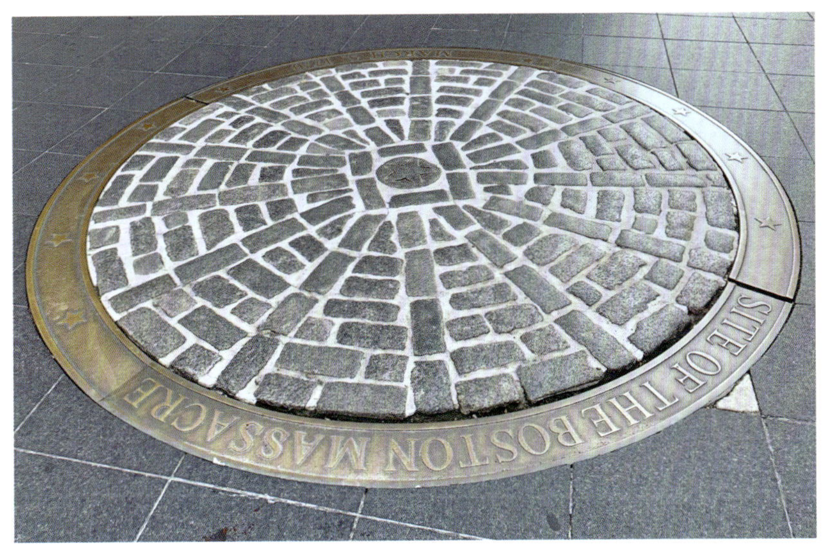

The Boston Massacre of March 5, 1770, in which British soldiers fired on an angry crowd of colonists, took place in front of the Old State House. A cobblestone circle *(above)* memorializes the event. The former State House *(below)* dates to 1713, making it the oldest of the public buildings in Boston that has survived to the present day. It currently houses a museum.

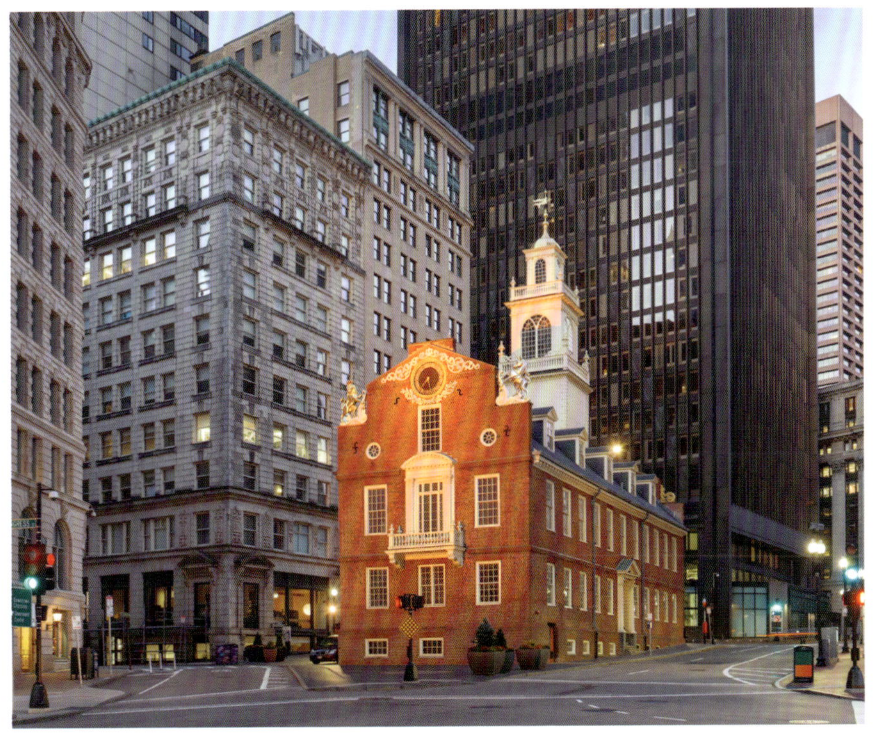

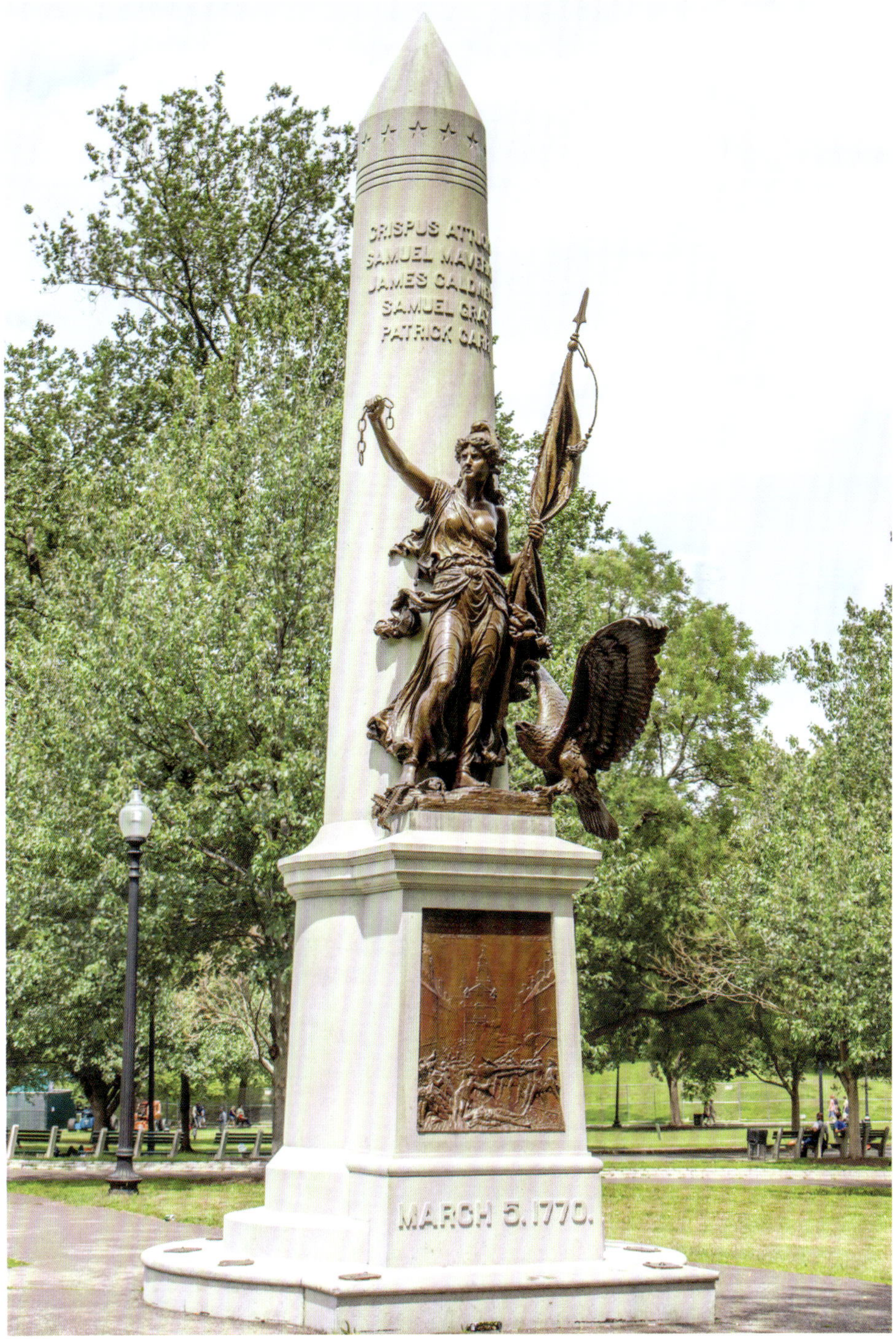

Boston Common is one of a series of parks designed by landscape architect Frederick Law Olmsted and dubbed the Emerald Necklace. Visitors can see an Augustus Saint-Gaudens monument to Robert Gould Shaw and the Black 54th Massachusetts Volunteer Infantry soldiers, a Soldiers and Sailors Monument, and this monument to the Boston Massacre.

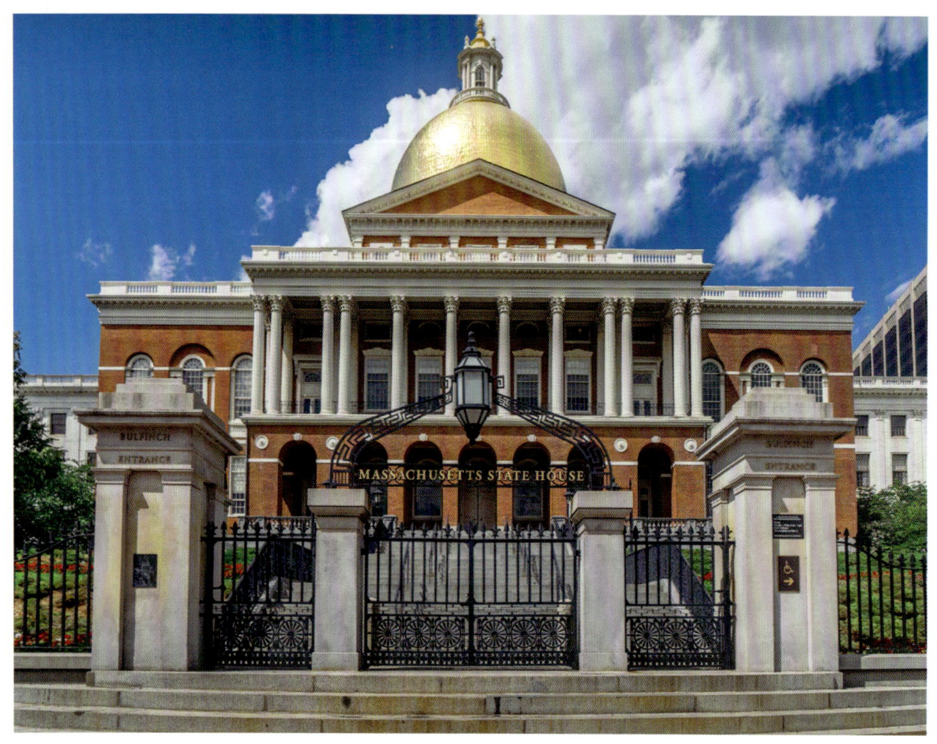

The current Massachusetts State House is home to the state legislature and the governor. It was designed by legendary architect Charles Bulfinch. The cornerstone was laid in 1795, with noted patriot Paul Revere presiding.

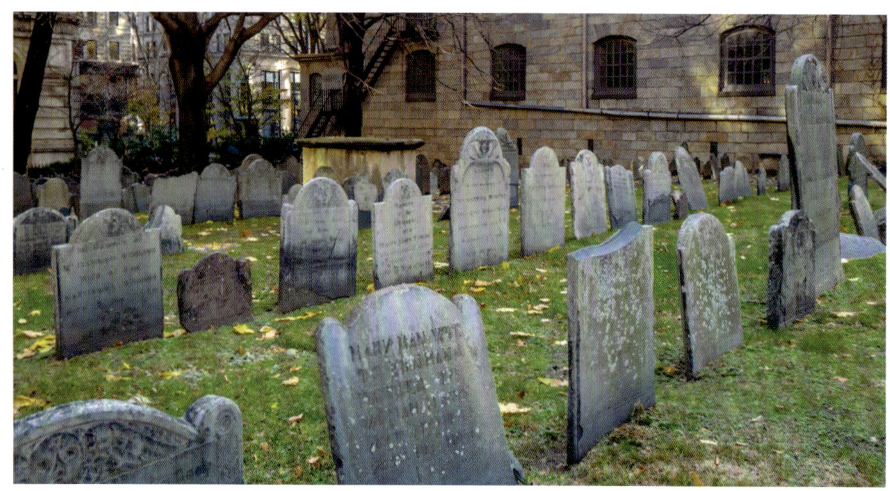

King's Chapel Burying Ground is the oldest cemetery in Boston, dating to 1630. The grave of Ralph Waldo Emerson's father William is found there, as is the grave of Mary Chilton, a Plymouth pilgrim who was reportedly the first of the *Mayflower* passengers to step ashore on Plymouth Rock.

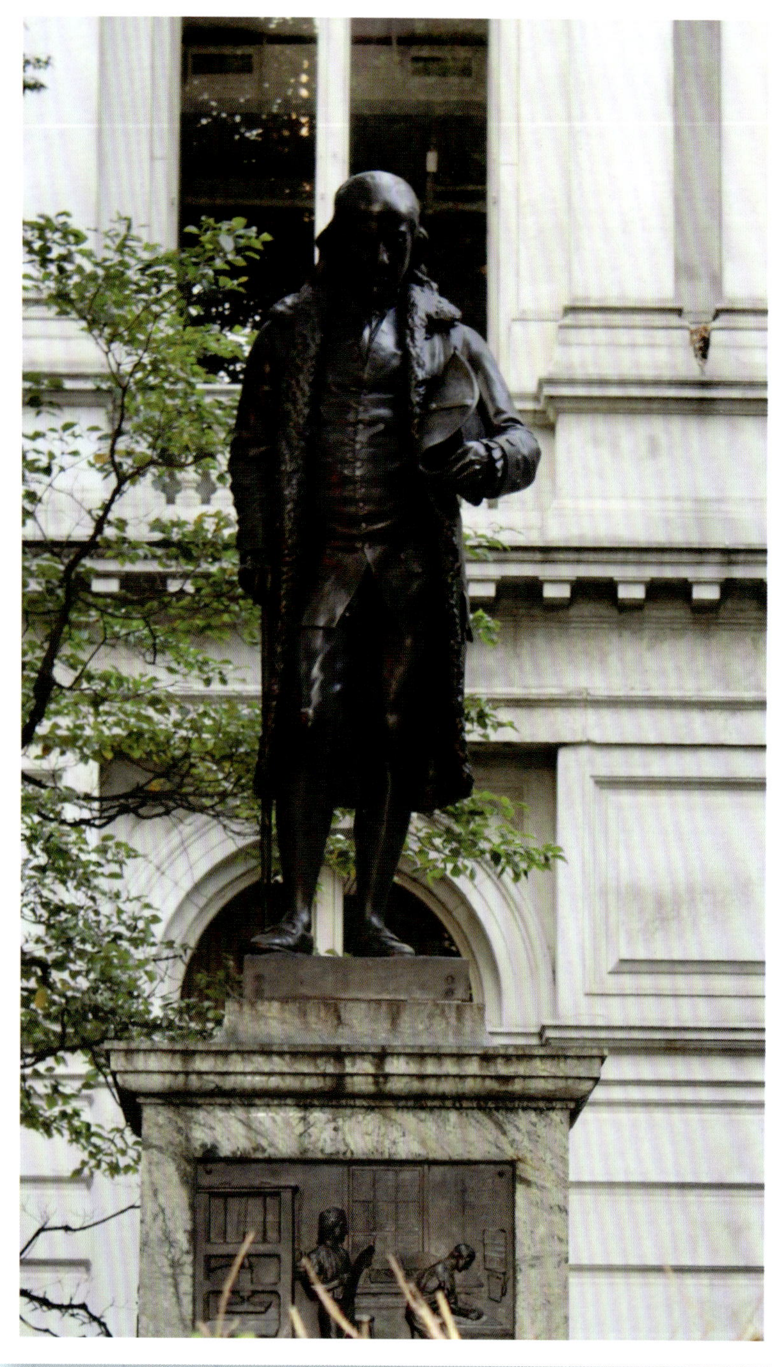

Founding Father Benjamin Franklin was born in Boston, baptized in the Old South Meeting House, and attended Boston Latin School before moving to Philadelphia at the age of 17. His statue is found in front of the Old City Hall building, which was the first location of the Boston Latin School that was founded in 1635 and continues as an educational institution today.

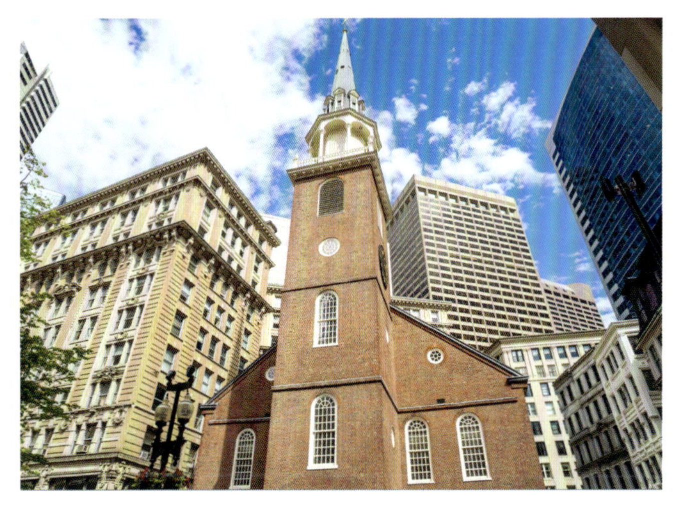

A Congregational church built the Old South Meeting House, which was completed in 1729. In the 1770s, colonists held political meetings in this large space that could fit hundreds and even thousands of people. One such meeting in 1773 was the impetus for the Boston Tea Party. Today, the building houses a museum.

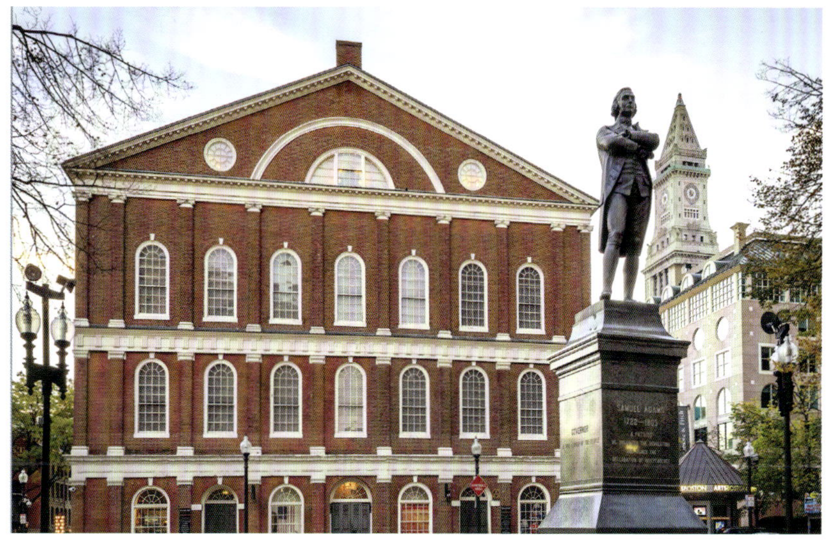

Faneuil Hall, named after merchant Peter Faneuil, was a public marketplace that also served as a place where Samuel Adams and other patriots made speeches promoting independence. Throughout the following centuries, other politicians and speakers have held events there as well.

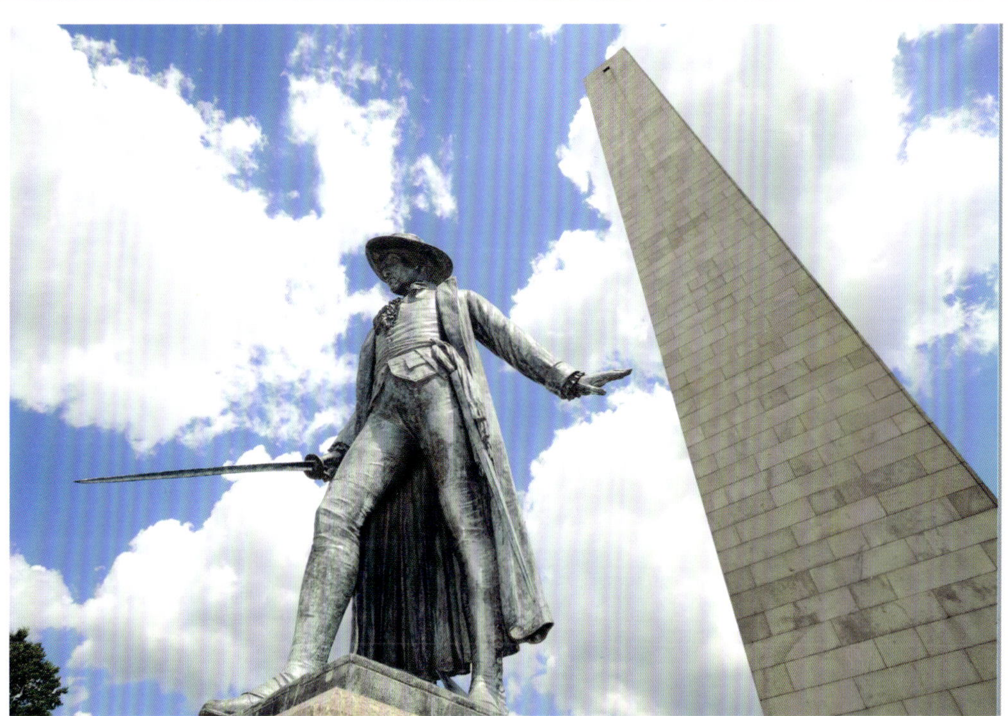

The Bunker Hill Monument in Charleston rises 221 feet. The statue portrays Colonel William Prescott, who led colonial troops during the Revolution's Battle of Bunker Hill.

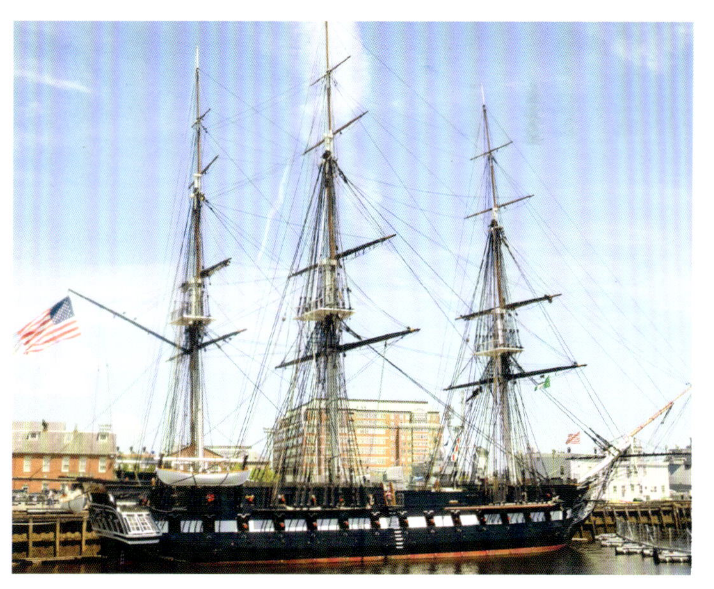

The USS *Constitution* was launched in 1797. Though retired from active service in 1881, she is still considered an active, commissioned Navy ship, and her crew is comprised of active-duty Navy members. She is most famous for her defeat of the HMS *Guerriere* during the War of 1812.

Three Museums Via Central Park

Location: Manhattan, New York City, New York
Length: 1.9 miles (museums only via Fifth Avenue); about 3 miles via Central Park paths
Start point: Museum of Modern Art
End point: Solomon R. Guggenheim Museum

For a long but satisfying day in Manhattan that intersperses artwork and natural beauty, begin at the Museum of Modern Art (MoMA), located on 53rd Street between Fifth and Sixth Avenues, where you can see famous works by Monet, Kahlo, Magritte, Matisse, Picasso, and Warhol. MoMA is the permanent home of Vincent van Gogh's *The Starry Night*, a must-see.

After your visit there, one option is to make your way directly to the Metropolitan Museum of Art, a mile and a half away via Fifth Avenue. The Metropolitan Museum of Art, familiarly known as the Met, is the largest art museum in North America, with over a million works, and you could spend several days touring its extensive holdings that include both ancient and modern art from around the world.

The Solomon R. Guggenheim Museum is also on Fifth Avenue, only a third of a mile away from the Met. The museum focuses on Impressionist, Post-Impressionist, Modern, and contemporary art. The building itself is a sight to see, as its unique architecture was designed by Frank Lloyd Wright. Fifth Avenue forms the eastern border of Central Park, so you'll get some beautiful views on your way.

For a longer day, wander through Central Park as you make your way from MoMA to the Met. Though there are larger urban parks in New York, Central Park is the most visited—not only in New York but in the United States. Central Park features nature walks, recreational activities like carriage-horse tours and the Central Park Carousel, a zoo, playgrounds, sculptures, and Belvedere Castle, which serves as both a visitor center and the home of a weather station. There are a number of food options available in Central Park, from food carts to sit-down cafés, so you can stop for a bite to eat and enjoy nature between museum visits.

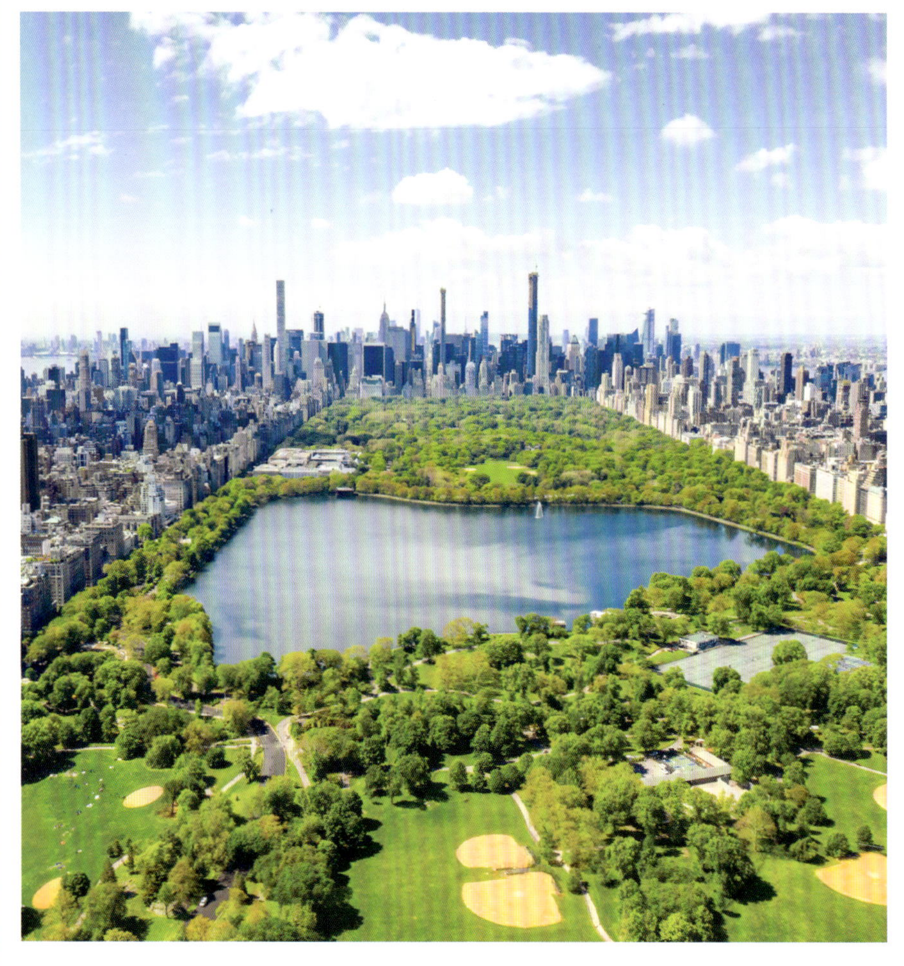

The construction of Central Park began in 1857, the work of landscape architects Frederick Law Olmsted and Calvert Vaux.

Points of Interest

Museum of Modern Art
Wollman Rink
Central Park Zoo
Central Park Carousel
Balto Statue
Sheep Meadow
Bethseda Terrace and Fountain
The Mall and Literary Walk
Belvedere Castle
Metropolitan Museum of Art
Solomon R. Guggenheim Museum

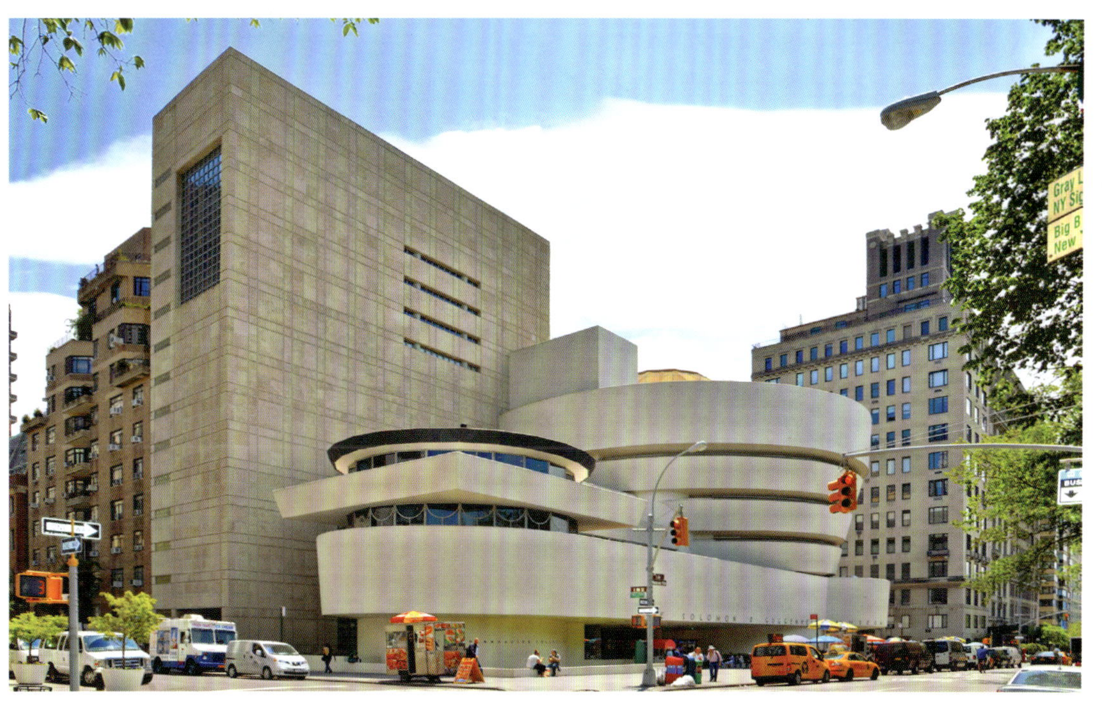

Frank Lloyd Wright worked on the Guggenheim building between 1943 and his death in 1959. It, along with seven other buildings he designed, collectively form a UNESCO World Heritage Site.

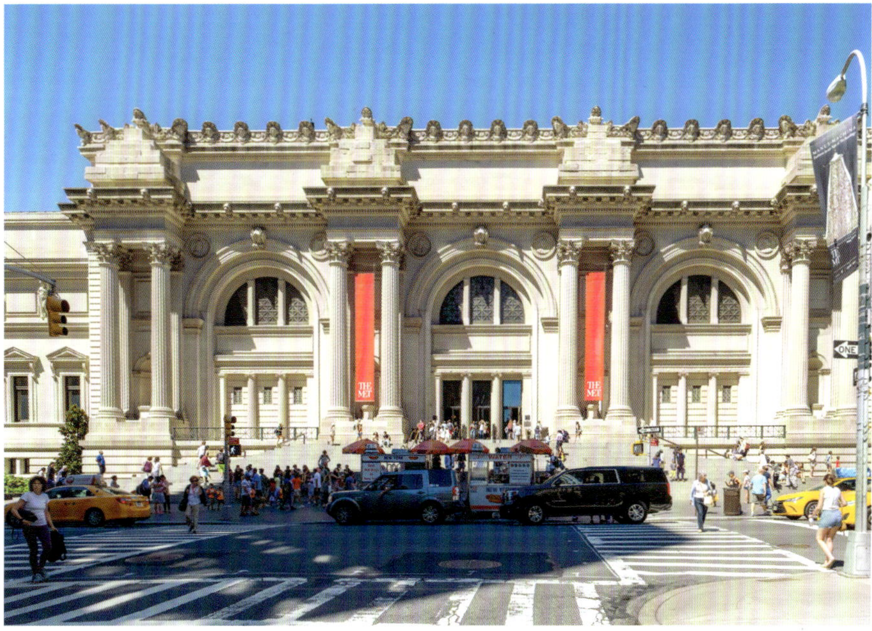

The Met was established in 1870. Its collections include paintings, sculpture, armor, pottery, costumes, and more.

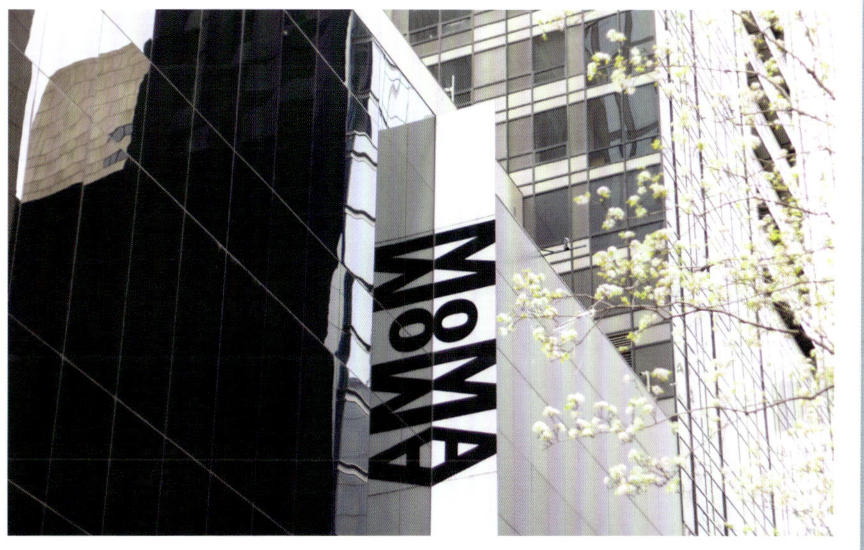

The Museum of Modern Art opened in 1929 as an institution, moving to its current home in 1939.

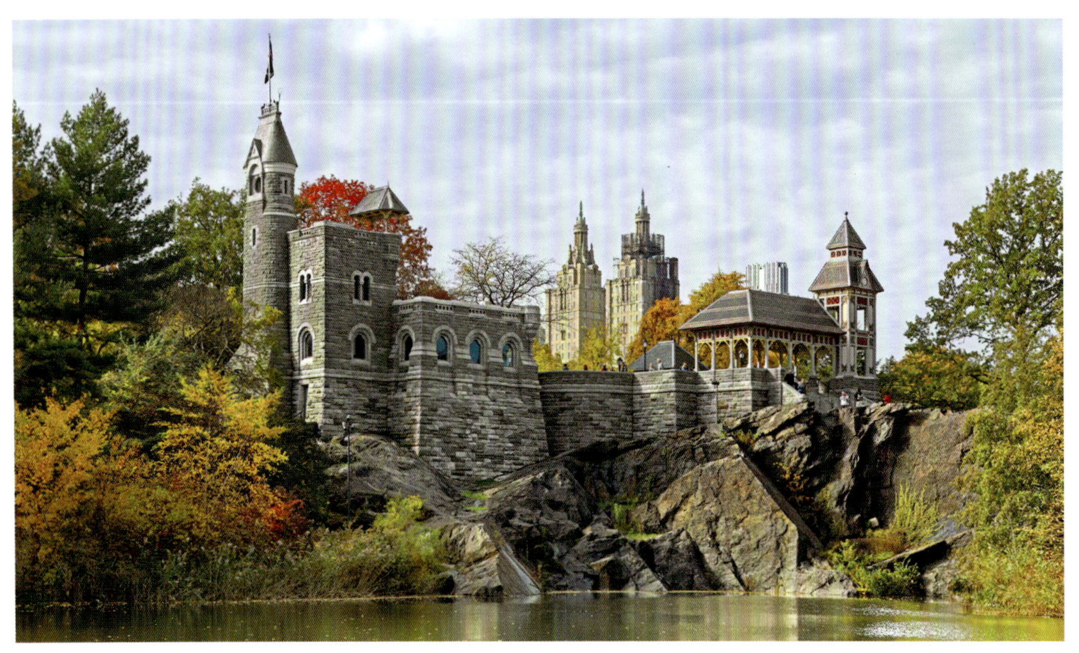

Belvedere means "beautiful view" in Italian, a fitting name for the structure designed by architects Calvert Vaux and Jacob Wrey Mould.

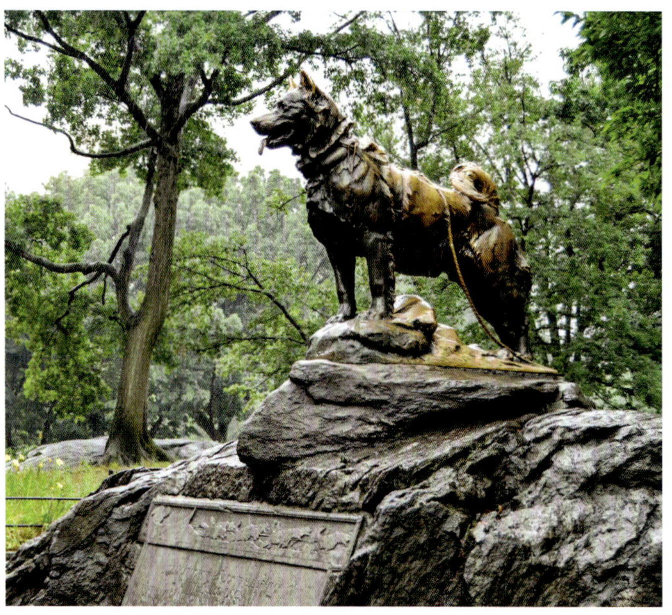

In early 1925, the Alaskan husky Balto became a canine hero when he led a team of sled dogs carrying diphtheria antitoxin to Nome, Alaska. In December 1925, his statue was erected in Central Park.

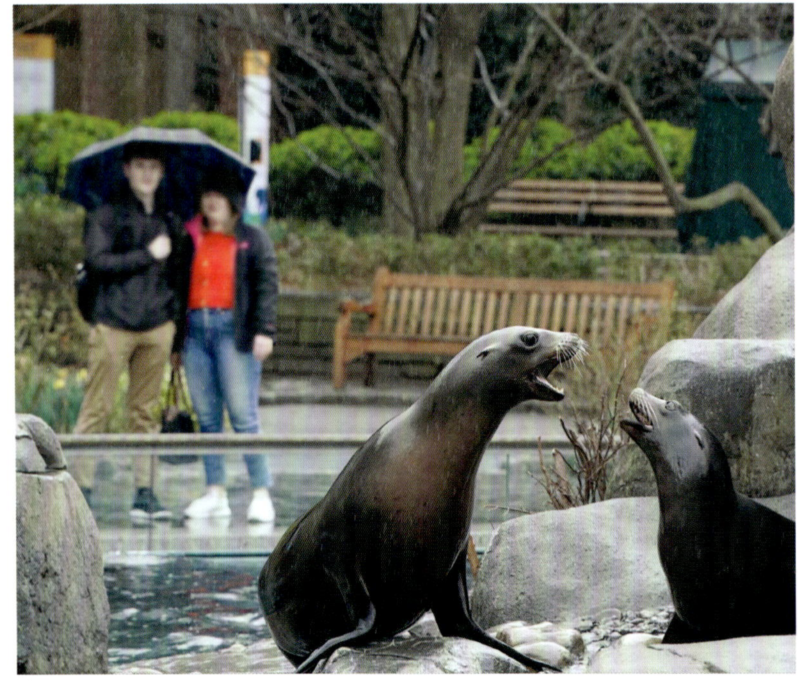

A menagerie opened in Central Park in 1864. The zoo followed in 1934.

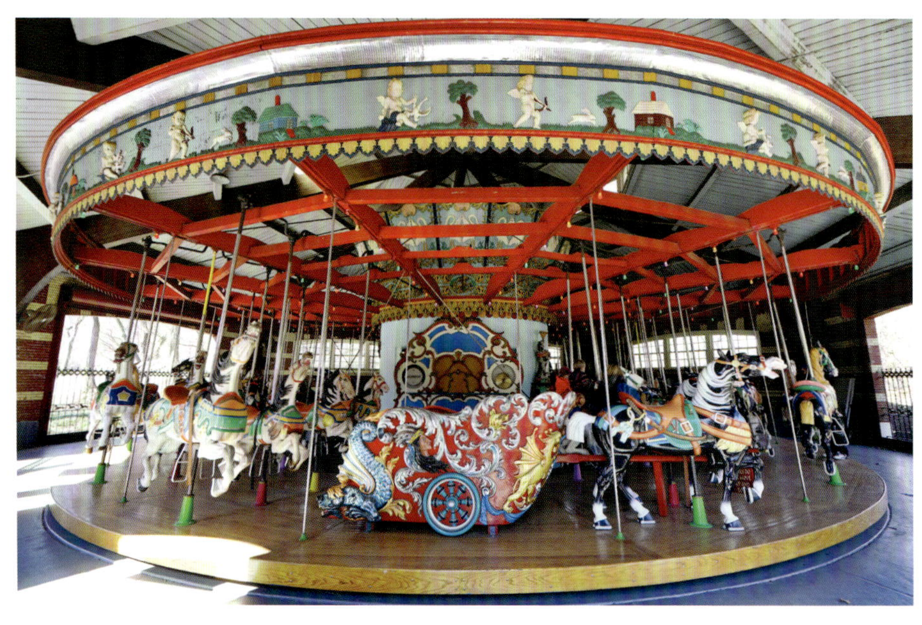

The Central Park carousel

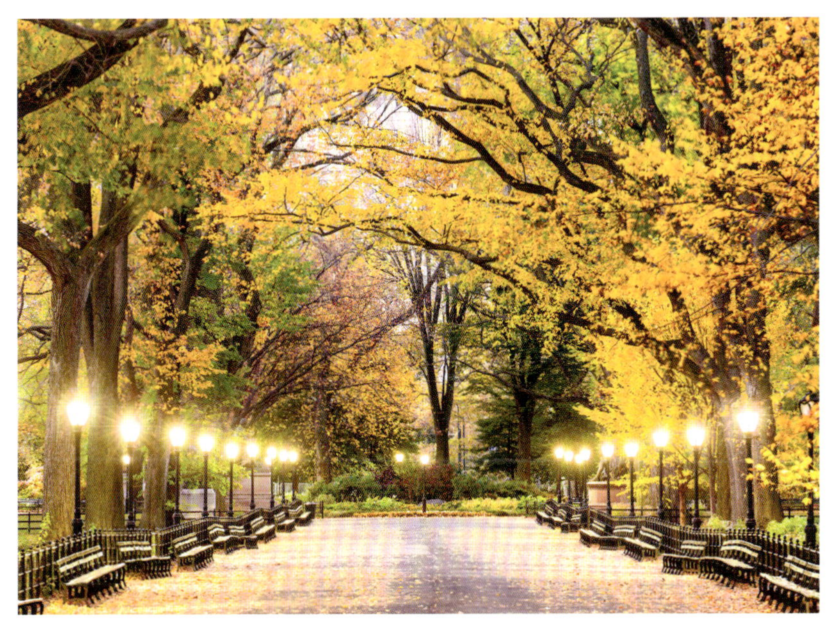

The Mall, a pedestrian walkway, is beautiful in autumn. Visitors will see a number of statues, especially statues of writers.

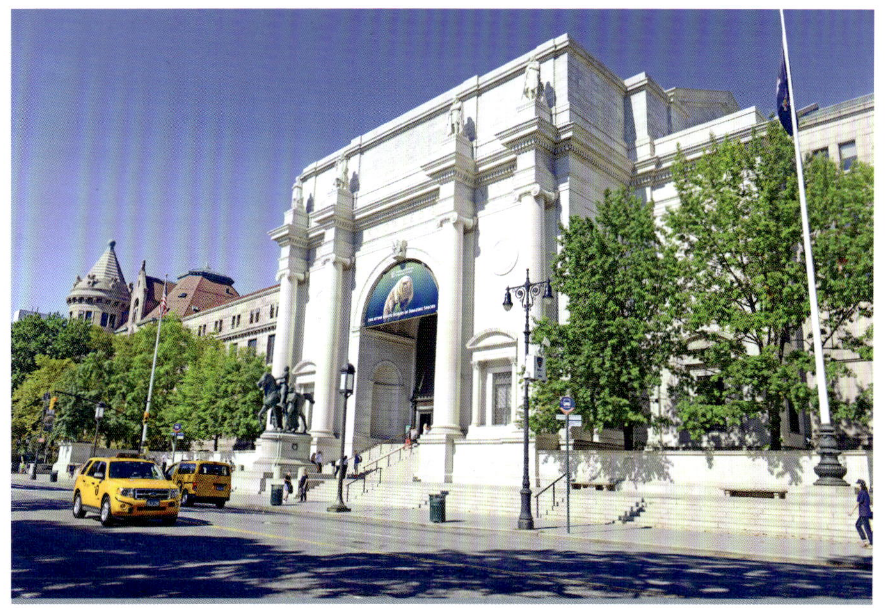

If you're interested in history rather than art, a trip to Central Park also offers options on that front. The Jewish Museum and the Museum of the City of New York are both found along Fifth Avenue, north of the Guggenheim. Across from Central Park on its western border, you can find the American Museum of Natural History *(above)*, with more than 35 million specimens, including dinosaur fossils.

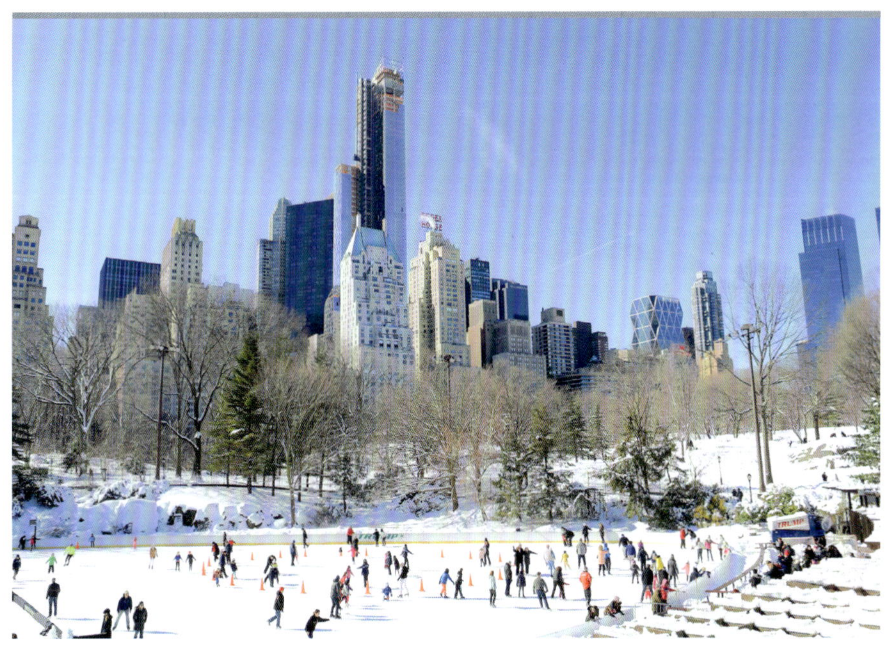

Wollman Rink opens between late October and early April. During the summer months, the space has variously hosted concerts, a children's amusement park, and pickleball courts.

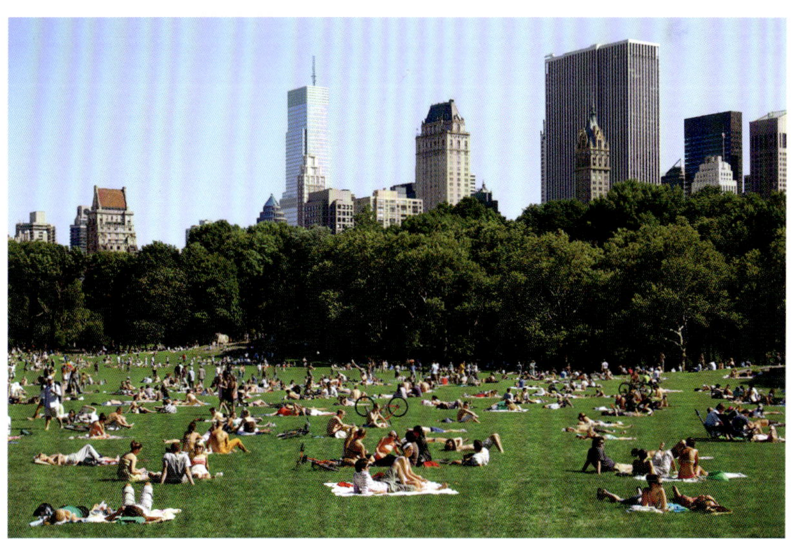

Sheep Meadow is a popular open space at Central Park, able to host large events and gatherings.

High Line

Location: Manhattan, New York City, New York
Length: 1.45 miles
Start point: Gansevoort Street
End point: 34th Street

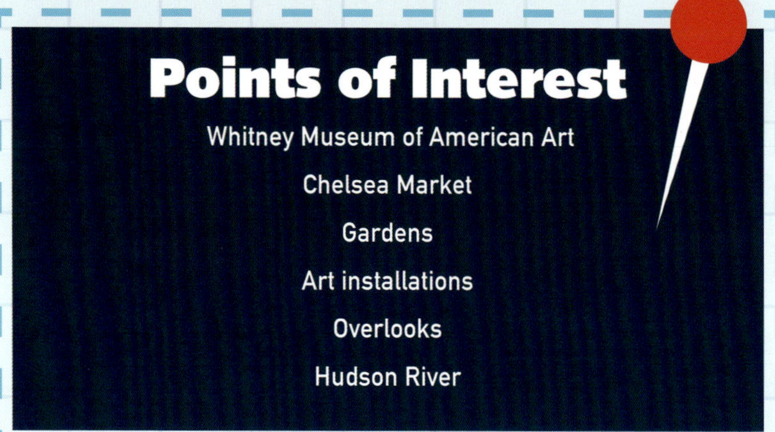

Points of Interest

Whitney Museum of American Art
Chelsea Market
Gardens
Art installations
Overlooks
Hudson River

From the abandoned section of a railway line, New Yorkers created a space of greenery and beauty, an elevated park where walkers can stroll to see plants, art, views of the city, and more. The High Line opened in 2009 and has expanded several times since.

The park can be reached from several entrances along its length, though some are stairway only, without elevator access. Restrooms are also found at various access points. A complete list of access points and notes about wheelchair accessibility is maintained at the High Line web site run by the Friends of the High Line.

The southern access point is found at Gansevoort Street in the Meatpacking District, not far from the Whitney Museum of American Art. As visitors proceed north, they may want to stop for a bite at the Chelsea Market food hall, where the High Line passes through the building. Between 30th and 34th Streets, the High Line approaches the Hudson River, providing good views of it. The route's other end is found near the Jacob Javits Convention Center, so if you're in town for a convention there, take a break to hop on the High Line.

As visitors walk the High Line, they will encounter various gardens, rotating art exhibitions, play areas, rest areas, and overlooks and observation decks. The park has become a tourist attraction that draws millions of visitors each year, and the Friends of the High Line offer public tours throughout the year. These tours take about 90 minutes and are a great way to learn more about the park's history and landscaping. Private group tours are also available for a fee.

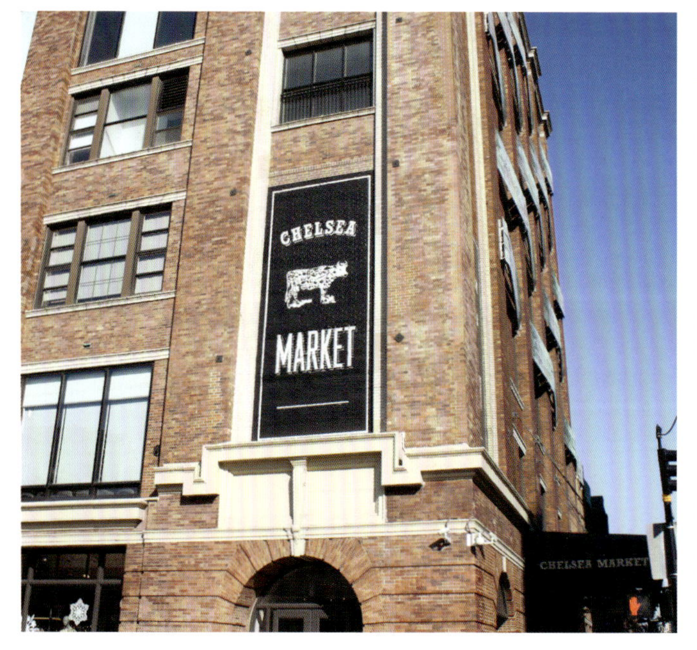

As well as a food hall, the Chelsea Market complex offers lots of shopping opportunities. Eat there, or pick up treats or baked goods for a picnic on the High Line!

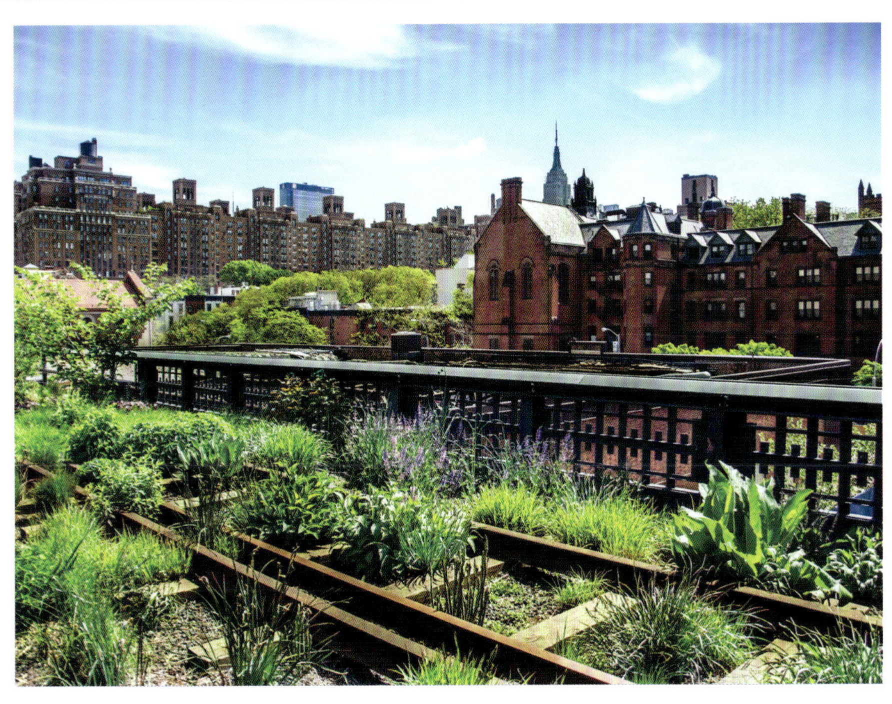

The designers of the High Line planted greenery that is sustainable for the outdoor space.

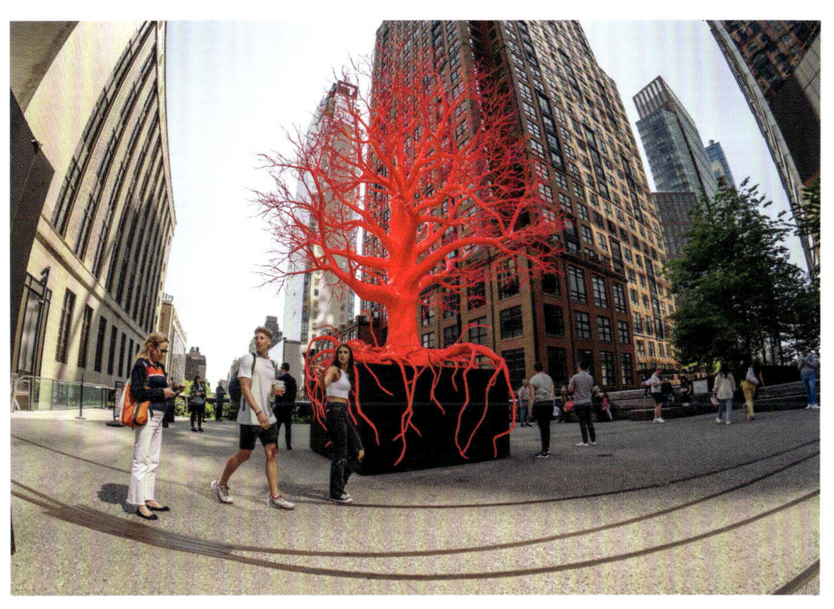

Pamela Rosenkranz's *Old Tree* was a 2023 installation on the High Line.

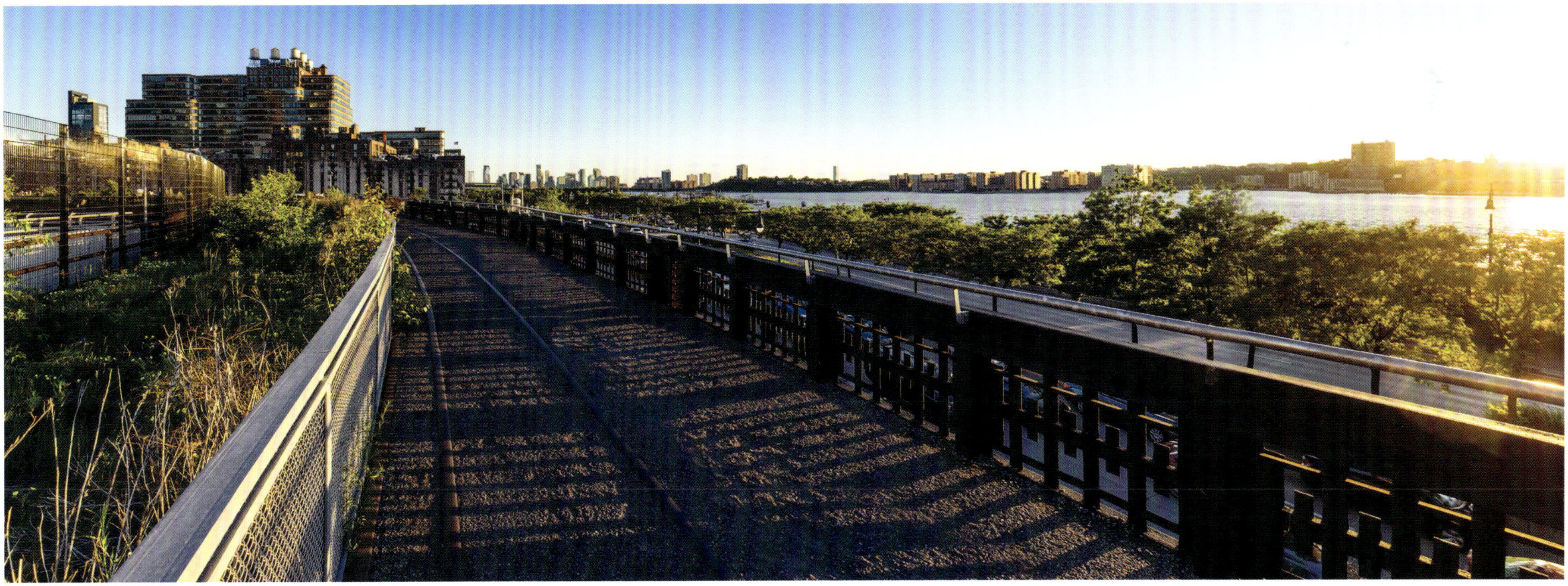

From the High Line, walkers can see the Hudson River.

Brooklyn Bridge

Location: East River between Manhattan and Brooklyn
Length: 1.1 miles
Start point: City Hall Park, Manhattan
End point: Cadman Plaza Park, Brooklyn

Points of Interest

One World Trade Center
Statue of Liberty
Empire State Building
Chrysler Building

Not only does Brooklyn Bridge offer stunning views of New York City, but it itself is a historical landmark that plays a part in Brooklyn and New York history.

In the 1870s and 1880s, while the Brooklyn Bridge was being built, Brooklyn was considered a separate city from New York, and people had to use ferries or boats to traverse the East River between them. The bridge opened in 1883, firmly linking Manhattan with Brooklyn. The ability to travel by foot, horse-drawn carriage, and cable car made travel between the two locations much easier. Not that long afterward, in 1898, Brooklyn became a borough in New York City.

In 1867, New York approved a $15.1 million plan created by John Roebling to build the Brooklyn Bridge. It was the first suspension bridge to use steel for its cable wire and to employ explosives underwater during construction. Just before construction began in 1869, Roebling died of tetanus from an injury he had incurred while taking measurements for the bridge. Roebling's son Washington Roebling took over his father's work. He too suffered, falling prey to compression sickness while working underwater. Bedridden, Washington Roebling sent construction tasks through his wife Emily, herself an engineer.

On May 24, 1883, Emily Roebling took the first carriage ride over the completed bridge, followed by roughly 200,000 people who paid a penny to walk the large, paved walkway her father-in-law had designed. Today, visitors can cross the landmark bridge by car, bicycle, and foot to view the city skyline.

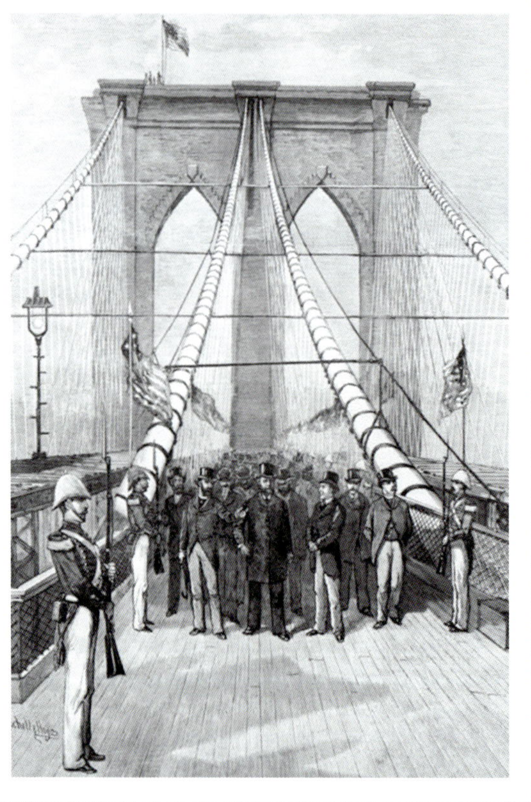

President Chester Arthur, who had lived in New York before his presidency, returned to the city to attend the first bridge crossing. *Harper's Weekly* illustrated the occasion.

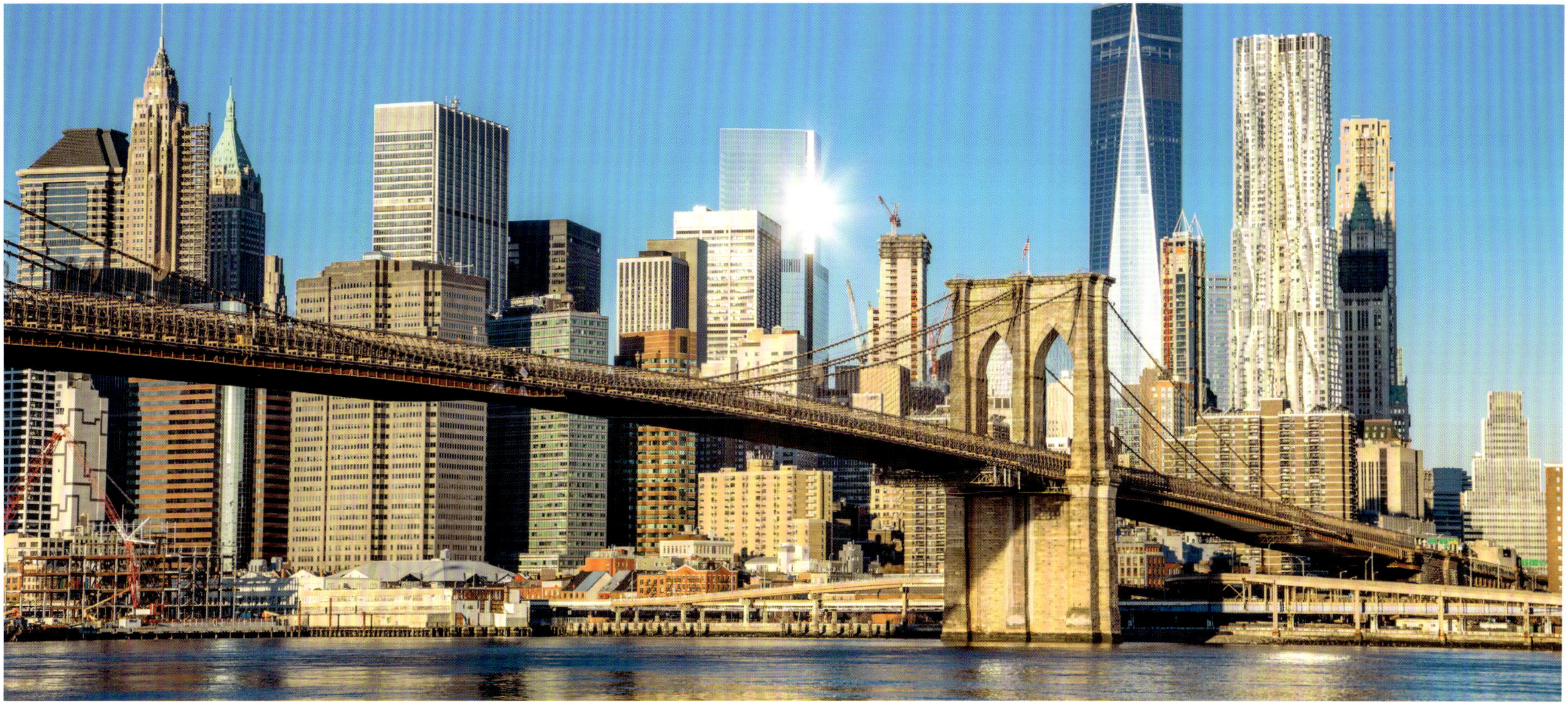

At the time it was built, Brooklyn Bridge was the longest suspension bridge in the world.

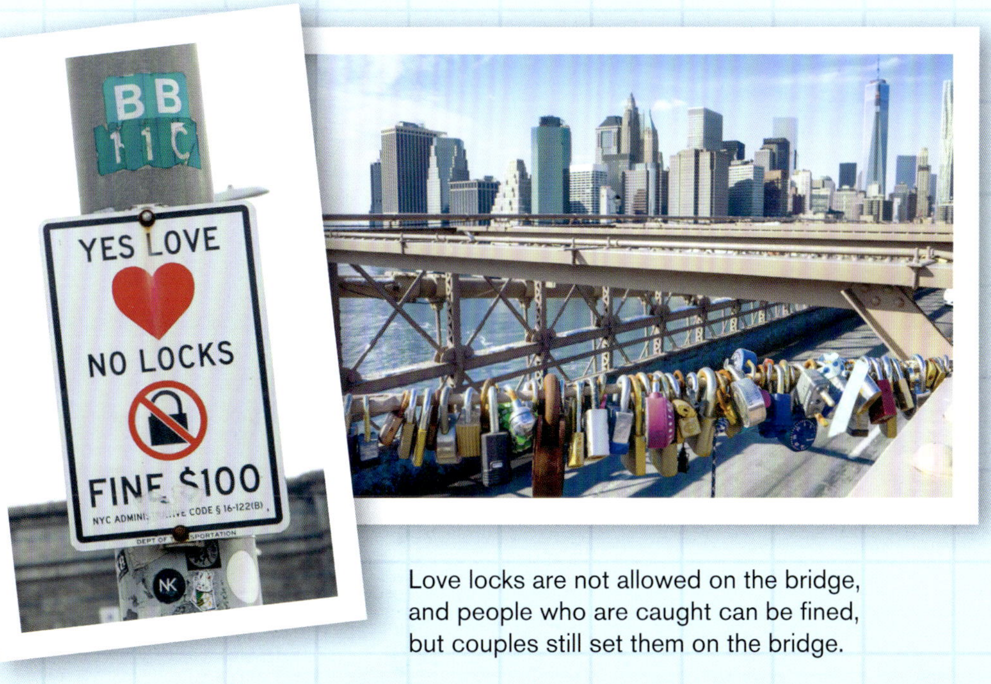

Love locks are not allowed on the bridge, and people who are caught can be fined, but couples still set them on the bridge.

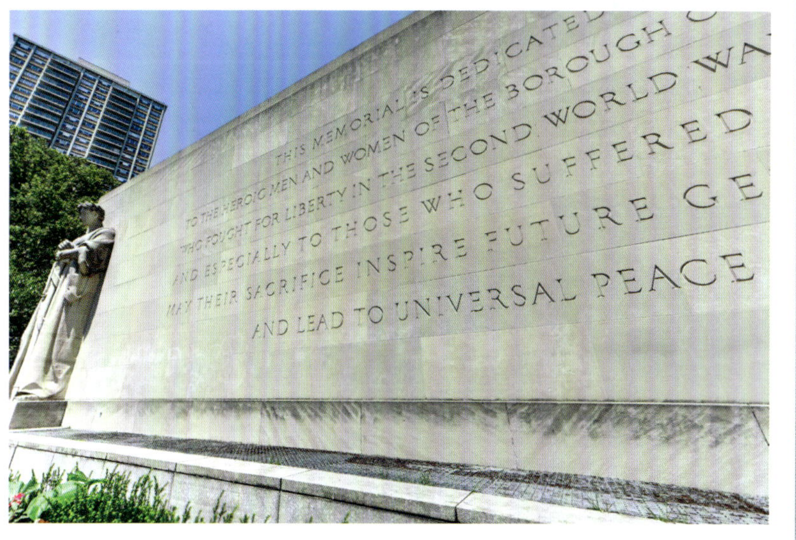

In Brooklyn, the bridge ends near Cadman Plaza Park, which includes the Brooklyn War Memorial that honors those soldiers from Brooklyn who fought in World War II.

Greenwich Village

Location: Greenwich Village, New York City, New York
Length: 1.1 miles
Start point: Merchant's House Museum
End point: Bedford Street

New York's Greenwich Village and West Village have long been a home to writers, artists, dreamers, and activists. In a walk of just over a mile, you can see the layers of this rich cultural history by visiting a number of fascinating places from different eras.

Start in the NoHo neighborhood with the Merchant's House Museum at 29 E. Fourth Street. Built in the 1830s as a family home, the museum shows how that family lived, providing a glimpse into the past. Departing the museum, as you head along Fourth Street, you'll be passing through part of the New York University campus, so expect to see students out and about!

On the south side of Washington Square Park, you'll find Judson Memorial Church, a beautiful church with a bell tower. Washington Square Park itself provides both a lovely walk and its own rich history. It's long been a place where street musicians and buskers have performed, as well as a gathering place for protests and demonstrations. In 1912, for example, a year after the Triangle Shirtwaist Factory Fire, 20,000 workers gathered there on Labor Day.

On Washington Square North, a set of red brick townhouses called The Row date back to the 1830s. Inhabitants over the years have included Henry James, Edith Wharton, and Edward Hopper. Not far from The Row is Electric Lady Studios on Eighth Street, which musician Jimi Hendrix set up and where he recorded shortly before his death. Stevie Wonder, Led Zeppelin, and Patti Smith have also recorded there. From there, take Sixth Avenue up to Tenth Street, where you'll see

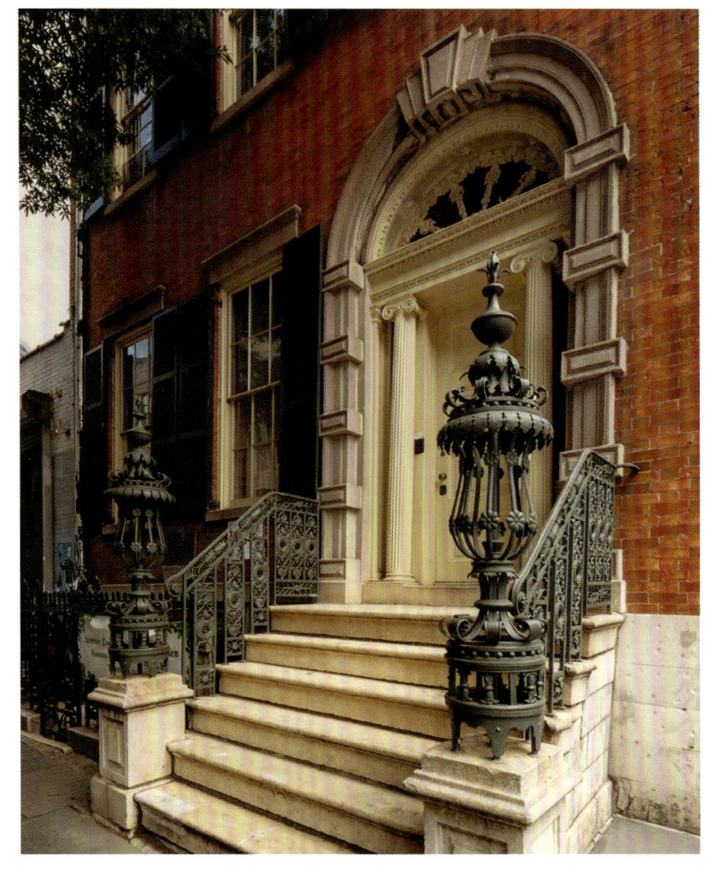

In 1835, a merchant named Seabury Tredwell moved his household and their servants to this four-story home. The house remained in the family for close to a century before becoming a museum.

the magnificent architecture of the Jefferson Market Library. Nearby, pass by the gated cul-de-sac of Patchin Place, home of writers like Theodore Dreiser and e.e. cummings, on your way to Christopher Park and the Stonewall Inn, both critical sites in the movement for LGBTQ+ rights and part of Stonewall National Monument. Wrap up your tour on Bedford Street, where 77 Bedford dates back to 1799, making it the oldest extant house in Greenwich Village, while 75 ½ Bedford was once home to poet Edna St. Vincent Millay.

Points of Interest

Merchant's House Museum

Judson Memorial Church

Washington Square Park

The Row

Electric Lady Studios

Jefferson Market Library

Patchin Place

Christopher Park

Stonewall Inn

Bedford Street

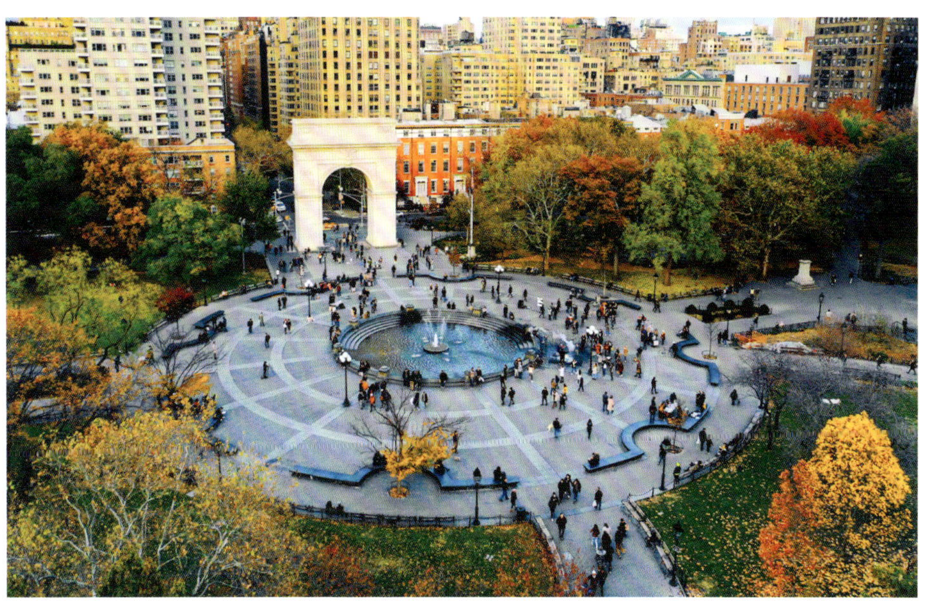

In various eras, visitors to Washington Square Park could have met Mark Twain, who lived nearby; folk singers; and the musician Buddy Holly.

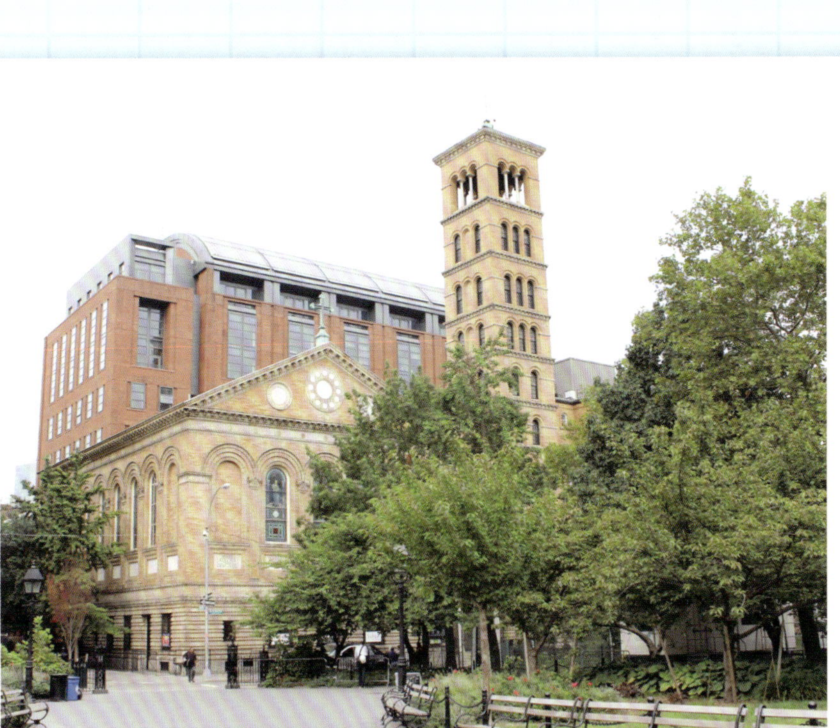

Construction on Judson Memorial Church began in 1888, with the bell tower complete in 1896. Over the years, the church has sponsored and provided space for various artistic endeavors, including dance and poetry.

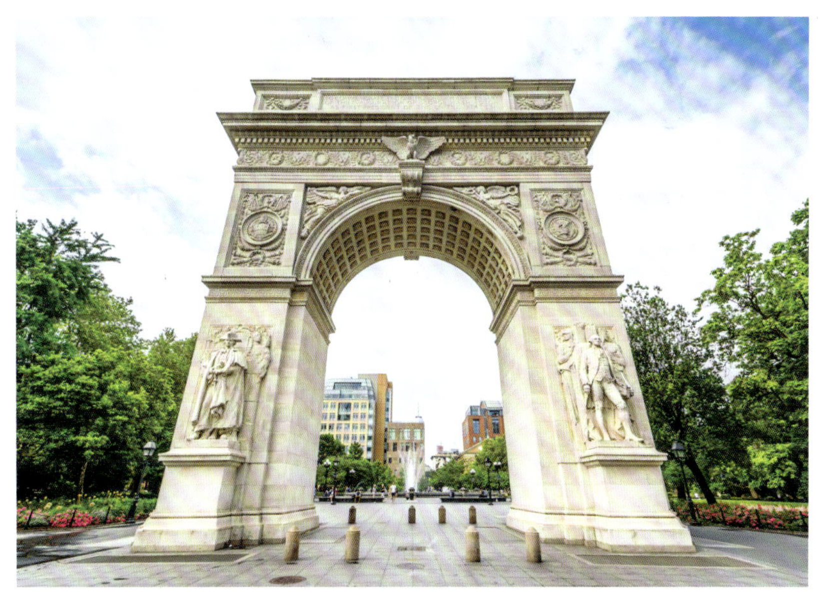

The Washington Square Arch was erected in the 1890s, with two sculptures of George Washington added later.

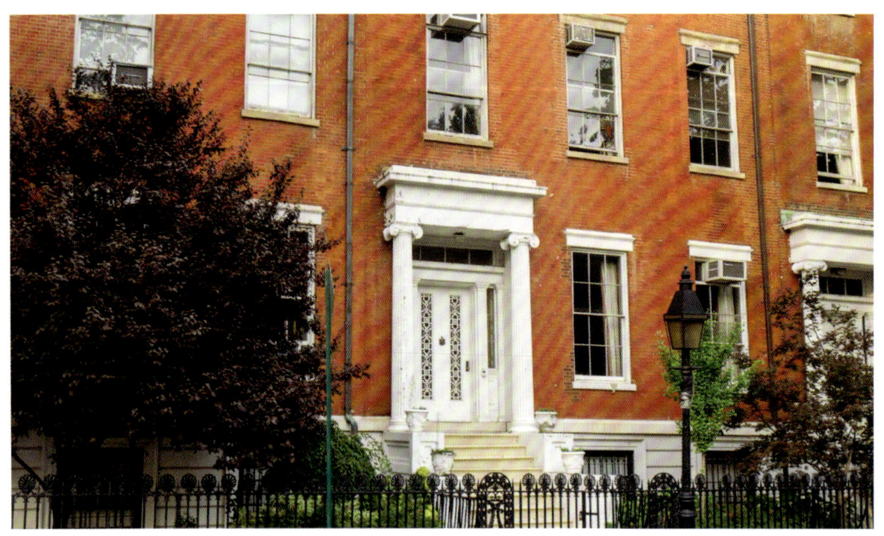

The townhomes of "The Row" are right off Washington Square Park. Henry James set his 1880 novel *Washington Square* in this area.

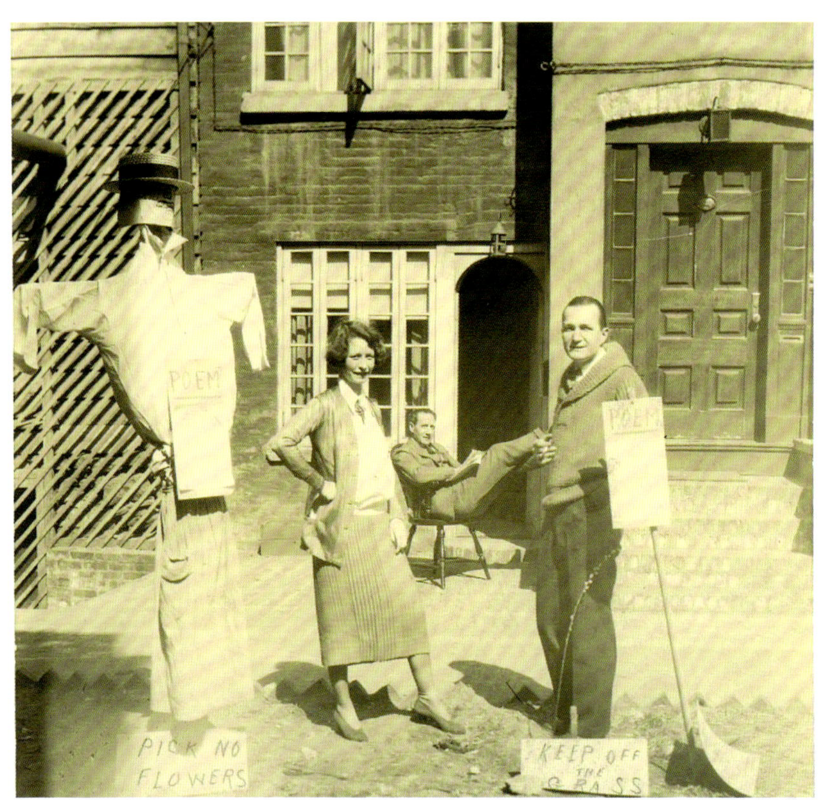

This photograph from the 1920s shows poet Edna St. Vincent Millay in front of her home at 75 ½ Bedford Street.

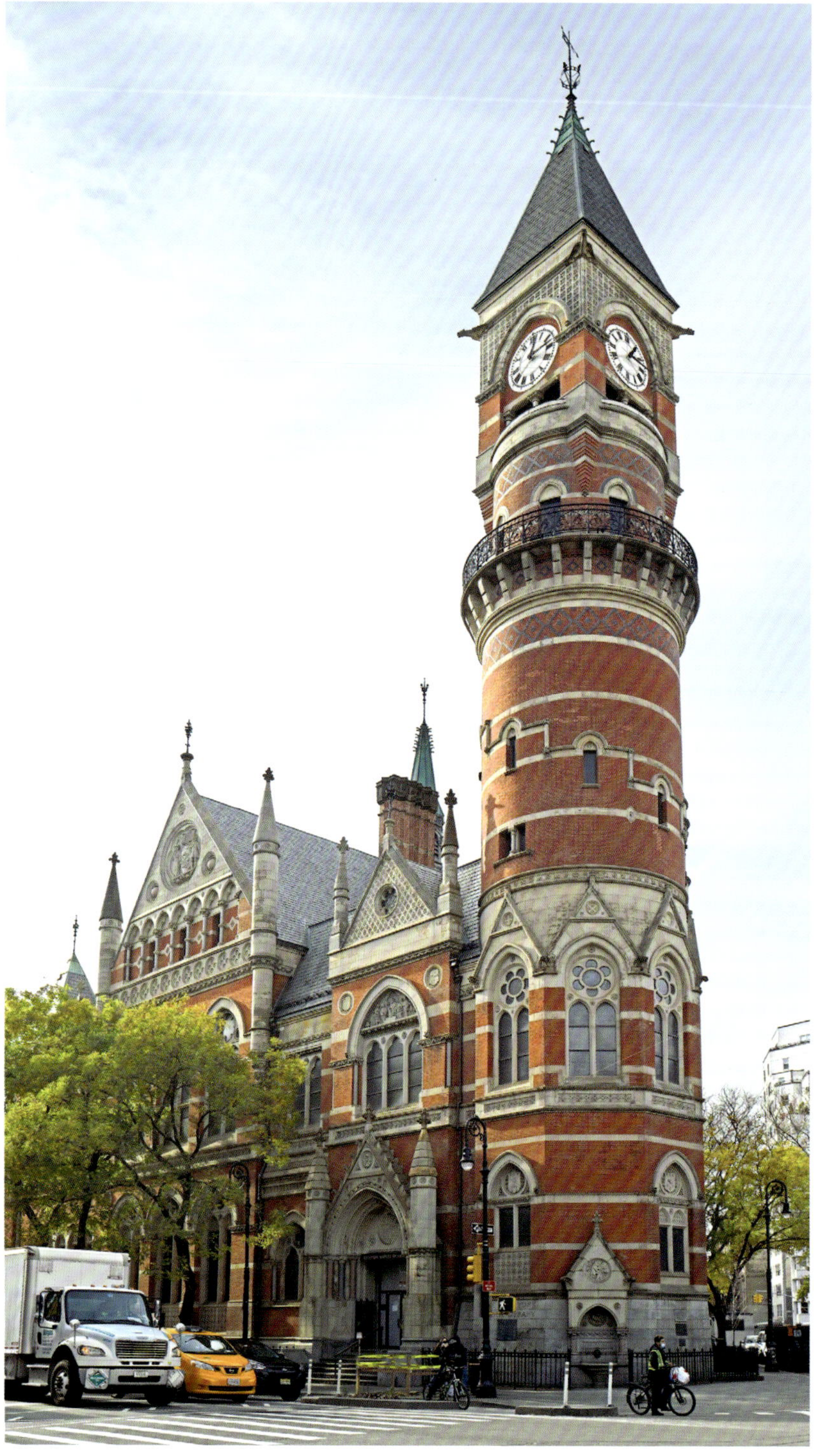

Today part of the New York Public Library system, the Jefferson Market Library building was once a courthouse.

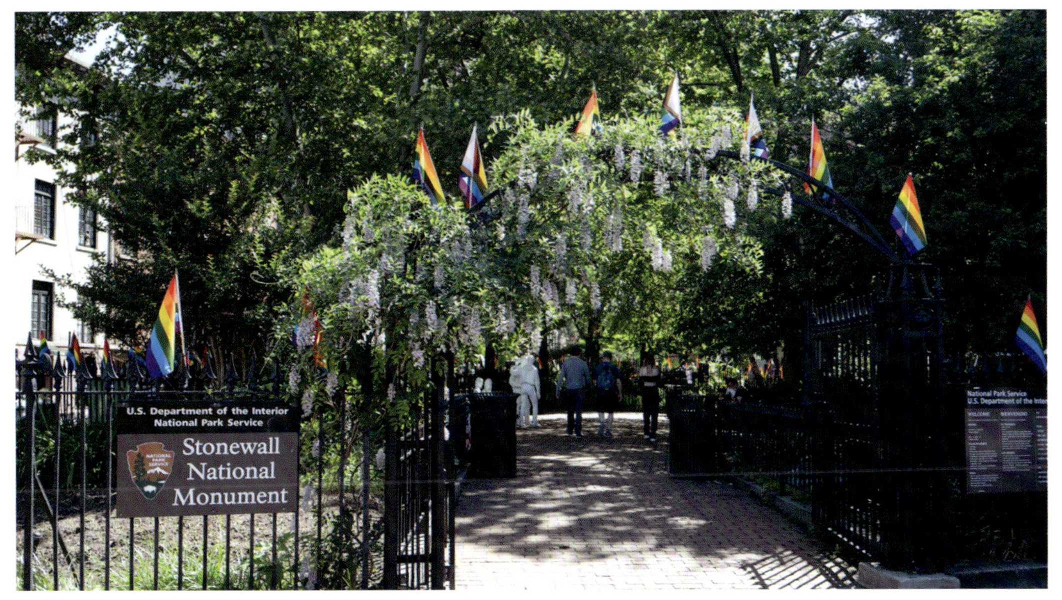

During the time of the Stonewall riots in 1969, activists gathered at Christopher Park.

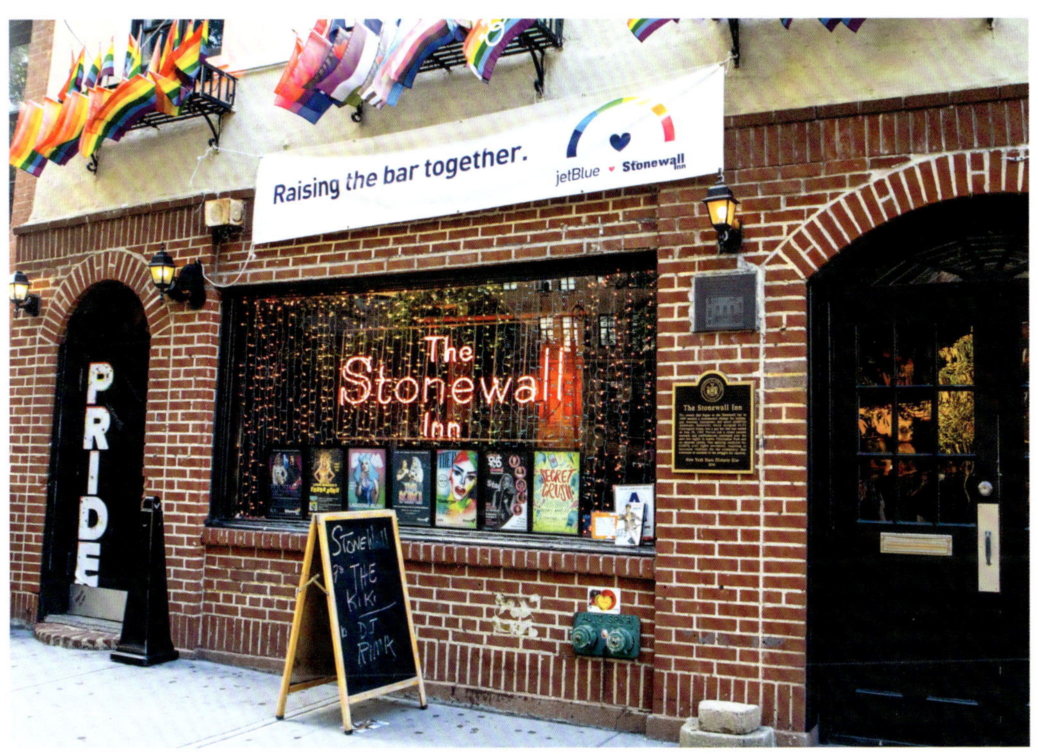

The Stonewall Inn changed ownership, names, and purposes several times after the Stonewall riots, but was renamed the Stonewall Inn again in 2006.

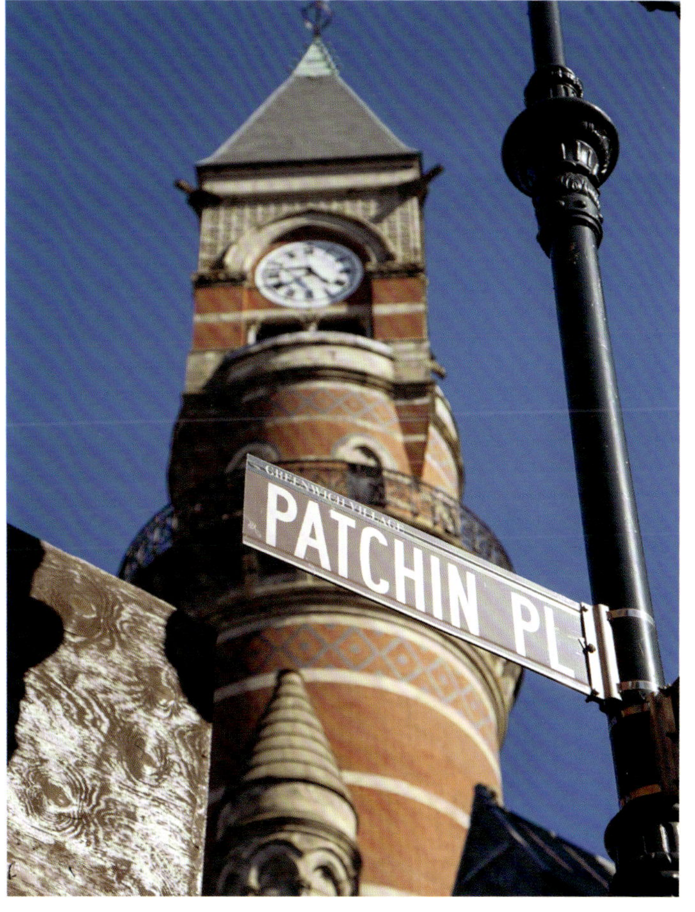

Patchin Place contains ten three-story houses. Poet e.e. cummings lived there for decades between 1923 and 1962.

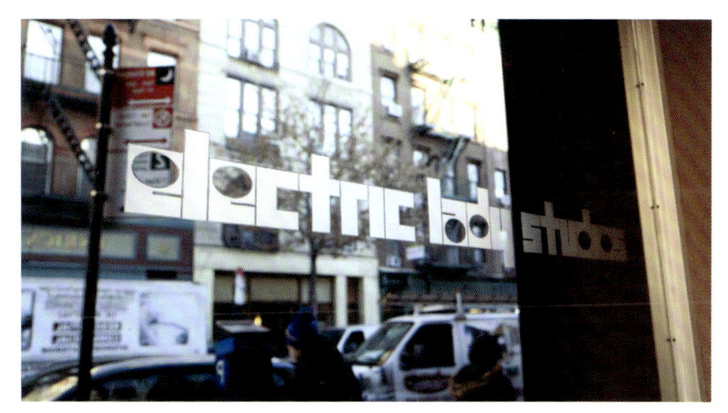

Electric Lady Studios has seen countless musical greats, including David Bowie, the Rolling Stones, Billy Idol, Adele, and Taylor Swift.

Atlantic City Boardwalk

Location: Atlantic City, New Jersey
Length: Variable, about 4 miles
Start point: Variable
End point: Variable

Points of Interest

Absecon Lighthouse
Steel Pier
Jim Whelan Boardwalk Hall
Atlantic City Historical Museum
Kennedy Plaza
Shops, casinos, and arcades

The summer of 1870 saw the first boardwalk in the United States open for business: the Atlantic City Boardwalk in New Jersey. The iconic Boardwalk is still a huge tourist draw today. It extends for about four miles in Atlantic City, but then continues another mile and a half into Ventnor City. Along the way, you'll see beautiful ocean views on one side, and be able to pop into any number of shops, casinos, restaurants, arcades, and hotels.

You might start your walk at Absecon Lighthouse, the tallest lighthouse in New Jersey, on Pacific Avenue, before proceeding to the Boardwalk. For family fun, check out the amusement park at Steel Pier, which offers more than twenty rides.

For visitors who want to learn more about the Boardwalk and Atlantic City, the Atlantic City Historical Museum is located in Jim Whelan Boardwalk Hall. Boardwalk Hall, the home of both the Miss America Pageant and the world's largest pipe organ, is also a notable concert venue, so check out its event page to book tickets before your arrival. Across from Boardwalk Hall is Kennedy Plaza, which features miniature golf and an outdoor amphitheater with frequent free shows during the summer.

Inexpensive trams run along most of the Boardwalk, so one option is to walk down the Boardwalk, then take a tram for an easy return trip back to your car.

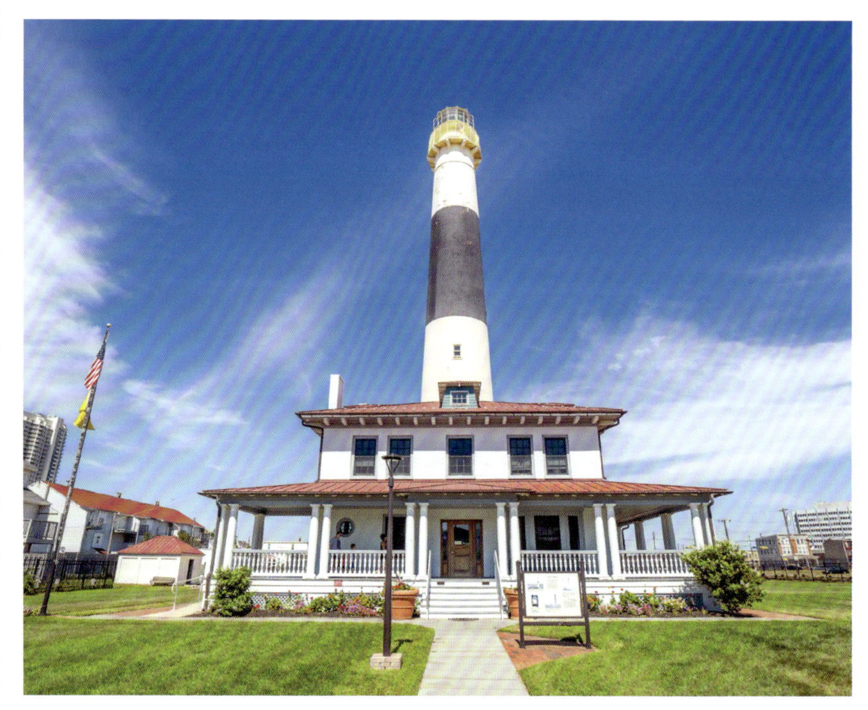

Absecon Lighthouse is one of the oldest in the United States, opening in 1856.

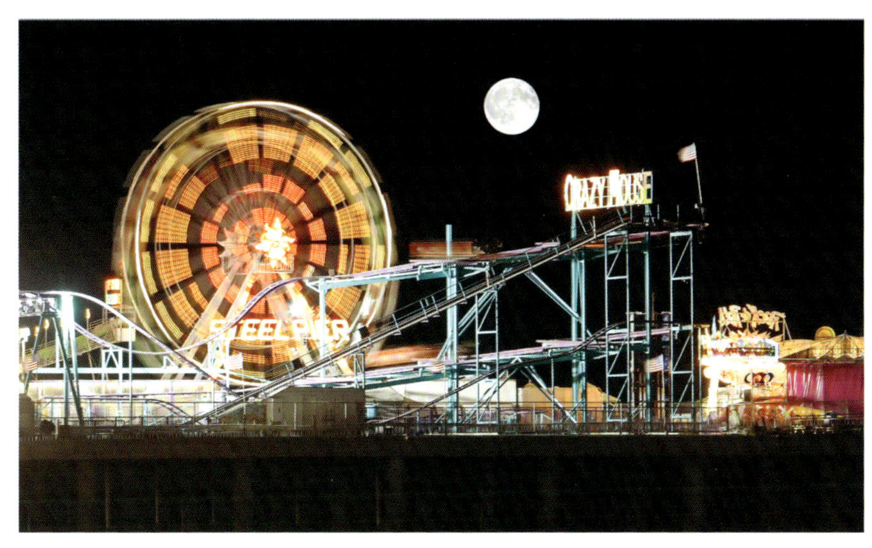

Steel Pier

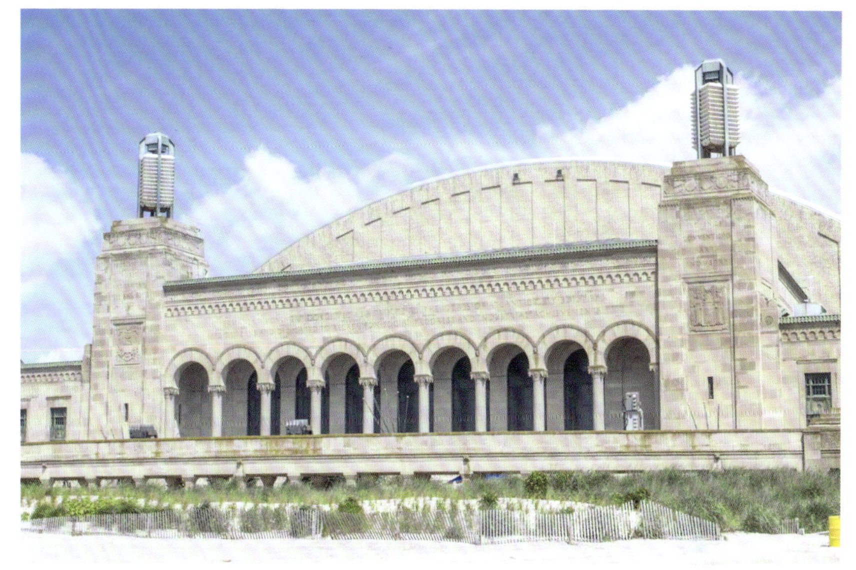

Boardwalk Hall was opened in 1929.

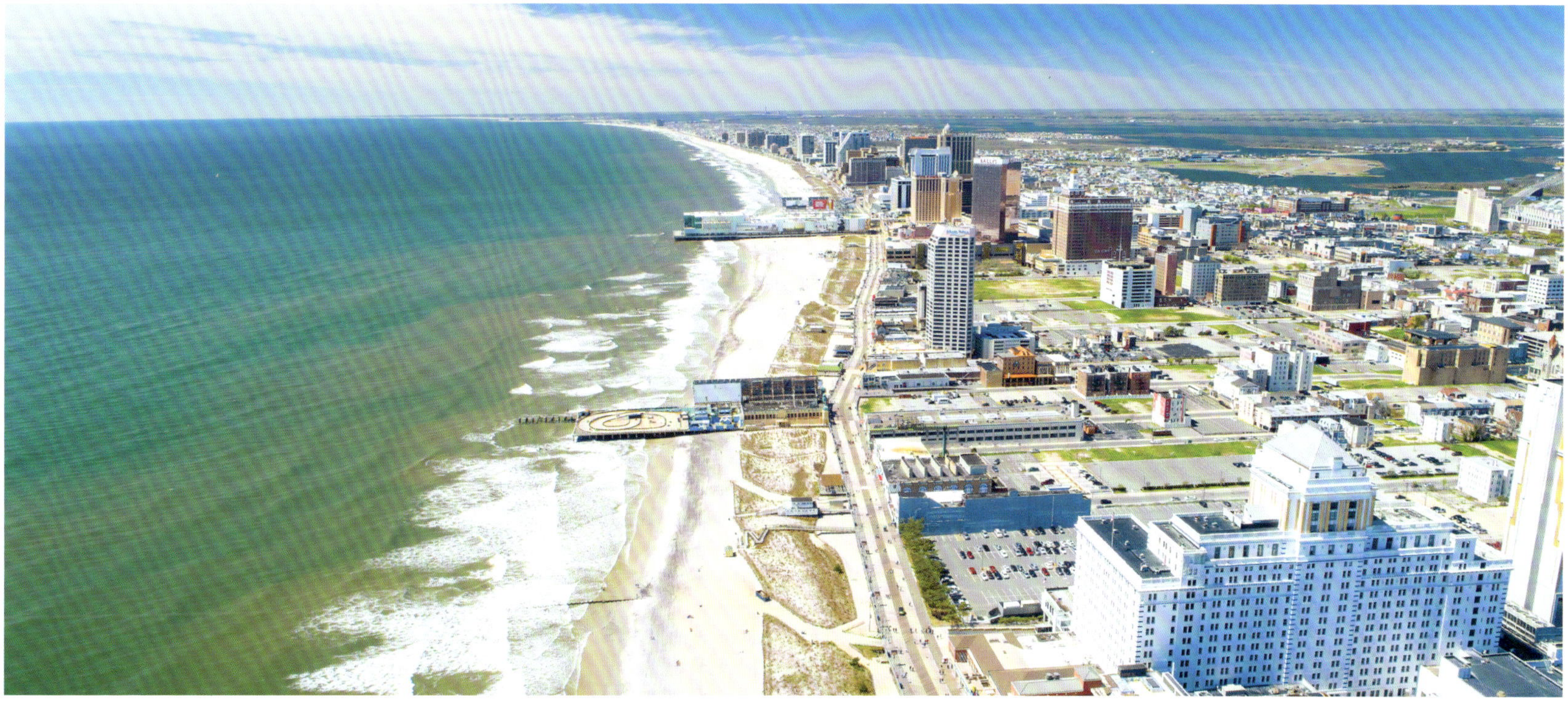

There's no shortage of places to eat or shop along the Boardwalk.

Historic District

Location: Philadelphia, Pennsylvania
Length: About 4 miles
Start point: Independence Visitor Center
End point: National Liberty Museum

The city of Philadelphia was founded in 1682, and played a significant role in the American Revolutionary War and the early days of the United States. It hosted both the First and Second Continental Congresses, was the signing place of the Declaration of Independence, and was one of the cities that preceded Washington, D.C., in serving as the nation's capital. Philadelphia's Historic District honors that era of history with an Official Trail that contains more than twenty locations. Though the sites are clustered relatively close together, you'll likely want to take two days to explore at your leisure.

Start at the Independence Visitor Center to pick up maps and buy tickets. Within just a couple of minutes of walking, you can see the site of the President's House, where George Washington and John Adams lived before the White House was constructed; the Liberty Bell Center; and Independence Hall, the birthplace of the Constitution. Many other sites on the trail are also devoted to the struggle for independence and the early days of the fledgling nation, from Carpenters' Hall where the First Continental Congress was held to Declaration House, where Thomas Jefferson wrote the nation's founding document. Philadelphia's famous Founding Father is honored at the Benjamin Franklin Museum, and his grave can be found at Christ Church Burial Ground.

While the trail is heavy on Revolutionary War history, it's not limited to it. Elfreth's Alley, one of the oldest residential streets in the country, gives a glimpse into working class houses and lives from the colonial time period. Other sites on the trail provide insight into different aspects of Pennsylvanian and American history, like the Weitzman National Museum of American Jewish History; the Independence Seaport Museum where you can tour a warship and a submarine; and the African American Museum. Franklin Square, with a carousel, a miniature golf course, and a playground, makes a good break for kids.

Points of Interest

Independence Visitor Center
The President's House
The Liberty Bell Center
Independence Hall & Congress Hall
American Philosophical Society Museum
Weitzman National Museum of American Jewish History
Museum of the American Revolution
Benjamin Franklin Museum & Franklin Court
Second Bank of the United States
Carpenters' Hall
Independence Seaport Museum
Delaware River Waterfront
Christ Church & Christ Church Burial Ground
Elfreth's Alley
The Betsy Ross House
National Constitution Center
Franklin Square
The African American Museum in Philadelphia
Declaration (Graff) House
Washington Square
Mother Bethel African Methodist Episcopal Church
Hill-Physick & Powel Houses
National Liberty Museum

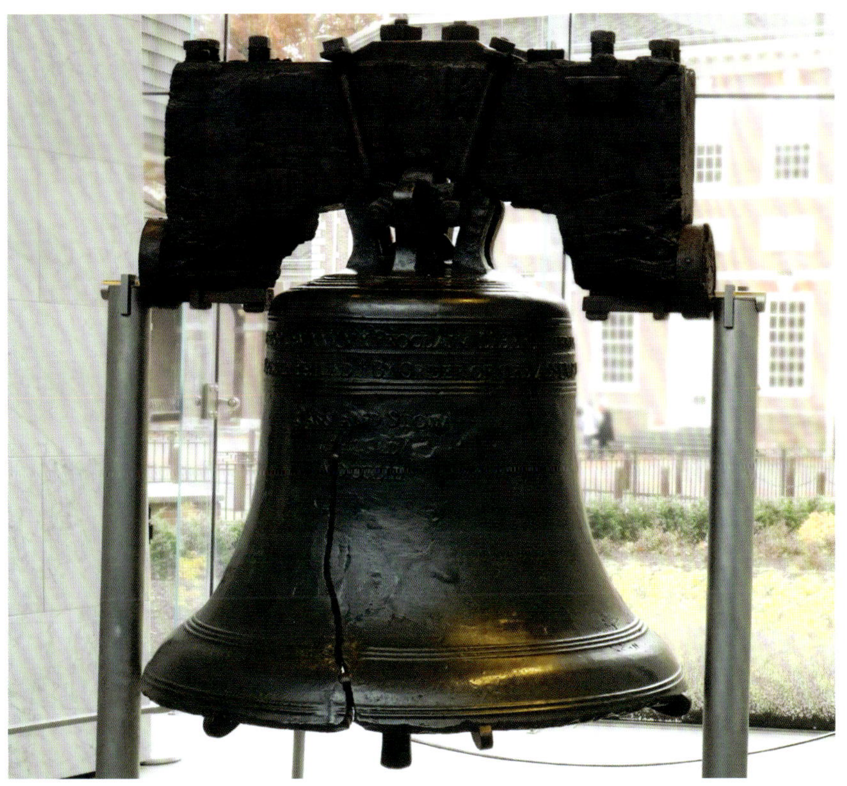

The Liberty Bell and Independence Hall across the way are both part of Independence National Historical Park.

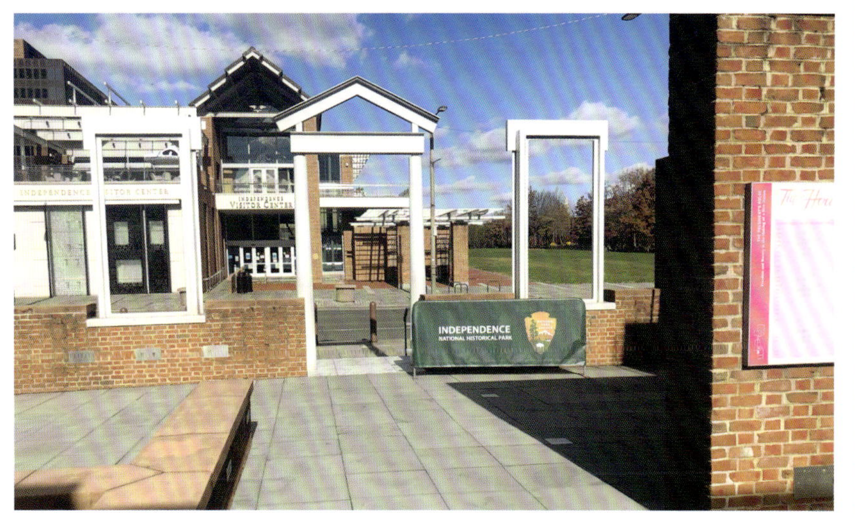

The President's House is an open-air site.

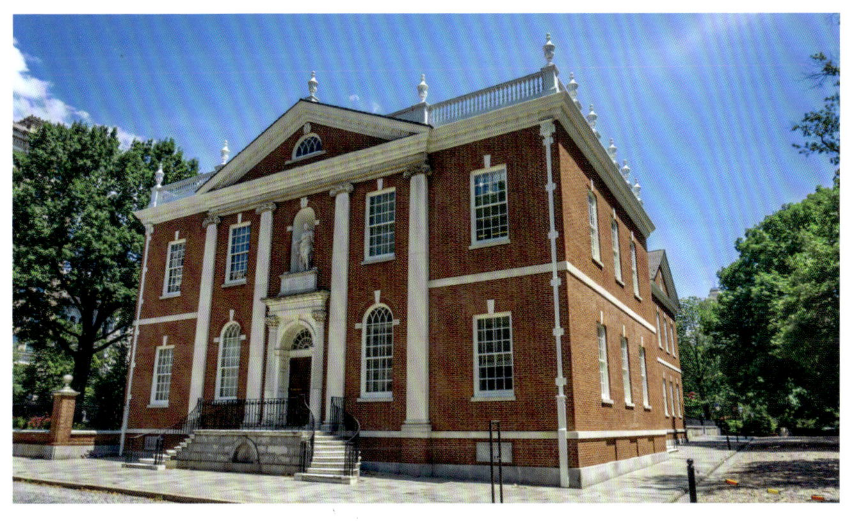

Benjamin Franklin was one of the founders of the American Philosophical Society in 1743. Today the site is a museum.

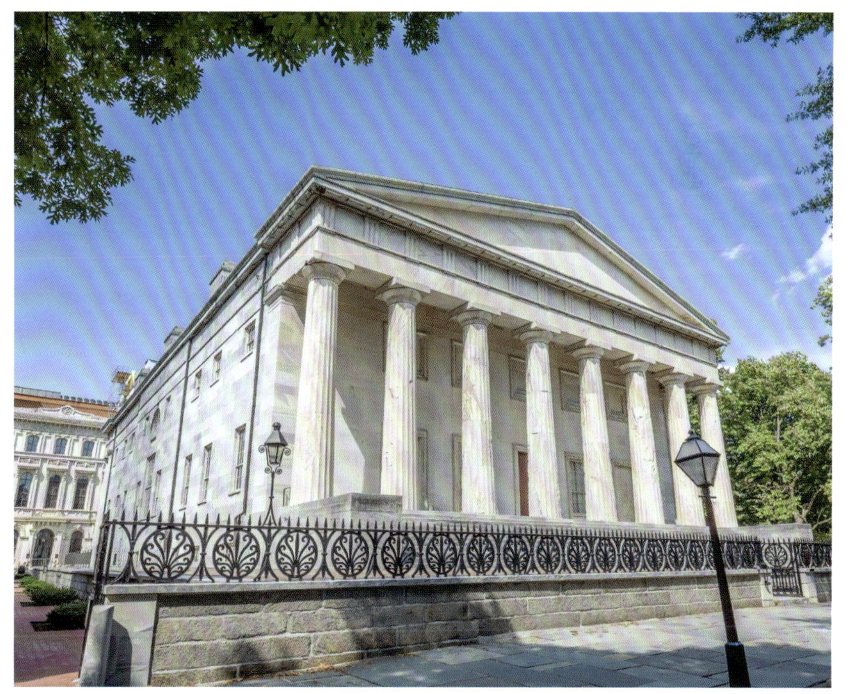

The building that once housed the Second Bank of the United States is now part of Independence National Historical Park and hosts a portrait gallery.

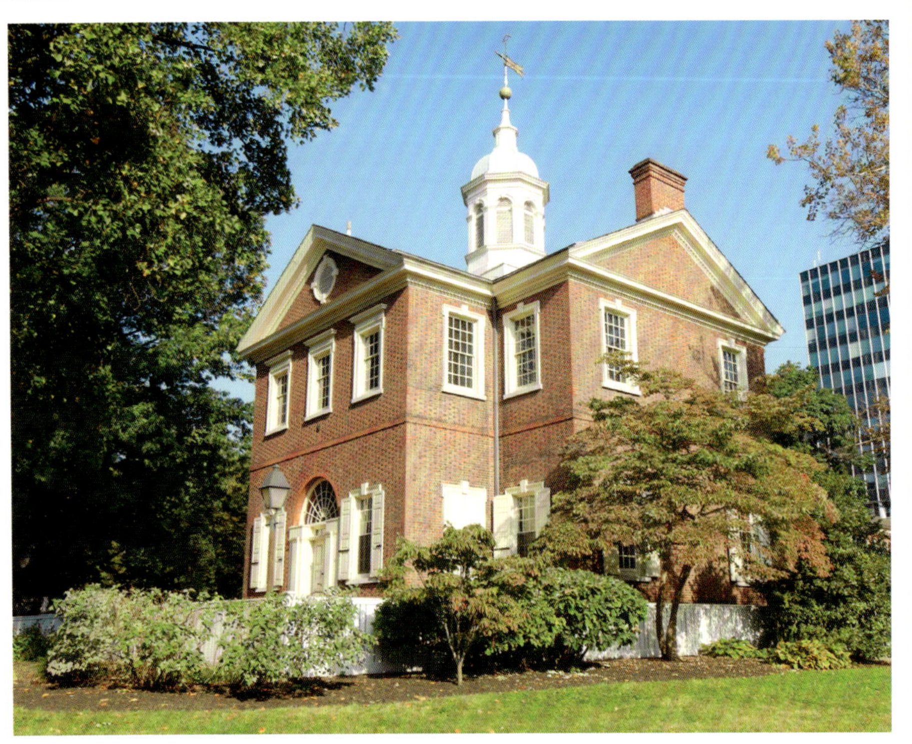

Carpenters' Hall

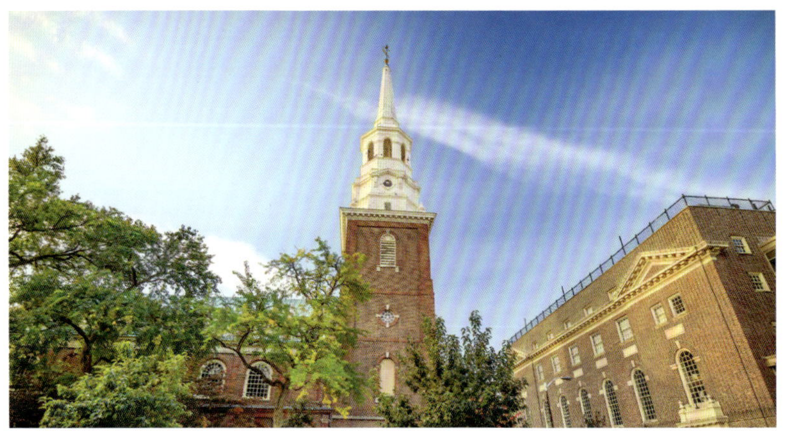

Christ Church, an Episcopal church, was founded in 1695. Betsy Ross was one famous attendee.

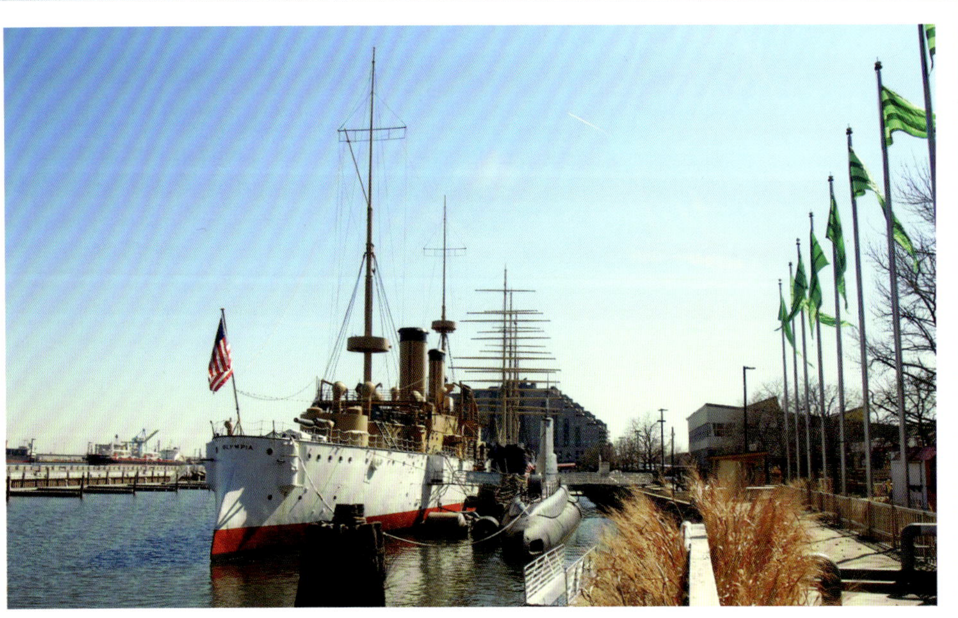

The USS *Olympia* was active between 1895 and 1922, serving in both the Spanish-American War and World War I. She now serves as a museum ship at the Independence Seaport Museum.

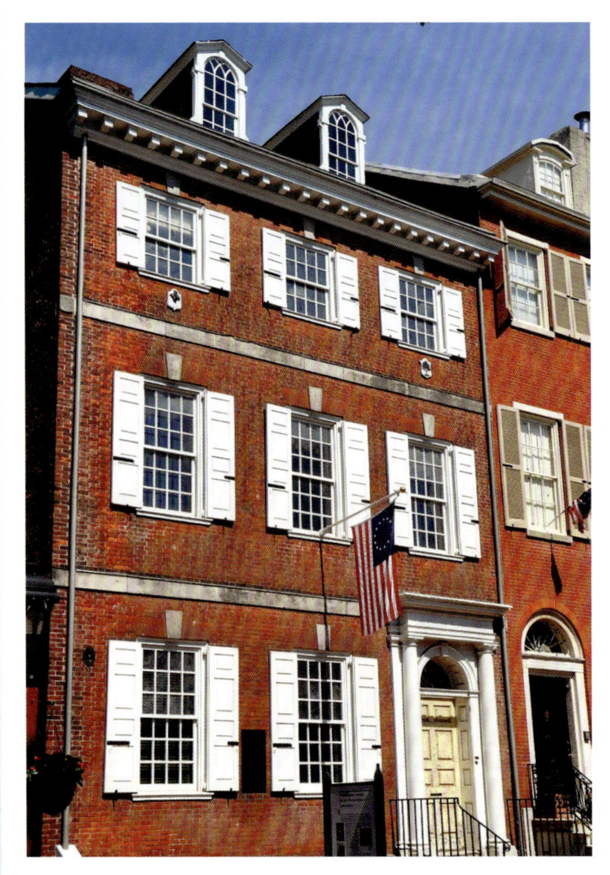

The Powels were a wealthy couple who counted George and Martha Washington as friends, and hosted the Washingtons for their 20th wedding anniversary. Powel House dates to 1765 and today serves as a museum.

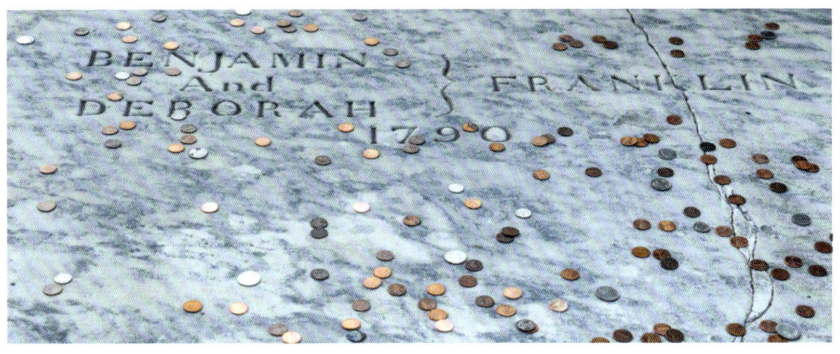

Benjamin Franklin's burial place at Christ Church Burial Ground

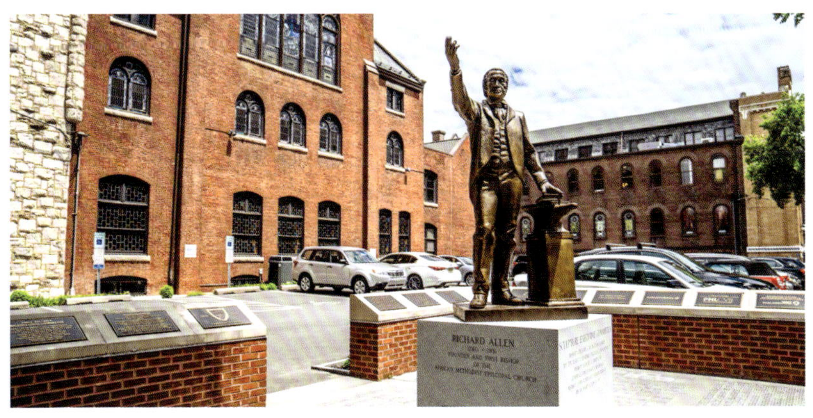

A statue in front of Mother Bethel AME Church honors Bishop Richard Allen, who founded the African Methodist Episcopal Church.

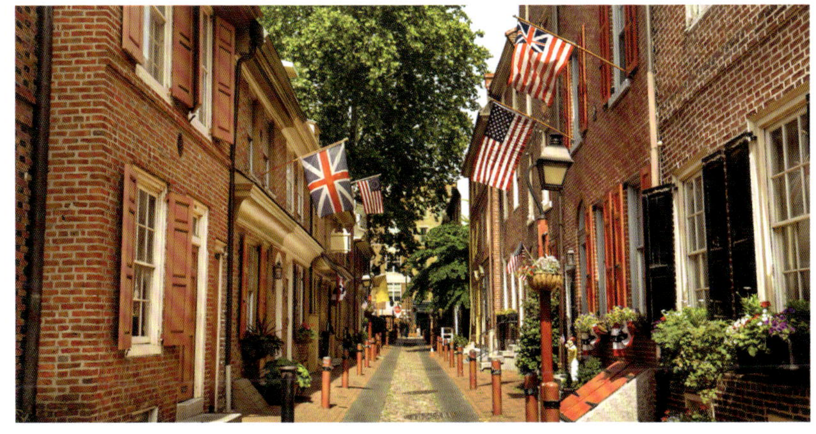

Elfreth's Alley is a showcase of houses built between 1720 and 1836. Two of them are used by the Elfreth's Alley Museum, but most homes on the street are private residences, so take care to be respectful.

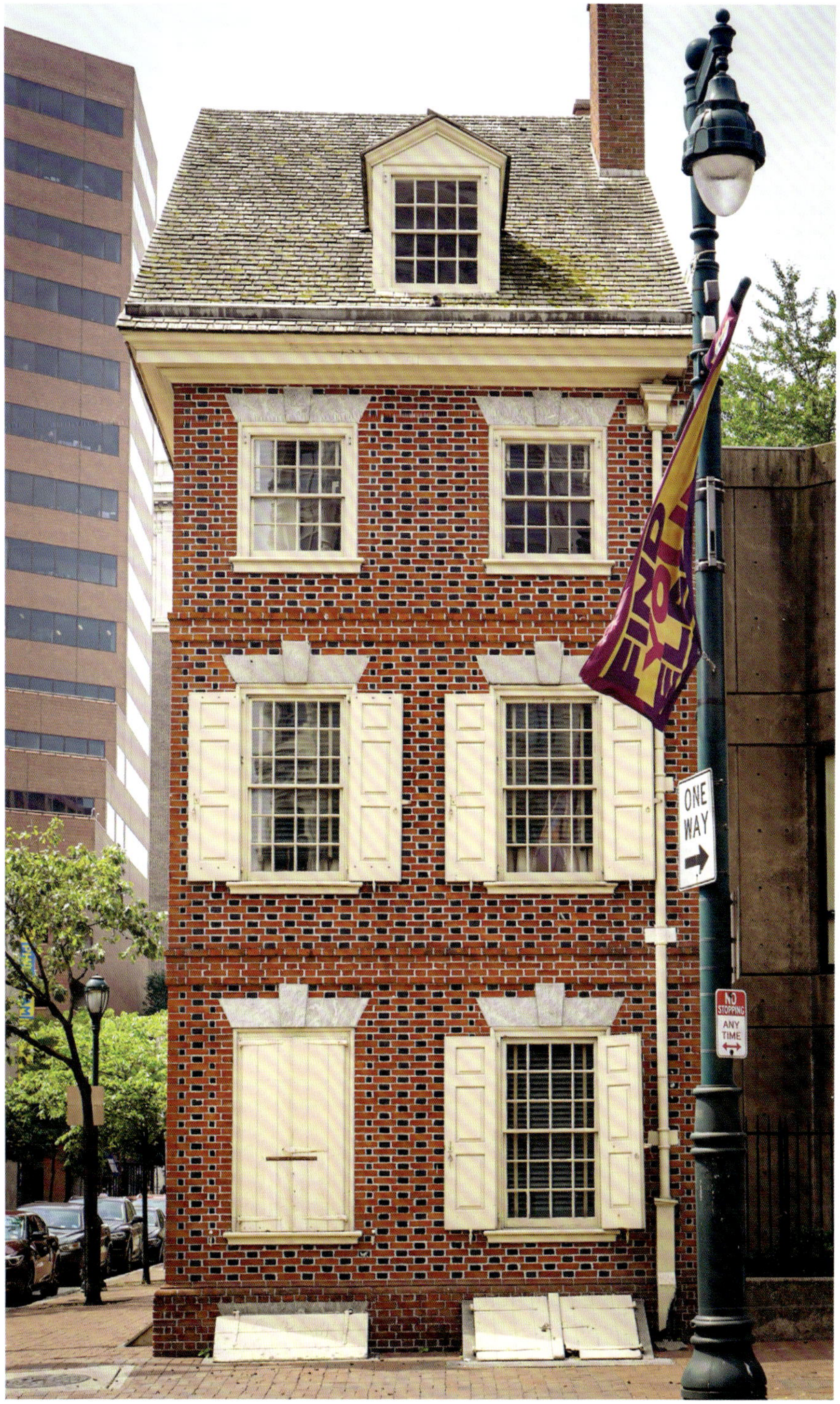

Philadelphia's Declaration House is a reconstruction of the place where Jefferson drafted the Declaration of Independence.

Jack Markell Trail

Location: Wilmington to New Castle, Delaware
Length: 5.5 miles (Jack Markell Trail only); up to 10 miles if the Wilmington Riverwalk and Battery Park Trail are included
Start point: DuPont Environmental Education Center, Wilmington
End point: New Castle Battery Park

Points of Interest

Wilmington Riverwalk
Russell Peterson Wildlife Refuge
Christina River
Amstel House Museum
Dutch House Museum
First State National Historical Park

Wilmington, Delaware's largest city, has a fascinating history that includes being the location of the first Swedish settlement in North America at Fort Christina in 1638. Not far from Wilmington is New Castle, first settled by the Dutch in 1651, then claimed by New Sweden, then absorbed by the Dutch again. Not long after, the British claimed New Castle as part of Delaware Colony, and made it into the capital. Visitors can get their fill of both history and natural beauty as they travel from Wilmington to New Castle via the Jack Markell Trail that links the two locations.

The Jack Markell Trail itself is 5.5 miles. However, it connects to trails on both sides: the 1.4-mile Wilmington Riverwalk on one side and the 2.1-mile Battery Park Trail on the other side. Between the trails and various sites in Historic New Castle, you might walk close to 10 miles.

The Wilmington Riverwalk borders the Christina River and provides beautiful views, as well as a children's museum and restaurants. From there, head into the wetlands to pick up the Jack Markell Trail at the DuPont Environmental Education Center in the Russell Peterson Wildlife Refuge. The path is used by both pedestrians and bicyclists, so be aware as you hike. Information kiosks are found along the way, and you'll cross the Christina River at one point.

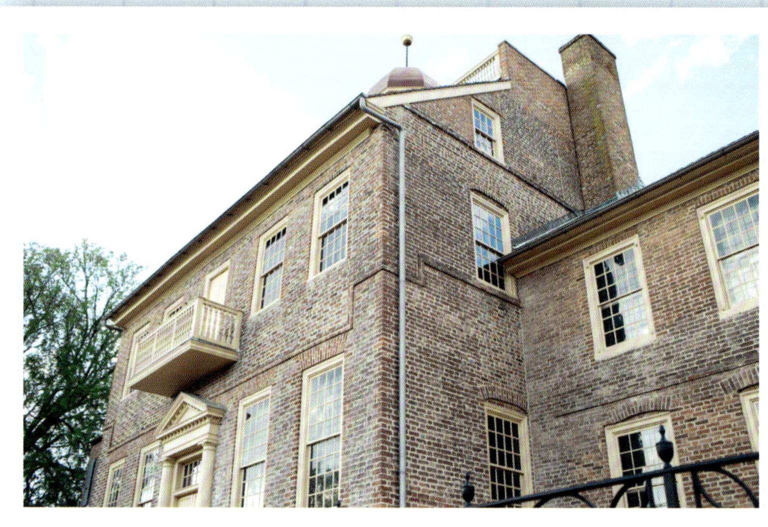

The New Castle Court House Museum was built in 1730.

At the end of the trail, you'll find yourself in Historic New Castle, where attractions include the Amstel House Museum based in a house built in the 1730s; the Dutch House Museum from the late 1600s; and the New Castle Court House Museum found in First State National Historical Park.

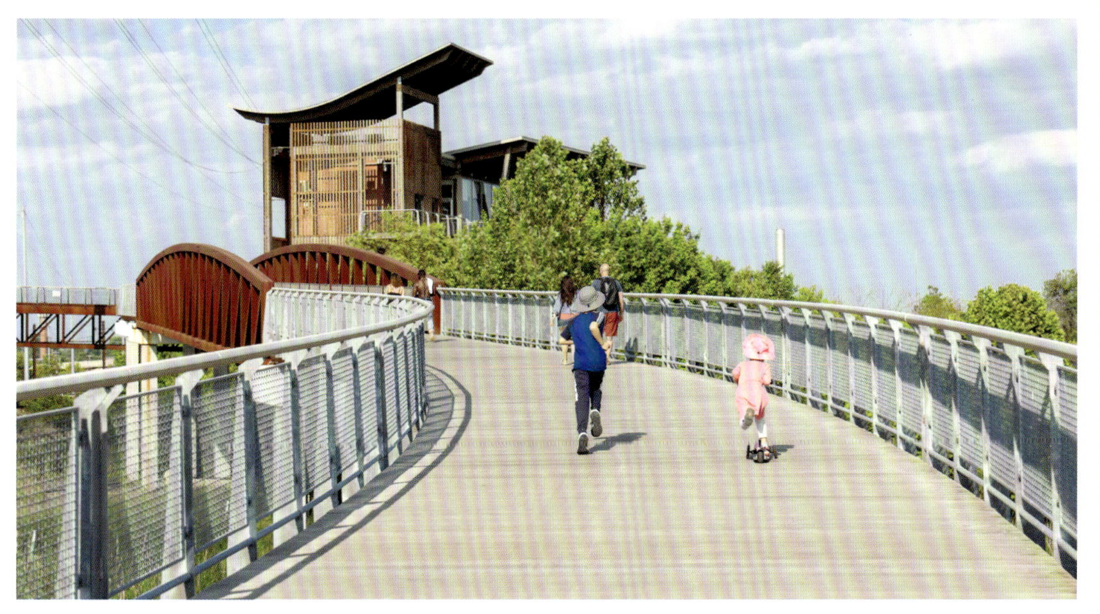

The Russell Peterson Wildlife Refuge is named after a former governor of the state of Delaware. Jack Markell was another Delaware governor.

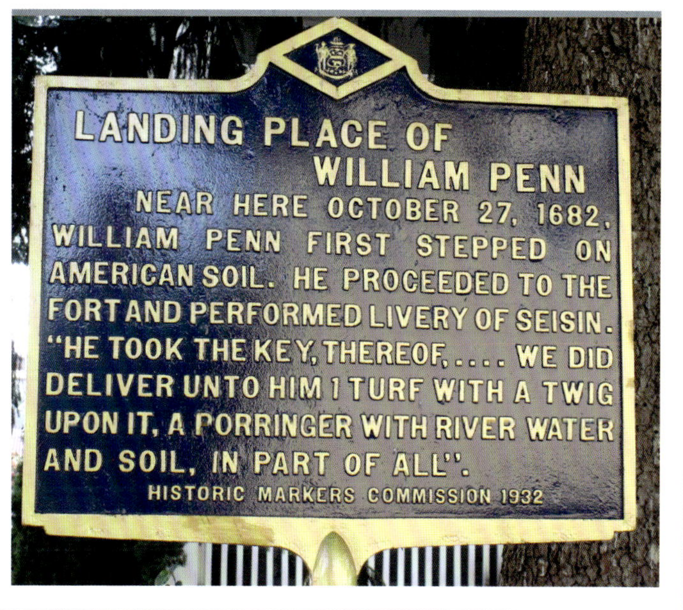

William Penn, the Quaker who founded Pennsylvania, landed in New Castle in 1682.

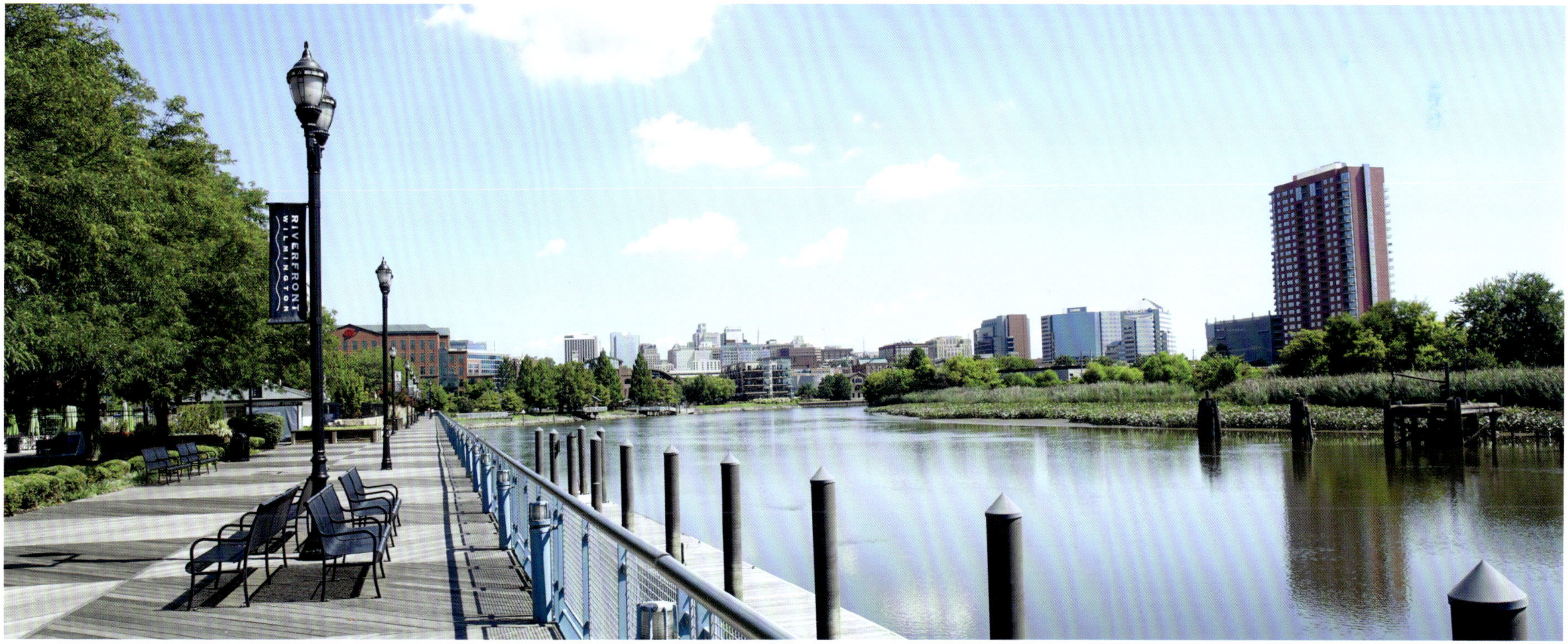

The Wilmington Riverwalk offers a tranquil place to see the Christina River.

Heritage Walk

Location: Baltimore, Maryland
Length: 3.2 miles
Start point: Baltimore's Inner Harbor
End point: Alex. Brown & Sons Building

The sites on the Heritage Walk in downtown Baltimore point towards the importance of the city at several different eras in the nation's history. Perhaps most notably, it was in Baltimore that our national anthem was born: Francis Scott Key wrote the lyrics of the "Star-Spangled Banner" while observing the Battle of Baltimore in 1814 during the War of 1812. The National Park Service has designated certain parts of Baltimore as the Baltimore National Heritage Area, and the Baltimore Heritage Area Association has established several heritage trails for residents and visitors to explore the area's history.

Many of the sites on the Heritage Walk trail are clustered on or near Baltimore's Inner Harbor on the Patapsco River. You might want to start at the Baltimore World Trade Center, where the Observation Deck offers a panoramic view of the city, before you go down to the Historic Ships in Baltimore maritime museum to see ships that include the USS *Constellation*, a sloop-of-war; a World War II submarine; and a Coast Guard cutter that fought in Pearl Harbor.

Some of the sites focus on specific eras of history. The Star-Spangled Banner Flag House, for example, was the home of Mary Young Pickersgill, who sewed the massive flag that Francis Scott Key saw flying over Fort McMenry during the War of 1812. Other places provide a wealth of information about different Maryland eras, like the Reginald F. Lewis Museum of Maryland African American History & Culture; and the Jewish Museum of Maryland, which includes two historic synagogues. The Peale Museum has a focus on the local community, providing various exhibits about Baltimore and Chesapeake Bay. Historic mansions, churches, a school building, and various monuments add depth to the tour.

The Baltimore Heritage Area Association offers various walking tour apps through their web site, and printed guides are available at the Baltimore Visitor Center, conveniently located at the Inner Harbor.

Points of Interest

Baltimore World Trade Center / Top of the World Observation Deck
Historic Ships in Baltimore
Public Works Experience
President Street Station Civil War Museum
Star-Spangled Banner Flag House
Reginald F. Lewis Museum of Maryland African American History & Culture
Carroll Mansion
Jewish Museum of Maryland
McKim's Free School
Old Town Friends' Meetinghouse
Nine North Front Street
Phoenix Shot Tower
St. Vincent de Paul Roman Catholic Church
War Memorial Plaza
Zion Church of the City of Baltimore
Peale Museum
Baltimore City Hall
Battle Monument (War of 1812)
Alex. Brown & Sons Building

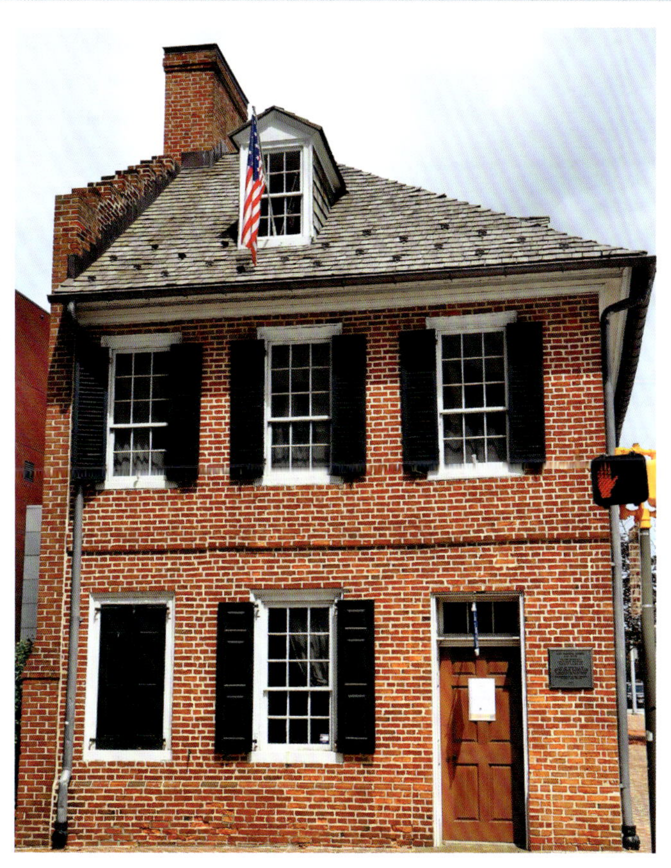

The Star-Spangled Banner Flag House was built in 1793. Seamstress Mary Young Pickersgill lived there in 1813, when she sewed the massive 30-by-42-foot flag that would be flown from Fort McHenry during the 1814 Battle of Baltimore.

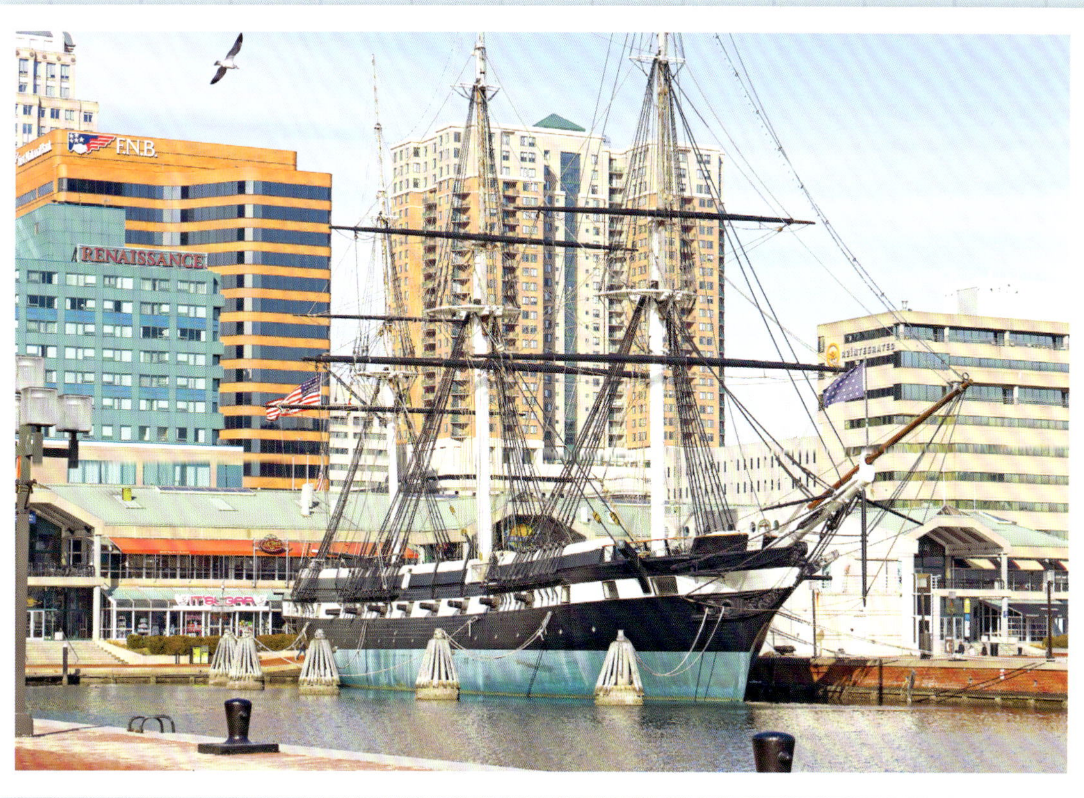

Launched in 1854, the USS *Constellation* now serves as a museum ship.

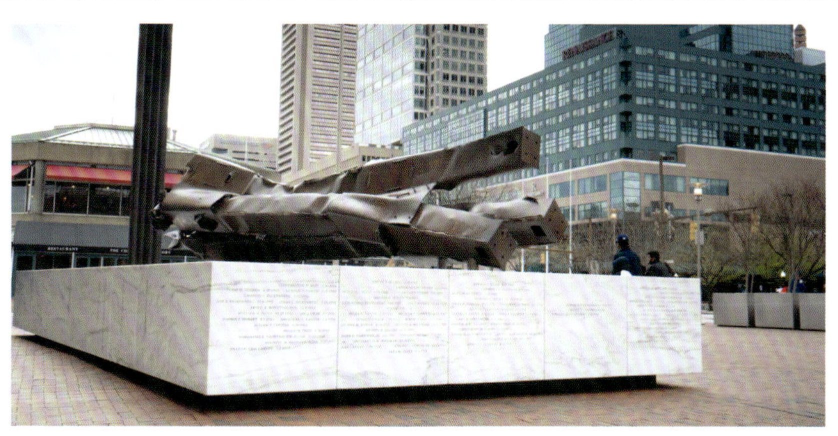

Baltimore World Trade Center is home to a 9/11 Memorial.

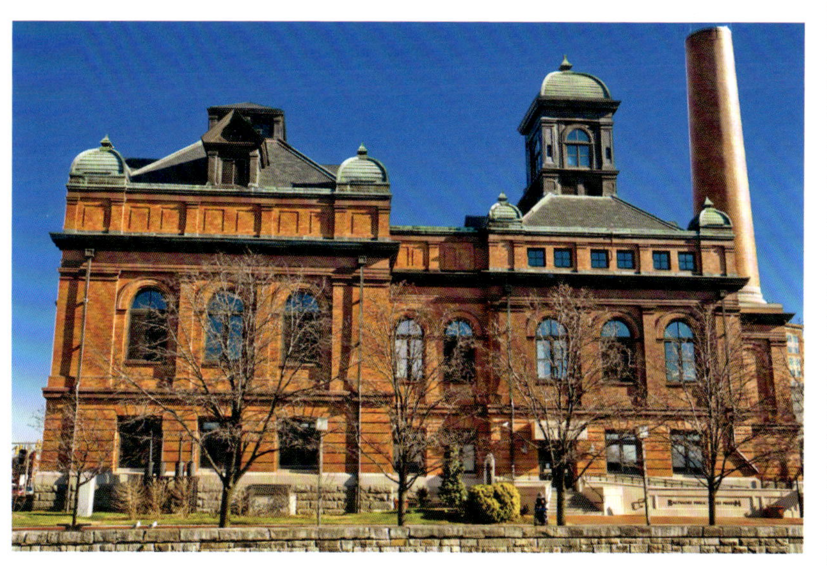

The Public Works Experience, formerly the Baltimore Public Works Museum, opens its Eastern Avenue Pumping Station for one Saturday a month for tours, and also offers the space for rentals.

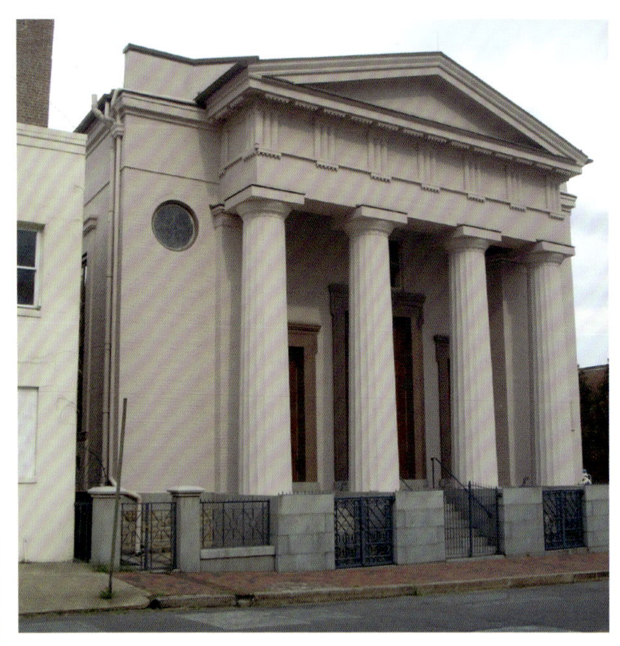

The Lloyd Street Synagogue, part of the Jewish Museum of Maryland, is one of the oldest synagogue buildings in the United States, opening in 1845.

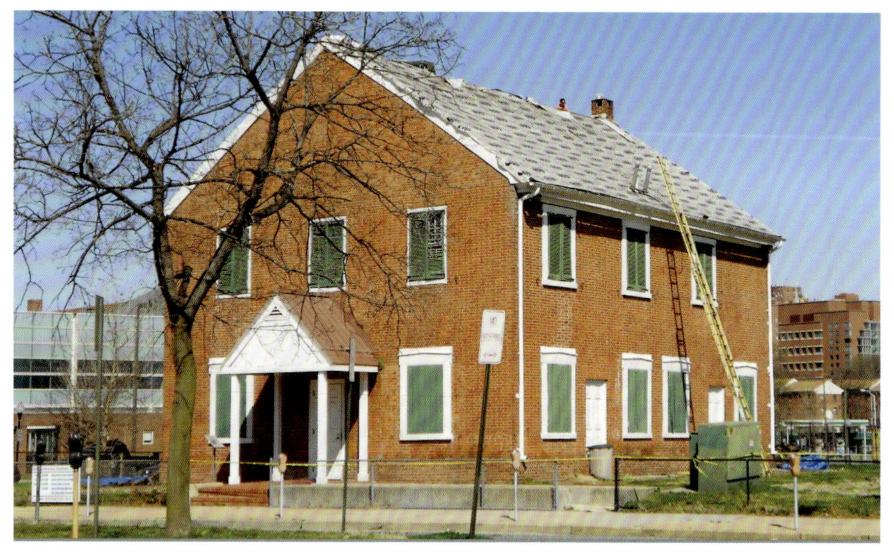

This Old Town Friends' Meetinghouse was built as a Quaker meetinghouse in 1781.

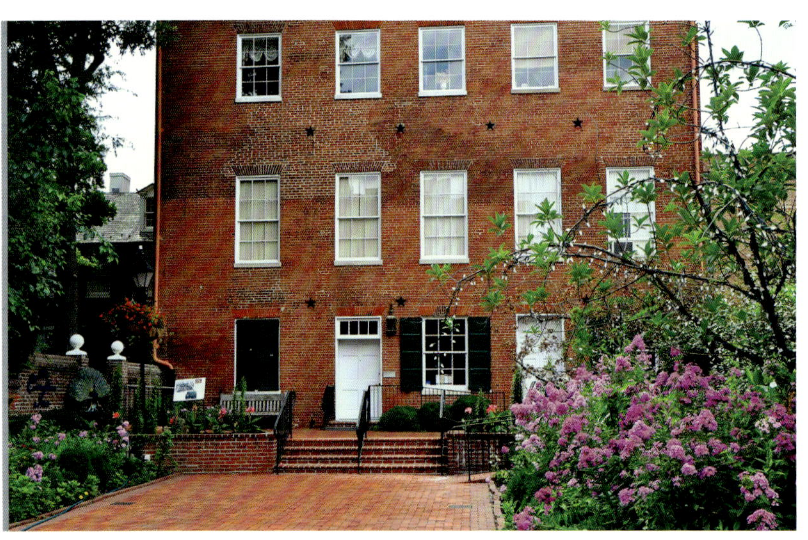

Built in 1811, the house now known as the Carroll Mansion was bought in 1818 by Richard Caton. Caton lived there with his wife Mary and his father-in-law, Charles Carroll, one of the signers of the Declaration of Independence. The house has served as a family home, an apartment building for immigrants, a saloon, a store, a vocational school, and now a museum.

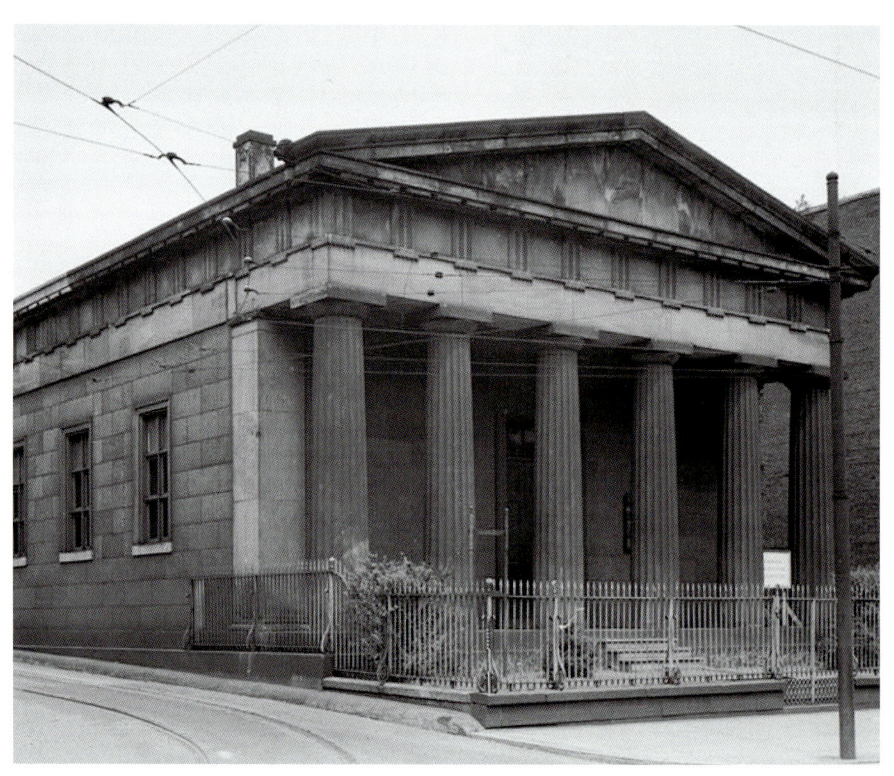

McKim's Free School, built in 1833 by Quaker merchant Jon McKim, was modeled after a Greek temple. It is pictured here in 1936.

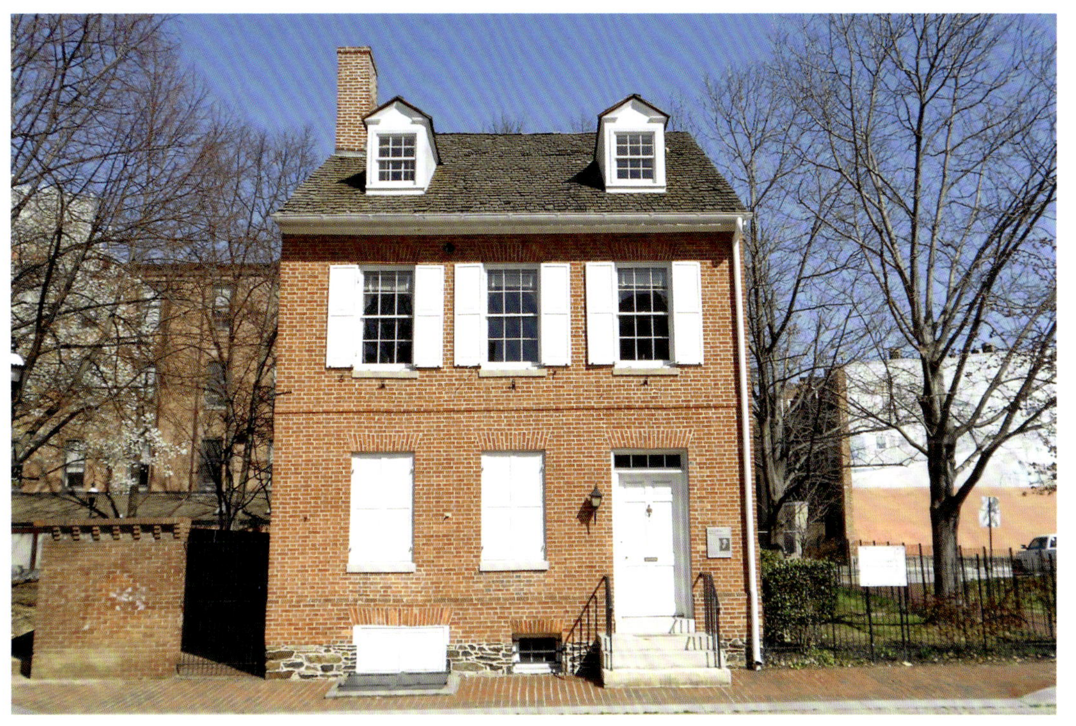

The house at Nine North Front Street, built around 1790, served as the home to the second mayor of Baltimore, Thorowgood Smith.

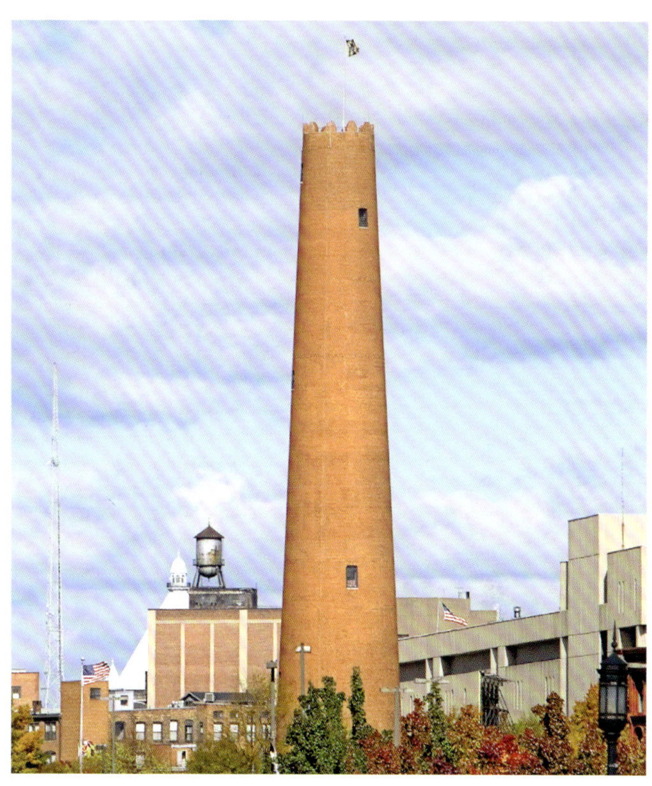

Built in 1828, the Phoenix Shot Tower was used to produce drop shot for muskets. Standing 234.25 feet, the tower held the record of tallest structure in the United States until it was superseded in 1846.

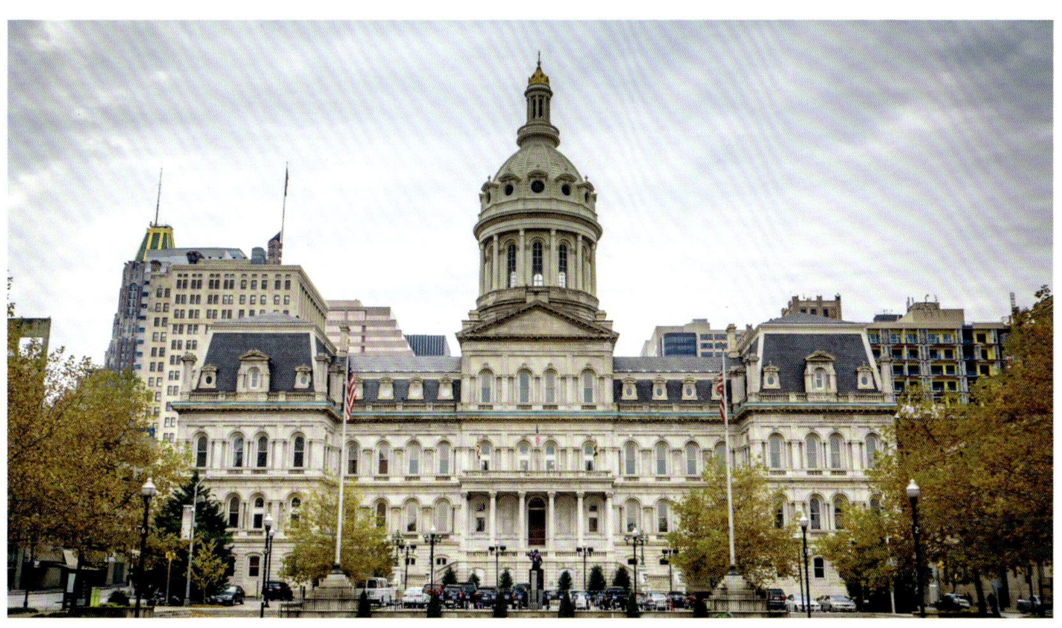

Baltimore City Hall was built between 1867 and 1875. It is immediately next to the War Memorial Plaza.

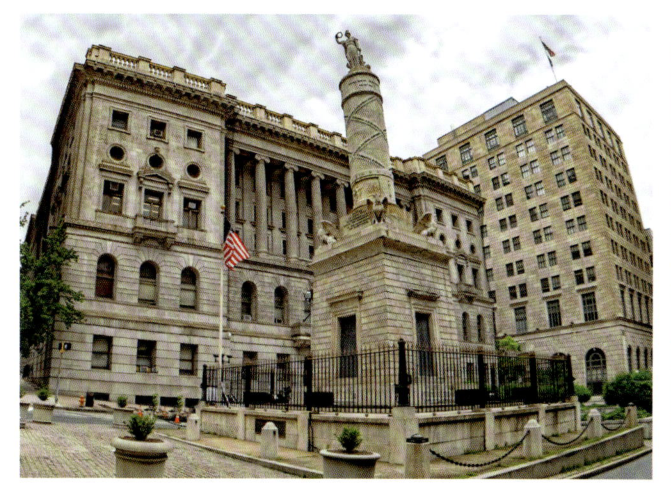

The Battle of Baltimore took place in 1814. Work on the Battle Monument to honor the dead began in 1815 and was completed in 1825.

Capitol Hill and the National Mall

Location: Washington, D.C.

Length: Variable

- 2.6 miles from United States Capitol Building to the Lincoln Memorial
- 3.9 miles from the Capitol to the Lincoln Memorial via the Tidal Basin

Easternmost point: United States Capitol Building

Westernmost point: Lincoln Memorial

Southernmost point: Jefferson Memorial

The National Mall is a national treasure, a beautiful landscape packed with monuments, memorials, and museums. Eleven of the Smithsonian Institution's museums and galleries are located on the Mall, offering opportunities to explore collections of artwork and learn more about history, science, and culture. Admission to those museums is free, though timed-entry passes may be required.

Various memorials, monuments, and sculptures showcase the ideals of American freedom, as they commemorate leaders who provided a vision of what America could be. War memorials remember those veterans who fought and died for our country.

Book plenty of time to visit the National Mall. One option is to take a night tour, which can be less crowded than during the daytime. Many of the monuments look splendid at night, too.

Points of Interest

Beginning at the U.S. Capitol Building and moving clockwise

U.S. Capitol Building
Ulysses S. Grant Memorial
Garfield Monument

Along Independence Avenue

U.S. Botanic Garden
National Museum of the American Indian
National Air and Space Museum
Hirshhorn Museum & Sculpture Garden
Arts & Industries Building
National Museum of African Art
Smithsonian Institution Building (the Castle)
National Museum of Asian Art (Sackler Gallery and Freer Gallery)
Washington Monument

Around the Tidal Basin

U.S. Holocaust Memorial Museum
Tidal Basin
Jefferson Memorial
Franklin Delano Roosevelt Memorial
Martin Luther King Jr. Memorial
District of Columbia War Memorial
Korean War Veterans Memorial

Westernmost point

Lincoln Memorial

Along Constitution Avenue

Vietnam Veterans Memorial
Constitution Gardens
World War II Memorial
National Museum of African American History and Culture
National Museum of American History
National Museum of Natural History
National Sculpture Garden
National Gallery of Art
Peace Monument

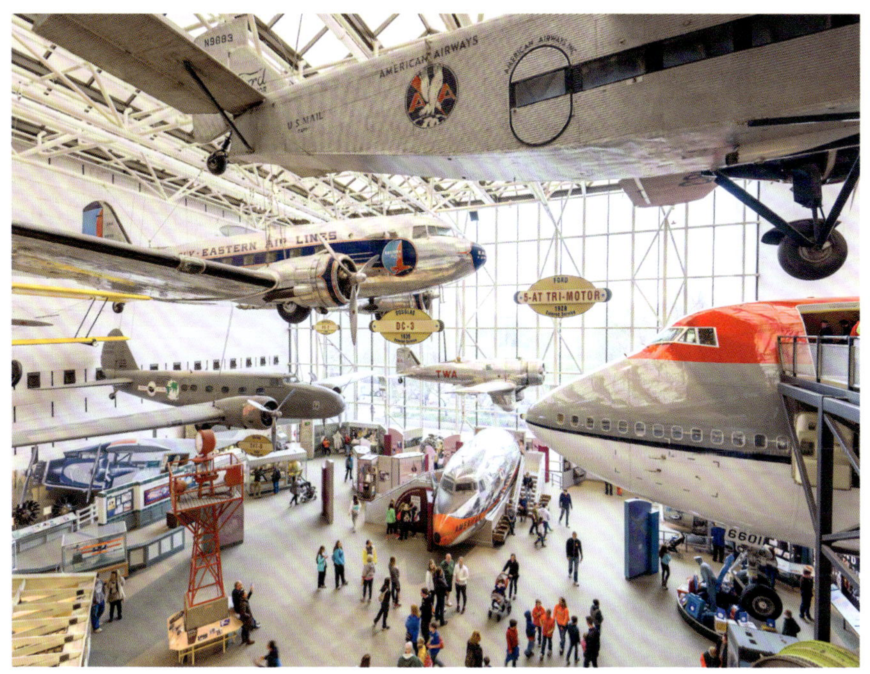

The National Air and Space Museum is a crowd pleaser for all ages.

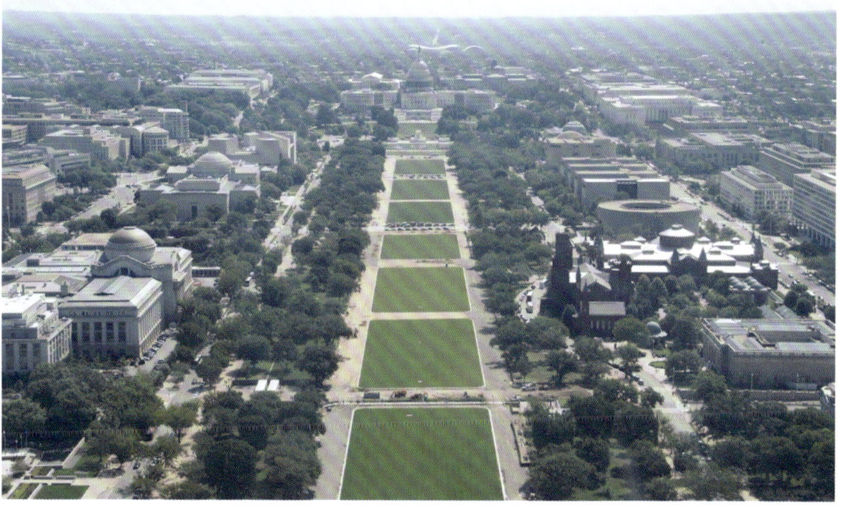

The Capitol Building is seen here from the Washington Monument, with much of the National Mall in view. The National Mall is bordered by Constitution Avenue on one side and Independence Avenue on the other.

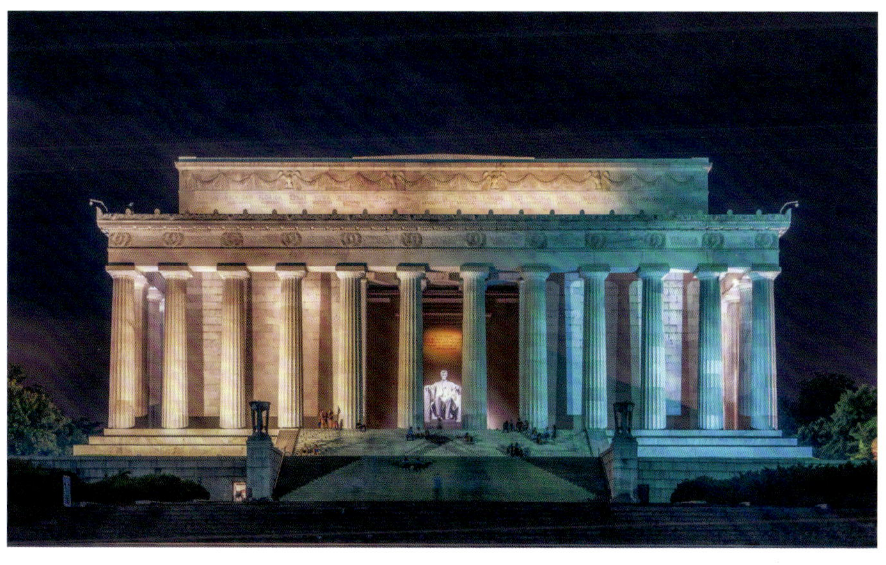

The Mall is bracketed by monuments honoring two Civil War heroes. At one end of the Mall stands an equestrian statue of Ulysses Grant, the Civil War general. At the other end is the iconic Lincoln Memorial.

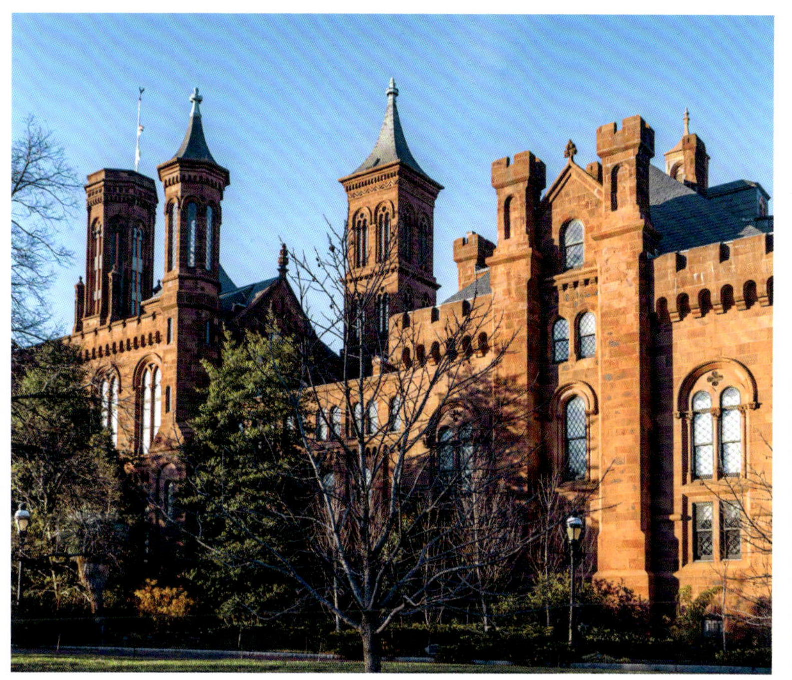

The Smithsonian Institution Building, familiarly known as the Castle, dates to 1855 and houses the Smithsonian Institution's administrative offices.

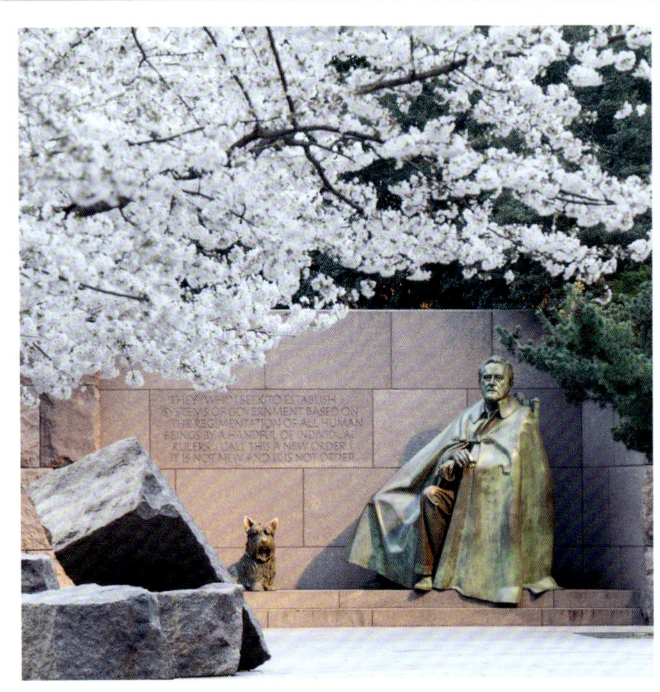

The Franklin Delano Roosevelt Memorial includes depictions of the president and First Lady Eleanor Roosevelt, water features, and inscriptions from Roosevelt's speeches.

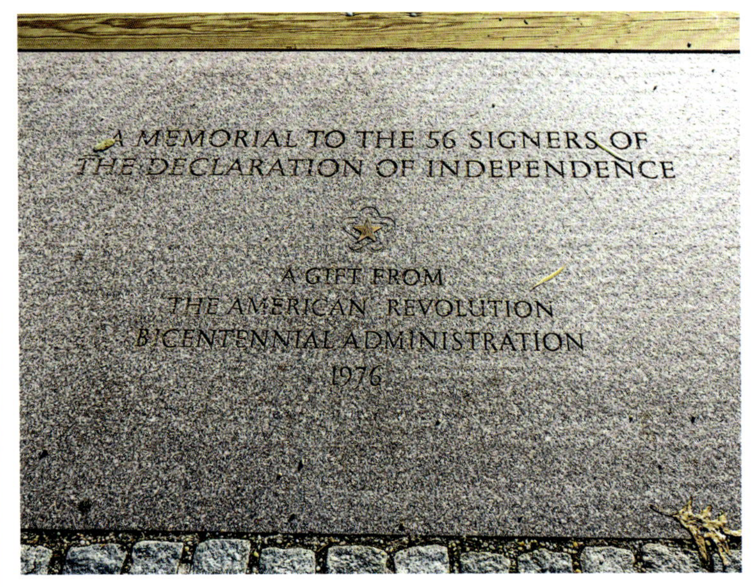

At Constitution Gardens, see a memorial to the signers of the Declaration of Independence.

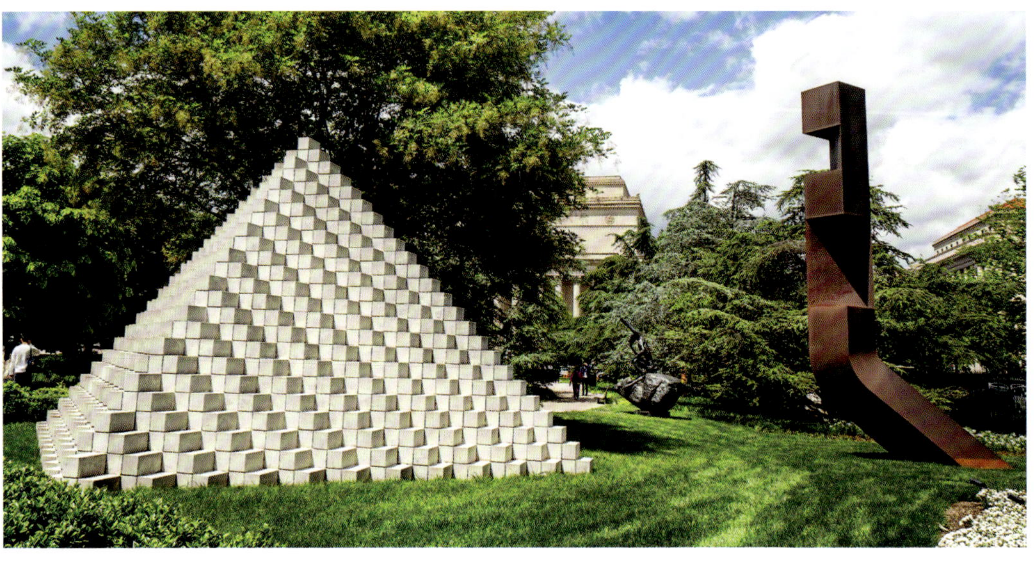

The National Gallery of Art and its accompanying sculpture garden are free to the public.

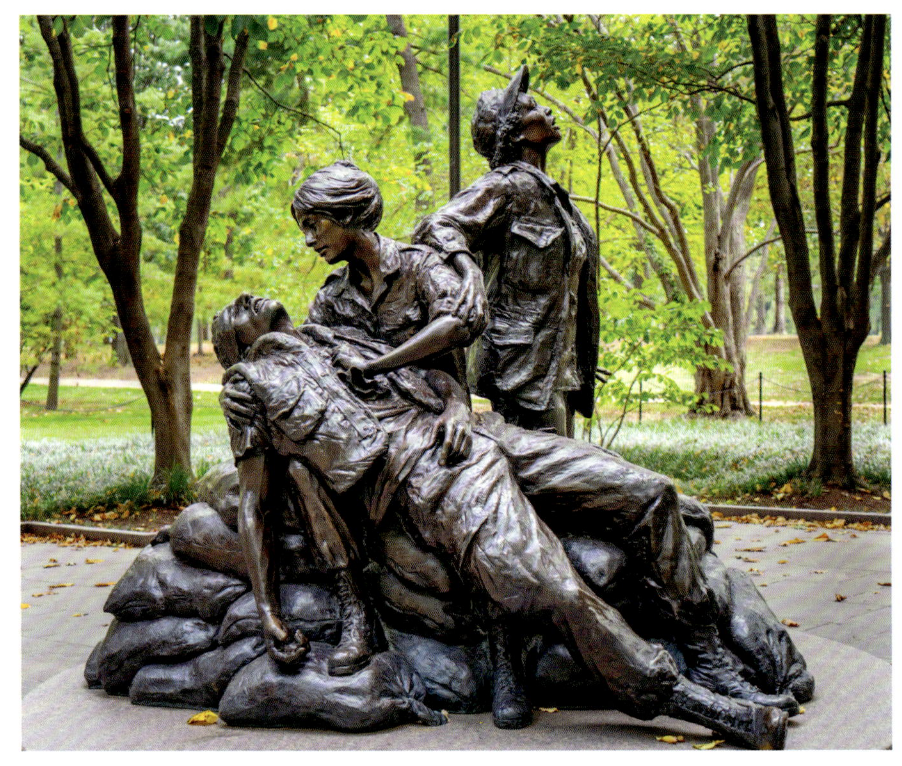

The Vietnam Women's Memorial, sculpted by Glenna Goodacre, can be seen at the larger Vietnam Veterans Memorial.

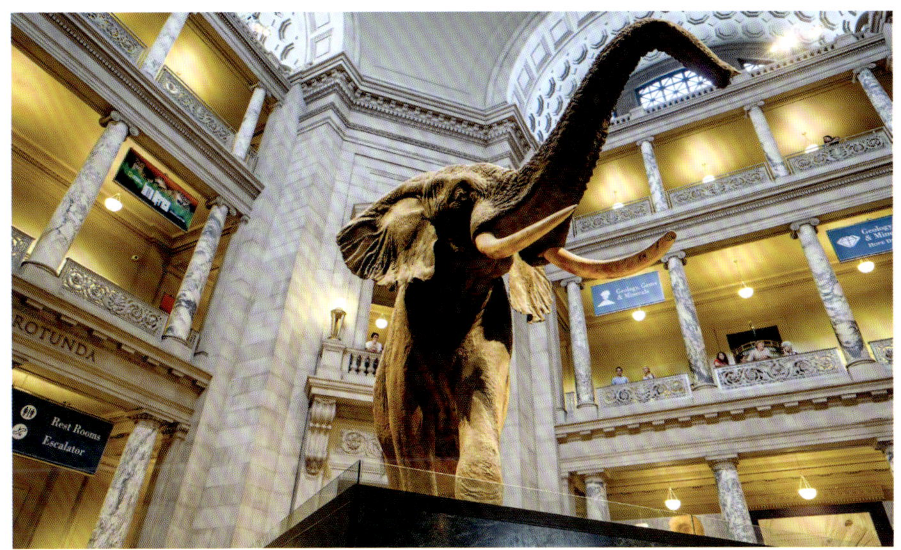

The National Museum of Natural History has a collection of more than 145 million objects, including animal and plant specimens as well as meteorites and things made by humans.

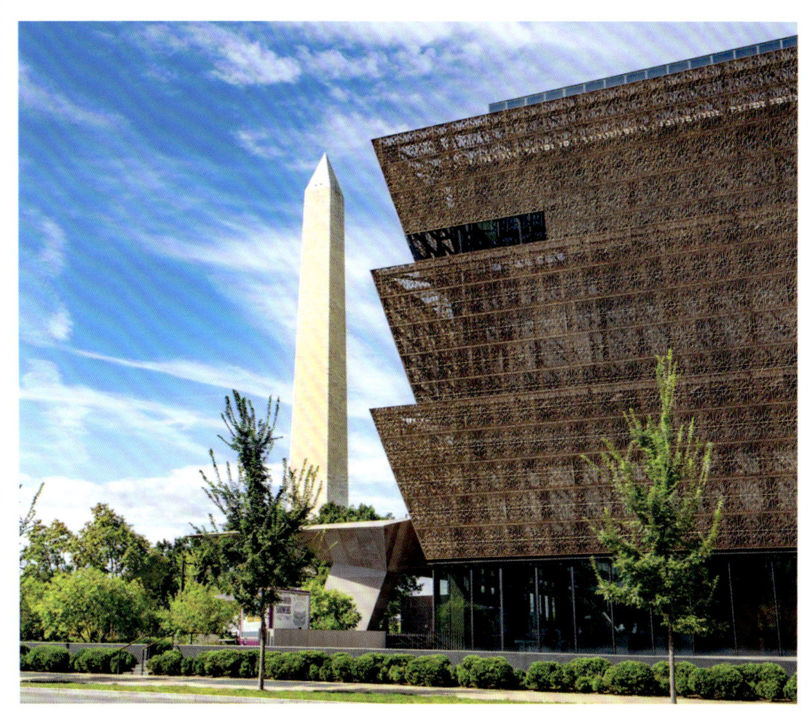

The National Museum of African American History and Culture opened in 2016.

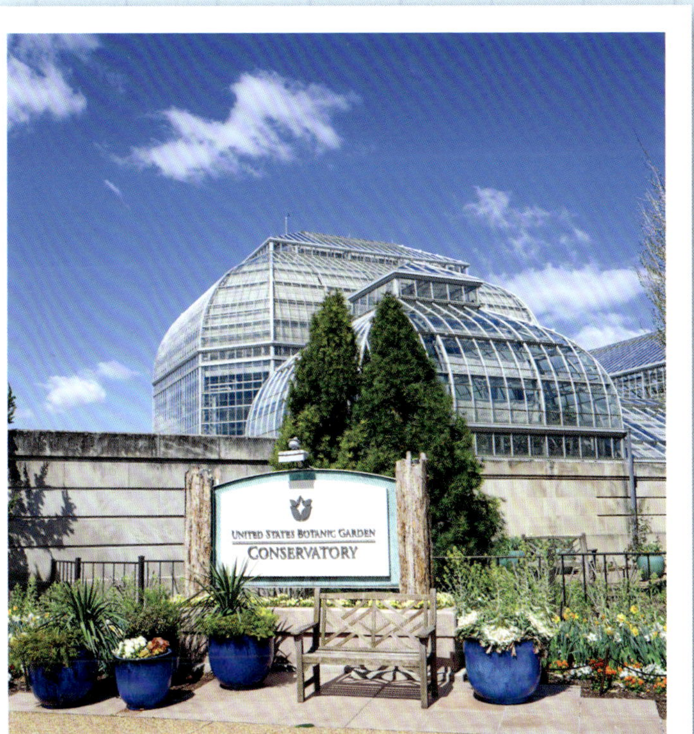

The greenhouse of the United States Botanic Garden was built in 1933.

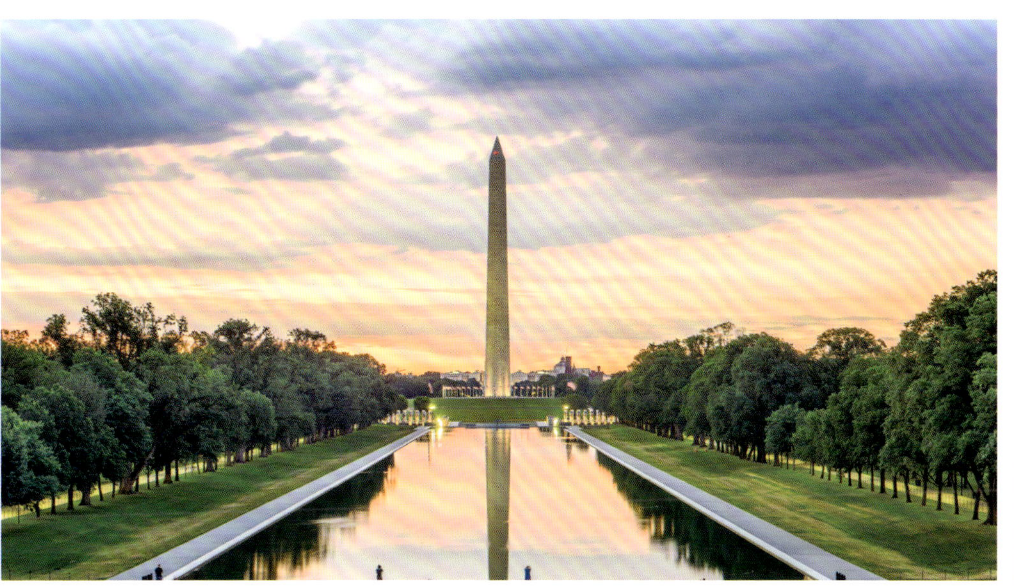

The Washington Monument is seen here from the Lincoln Memorial Reflecting Pool. The obelisk stands almost 555 feet high.

Liberty Trail

Location: Richmond, Virginia

Length: 6.2-mile loop

Start point: Any, but you may want to start at the Richmond Region Visitor Center

Virginia's capital city Richmond was founded in 1737 and later became the capital of the colony of Virginia before the Revolutionary War. After the war, it became the state's capital. The city's important role in the history of Virginia, the fledgling United States, and later as the capital of the Confederacy during the Civil War, is highlighted in the abundance of historic sites found along the Richmond Liberty Trail.

The trail is a loop—one potential starting point is the Visitor Center—with helpful sidewalk markings that take you through Richmond's downtown area. Along the way, you pass by museums, monuments, churches, historic buildings, and more. Capitol Square houses both the Capitol Building and the Executive Mansion, which are historically significant buildings even as they serve today as the home of Virginia's government. The Capitol Building is one of the oldest in the United States, dating back to the 1780s; one of its architects was Thomas Jefferson. The Executive Mansion dates to 1811. Another must-see on the trail is St. John's Church. An active Episcopalian church, the 1741 church was the gathering place of the Second Virginia Convention in 1775, and thus saw Patrick Henry thunder, "Give me liberty or give me death." Reenactments of those events are held on Sundays during the summer months.

Along with the city sights, you'll get some glimpses of nature. At one point the walk takes you along the James River, so you can relax and appreciate beautiful views of the water.

Points of Interest

Hippodrome Theater

Black History Museum and Cultural Center of Virginia

Virginia Repertory Sara Belle and Neil November Theatre

Bolling Haxall House

Richmond Ballet

Historic Tredegar Park and American Civil War Center

Riverfront Plaza

Brown's Island

Christopher Newport Cross

Henry "Box" Brown Monument

Virginia Holocaust Museum

St. John's Church

Edgar Allan Poe Museum

Main Street Station

Old Fellows Hall

First Freedom Center

St. Paul's Episcopal Church

Virginia Capitol and Executive Mansion

Virginia Civil Rights Monument

City Hall

Monumental Church

First African Baptist Church

Valentine Richmond History Center

Library of Virginia

National Theater

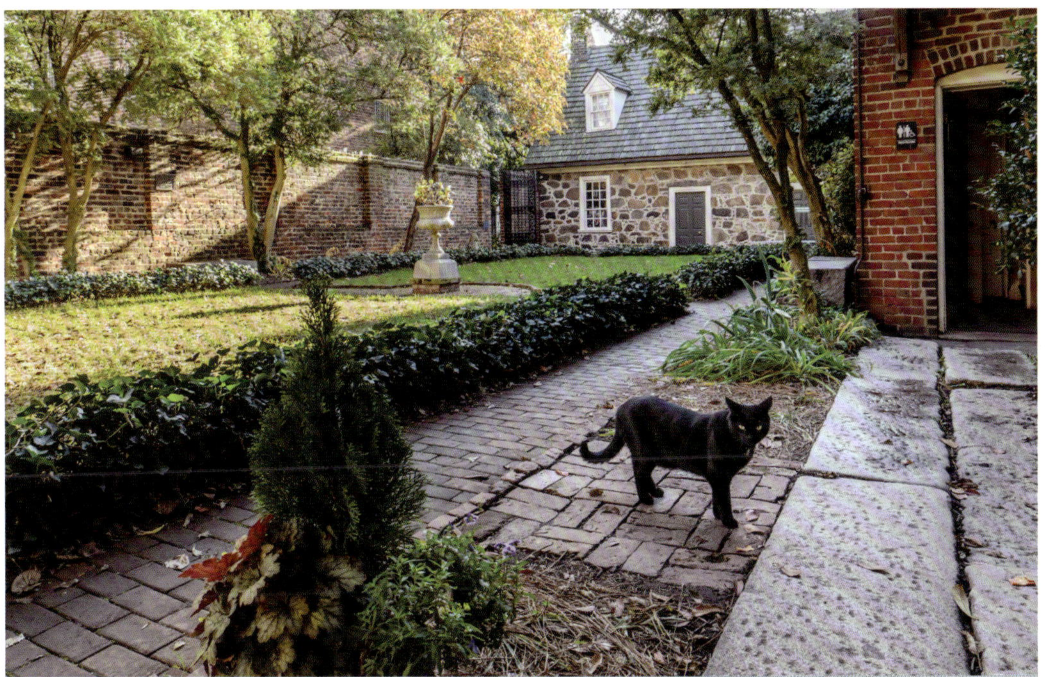

The Edgar Allan Poe Museum honors the famous author, who lived in Richmond during portions of his life. Visitors can see collections that include his writings, furniture, and possessions–and possibly one of the cats that have made the museum gardens their home.

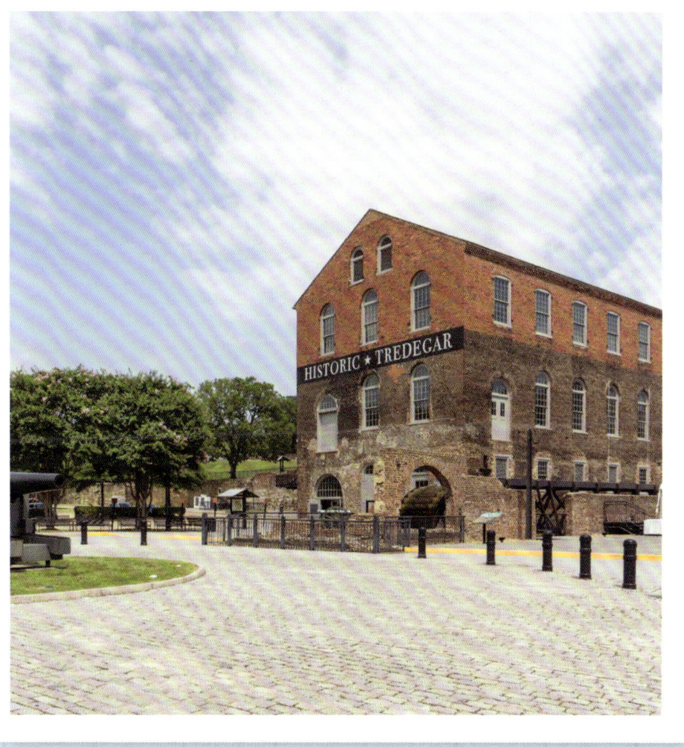

During the Civil War, the Tredegar Iron Works *(above)* supplied the Confederacy with artillery. Today, the site is part of Richmond National Battlefield Park. The American Civil War Center, a museum, is found at the site.

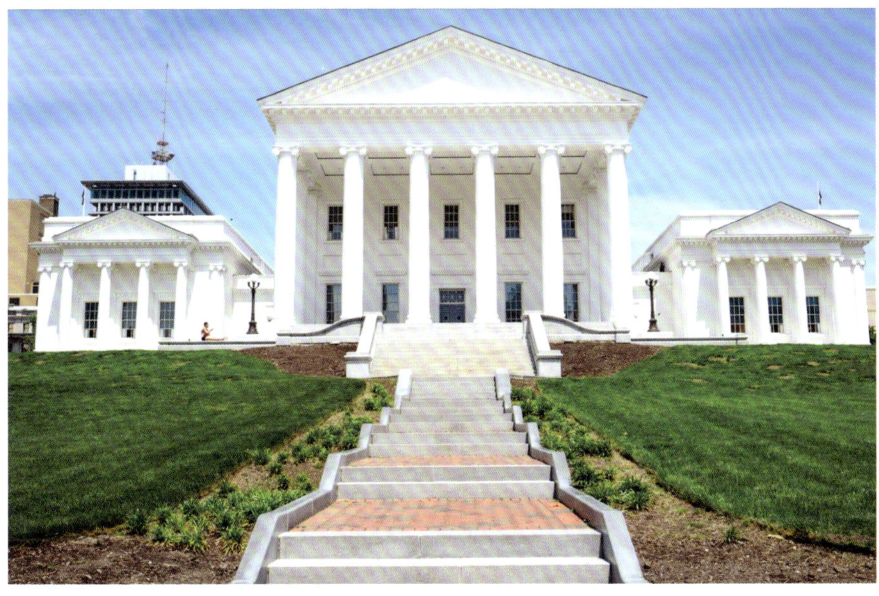

Construction on the State Capitol began in 1785 and was completed three years later. The two wings were added in 1904.

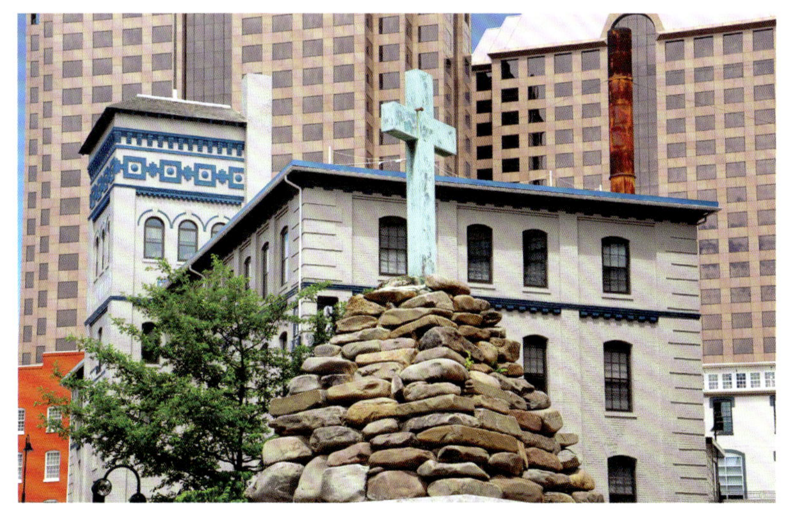

The Christopher Newport Cross remembers the captain of one of the ships that brought settlers to Jamestown, Virginia, in 1607.

Liberty Walk

Location: Charlotte, North Carolina
Length: About 1 mile
Start point: Battle of Charlotte Monument
End point: Mecklenburg Resolves

Stroll along the self-guided Charlotte Liberty Walk to view close to twenty markers that indicate places of importance during Charlotte's early history, especially during the American Revolutionary War. Brochures outlining the route and giving more historical information about each site can be found at the Charlotte Liberty Walk web site.

European colonists came to Charlotte and the surrounding area of Mecklenburg County in the mid-1750s. One early settler, considered the founder of Charlotte, was Thomas Polk, who later served in the Continental Army. Along the walk, people can see the former location of his home, where George Washington visited before a stay at the nearby Cook's Inn; and view Polk's gravesite at the Settlers' Cemetery. Other prominent patriots like Ephraim Brevard and James Jack are also honored with markers along the route.

Some of the sites commemorate military occasions, while others focus on political moments. The route finishes with one such marker, which focuses on the creation of the Mecklenburg Resolves on May 31, 1775. Early in the Revolutionary War, colonists produced these resolves, which were documents stating that the Crown's power would not be recognized and annulling laws previously established by the British king.

The first few markers on the route are located near the intersection of Martin Luther King Jr. Bouvelard and South Tryon Street, very close to the Levine Center for the Arts, if you'd like to get your culture fix before heading on your historical walk. Check out the Bechtler Museum of Modern Art, the Harvey B. Gantt Center for African-American Arts + Culture, the Knight Theater, and the Mint Museum Uptown.

Points of Interest

Battle of Charlotte Monument
Ishmael Titus Marker
Catawba Indians & Indian Trading Path Marker
Liberty Hall DAR Marker
Site of Queens College
Site of British Camp
Battle of Charlotte State Historical Marker
Mecklenburg Declaration of Independence
Cook's Inn
Captain Jack Homesite
First Presbyterian Church
Settlers' Cemetery
Line of Patriots' Retreat
Queen Charlotte Statue
Ephraim Brevard Marker
Thomas Polk Homesite
Nathanael Greene State Historical Marker
Mecklenburg Resolves Marker

**Older maps or listings may show Thomas Polk Park, which closed in 2023, as part of this walk.*

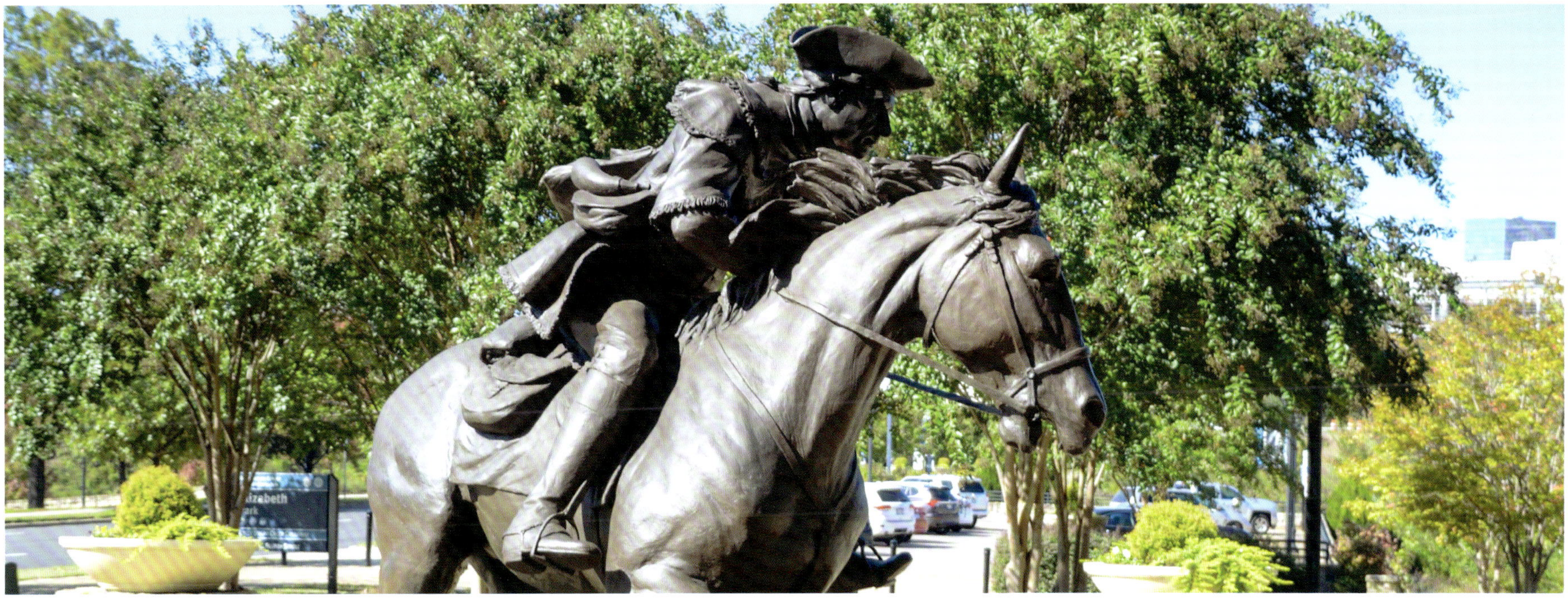

A Charlotte statue memorializes James Jack, who reportedly made a ride carrying the "Mecklenburg Declaration of Independence."

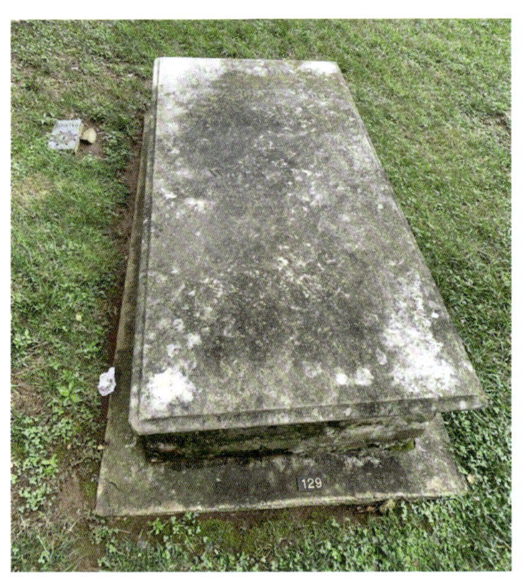

Settlers' Cemetery, sometimes called Old Settlers' Cemetery, contains the grave of Thomas Polk. Along with his accomplishments in Charlotte history, Polk was the uncle of President James Polk.

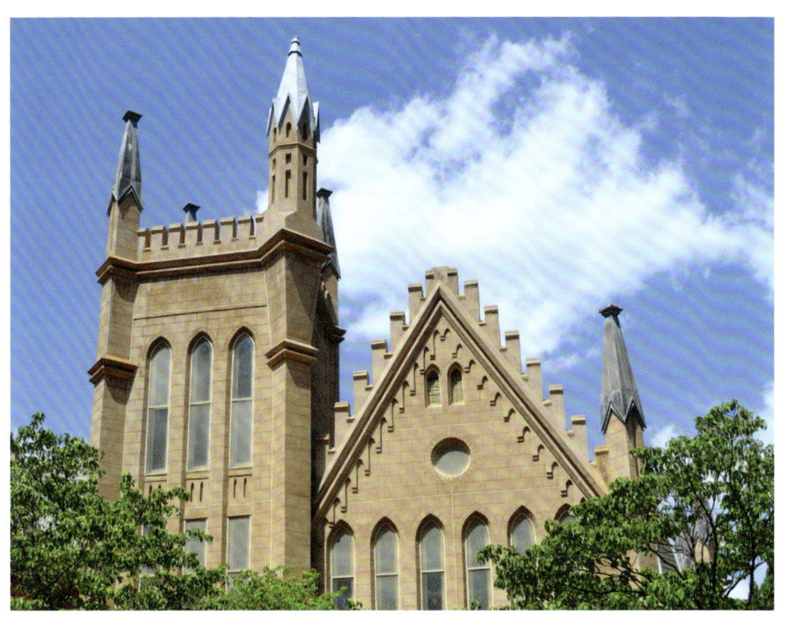

Land was set aside for a church as far back as 1815 in the location where Charlotte's First Presbyterian Church now stands. The current building dates to 1857.

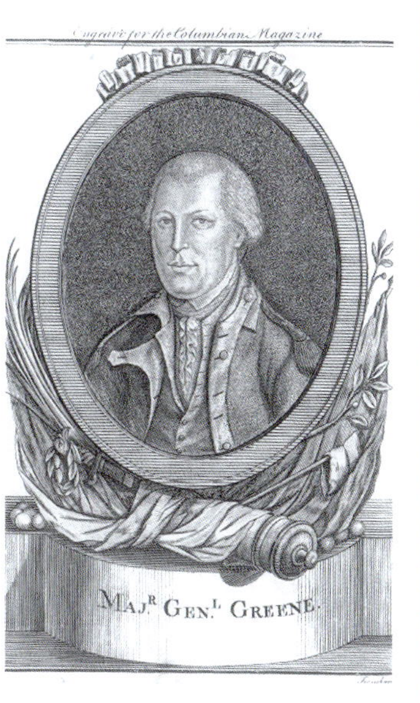

Nathanael Greene was an officer of the Continental Army who assumed command of the southern part of the Army in 1780, countering General Cornwallis.

Eastside Trail

Location: Atlanta, Georgia

Length: 2 miles (main stretch), 3 miles with extensions

Start point: Piedmont Park

End point: Variable

The Atlanta BeltLine is a huge project with the goal of turning more than 20 miles of a former railroad corridor into a collection of parks and multi-use trails, with eventual aims that also include a system of light rail streetcars and affordable housing. Development began in 2005, and there are now a number of completed trails, with others in progress. The Atlanta BeltLine Partnership offers both walking and biking tours of some of the trails, and people can hike or bike them on their own, often spotting both official public art installations and unofficial street art along the way.

The Eastside Trail is part of that larger project, a paved stretch through several of Atlanta's neighborhoods. Along the route, walkers can ramble through parks, including the Historic Fourth Ward Skatepark, the first public skatepark in the United States. There are also tons of opportunities for shopping and eating at the Ponce City Market and the Krog Street Market. At the Ponce City Park, pop upstairs to the rooftop, known as Skyline Park, to get great views of the city. Toward the end of the trail, check out the Krog Street Tunnel, known for its quirky street art.

For a longer day, walkers can visit two historic sites that are quite close to the trail. About a half mile from the skatepark, walkers can take a slight detour east via the Freedom Park Trail to arrive at the Jimmy Carter Library and Museum. When walkers reach Irwin Street near Krog Market, they're less than a mile's walk from Martin Luther King Jr. National Historical Park, which includes his childhood home, Ebenezer Baptist Church where he was a pastor, and the King Center for Nonviolent Social Change, where he and Coretta Scott King are buried.

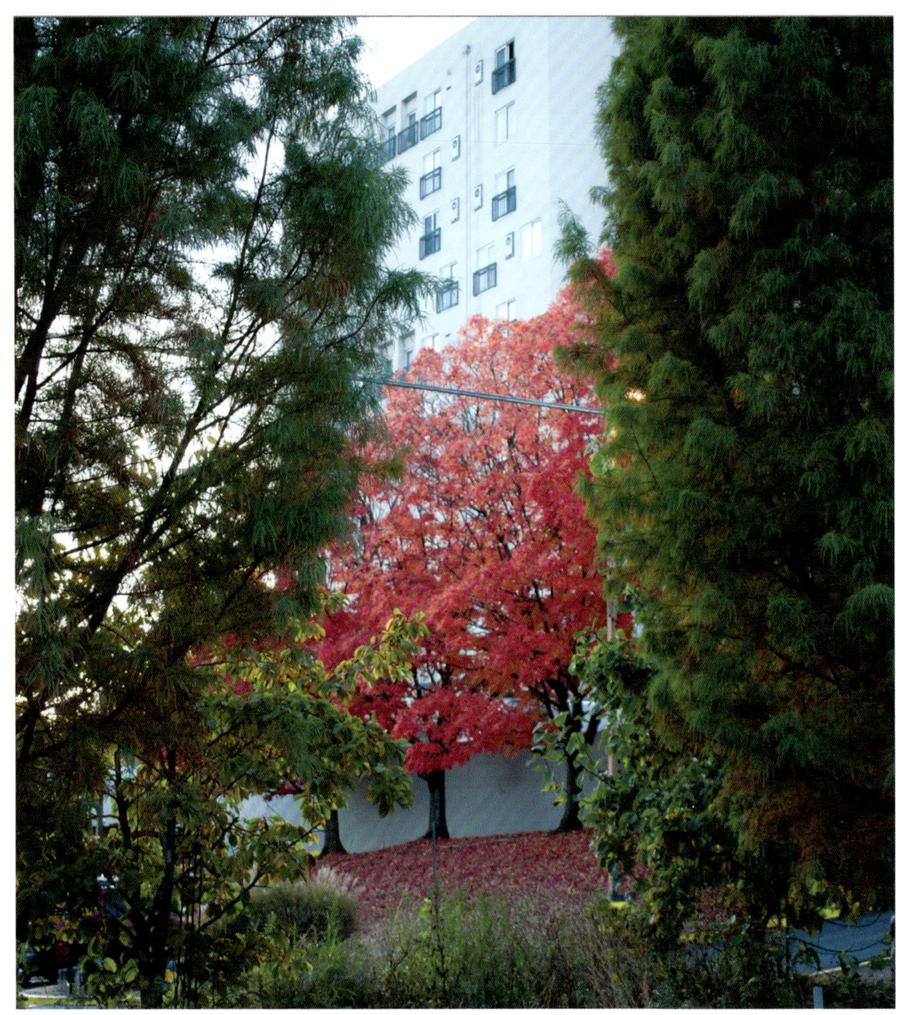

The Eastside Trail provides views of the city, nature, art, and architecture.

Points of Interest

Piedmont Park
Ponce City Market
Historic Fourth Ward Park
Historic Fourth Ward Skatepark
Krog Street Market
Krog Street Tunnel
Carter Center / Jimmy Carter Library and Museum *(nearby)*
Martin Luther King Jr. National Historical Park *(nearby)*

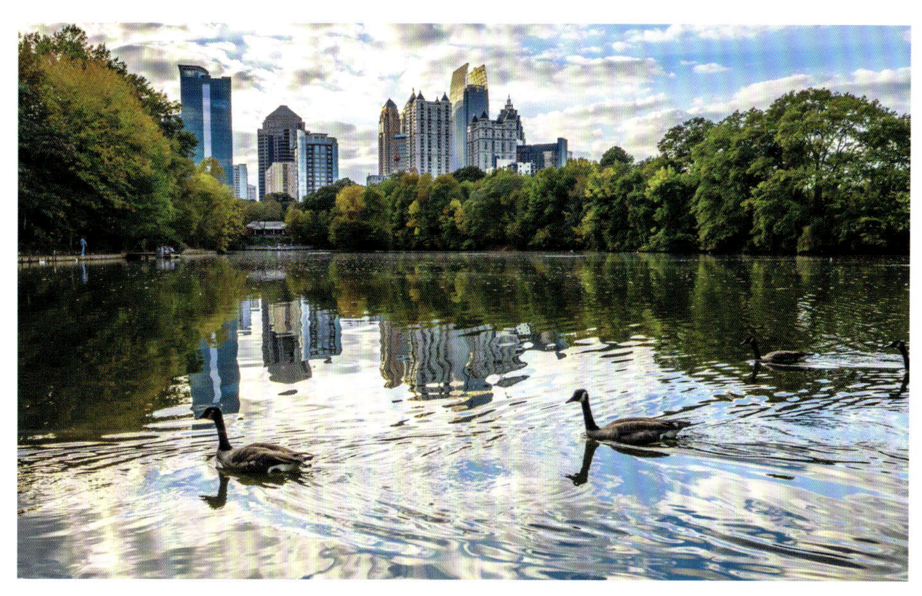

Piedmont Park covers more than 185 acres and includes a playground, paths, picnic areas, and lake fishing. In the summer, concerts and movies are offered.

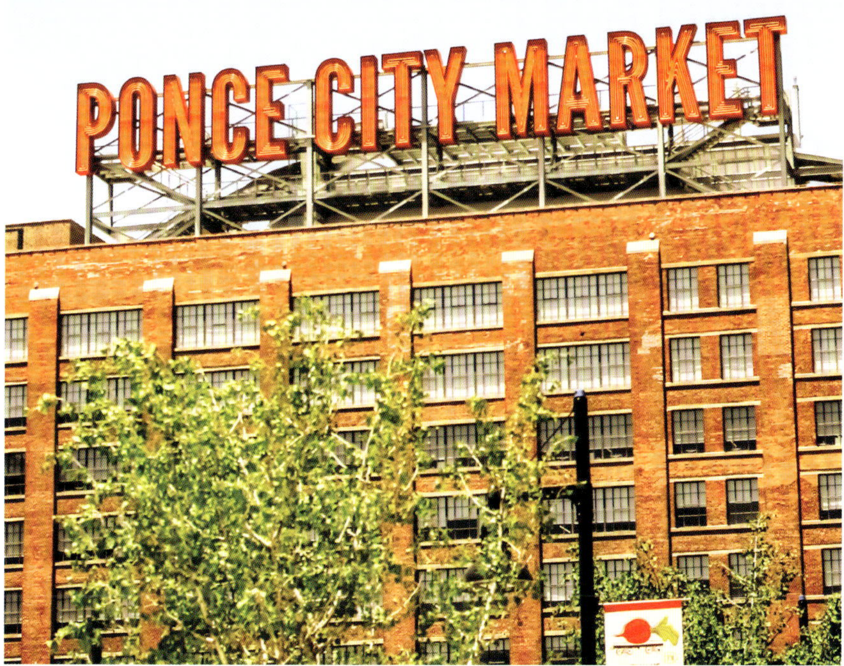

Ponce City Market contains apartments, restaurants, stores, and a food hall.

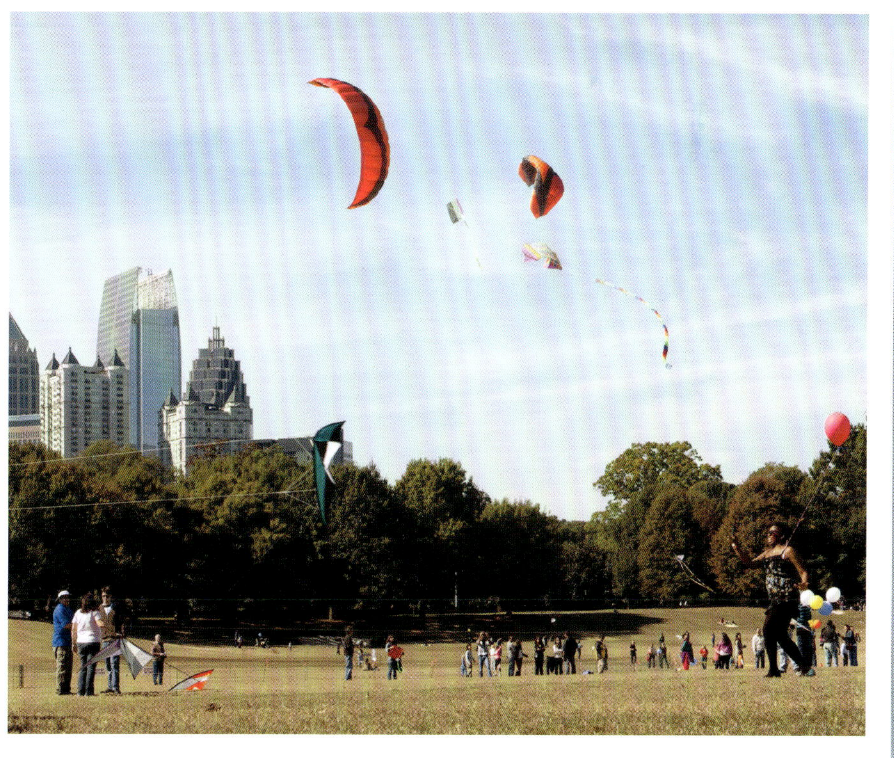

Piedmont Park hosted a kite festival in 2013.

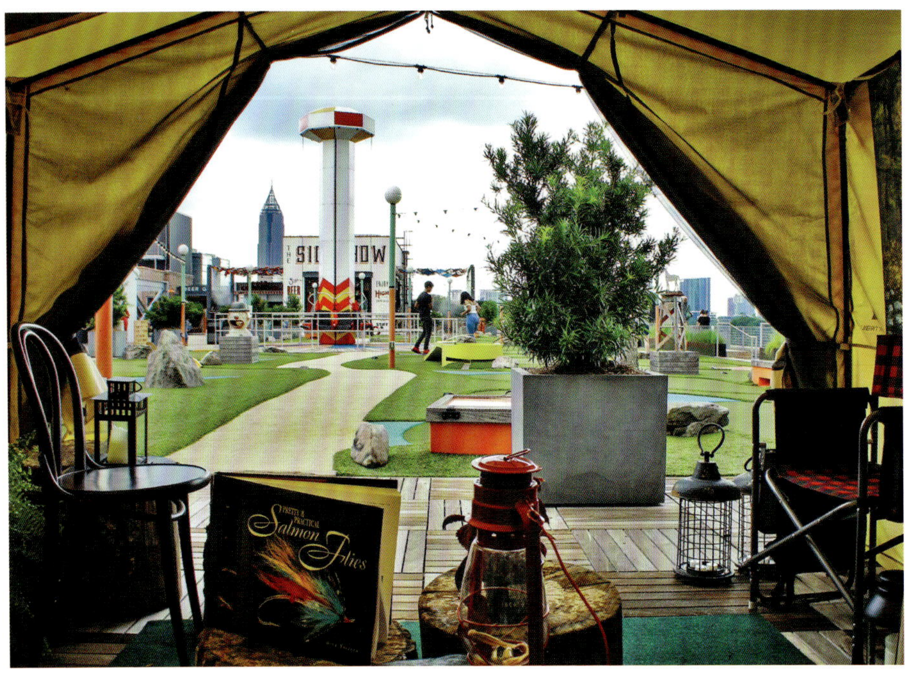

Skyline Park is a rooftop amusement park at Ponce City Market.

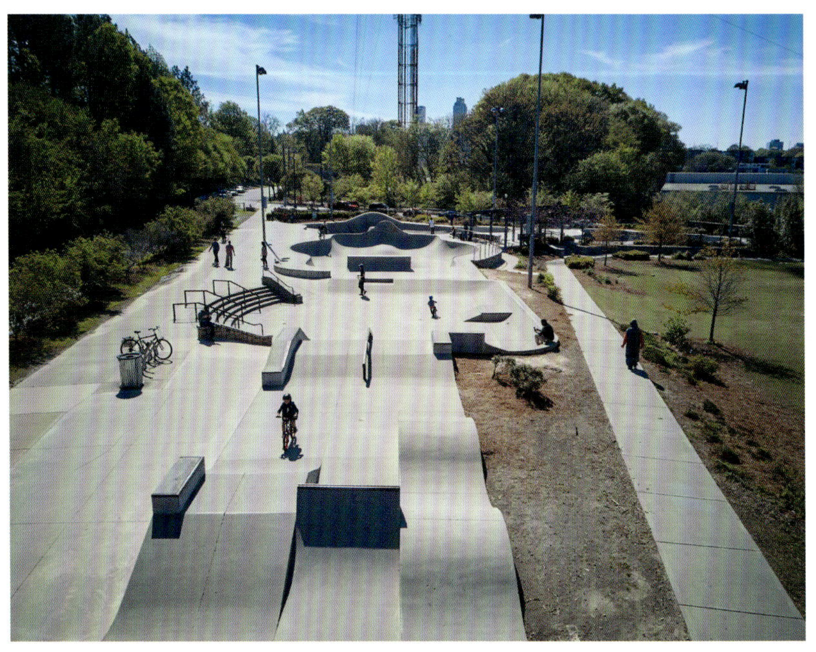

The Historic Fourth Ward Skatepark opened in 2011 as the first public skatepark in the United States.

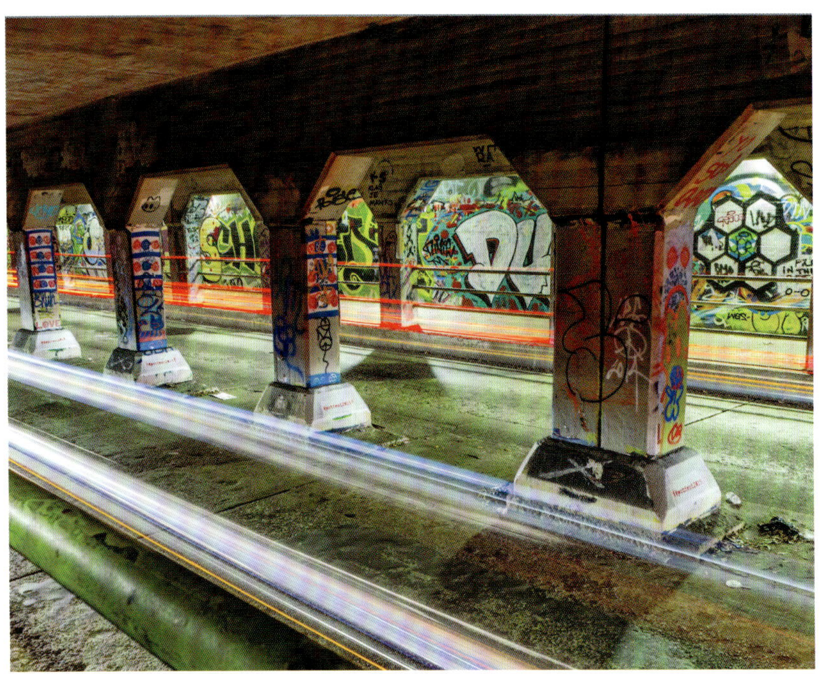

Walkers can pause to check out the street art in the Krog Street Tunnel. Ramble the nearby areas to see more street art and murals.

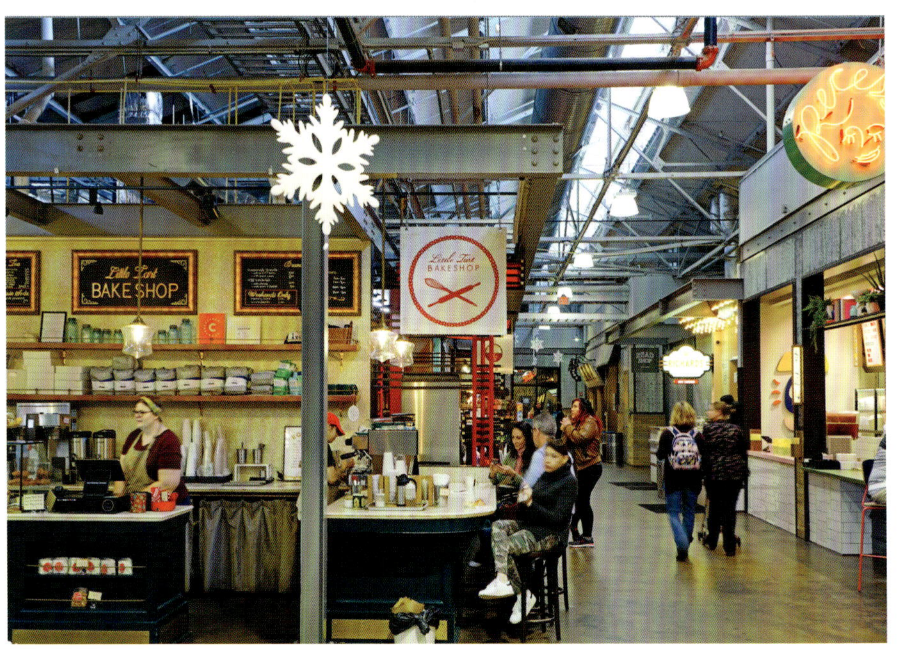

If walking makes you hungry, stop off for a bite to eat at the Krog Street Market.

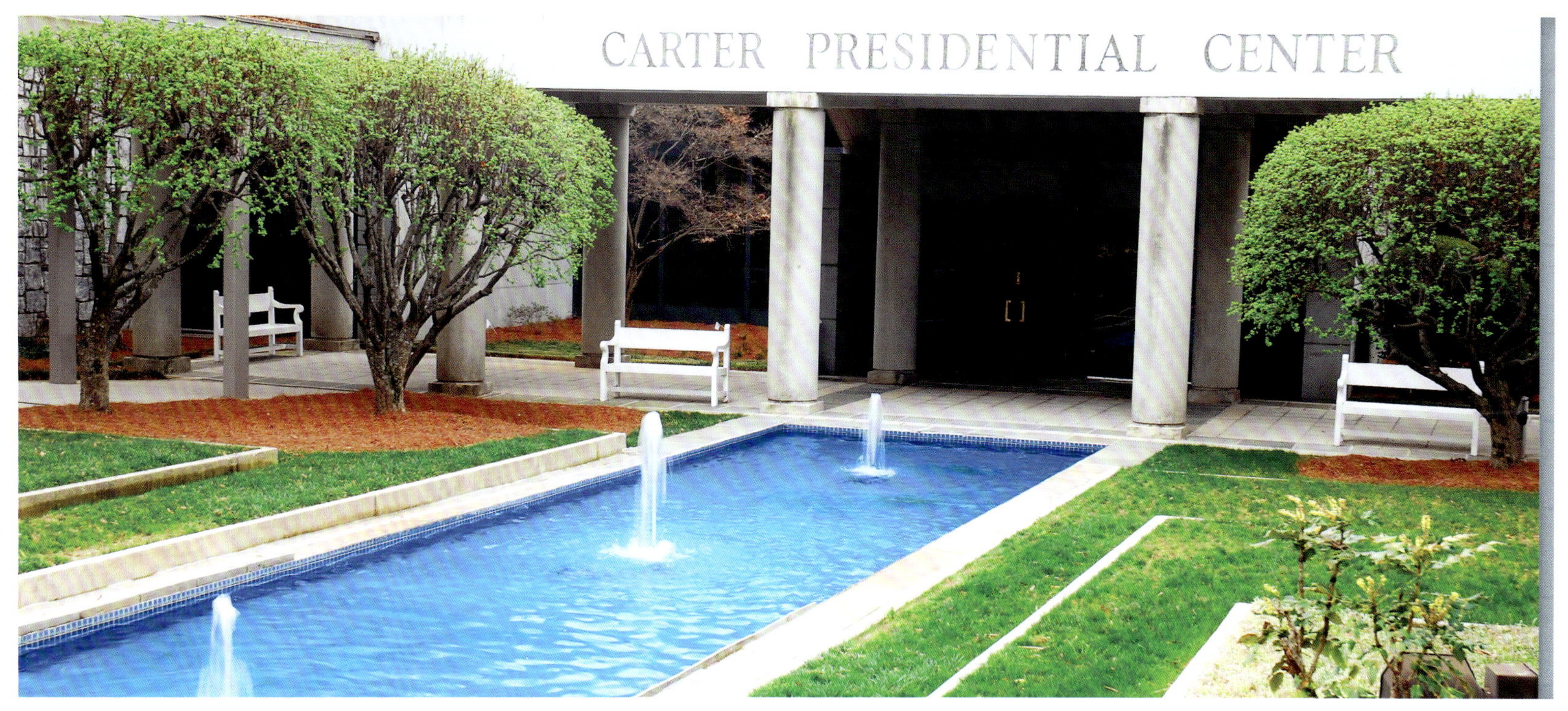

The Jimmy Carter Library and Museum is easily reached from the Eastside Trail. It's adjacent to the Carter Center, the organization created by former President Jimmy Carter and his wife Rosalynn that has a focus on election monitoring, democracy, human rights, and health.

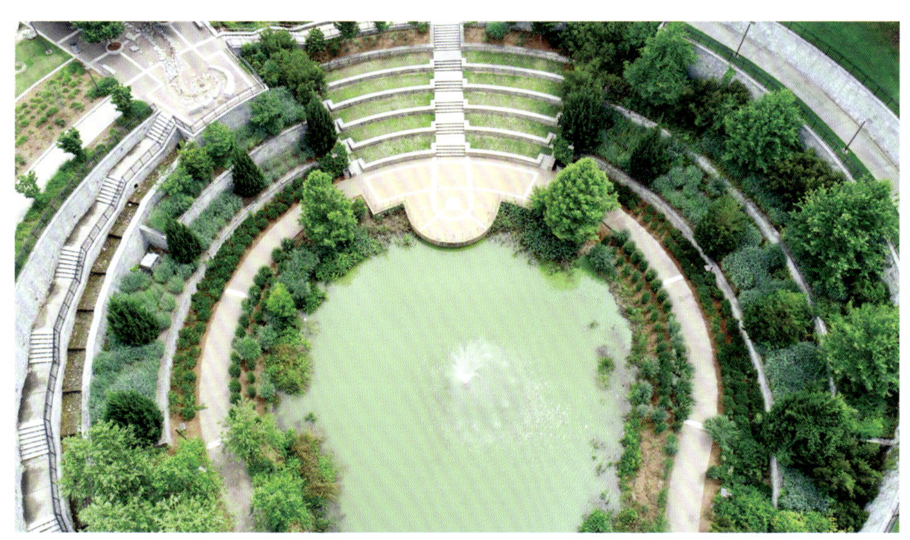

The Historic Fourth Ward Park contains an amphitheater, playground, splash pad, and lots of landscaped beauty.

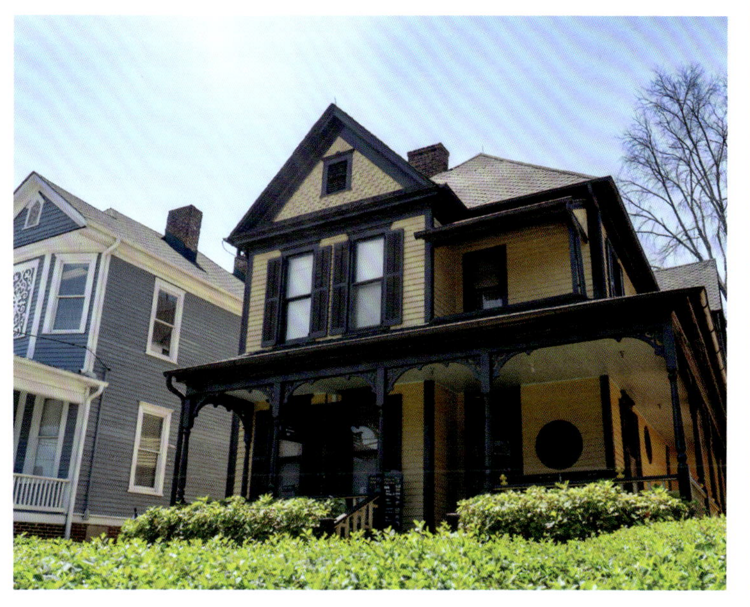

Martin Luther King Jr.'s childhood home is one site of several in Martin Luther King Jr. National Historical Park.

Historic St. Augustine

Location: St. Augustine, Florida
Length: 1.2 miles
Start point: Castillo de San Marcos National Monument
End point: Ximenez-Fatio House Museum

St. Augustine was founded in 1565 by Spanish explorer Pedro Menéndez de Avilés, and has been continuously inhabited ever since, making it the oldest continuous settlement by Europeans in the contiguous United States. By travelling a little more than a mile in the downtown area, tourists can get an overview of several layers of St. Augustine history, from the original Spanish settlement, to a period of British rule, to a second period of Spanish rule before Florida became part of the United States.

Start on the waterfront of Matanzas River with the Castillo de San Marcos National Monument. The old masonry fort there—the oldest in the United States—dates to 1672. From there, head to the north end of St. George Street to see the City Gate, built in 1808. A short walk away, you'll find the Oldest Wooden Schoolhouse, which was built in the early 1700s. Not far from there, the Colonial Quarter is a living history museum, complete with blacksmithing demonstrations and musket drills.

Continuing on, walk down St. George Street, a pedestrian-only street with tons of boutique shops and restaurants, to the Cathedral Basilica of St. Augustine. The church building dates to 1793, with the parish community tracing its roots back to the 1565 settlement. Clustered nearby are the Plaza de la Constitución, a public square dating to 1573 with a number of monuments, and the Governor's House Cultural Center and Museum.

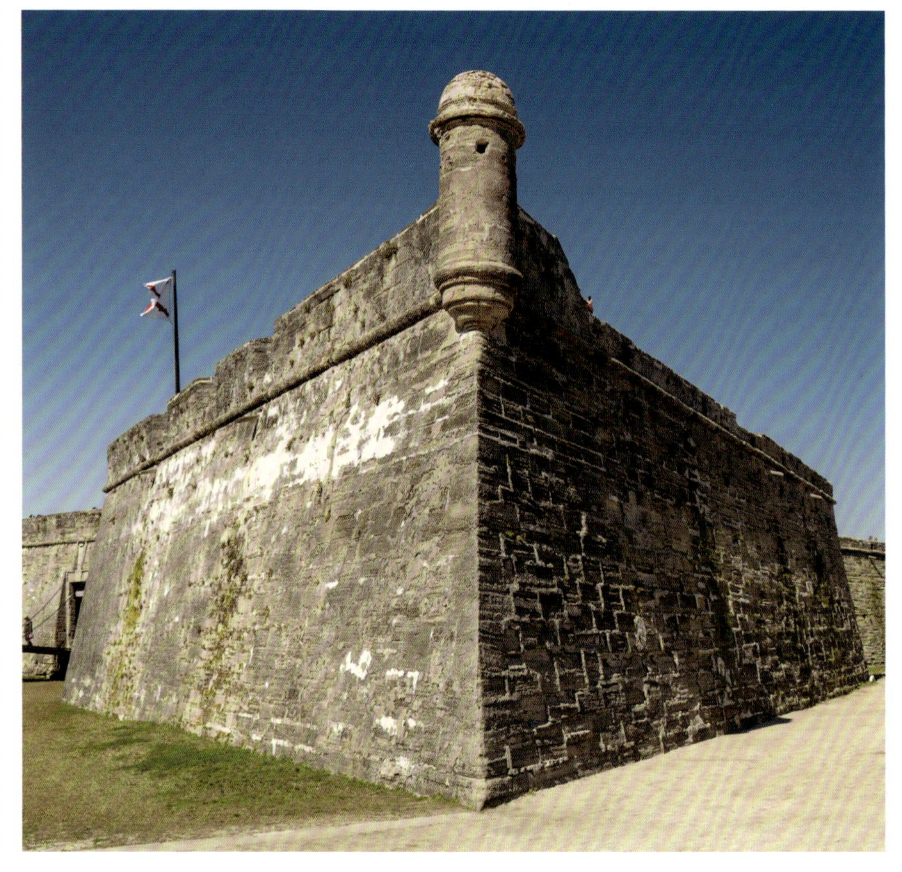

The Castillo de San Marcos National Monument was built between 1672 and 1695 in response to British piracy.

Two museums round out the tour: the Ximenez-Fatio House Museum dates to 1797, during the second period of Spanish rule, while the Lightner Museum is found in the former Alcazar Hotel. During the Gilded Age, industrialist Henry Flagler worked to make Florida and St. Augustine a tourist destination, opening the luxurious Hotel Alcazar as part of that project. The hotel became a museum in 1948.

Points of Interest

Castillo de San Marcos National Monument

City Gate

Oldest Wooden Schoolhouse

Colonial Quarter

St. George Street

Cathedral Basilica of St. Augustine

Plaza de la Constitución

Governor's House Cultural Center and Museum

Lightner Museum *(former Alcazar Hotel)*

Ximenez-Fatio House Museum

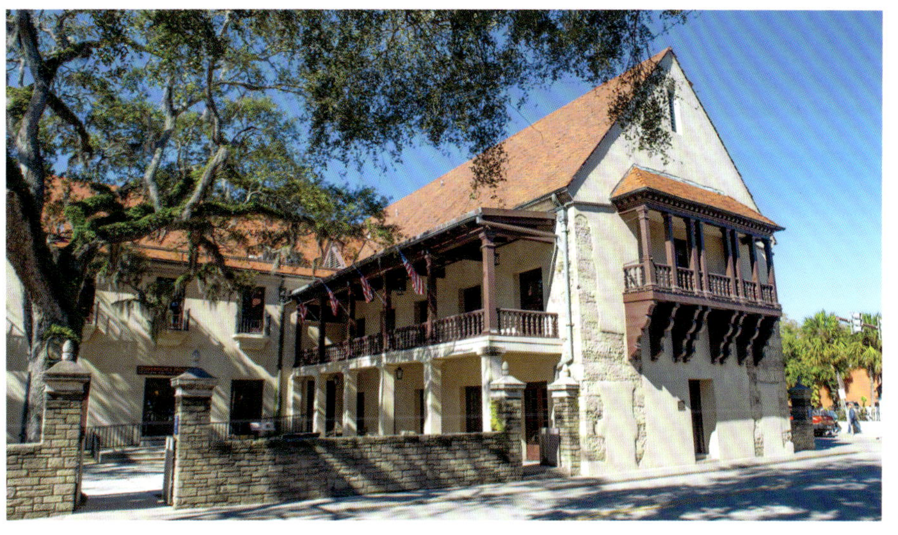

The Governor's House has been extensively remodeled several times. The oldest parts of the building come from its initial construction between 1706 and 1713.

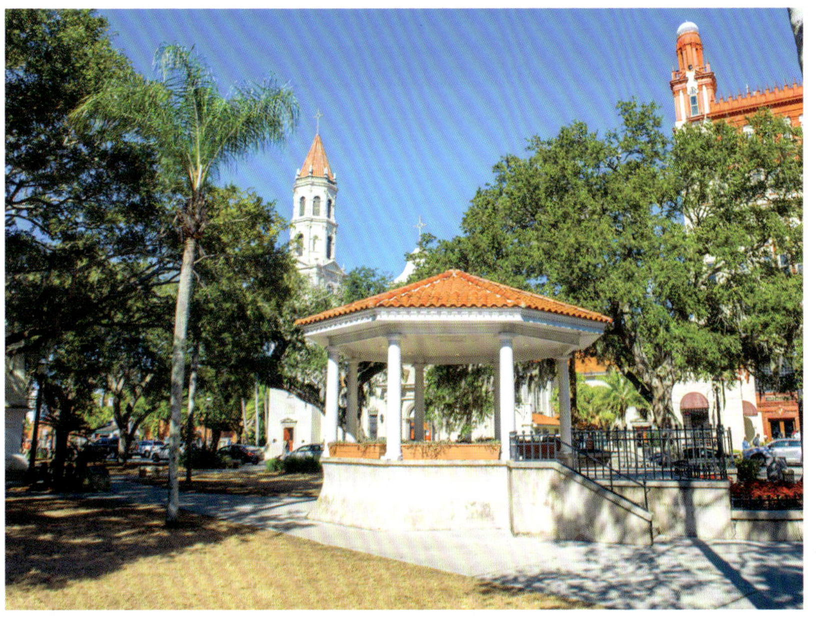

The Basilica can be seen in the background of this picture of the Plaza de la Constitución. The Plaza hosts concerts and a public market.

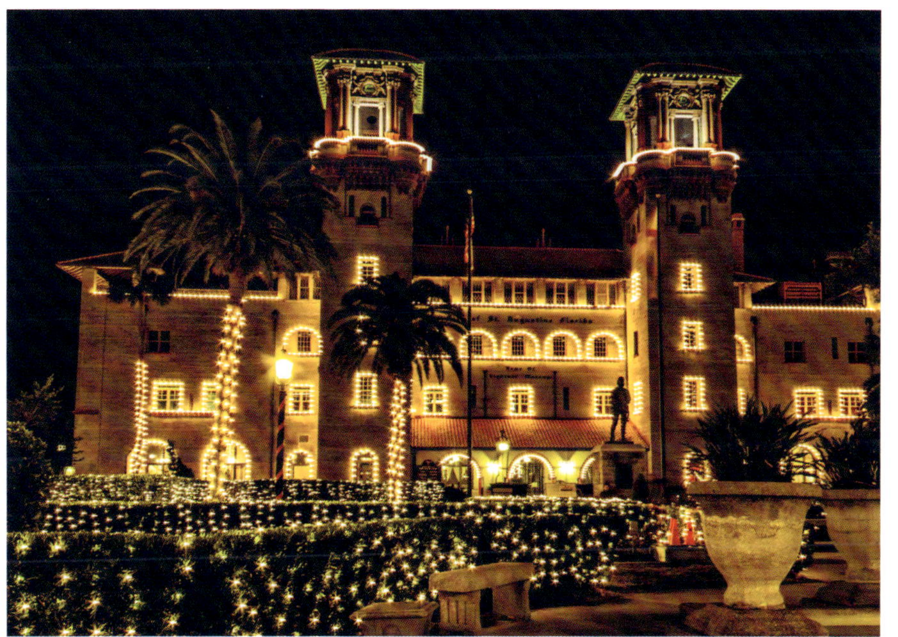

After the Alcazar Hotel closed, the building was purchased by an art collector named Otto Lightner, and became a museum in 1948.

Downtown Jacksonville

Location: Jacksonville, Florida

Length: 1 mile + optional 2 mile Northbank Riverwalk

Start point: Museum of Contemporary Art

End point: St. Johns River

This walk set in the Northbank area of Downtown Jacksonville is loaded with art, architecture, and places to eat. Start at the Museum of Contemporary Art (MOCA) on North Laura Street. For more art, you can check out the nearby Main Library building of the Jacksonville Public Library system, also on Laura Street, which features rotating art exhibits in its gallery space.

The museum is next to a large public park, James Weldon Johnson Park. The park features a number of food trucks, offering options for a bite to eat, and often hosts Jazz in the Park and other musical performances during the day. If you visit the park on the first Wednesday evening of the month, you can see the First Wednesday Art Walk. James Weldon Johnson Park is bordered on one side by Laura Street and on the other by Hogan. On the Hogan Street side, you'll see a Victorian mansion that houses Sweet Pete's Candy, home to an ice cream parlor and candy store. Tours of the mansion and the "candy kitchen" are available.

From James Weldon Johnson Park, head towards St. Johns River. Along the way, stop by to view the architecture of the Florida Theatre, built in 1927. At St. Johns River, check out the USS *Orleck* of the Jacksonville Naval Museum, although be sure to verify open hours first. (As of late 2024, the site is open Wednesdays through Sundays.) The destroyer was active from 1945 to 1982.

St. Johns River separates the Northbank and Southbank of Jacksonville, and there are various walking and biking trails along both sides of the river that offer beautiful views.

Points of Interest

Museum of Contemporary Art (MOCA)

James Weldon Johnson Park

Florida Theatre

Jacksonville Naval Museum and USS *Orleck*

St. Johns River *(link to Northbank Riverwalk)*

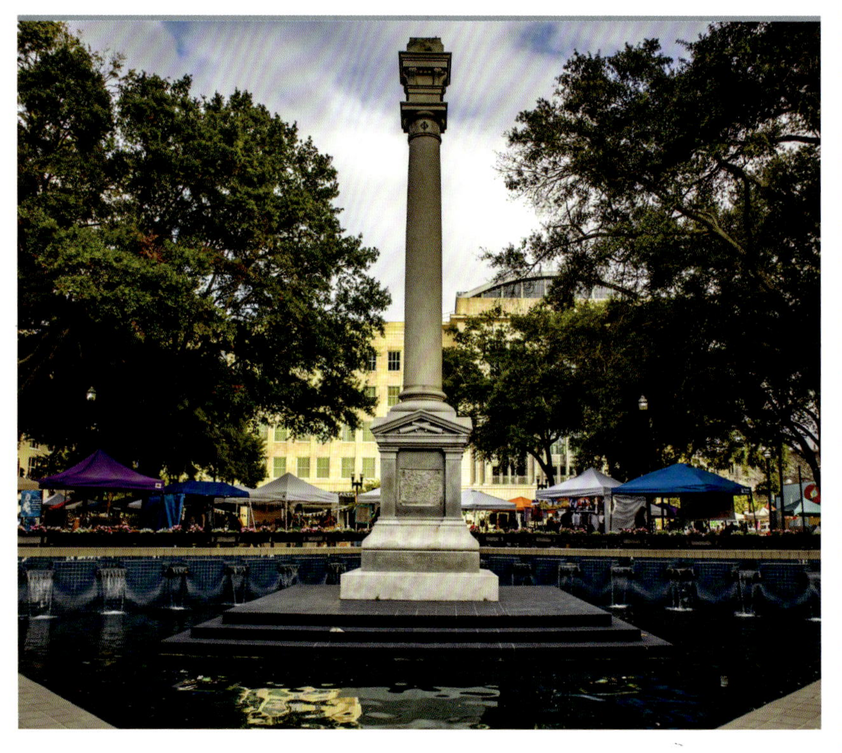

James Weldon Johnson Park, previously Hemming Park, was renamed to honor the civil rights activist in 2020.

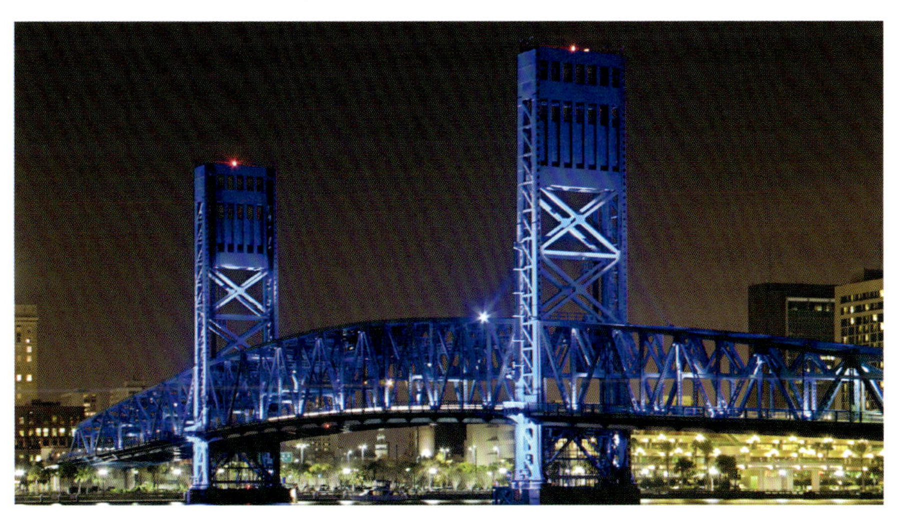

Jacksonville's Main Street Bridge, or John T. Alsop Jr. Bridge, crosses the St. Johns River near the USS *Orleck*.

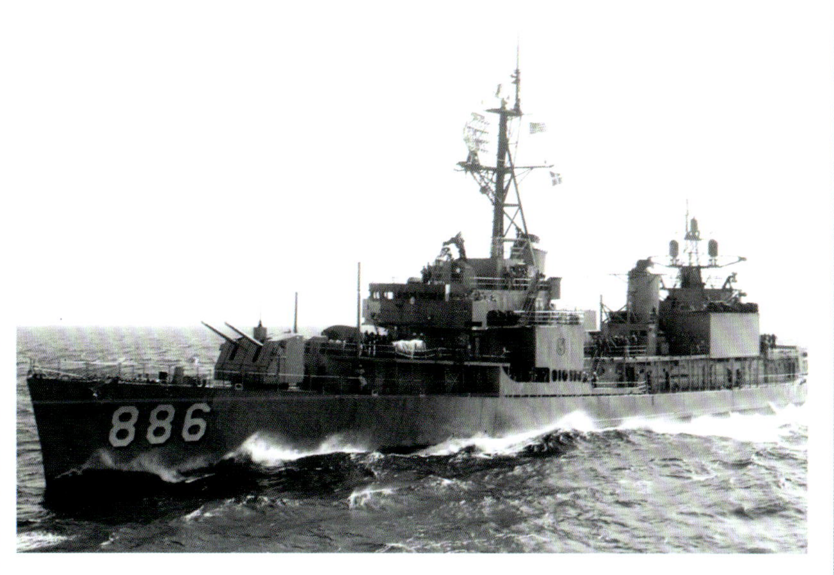

The USS *Orleck* is shown here in 1965.

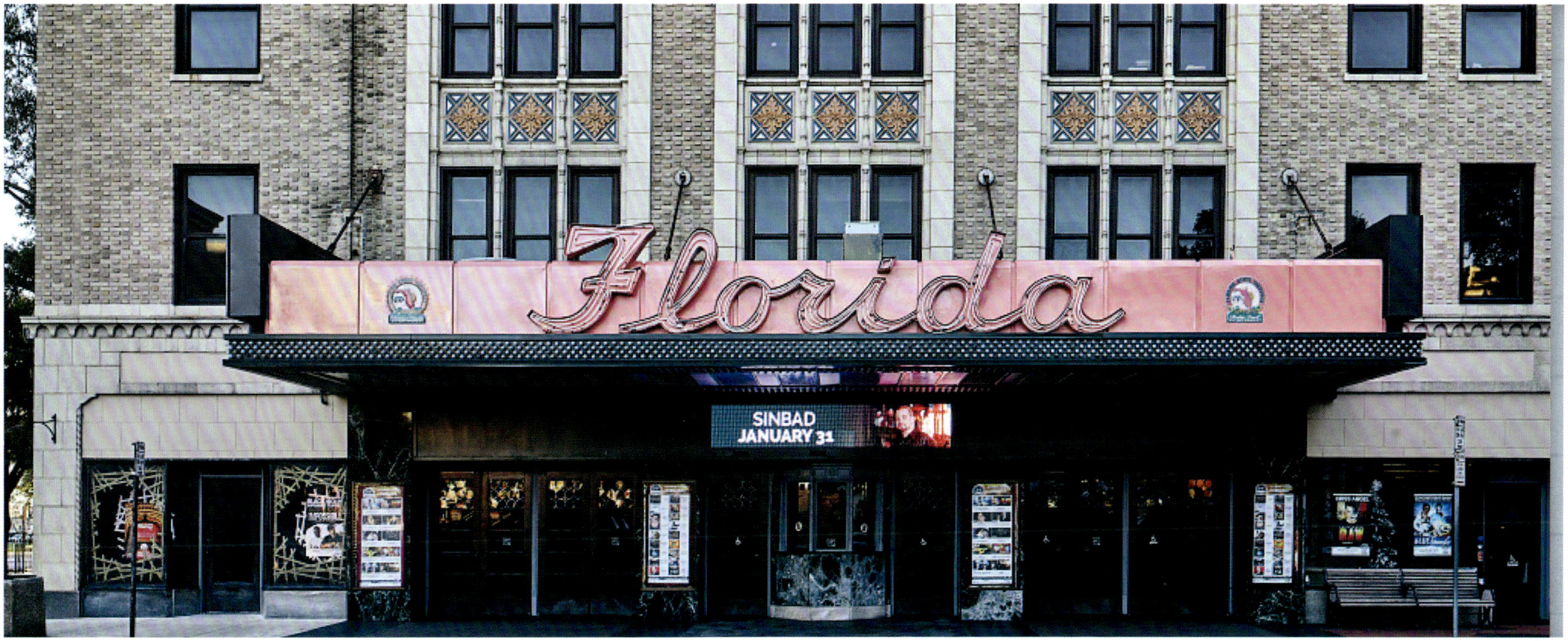

Fan of the supernatural? The Florida Theatre is reputedly haunted. The balcony in section 500 features the "Ghost Seat," where a ghost reportedly showed up on video.

Tampa Riverwalk

Location: Tampa, Florida
Length: 2.6 miles
Start point: Heights Market at Armature Works
End point: Sparkman Wharf

The Tampa Riverwalk runs along the Hillsborough River and offers a number of sights and attractions for the whole family. The walk itself is a pleasure: Murals and other pieces of public art are installed along the way, and alert walkers will also spot busts that honor prominent Tampa leaders, forming the Historical Monument Trail. For those interested in learning more about local history, the Tampa Bay History Center found near the end of the route contains exhibits on Florida and Tampa Bay history.

There are also a number of places to stop along the way in order to eat, shop, play, and learn. Armature Works near the start of the trail offers shopping and restaurants. Water Works Park and the Curtis Hixon Waterfront Park offer playgrounds, fountains, and dog parks. The Glazer Children's Museum gives kids the opportunity for interactive play and learning, and the Florida Aquarium is located near the end of the Riverwalk.

The Tampa Riverfront acts as a cultural hub for the city, with the Straz Center for the Performing Arts and the Tampa Museum of Art both found along the route. Sports fans will pass by Amalie Arena, the home of Tampa's hockey team, the Tampa Bay Lightning.

If you visit Tampa between mid-January and March, don't be surprised to see pirate ships along the Riverwalk. Each year, Tampa is home to the Gasparilla Pirate Festival, holding an assortment of events, including parades.

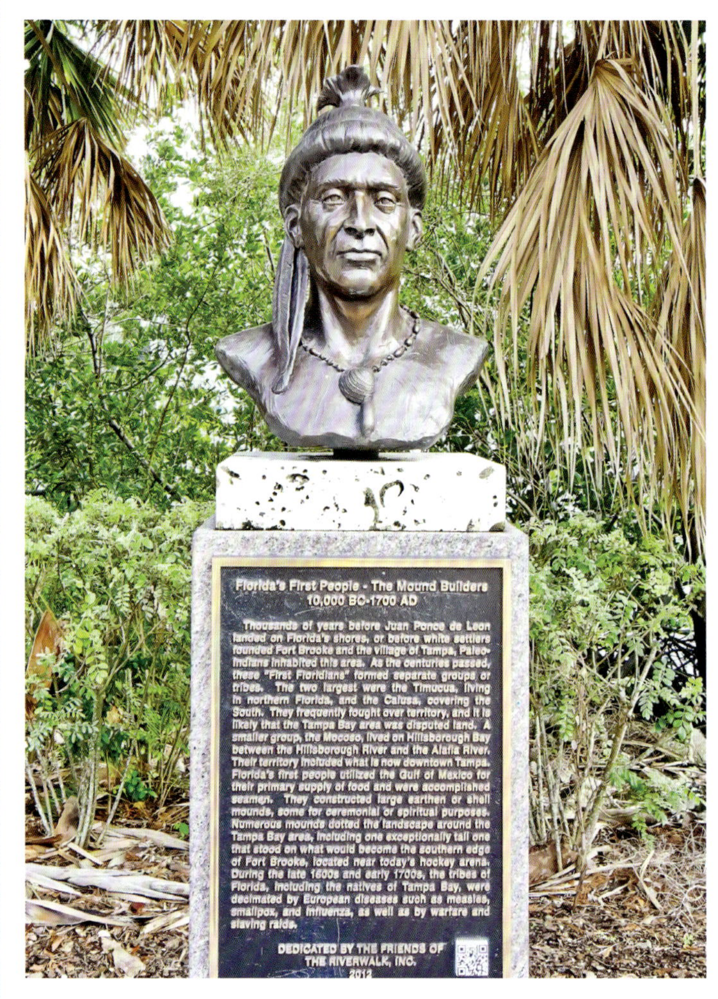

The Historical Monument Trail honors people from different eras of Floridian history.

The Friends of the Riverwalk organization works to develop the Riverwalk into an enjoyable experience. Their web site offers maps and more information about events and walking tours.

Points of Interest

- Historical Monument Trail
- Various public art installations
- Armature Works
- Water Works Park
- Straz Center for the Performing Arts
- Tampa Museum of Art
- Glazer Children's Museum
- Curtis Hixon Waterfront Park
- Tampa Convention Center
- Amalie Arena
- Tampa Bay History Center
- Sparkman Wharf
- Florida Aquarium

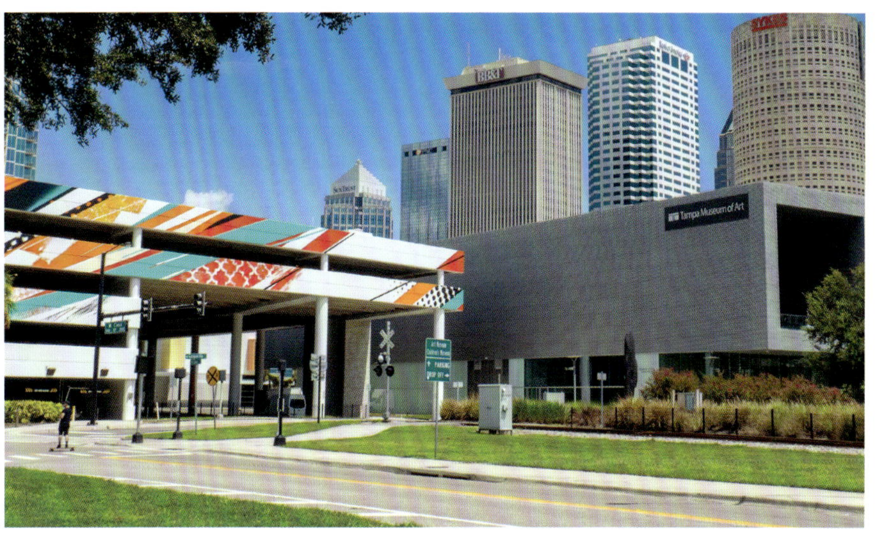

The Tampa Museum of Art, founded in 1979, moved to its current building along the Riverwalk in 2010.

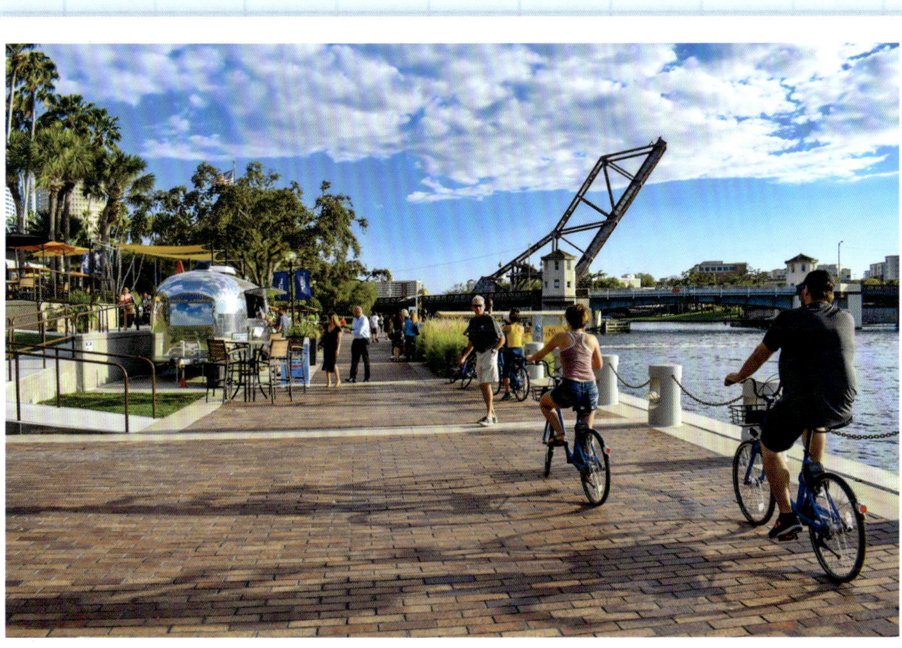

The Tampa Bay Riverwalk is used by both hikers and bikers.

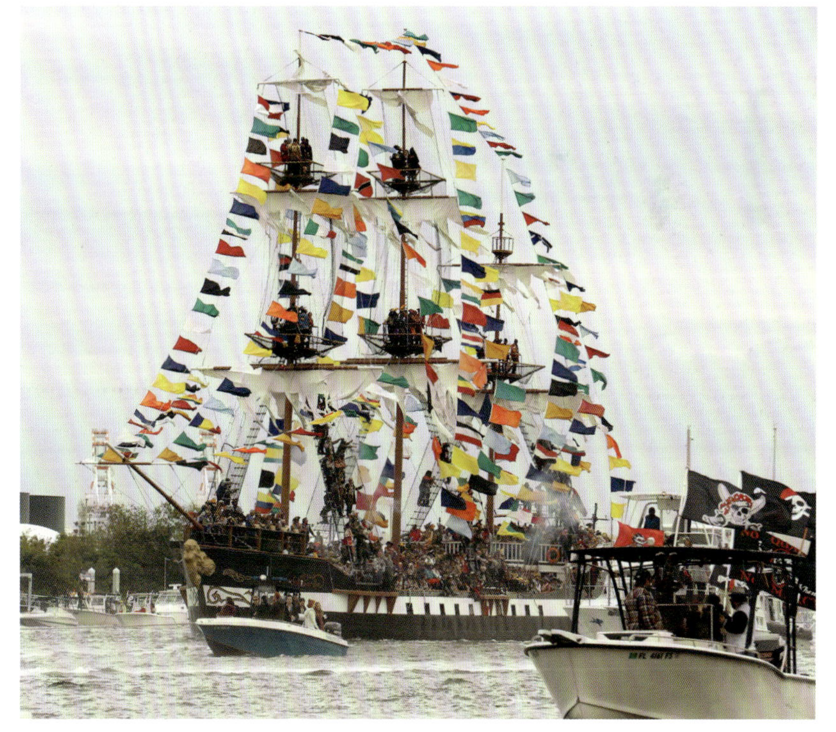

The Gasparilla Pirate Festival is an annual tradition. At one event near the Tampa Convention Center, the pirates demand the keys to the city from the mayor.

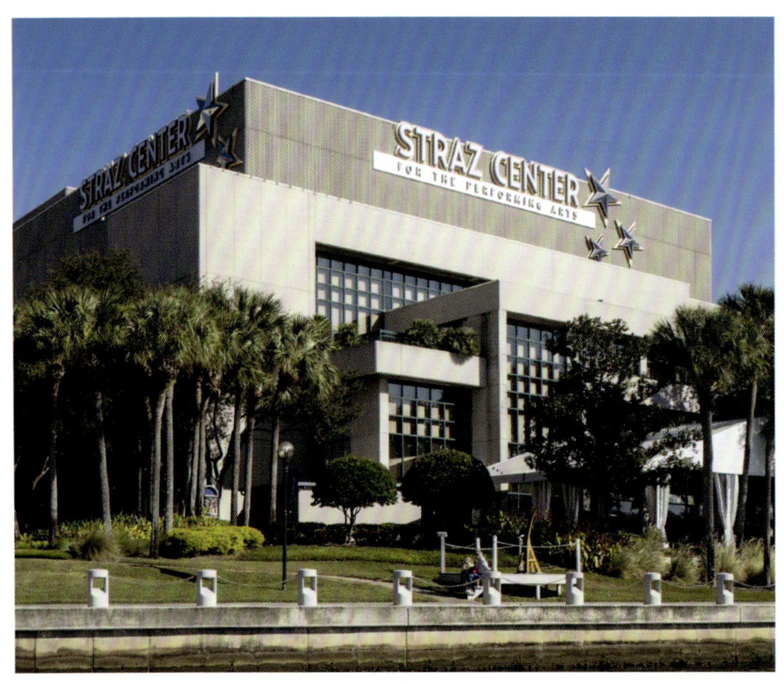

The Straz Center for the Performing Arts opened in 1987 and features five different theaters for audiences of various sizes. Choruses, dance groups, and the Opera Tampa regard the Straz as their home.

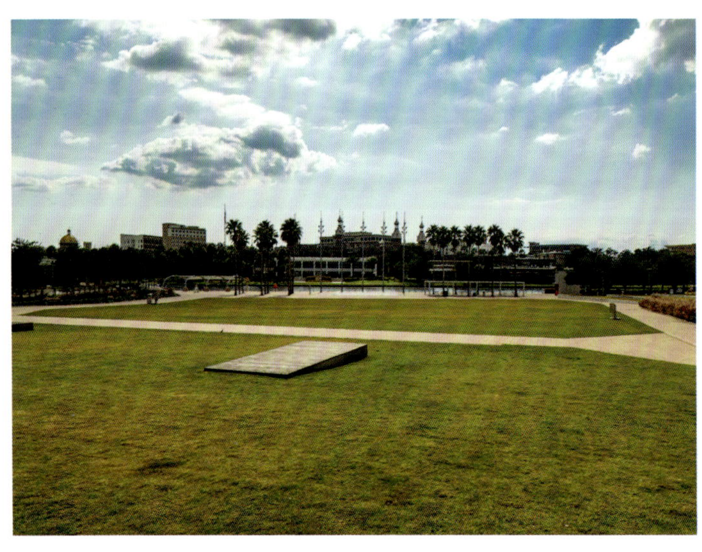

Curtis Hixon Waterfront Park is large enough to host assorted festivals and craft shows. Curtis Hixon was a former mayor of Tampa.

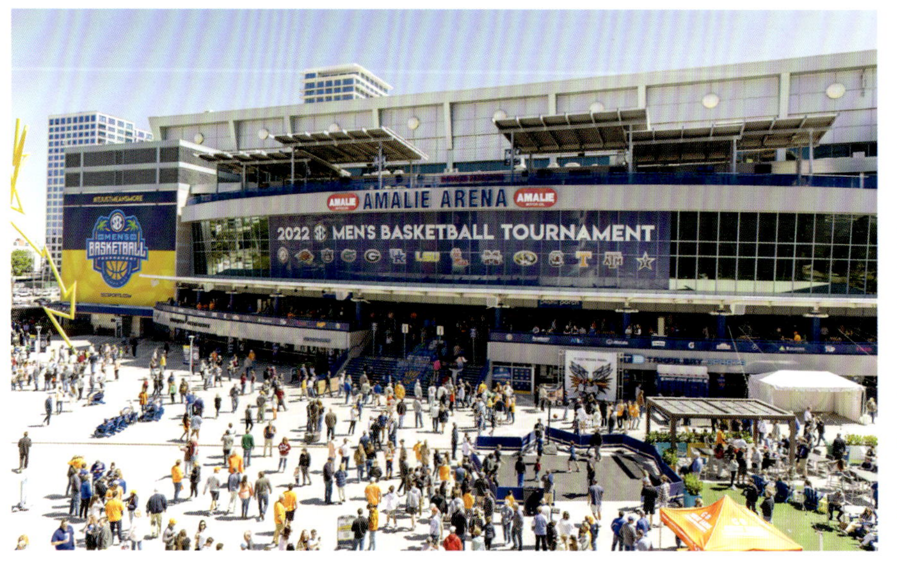

The Amalie Arena seats around 20,000 people and hosts concerts and various sporting events.

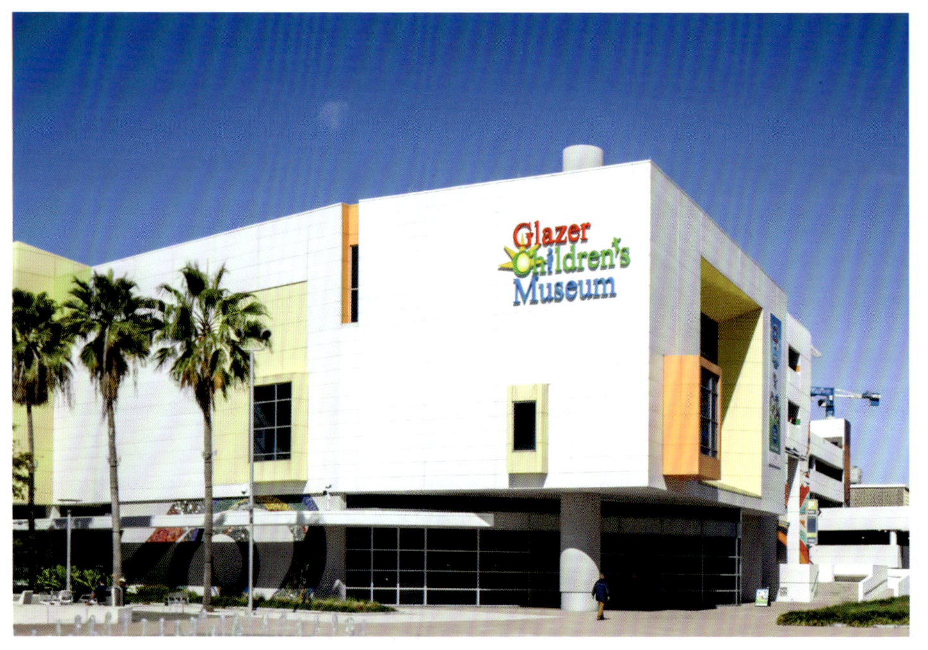

Tampa has had a children's museum in some form since 1986. The current facility opened in 2010. Both the Glazer Children's Museum and the Tampa Museum of Art are adjacent to the Curtis Hixon Waterfront Park.

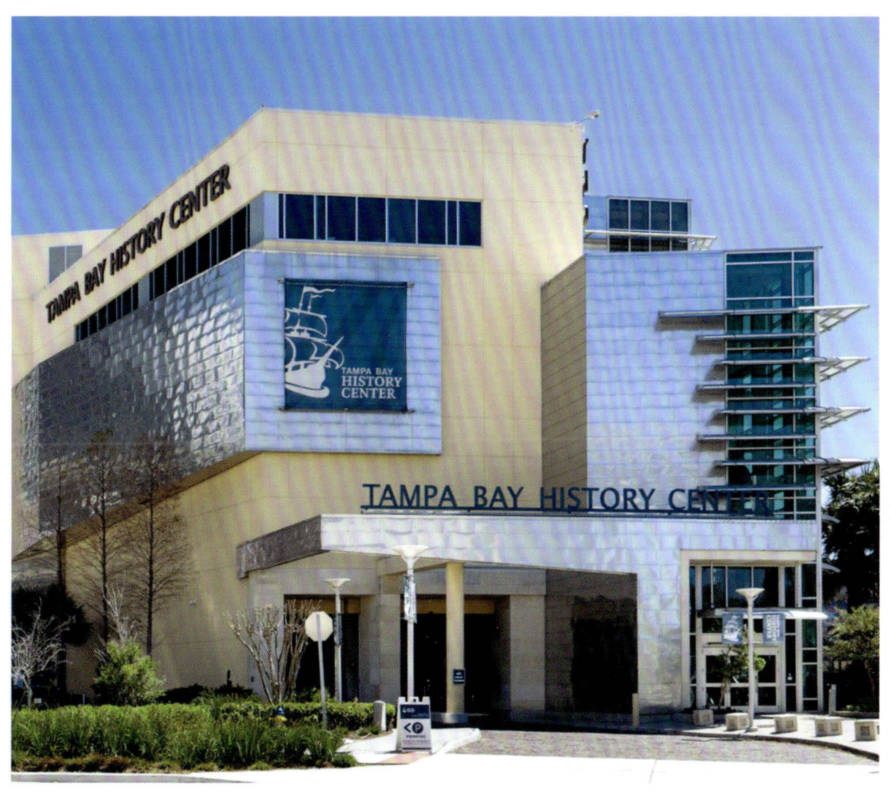

The Tampa Bay History Center provides exhibits on the history of different groups that have lived in the Tampa Bay area, from 12,000 years ago to more recent times.

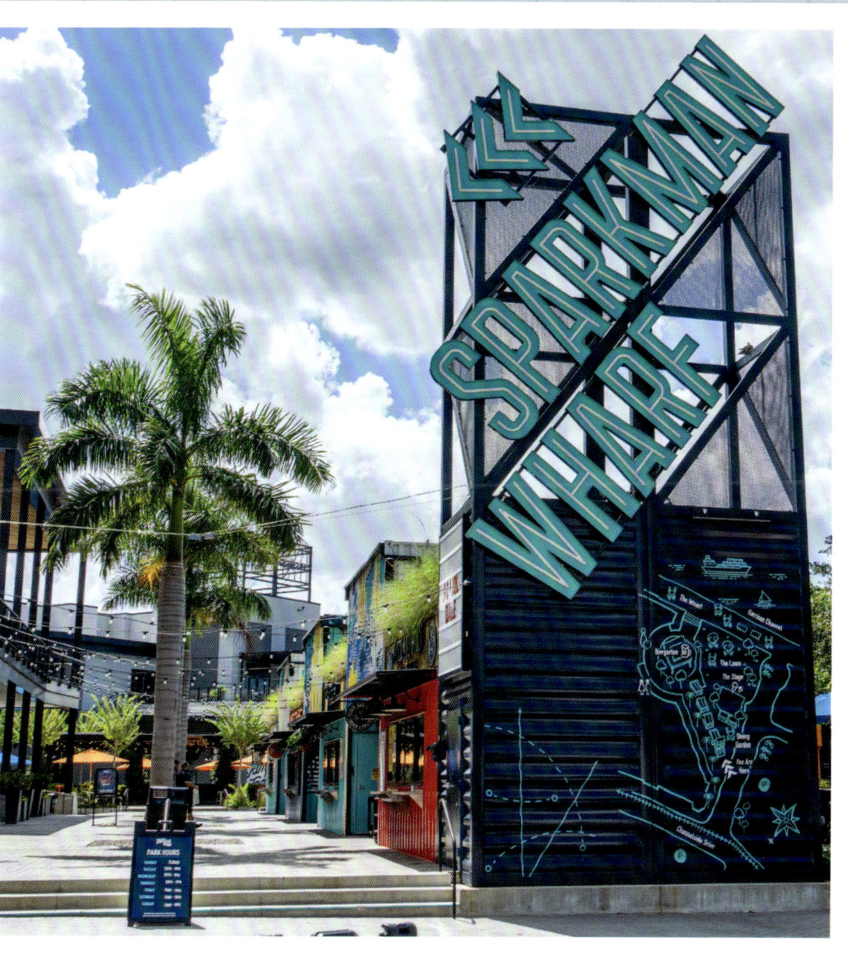

Sparkman Wharf contains shops and foods for a relaxing end to your journey.

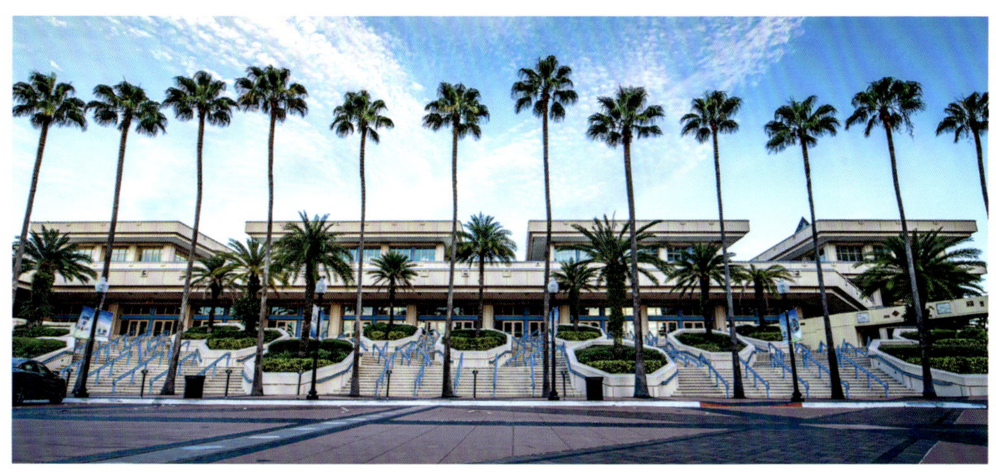

The Tampa Convention Center

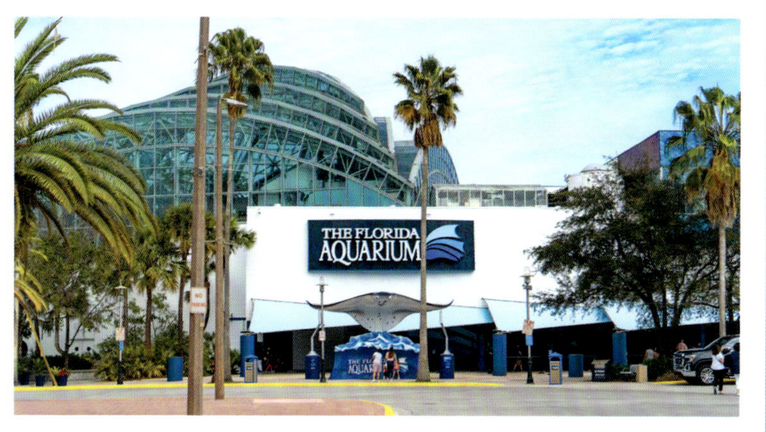

The Florida Aquarium isn't far from the end of the Tampa Riverwalk. One of its initiatives is the preservation of coral reefs.

Broadway

Location: Nashville, Tennessee
Length: 1.7 miles
Start point: 21st Avenue
End point: First Avenue South

Architecture, musical history, restaurants, shopping, and honky tonks: Broadway in Nashville has it all. Start where Broadway begins at 21st Avenue and stroll along until you reach its end at First Avenue near the Cumberland River. (If you want to go further, a pedestrian bridge takes you across the river to the spacious Cumberland Park.) The strip between Fifth and First Avenues, called Lower Broadway, is the heart of Nashville's entertainment district.

For architecture and history buffs, there's plenty to see. The landmark Union Station Hotel was built in 1900 as a train station. The Frist Art Museum is worth seeing not only for its exhibitions, but for the fact that it resides in a former U.S. Post Office building from the 1930s. Christ Church Cathedral, an Episcopal church, dates to 1894. A former Customs House building was built between 1876 and 1882.

Nashville is synonymous with music, though, and Broadway has been a critical part of that history. Bars and restaurants that play live music line the street, along with shops. Right off Broadway, on Fifth Avenue, you'll find a musical institution: the Ryman Auditorium that began as a church before it became the home of the Grand Ole Opry between 1943 and 1974. The Ryman still hosts musical performances, with the Grand Ole Opry returning at times. The Music City Walk is also just off Broadway, and includes markers that pay tribute to stars like Trace Adkins, Patsy Cline, and Reba McEntire. The nearby Johnny Cash Museum is a self-guided museum that contains memorabilia from the artist's life.

Points of Interest

The Union Station Hotel
Frist Art Museum
Christ Church Cathedral
Customs House
Bridgestone Arena
Ryman Auditorium *(on Fifth Avenue)*
Music City Walk of Fame Park *(on Fourth Avenue)*
Johnny Cash Museum *(on Third Avenue)*

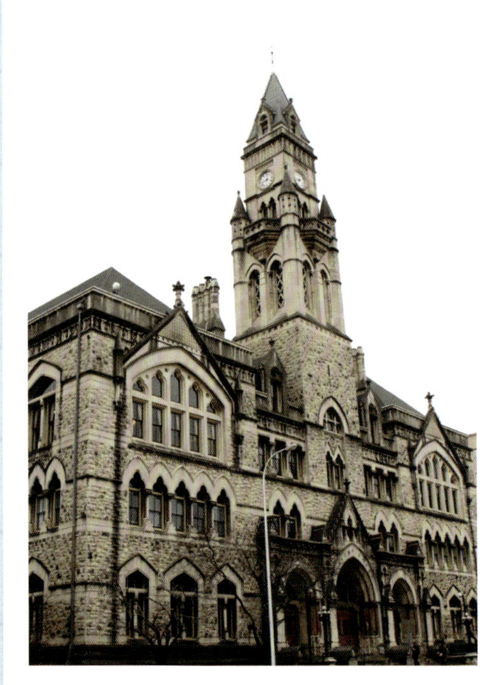

Now privately owned, this historic Customs House served several government functions, including as a District Court location.

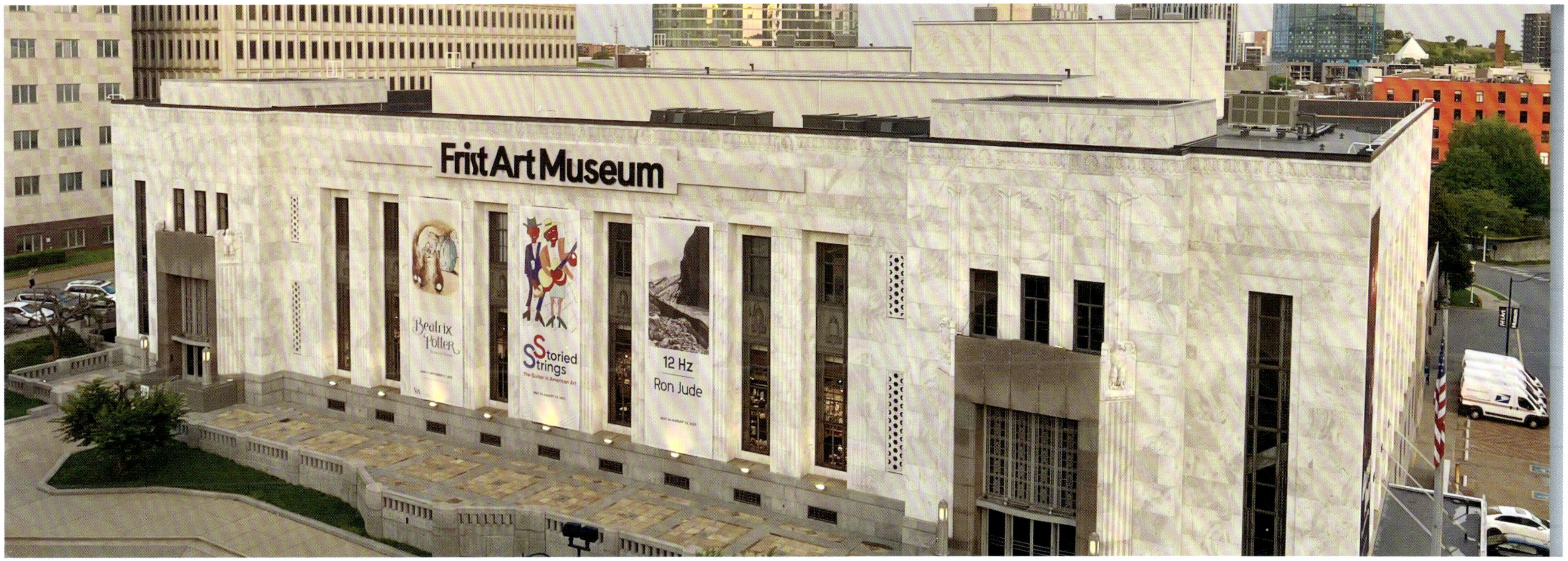

Nashville's Frist Art Museum opened in 2001 and exhibits traveling art collections rather than maintaining permanent collections, so there's always something new to see.

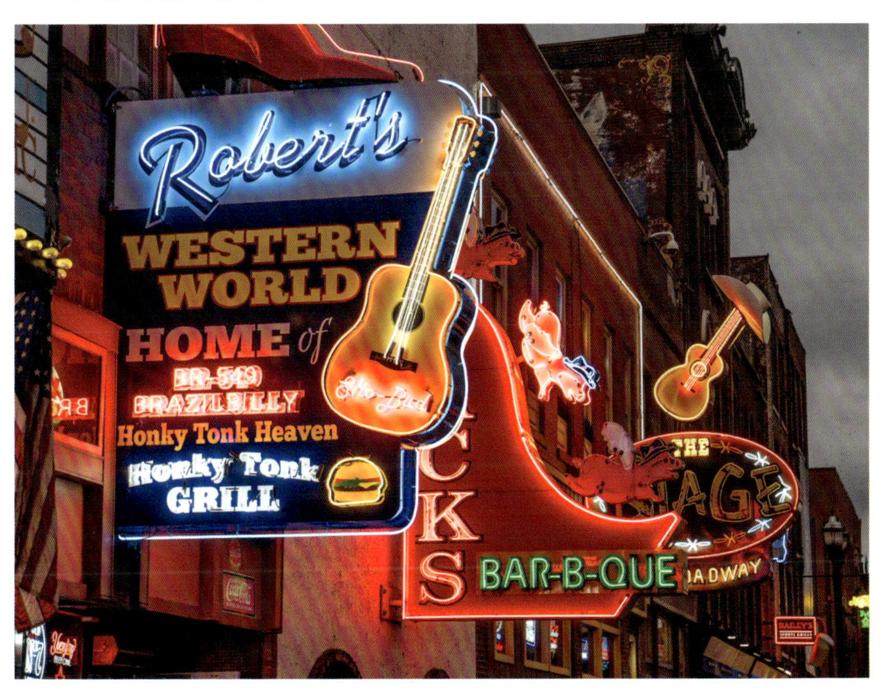

Colorful signs and storefronts line Broadway, inviting visitors to eat, buy, and hear live music.

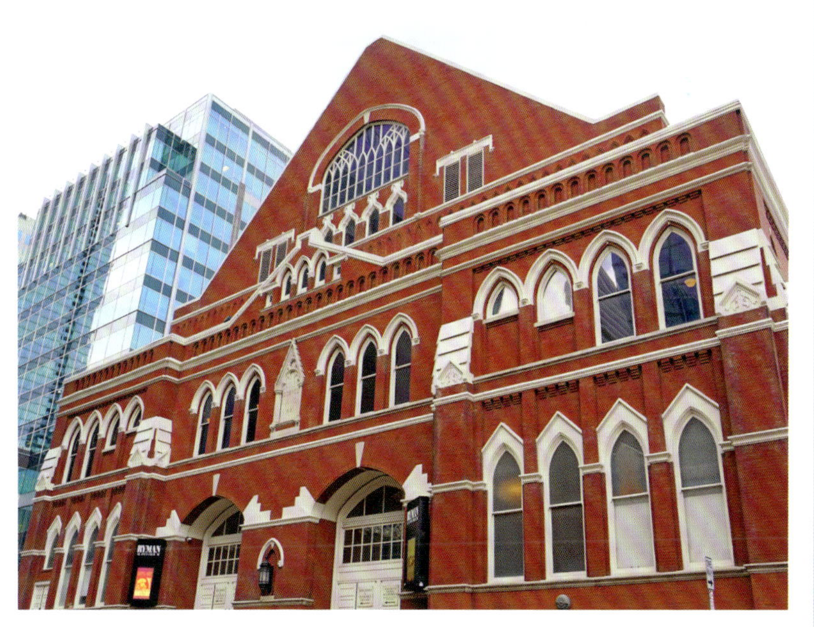

The Ryman Auditorium was built between 1885 and 1892.

Louisville Loop—Riverwalk

Location: Louisville, Kentucky

Length: Variable

- Big Four Bridge Trailhead to Lannan Park Trailhead is 3.2 miles
- Continuing to Shawnee Park Trailhead adds 3.3 miles
- Continuing to Chickasaw Park Trailhead adds another 1.5 miles

Start point: Big Four Bridge Trailhead

End point: Variable

The Louisville Loop is an ambitious project in progress, with an end goal of creating a network of 100 miles of multi-use trails. Parts of the loop are complete already, including a section that takes you along the Ohio River and Louisville's downtown area.

If you start at the Big Four Bridge Trailhead and move west, you'll begin at Louisville's Waterfront Park, a large public park that hosts festivals and contains playgrounds and a splash pad. Sights include a Lincoln Memorial statue and the Big Four Bridge, an older bridge from 1895 now reserved for pedestrians and bicyclists.

Continuing west, you'll be passing Louisville's downtown area and its Museum Row. The Muhammed Ali Center, the Kentucky Science Center, the Kentucky Center for the Performing Arts, the KMAC Contemporary Art Museum, the Frazier History Museum, and the Louisville Slugger Museum & Factory are all quite close to each other and the Ohio River if you hop off the trail for a bit.

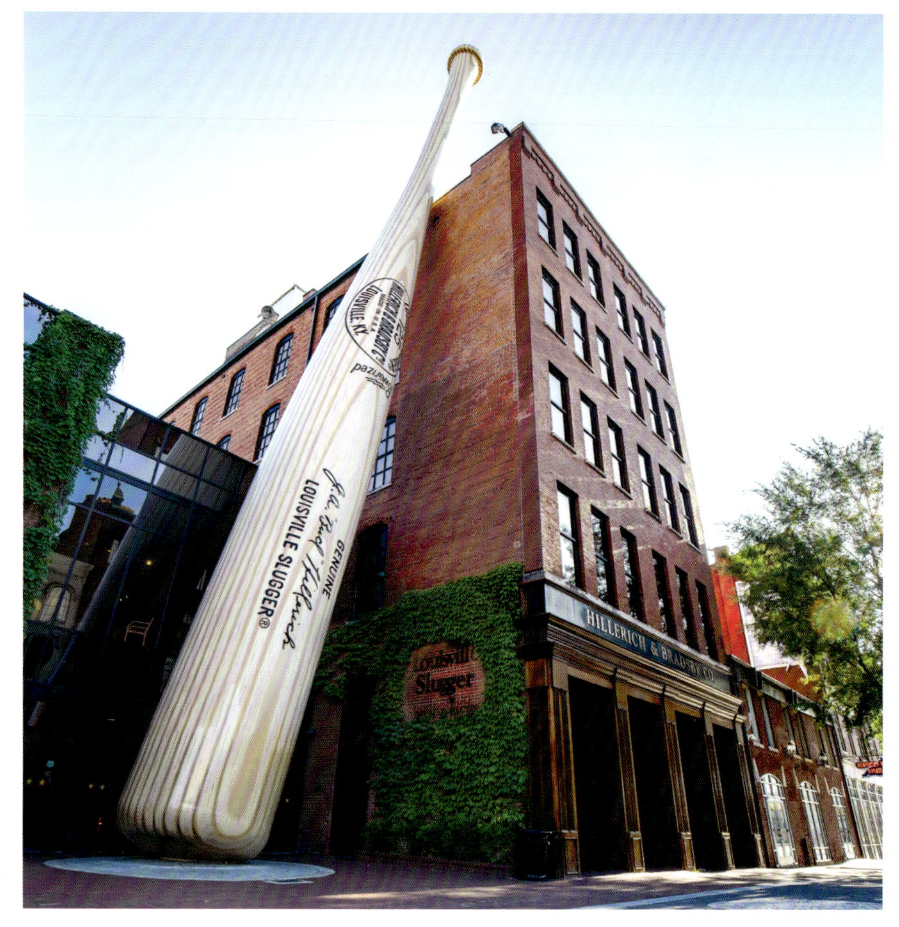

Baseball fans may want to take a side trip to the Louisville Slugger Museum & Factory, one of the many attractions clustered together in the Museum Row area.

As you meander along, you'll see various historic bridges, islands in the Ohio River, riverboats, and parks. You can adjust your route for a longer or shorter day, depending on which trailheads you choose as your starting and ending points.

Points of Interest

Waterfront Park

Ohio River and various bridges

Louisville Historic Wharf

Louisville Downtown and Museum Row

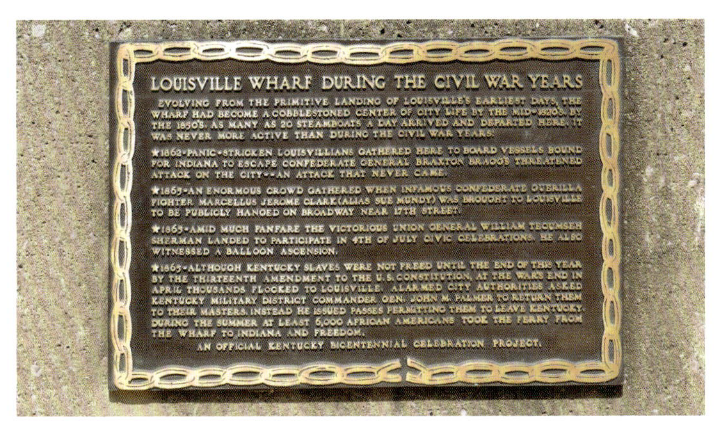

A historic marker at the Louisville Wharf explains the location's importance during the Civil War.

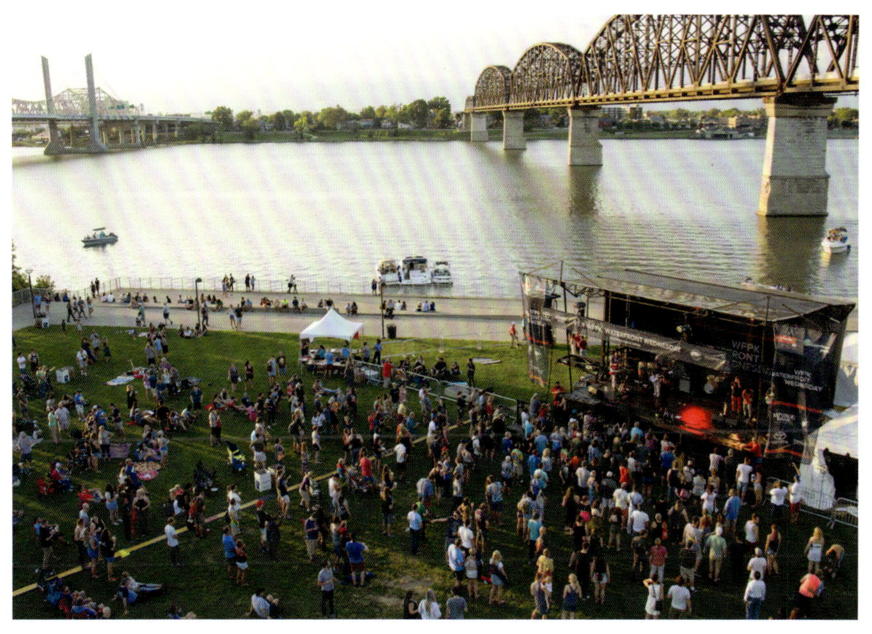

Louisville's Waterfront Park is shown here during a summer concert in 2018. By crossing the Ohio River, visitors would cross state lines to arrive in Jeffersonville, Indiana. The paired John F. Kennedy Memorial Bridge and the Abraham Lincoln Bridge *(left)* carry automobile traffic. The Big Four Bridge *(right)* carries pedestrian and bicycle traffic, although it was once a railroad bridge.

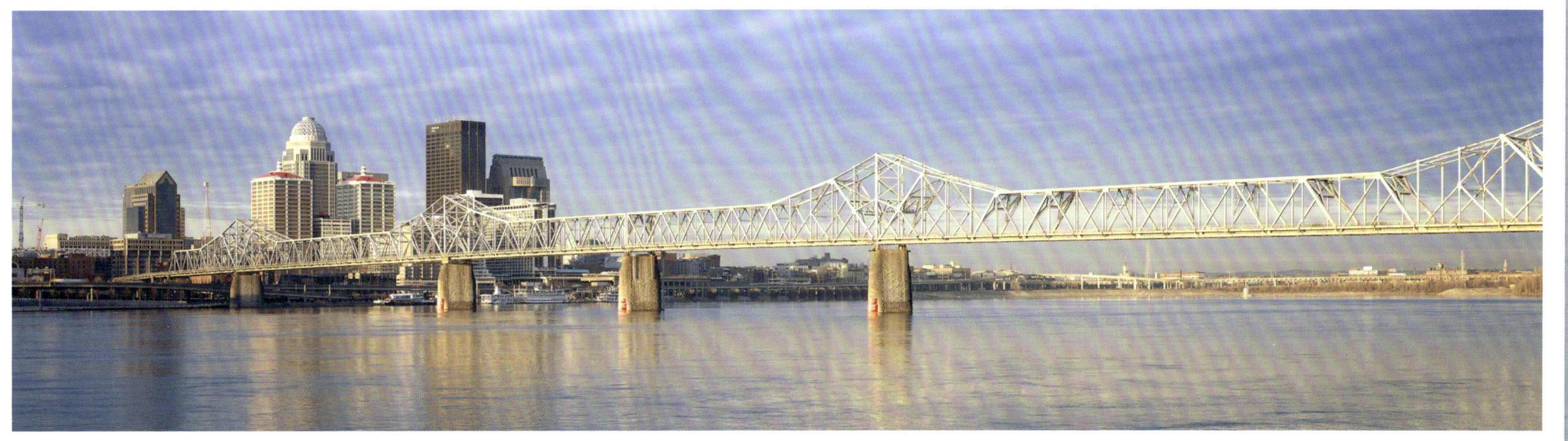

Another historic bridge, the George Rogers Clark Memorial Bridge, dates to 1928. The skyline of downtown Louisville can be seen in the background.

Memphis Heritage Trail

Location: Memphis, Tennessee
Length: Sites are spread across an 8.2-mile, 20-block area
Start point: Variable
End point: Variable

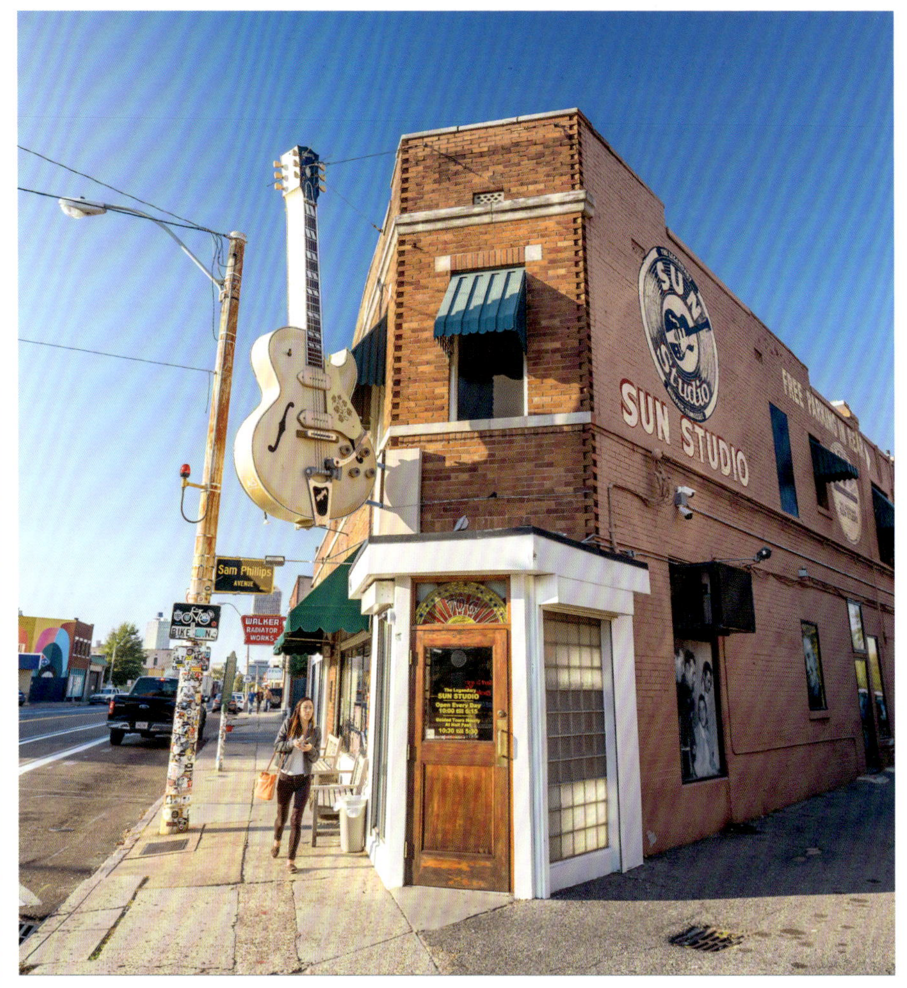

Sun Studio, opened in 1950, was the recording studio for famous blues artists that included B. B. King and Howlin' Wolf. Elvis Presley also recorded there.

Planning for the Memphis Heritage Trail (MHT) began in 2008, with the goal of creating a way to pay tribute to the contributions of African Americans to the city of Memphis. Ten years later, in 2018, the trail launched. The full Memphis Heritage Trail includes more than 50 sites, focused on the South City neighborhood in Memphis, with additional places of interest in the nearby Orange Mound and Soulsville districts. Sites include museums, churches, parks, businesses, historical markers, funeral homes, and private residences.

By going to the MHT web site, visitors can find maps and download an app that provides additional context about each site on the trail as they walk.

In the South City portion of the walk, the MHT is divided into four loops, each with a different emphasis. The Civil Rights Historic Loop includes the National Civil Rights Museum and the I AM A MAN Plaza. The Business-Entertainment Historic Loop contains Beale Street and several sites on it, like W. C. Handy Park, the Historic Old Daisy Theatre, the W. C. Handy House Museum, the Rock 'n' Soul Museum, and the Withers Collection Museum and Gallery. The Historic Commerce Loop includes several churches and funeral homes, the Solvent Savings Bank, Sun Studio, and the site of the NAACP Memphis Branch. The Historic Residential Loop features homes, churches, Booker T. Washington High School, and the former site of Martin Stadium, where the African American baseball team the Memphis Red Sox played for many years.

In the Orange Mound area, visitors can see churches, homes, schools, and the Whitten Brothers Hardware Company, founded in 1929. The Soulsville USA Historic District includes churches, LeMoyne-Owen College, a cemetery, a beauty salon, and Aretha Franklin's birthplace.

Points of Interest

National Civil Rights Museum
Blues Hall of Fame/Blues Foundation
Orpheum Theatre
The Cotton Museum
Beale Street Historic District
Historic Old Daisy Theatre
W. C. Handy House Museum
Withers Collection Museum and Gallery
Sun Studio

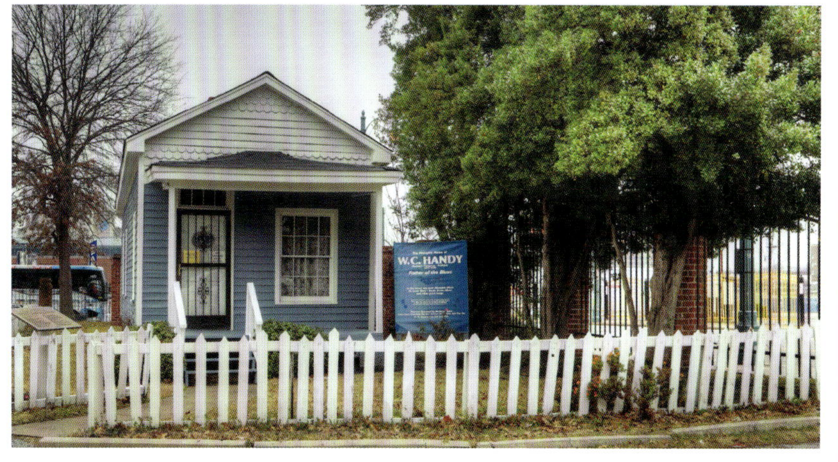

W. C. Handy, the "Father of the Blues," moved to Memphis, Tennessee, in 1909, and wrote the song "Memphis Blues" in 1912. He met his business manager at the Solvent Savings Bank and Trust, an African American-owned bank that is another site on the Memphis Heritage Trail.

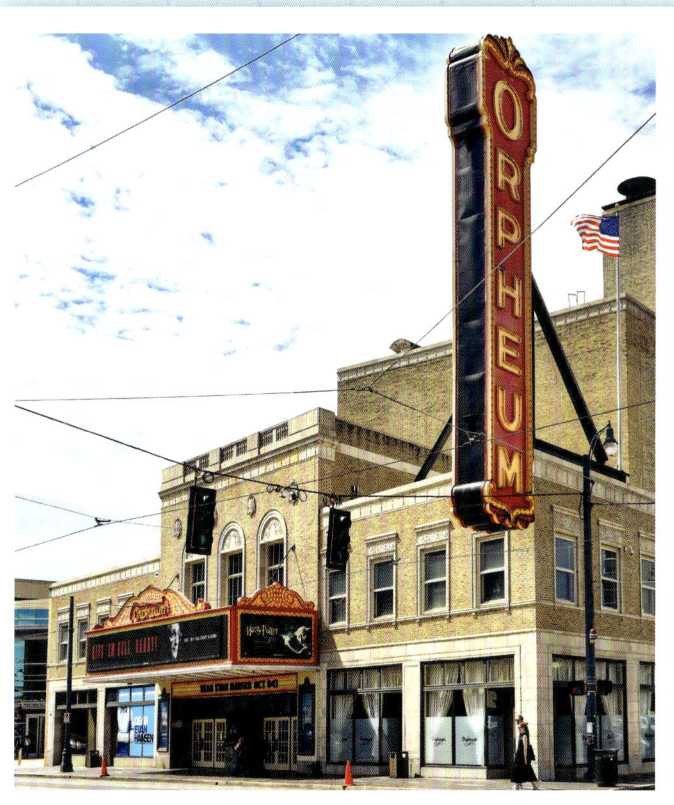

The Orpheum Theatre was originally opened in 1928.

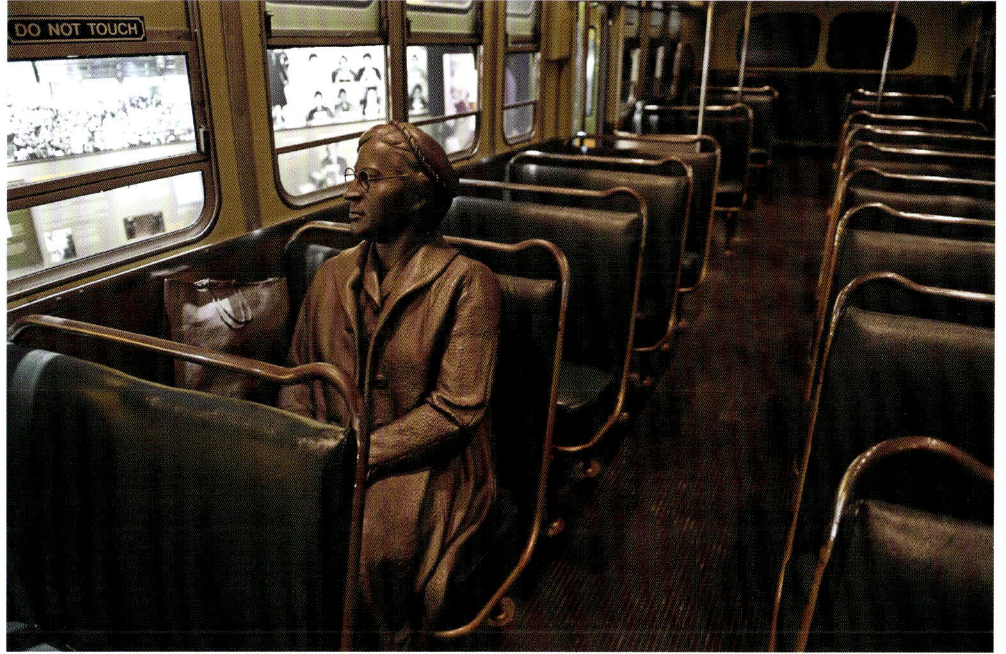

A sculpture of Rosa Parks at the National Civil Rights Museum. The museum complex includes the Lorraine Motel where Martin Luther King Jr. was assassinated.

Downtown Little Rock

Location: Little Rock and North Little Rock, Arkansas
Length: 2.2 miles
Start point: MacArthur Park
End point: North Little Rock

In a walk of less than two and a half miles, you can see up to seven museums and cross the Arkansas River, for a fairly full day of sightseeing. For a day heavier on walking, add some time on the Arkansas River Trail that runs 17 miles on either side of the river.

Start on the south side of the Arkansas River in MacArthur Park, a large public park situated in a neighborhood full of Victorian-era buildings. As well as playgrounds, ponds, and the Arkansas Korean War Veterans Memorial, it's also home to three museums. MacArthur Park was once the site of the U.S. arsenal at Little Rock, and the Tower Building of that arsenal now houses the MacArthur Museum of Arkansas Military History. The Arkansas Museum of Fine Arts can be found at the park, too, along with the Firehouse Hostel and Museum, a working hostel that also displays firefighting memorabilia.

From MacArthur Park, head towards the Arkansas River. The Historic Arkansas Museum (HAM) focuses on state history with collections that include art, furniture, jewelry, weaponry, pottery, and more. The Museum campus also includes several historic buildings from the 1800s. For more history, visit the Old State House Museum, located in the old state capitol building constructed between 1833 and 1842, while the Museum of Discovery is a family-friendly science museum.

From there, it's an easy walk through Julius Breckling Riverfront Park to the Arkansas River, although you'll likely want to meander to see various pieces of art. Cross the river using Junction Bridge, a former railroad bridge that has been converted for pedestrian and bicycle use. Right across the river in North Little Rock, you'll find the Arkansas Inland Maritime Museum, which features a World War II submarine, the USS *Razorback*, as well as a World War II tugboat.

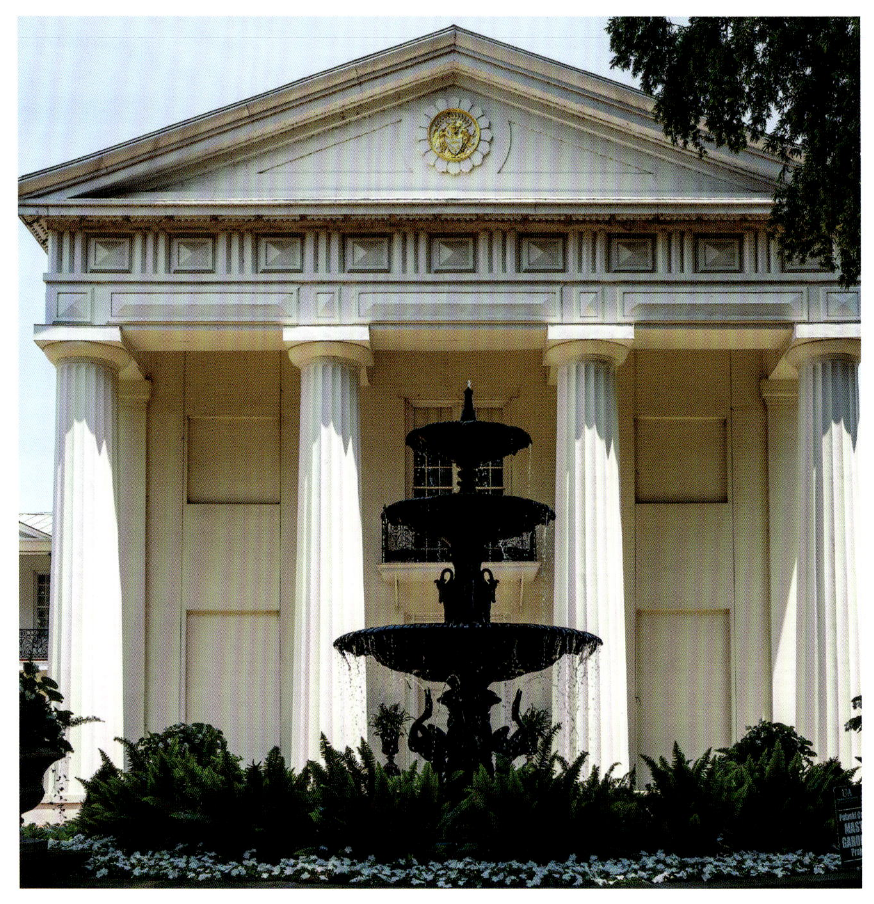

The original state capitol building was designed in the Greek Revival style. A newer building was constructed in 1912.

Points of Interest

MacArthur Park

Arkansas Museum of Fine Arts

MacArthur Museum of Arkansas Military History

Firehouse Hostel and Museum

Historic Arkansas Museum

Old State House Museum

Museum of Discovery

Julius Breckling Riverfront Park & Vogel Schwartz Sculpture Garden

Junction Bridge

Arkansas River

Arkansas Inland Maritime Museum

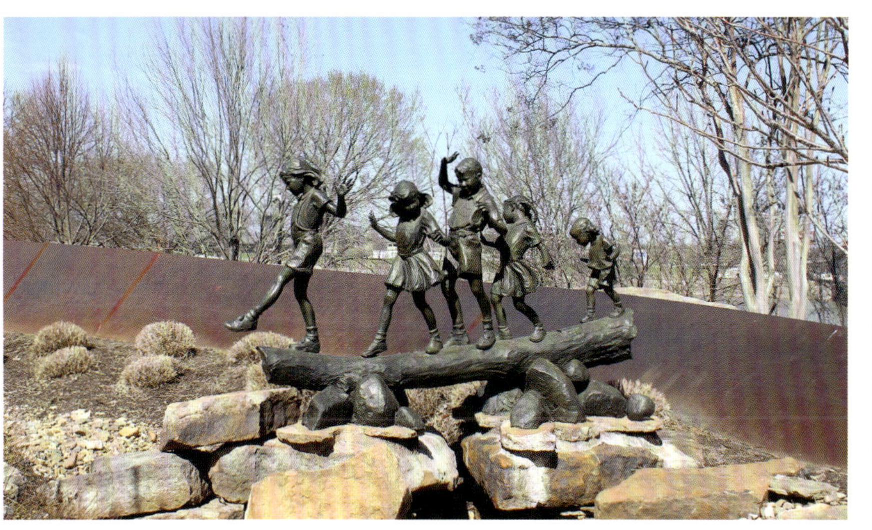

Art is found throughout the Julius Breckling Riverfront Park. One section, the Vogel Schwartz Sculpture Garden, has about 90 sculptures.

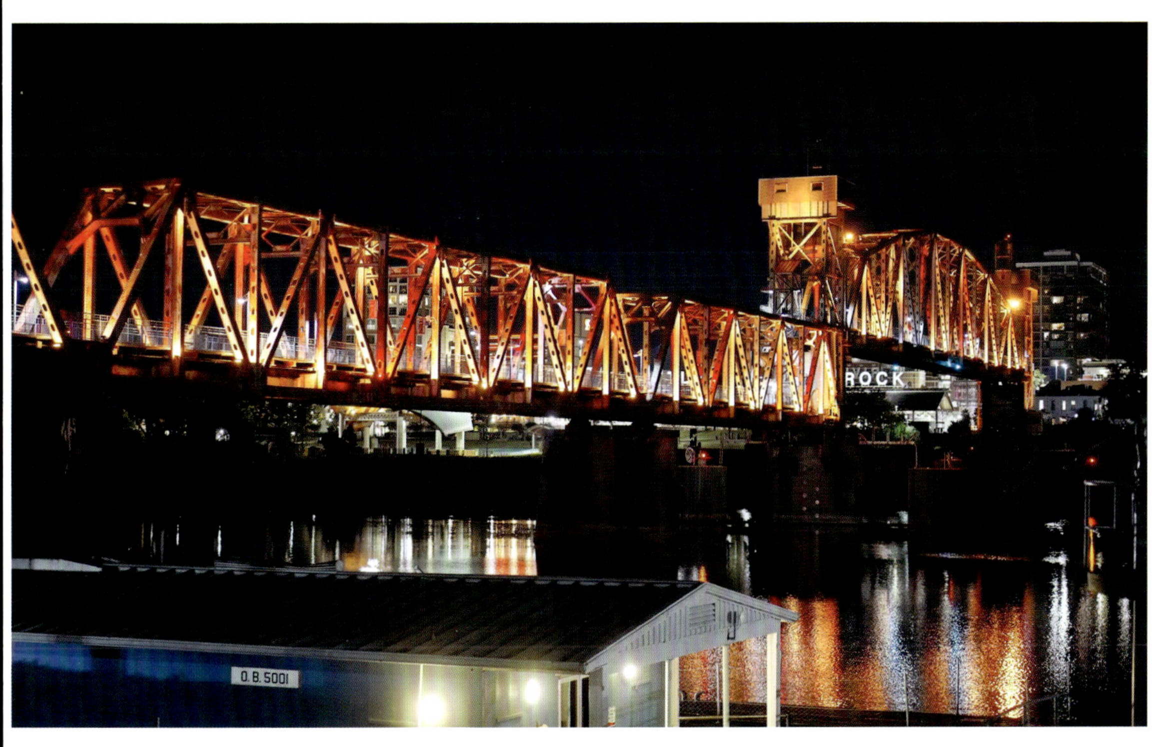

Junction Bridge connects Little Rock to North Little Rock.

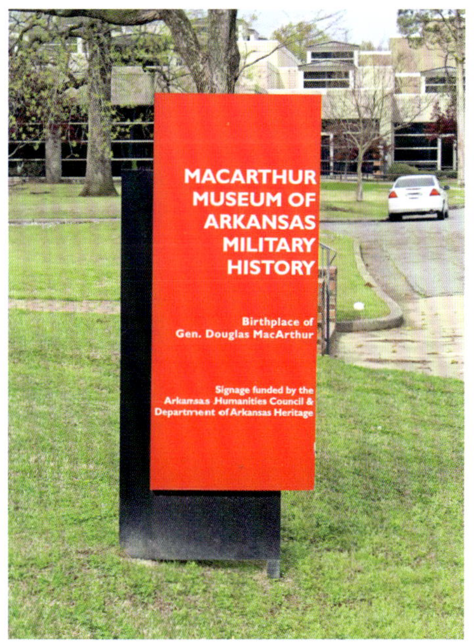

MacArthur Park is named after the military leader Douglas MacArthur, who was born in Little Rock, Arkansas—in fact, his father was stationed at the Little Rock Barracks that were the location of the current MacArthur Park.

A Taste of the French Quarter

Location: New Orleans, Louisiana
Length: About 1.5 miles
Start point: French Quarter Visitor Center
End point: Café du Monde

New Orleans's French Quarter is full of things to do and see, with this itinerary barely scratching the surface. Along the route, you'll spend time on three iconic New Orleans streets that run parallel to each other: Royal Street, Chartres Street, and Decatur Street. All have many shops and restaurants and feature historic buildings; Royal Street is especially well known for its art galleries.

The French Quarter Visitor Center is a good starting place, and not far from the quirky New Orleans Pharmacy Museum on Chartres. The museum dates to 1950, but the building is older, and was once an actual pharmacy between the 1820s and 1850s. From there, pop over to Royal Street to view the shops and visit the free Historic New Orleans Collection to discover more about the history of the area. If you continue wandering down Royal Street, keep an eye out for the LaBranche House at the corner of Royal Street and St. Peter, a historic building that's reputed to be haunted.

From there you're close to a cluster of sites adjacent to Jackson Square: St. Louis Cathedral; Pirates Alley; and two historic buildings that are part of the Louisiana State Museum system, the Cabildo and the Presbytère.

From Jackson Square, continuing further along Chartres Street will eventually take you to the Old Ursuline Convent Museum and the BK Historic House and Gardens. Moving toward the Mississippi River, you'll hit the French Market, and walking back in the direction of Jackson Square along Decatur Street will take you past Central Market, famous for its muffuletta sandwiches, and Café du Monde, famous for its beignets, to finish off your walk with a sweet treat.

Points of Interest

- New Orleans Pharmacy Museum
- The Historic New Orleans Collection
- St. Louis Cathedral
- Louisiana State Museum: the Cabildo and the Presbytère
- Jackson Square
- Old Ursuline Convent Museum
- French Market
- Joan of Arc Statue
- Central Grocery
- Café du Monde

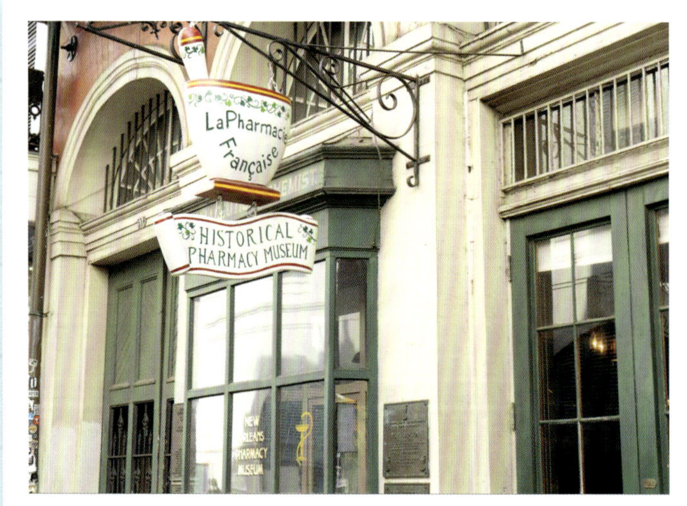

Louis Dufilho Jr., an early pharmacist, lived and worked in the building that today houses the New Orleans Pharmacy Museum. Guided tours are offered at specific times and days, with the museum open for self-guided tours at other times.

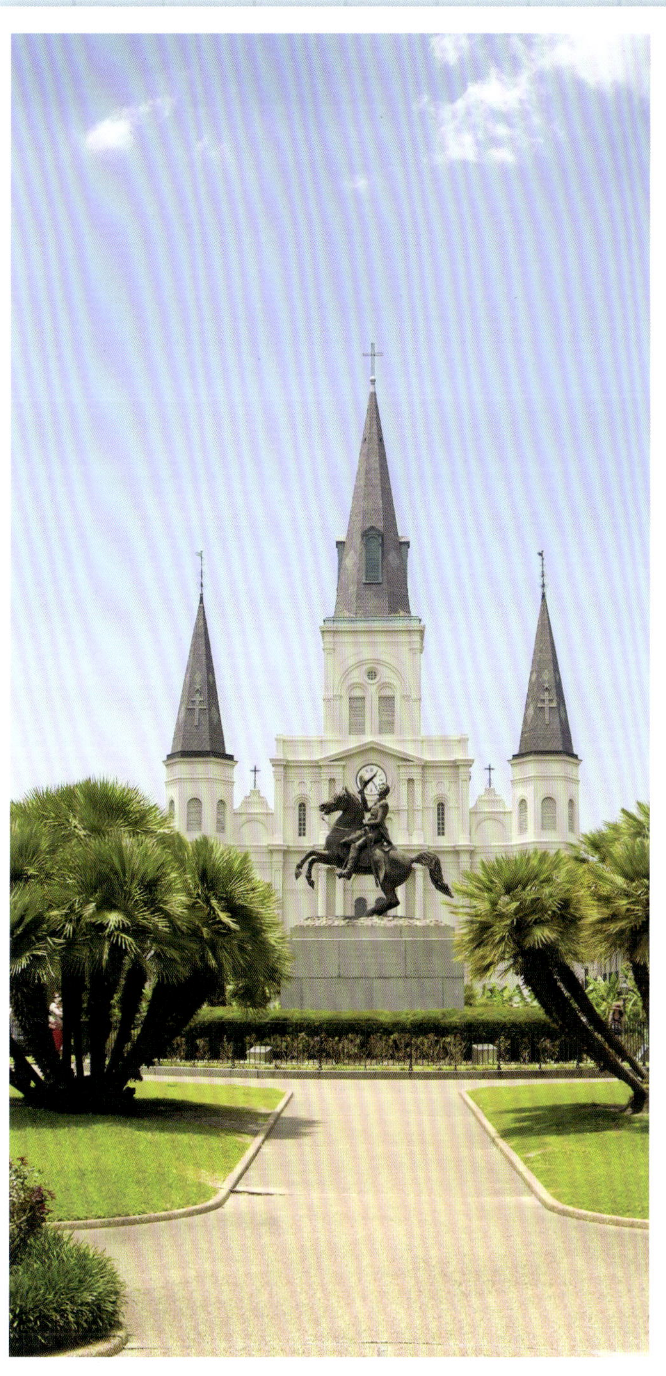

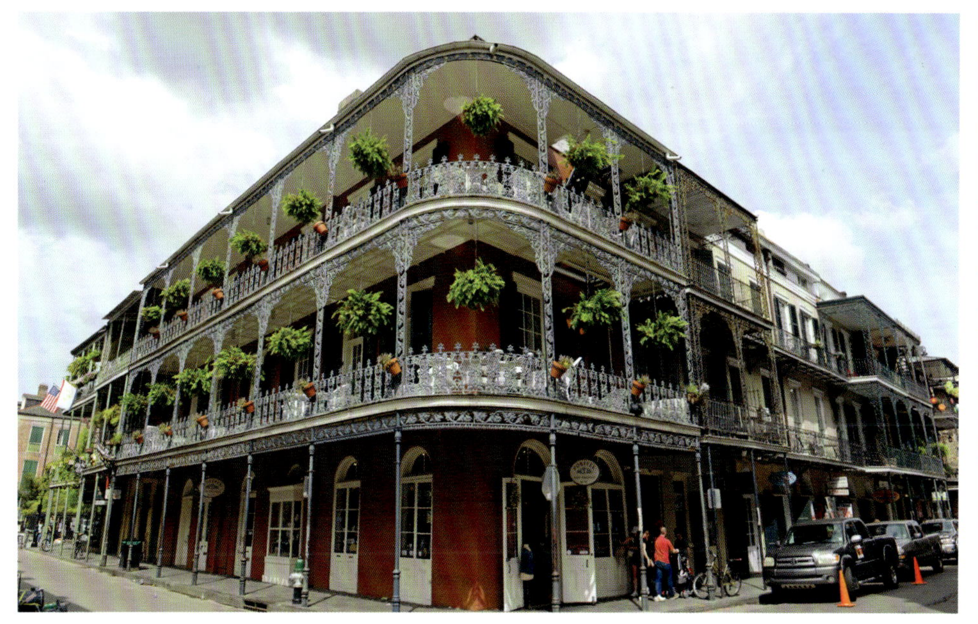

The LaBranche House is a classic example of 1830s architecture.

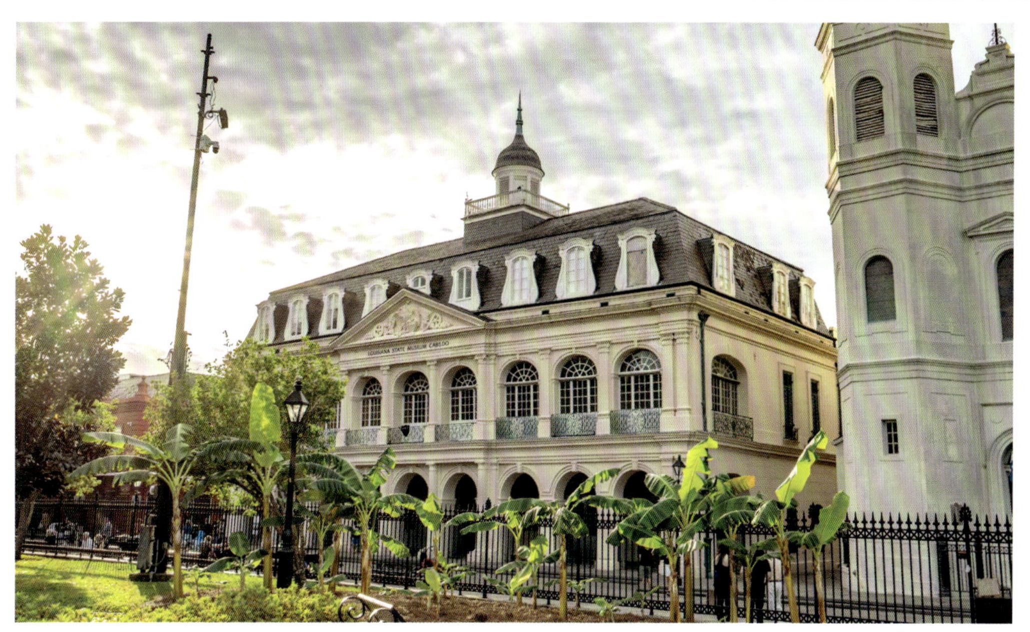

St. Louis Cathedral–officially the Cathedral Basilica of St. Louis–is seen here from Jackson Square. The building dates to 1914, and the interior relies heavily on mosaics for decoration.

The Cabildo *(above)*, adjacent to St. Louis Cathedral, was built between 1795 and 1799. At the time, New Orleans was under Spanish rule, and the building housed government offices. The building is now part of the Louisiana State Museum. The Presbytère, built in 1813, is a similar building on the other side.

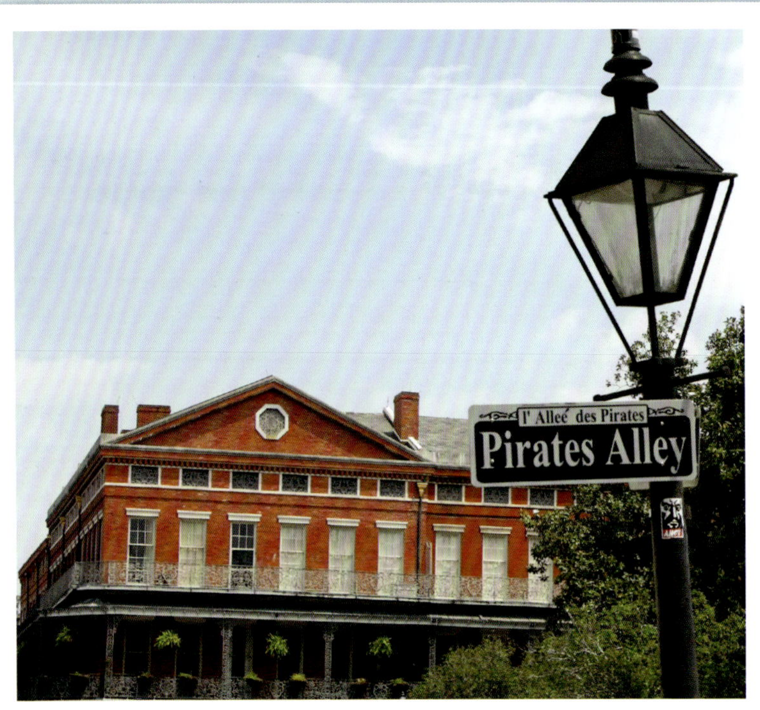

Pirates Alley near Jackson Square links Royal Street and Chartres Street. It's reportedly quite haunted.

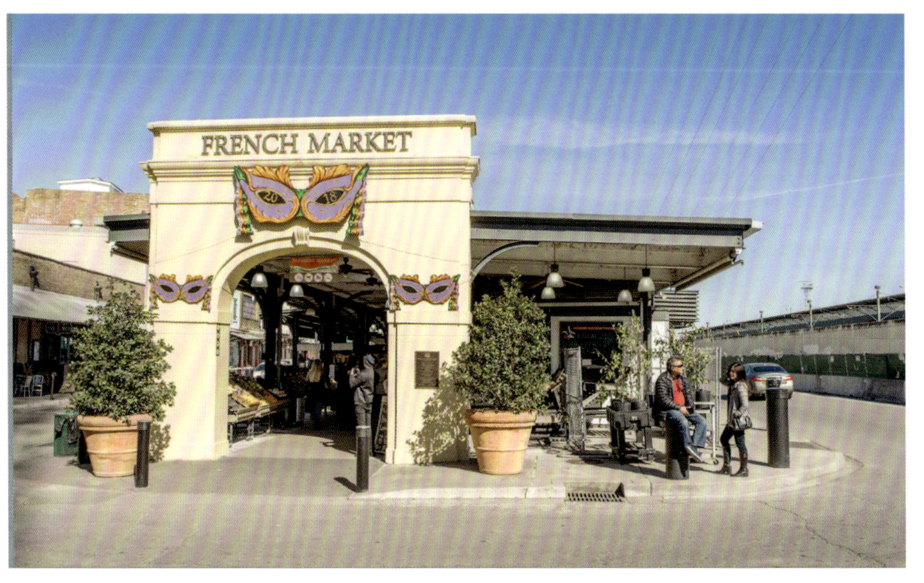

New Orleans's French Market features food stands, crafts, and a flea market where you can buy souvenirs from your trip.

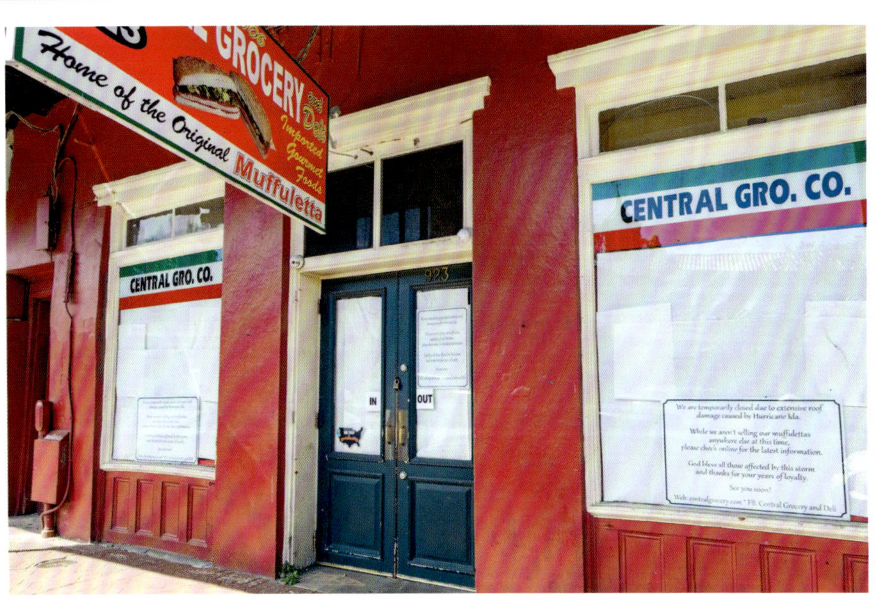

Italian immigrants brought muffuletta bread to Louisiana. The origins of the sandwich, which adds olive salad to meat and cheese, are uncertain, but one potential place of origin is the Central Grocery Co.

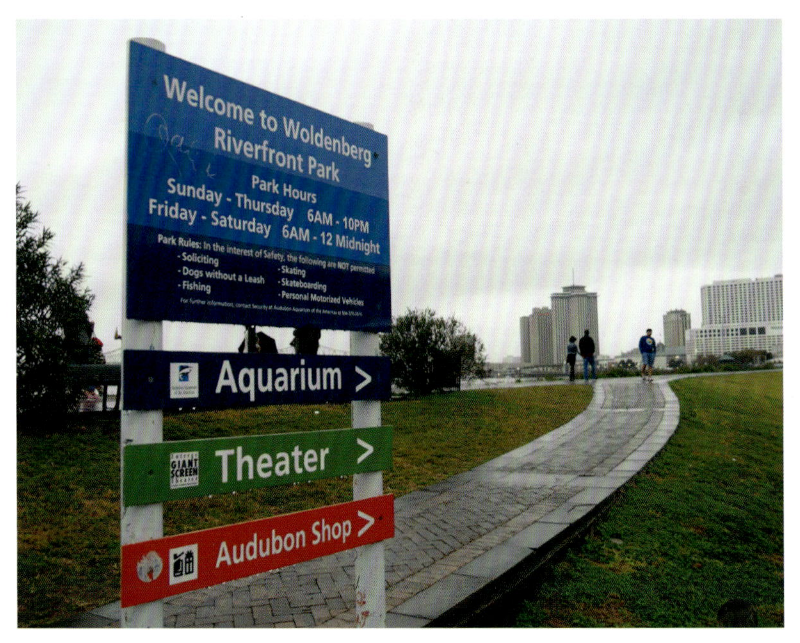

From Café du Monde, you can walk to the Mississippi River and wander down the French Quarter River Walk paths. Along the way, you'd spot statues, a gazebo, and various memorials. If you walked all the way to the Audubon Aquarium, you'll cover a distance of slightly more than three-quarters of a mile from Café du Monde.

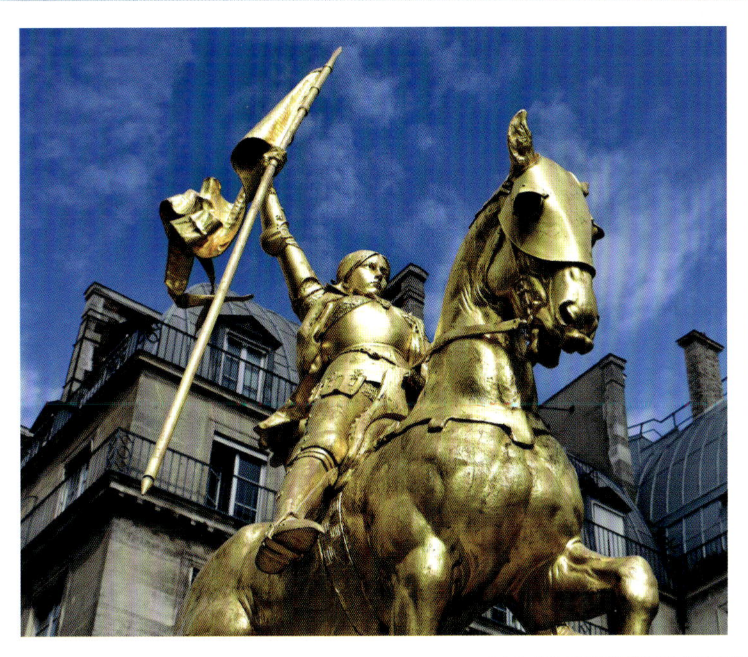

Joan of Arc, the "Maid of Orleans," is honored with a statue in New Orleans.

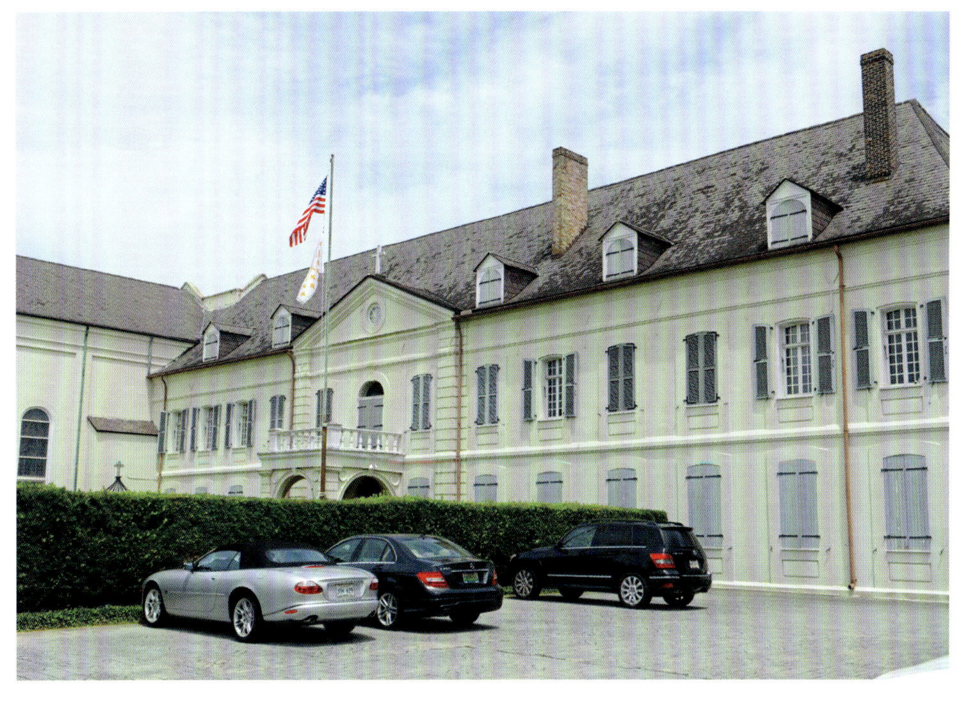

The Old Ursuline Convent Museum is the site of an Ursuline Convent that served as convent, orphanage, and girls' school between 1745 and 1824. The first building at the location dates to 1751.

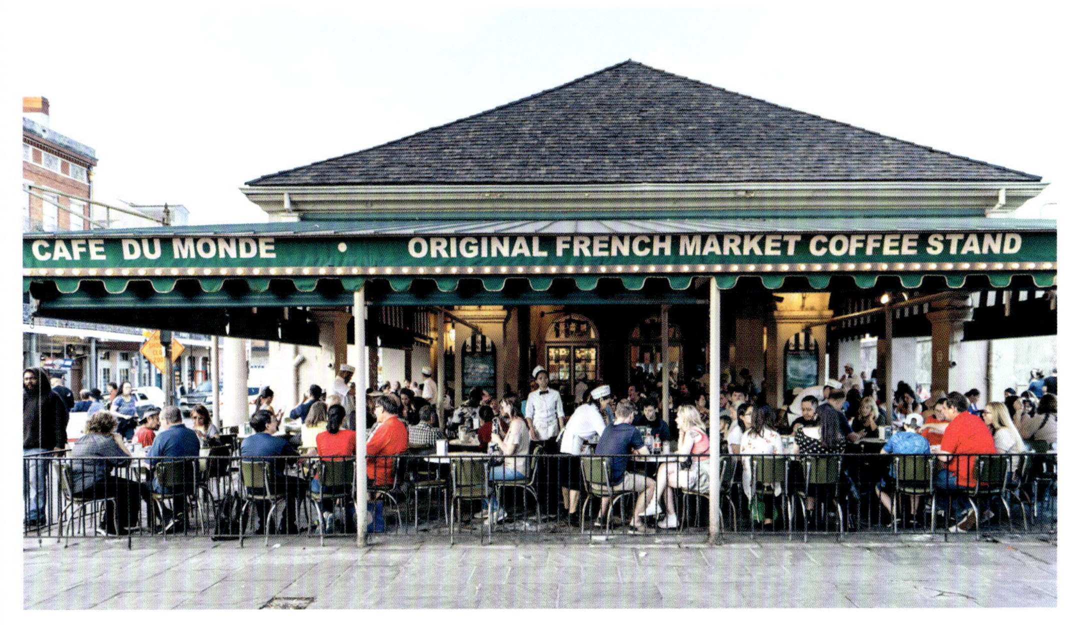

The Café du Monde is famous for its beignets, deep-fried pastries covered in powdered sugar.

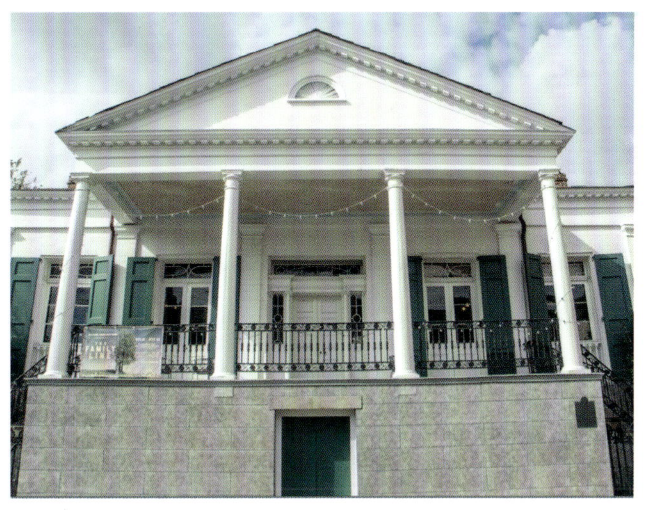

Keep an eye out for the BK Historic House and Gardens across the street from the Old Ursuline Convent Museum. The house was built in 1826 and is now a house museum.

Garden District Tour

Location: New Orleans, Louisiana
Length: About 2.3 miles
Start point: St. Charles Avenue and Eighth Street
End point: Magazine Street and Second Street

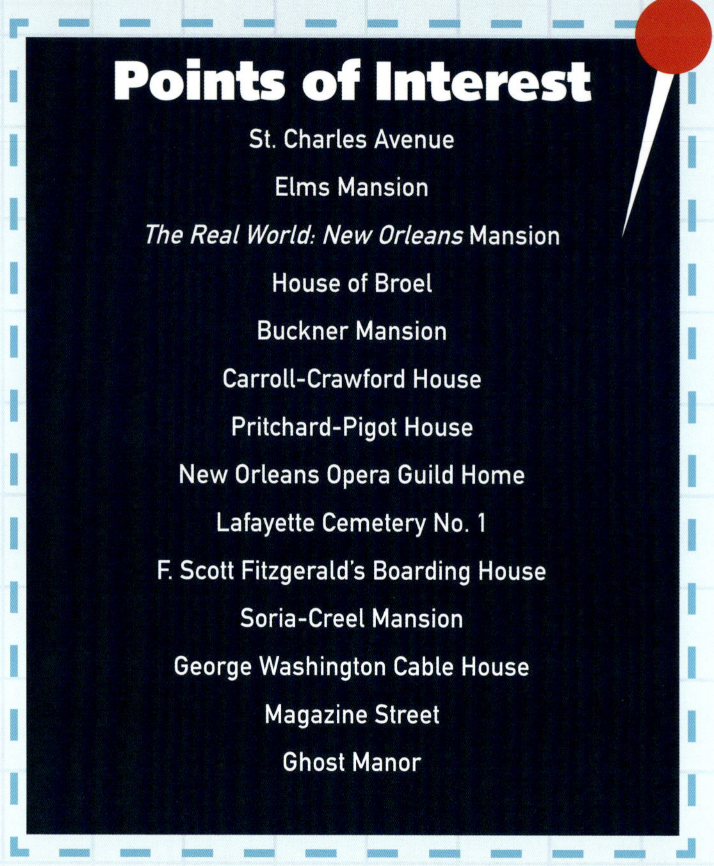

New Orleans's Garden District forms a roughly rectangular shape bordered by St. Charles Avenue on the north and Magazine Street on the south, with Magazine Street famous for its boutique shopping. Walking through the district, you'll see mansions, stately old oak trees, and the historic St. Charles Streetcar Line. Here's one route that shows you a number of historic homes.

Start at St. Charles Avenue and Eighth Street, going east. At 3029 St. Charles Avenue, spot the Elms Mansion from 1869. Once you pass Fourth Street, keep an eye out for the house at 2618 St. Charles Avenue. If you're a reality TV fan, you might recognize it as the house from *The Real World: New Orleans*. Continue until you reach 2220 St. Charles Avenue, the House of Broel. This Victorian-era mansion is open for tours, with a dollhouse museum on the second floor. Turn when you reach Jackson Avenue, keeping an eye out between Pyrtania Street and Coliseum Street for the 1856 Buckner Mansion that you may recognize as a familiar building from the third season of *American Horror Story*.

Take Coliseum Street to First Street, where you can find the 1869 Carroll-Crawford House at 1315 First Street and the Pritchard-Pigot House at 1407 First Street. Keep heading north on First Street until you reach Pyrtania Street, then swing a left. You'll see the 1859 New Orleans Opera Guild House at 2504 Pyrtania Street. Continue on Pyrtania until you reach Washington Avenue and Lafayette Cemetery. (As of late 2024, the cemetery was closed for repairs.)

Moving west on Pyrtania Street, you'll see the boarding house where F. Scott Fitzgerald briefly lived at 2900 Pyrtania, and the 1875 Soria-Creel Mansion at 3102 Pyrtania Street. Then head south on Eighth Street, keeping an eye out for the 1874 George Washington Cable House at 1313 Eighth Street, until you reach Magazine Street. Once you do, turn left and stroll along, popping into any shops you'd like to visit. As you approach Second Street, you'll see Ghost Manor, an 1892 Victorian at 2502 Magazine Street, which puts on extensive displays each October.

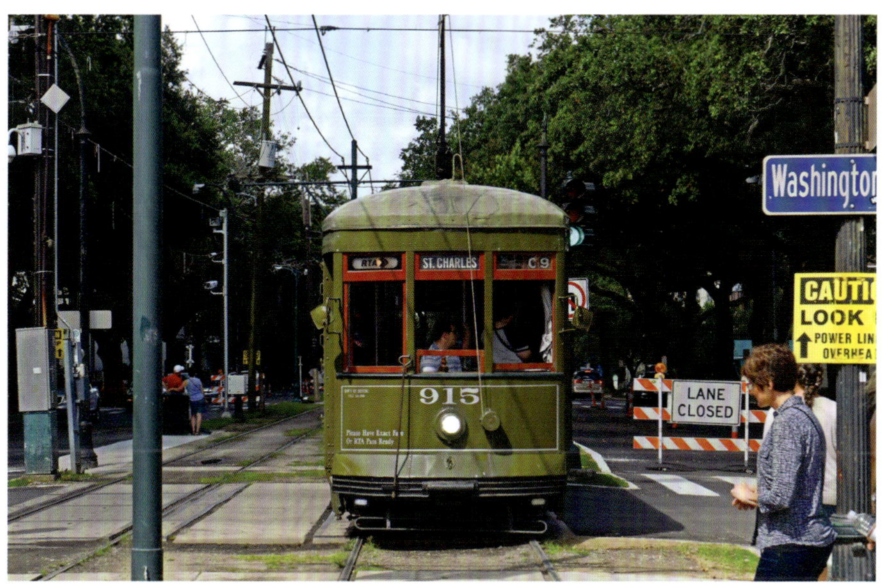

The St. Charles Streetcar Line has been running since 1835.

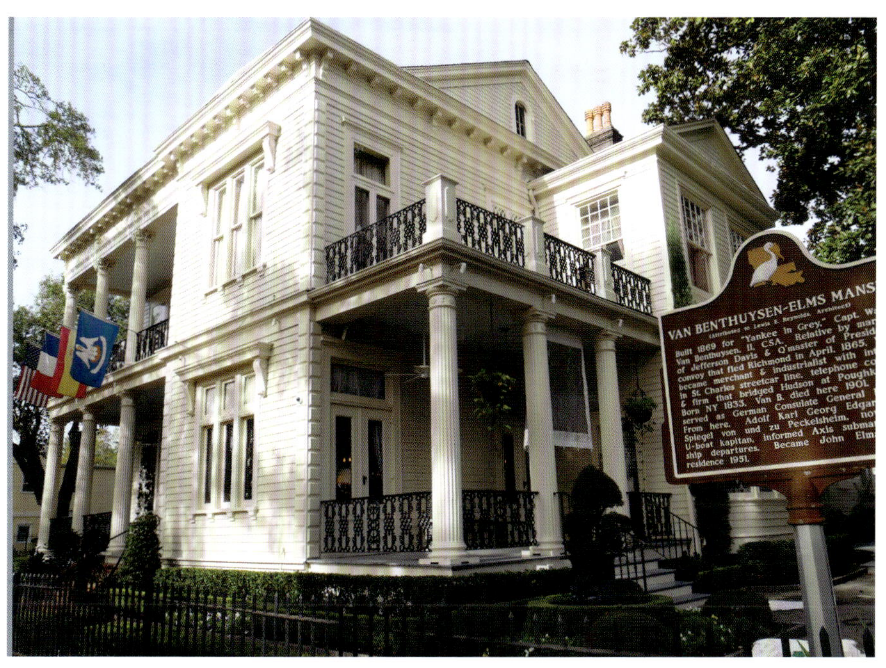

The Elms Mansion was built for a wealthy businessman in 1869, and today is an events venue.

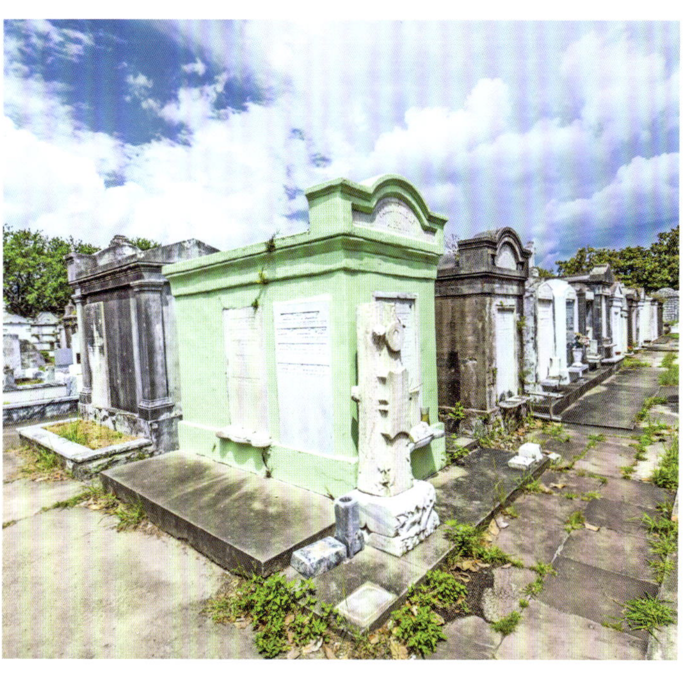

The historic Lafayette Cemetery No. 1 dates to 1833, and has shown up in mass media like the 1994 movie *Interview with the Vampire*.

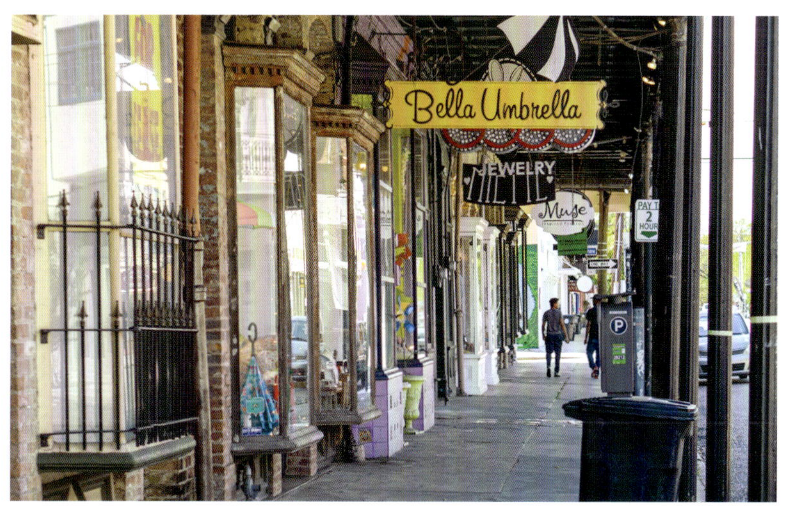

Magazine Street is lined with cute shops and restaurants.

Downtown Oklahoma City

Location: Oklahoma City, Oklahoma
Length: Minimum 3.1 miles
Start point: Oklahoma City National Memorial & Museum
End point: Skydance Bridge

This walk is a mix of history, art, architecture, natural beauty, and music. It starts in a somber place, at the Oklahoma City National Memorial & Museum, which commemorates the events and people of the Oklahoma City bombing in 1995. Among other elements, the Museum contains a reflecting pool, a Field of Empty Chairs that memorializes the victims of the bombing, and an orchard that represents rescuers.

From the memorial, head to the Oklahoma City Museum of Art, particularly notable for its large collection of Dale Chihuly's glass art. If you're an architecture fan, take a route that passes by the Oklahoma County Courthouse on Robert S. Kerr Avenue, a historic Art Deco building from 1937. The Oklahoma City Museum of Art is adjacent to City Hall Park, where you can see the City Hall or Municipal Building. Like the nearby Courthouse, it was funded by a U.S. Public Works Administration grant and done in Art Deco style.

From City Park, go to the Myriad Botanical Gardens for a dose of plant life and natural beauty, as well as sculptural art. From there, head east to the American Banjo Museum to learn more about the history of the banjo in North America throughout the centuries and see instruments from different eras.

Finish your walk by heading south along Thunder Drive, passing along the lovely Scissortail Park, until you reach the Skydance Bridge that crosses I-40. The architects were inspired by Oklahoma's state bird, the scissor-tailed flycatcher.

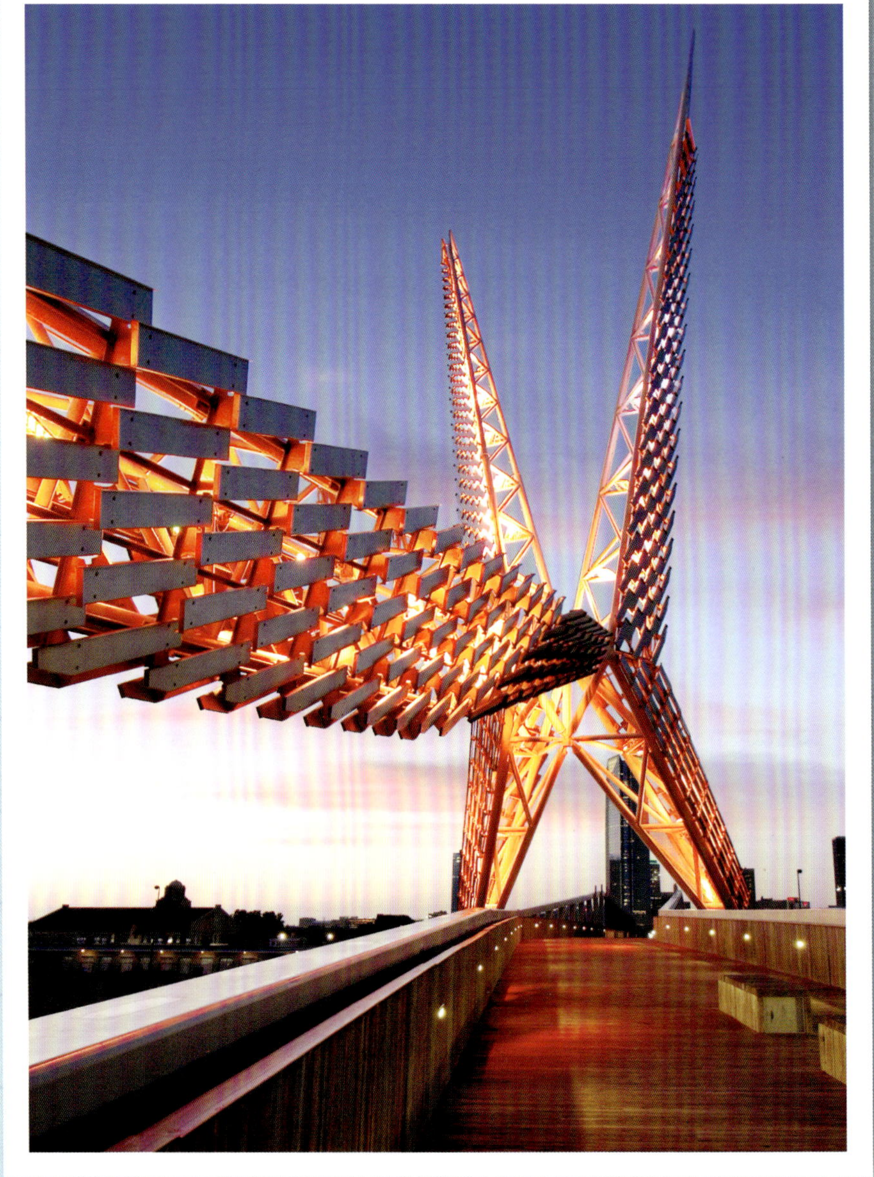

Skydance Bridge is a pedestrian bridge, so feel free to walk over it and catch different views.

Points of Interest

Oklahoma City National Memorial & Museum

Oklahoma County Courthouse

Oklahoma City Museum of Art

City Hall Park

Myriad Botanical Gardens

American Banjo Museum

Scissortail Park

Skydance Bridge

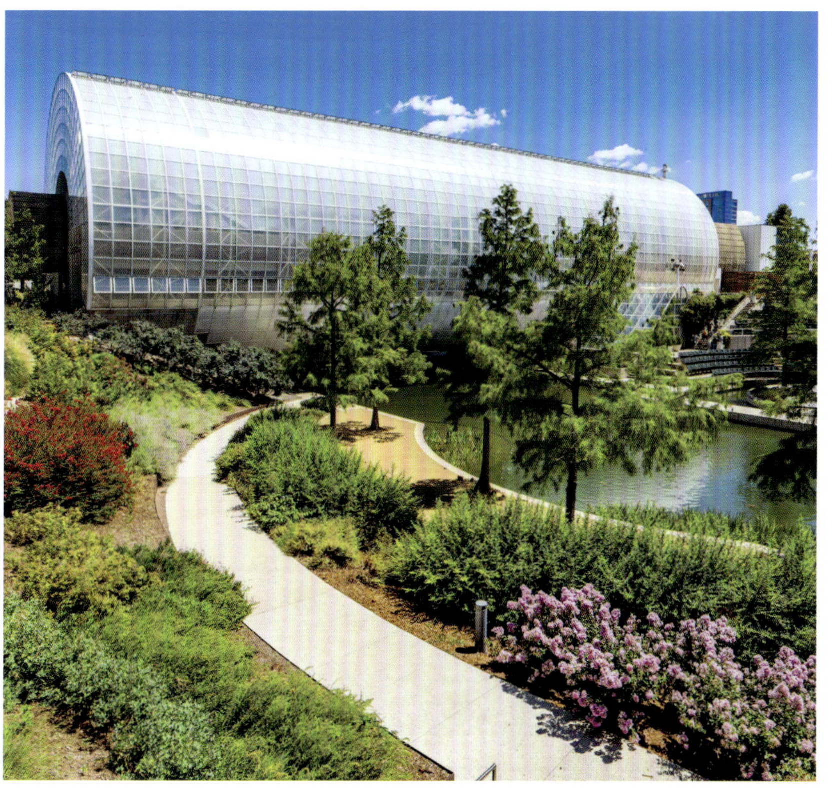

The Myriad Botanical Gardens cover about 15 acres.

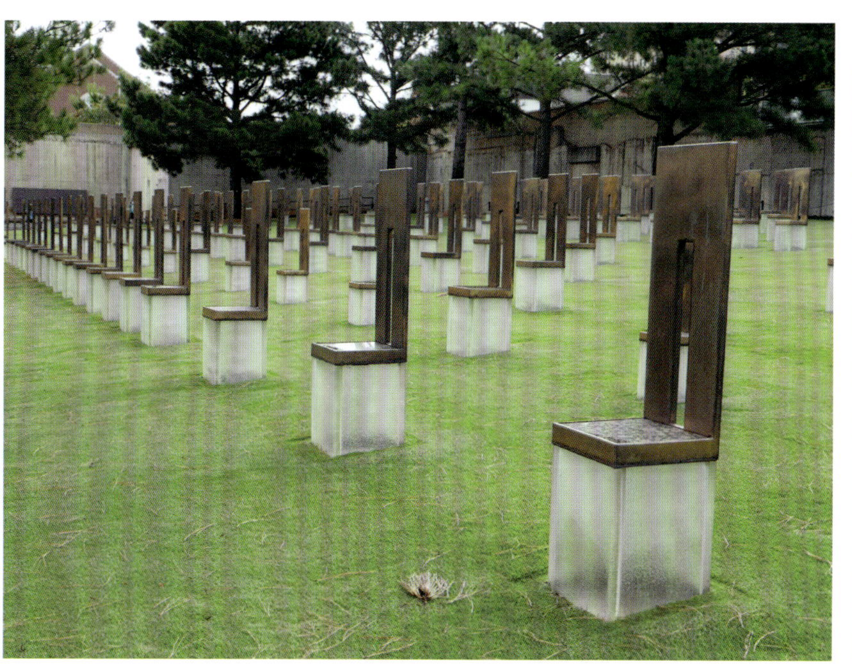

One hundred and sixty-eight chairs, acknowledging those who died, are placed at the former site of the Alfred P. Murrah building that was destroyed in 1995.

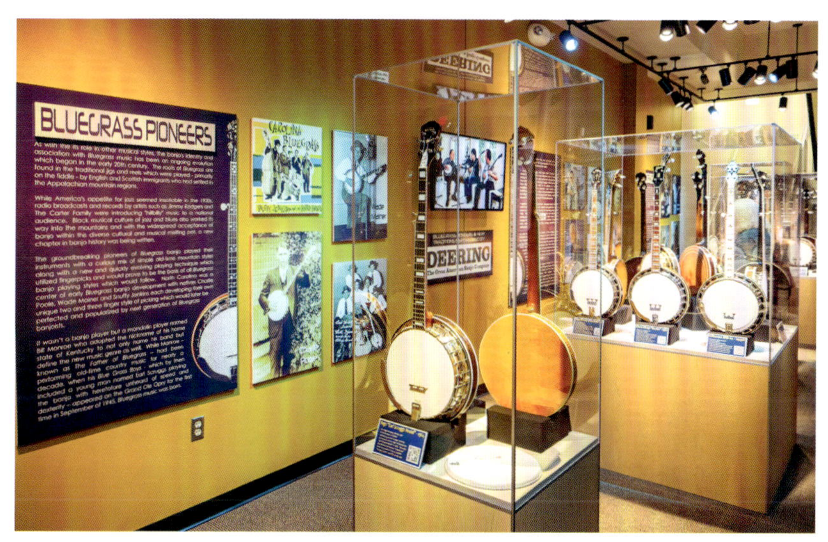

The American Banjo Museum has more than 400 instruments, with a focus on those from the 1920s and 1930s.

San Antonio River Walk

Location: San Antonio, Texas
Length: The River Walk runs 15 miles total, 5 miles downtown
Start point: Variable
End point: Variable

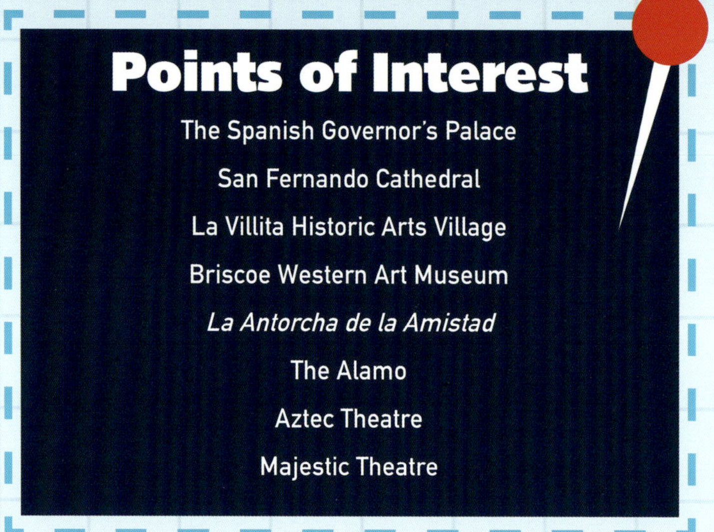

Points of Interest

The Spanish Governor's Palace
San Fernando Cathedral
La Villita Historic Arts Village
Briscoe Western Art Museum
La Antorcha de la Amistad
The Alamo
Aztec Theatre
Majestic Theatre

A fair amount of cities have developed river walks, many within recent decades. San Antonio's originated as far back as 1929, when an architect named Robert H. H. Hugman proposed the first version of an area around the river that would be set aside for "the shops of Romula and Aragon." The River Walk developed over time during the decades that followed, as both a draw for tourists and a way to manage the flow of water through the city. Today, the area is full of restaurants, hotels, and shops. The River Walk is also home to a number of art shows, festivals, and river parades. In February, you might see a parade for Mardi Gras; in March, for St. Patrick's Day. Fiesta San Antonio, held each April to commemorate the Battle of the Alamo and the Battle of San Jacinto, includes events throughout the city, such as a boat parade down the River Walk.

There are also a number of historical sites found on or very near the River Walk. The Spanish Governor's Palace, built in 1749, is a townhouse in Spanish Colonial style that now houses a museum. It's not far from Main Plaza and the San Fernando Cathedral. Much of the current architecture of the church dates to the 1860s, but parts of the building date back as far as 1738. A video show called "San Antonio–The Saga" is projected onto the Cathedral from Main Plaza in the evenings, for an immersive way to learn more about the city's history. And of course, no visit to San Antonio's downtown would be complete without a trip to the Alamo.

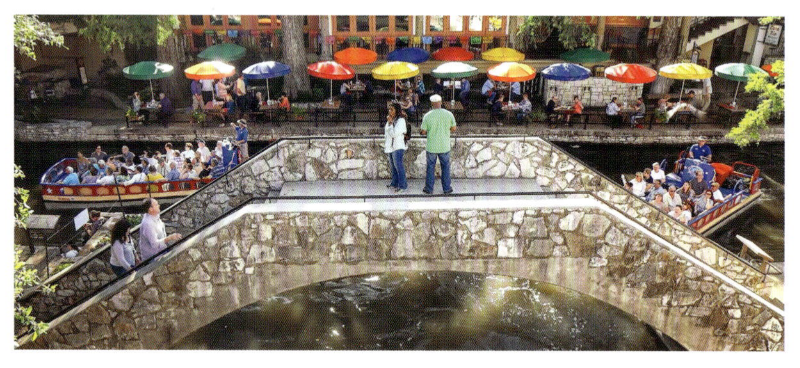

You might stroll down the River Walk in one direction, then take a tour boat back.

For those interested in art, La Villita Historic Arts Village on the River Walk features interesting architecture from several eras filled with shops and galleries. You can also tour the Briscoe Western Art Museum, featuring folk art and work by Western artists such as Frederic Remington. For architecture fans, the Aztec Theatre dates to 1926, while the huge Majestic Theatre found nearby dates to 1929.

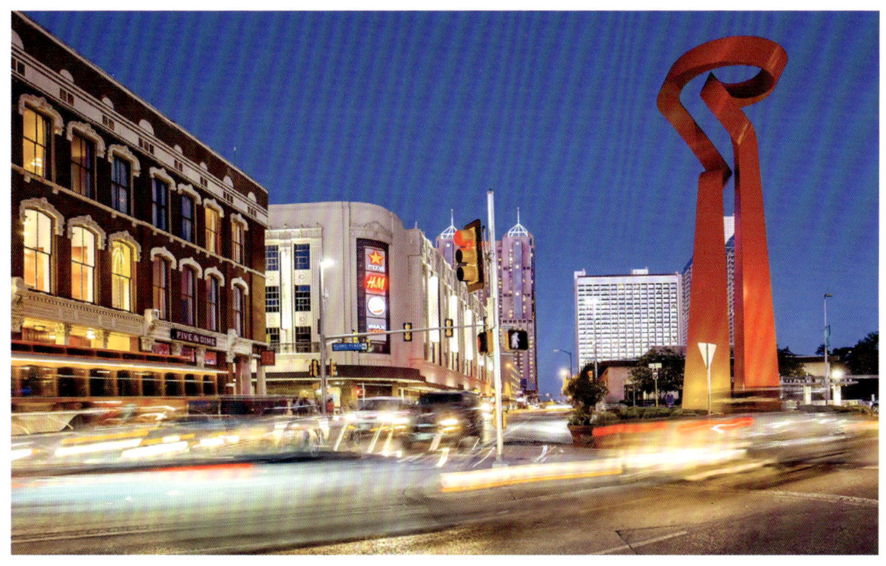

La Antorcha de la Amistad (meaning, the "Torch of Friendship"), by the Mexican sculptor Sebastián, was granted as a gift to San Antonio from the Mexican government in 2002.

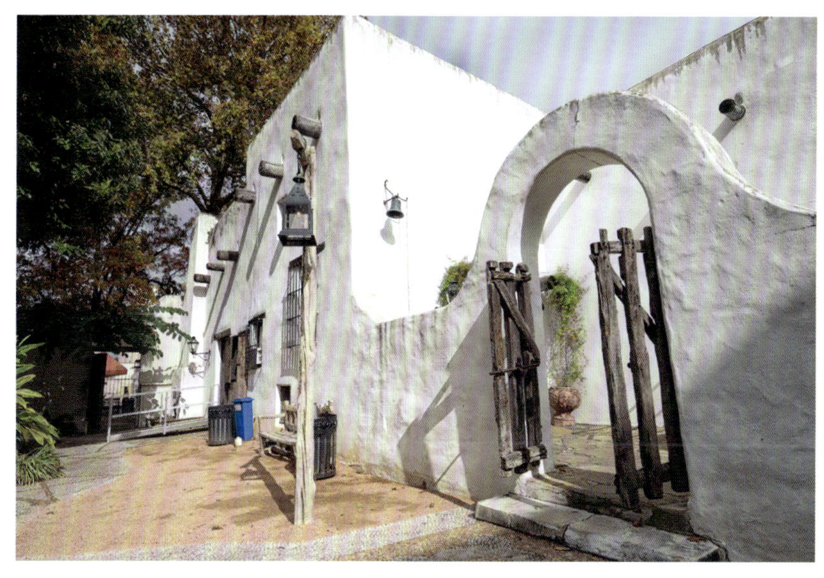

The adobe Spanish Governer's Palace was initially part of a Spanish fort, the Presidio de Béxar.

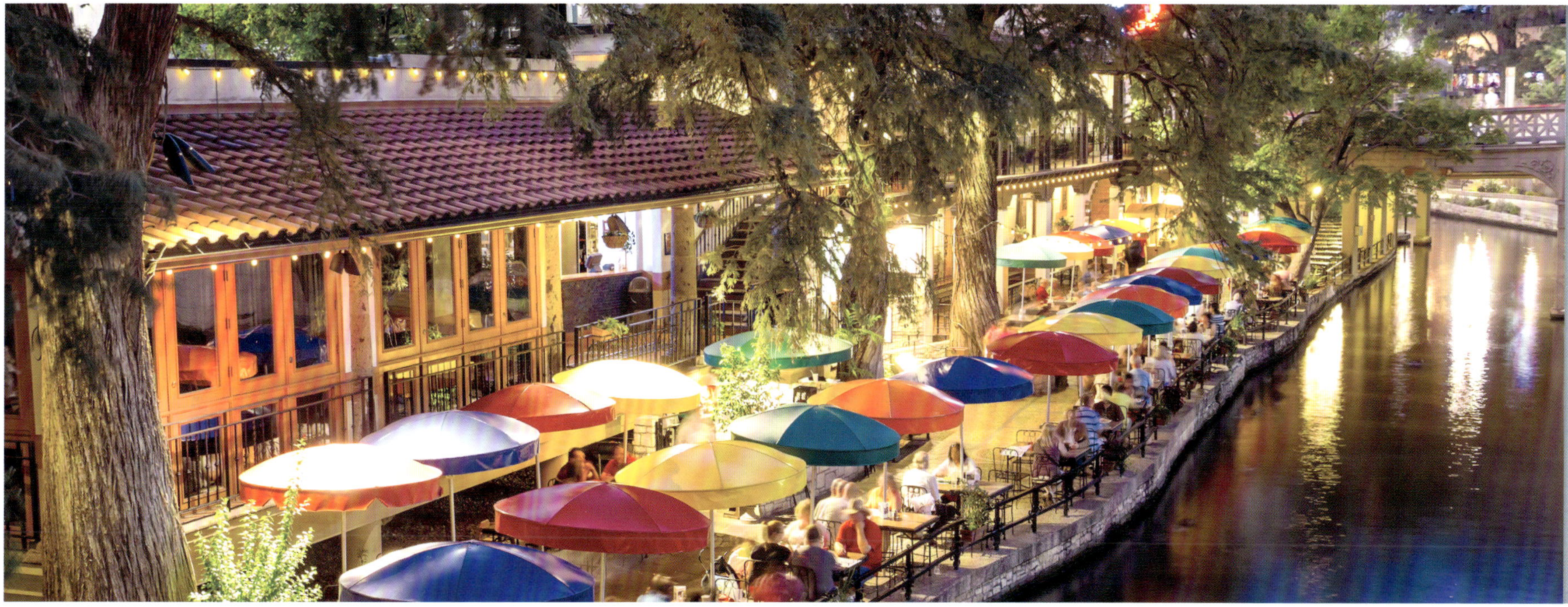

Catch a meal along the water, as restaurant options abound.

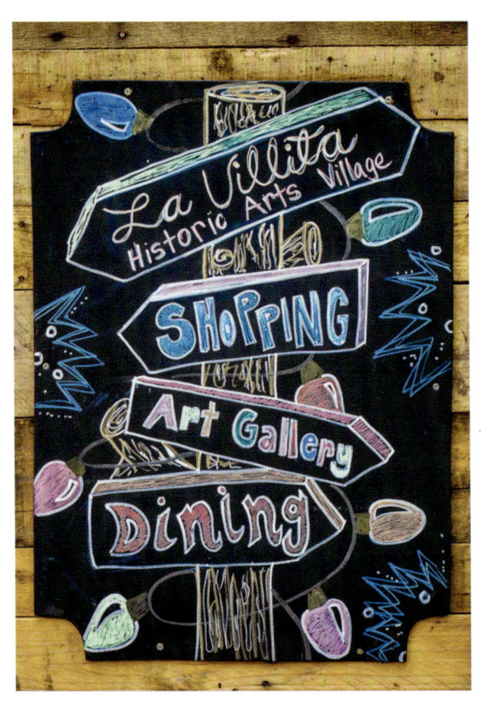

Buy jewelry, folk art, and pottery at La Villita Historic Arts Village. A number of buildings in the district date to the 1800s.

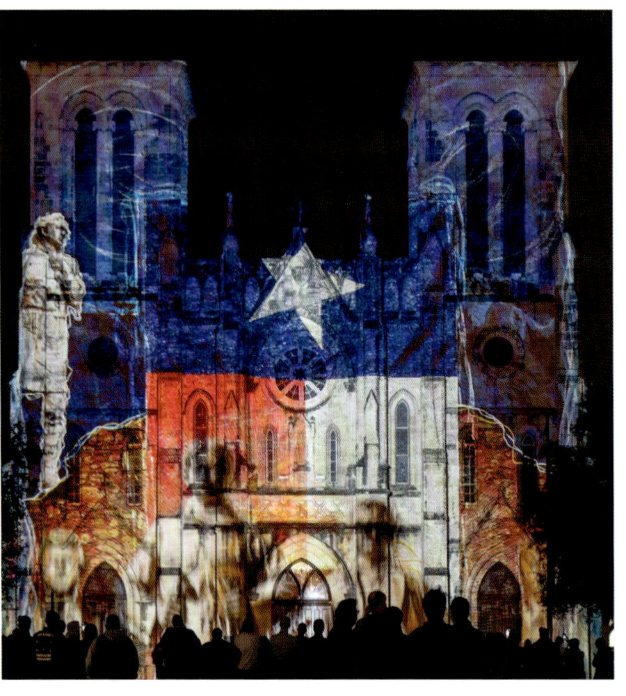

At night, San Fernando Cathedral becomes a projecting screen for "San Antonio–The Saga."

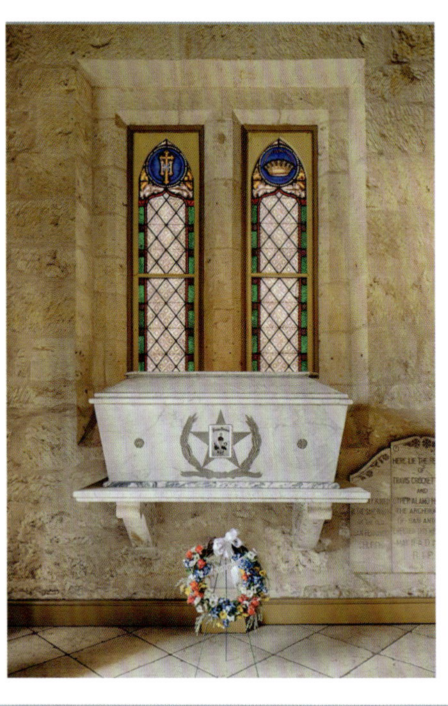

The ashes of some Alamo heroes are gathered at San Fernando Cathedral.

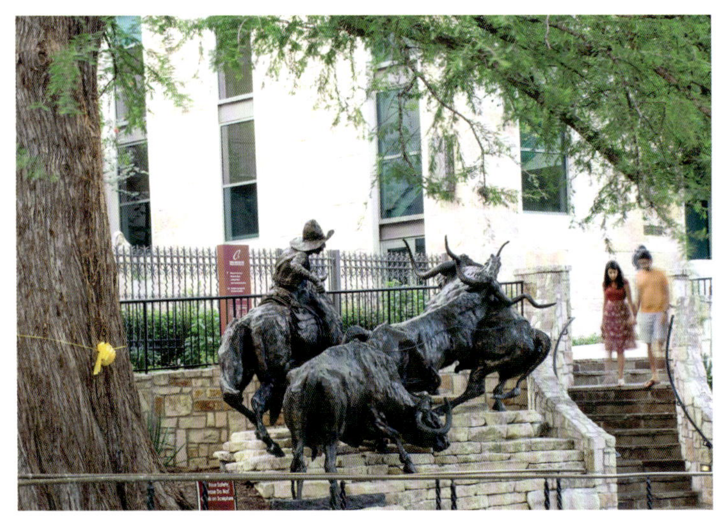

See artwork inside and outside the Briscoe Western Art Museum. This sculpture by T.D. Kelsey is named *Coming Home to the Briscoe.*

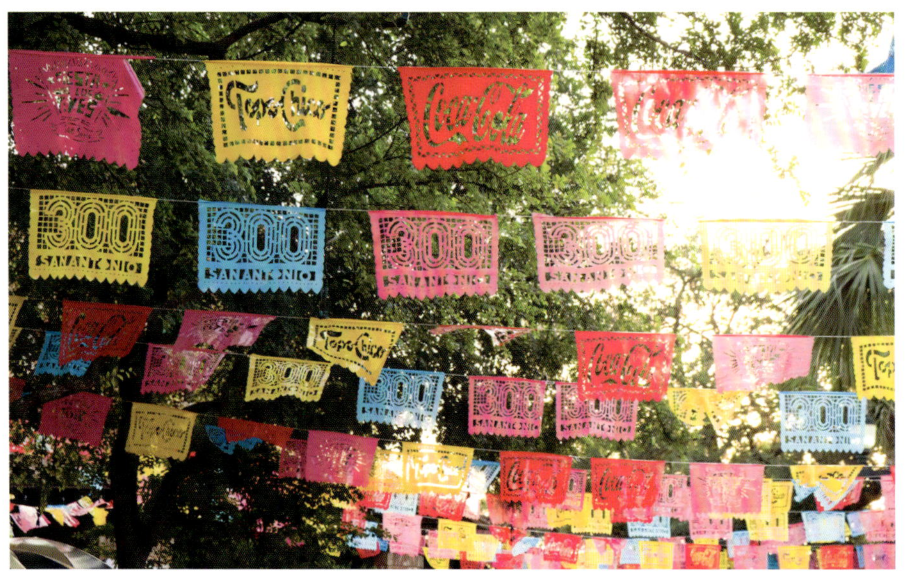

Fiesta San Antonio goes back as far as 1891, when San Antonio residents decided to put on a "Battle of Flowers" to honor their heroes from the Battle of the Alamo and the Battle of San Jacinto.

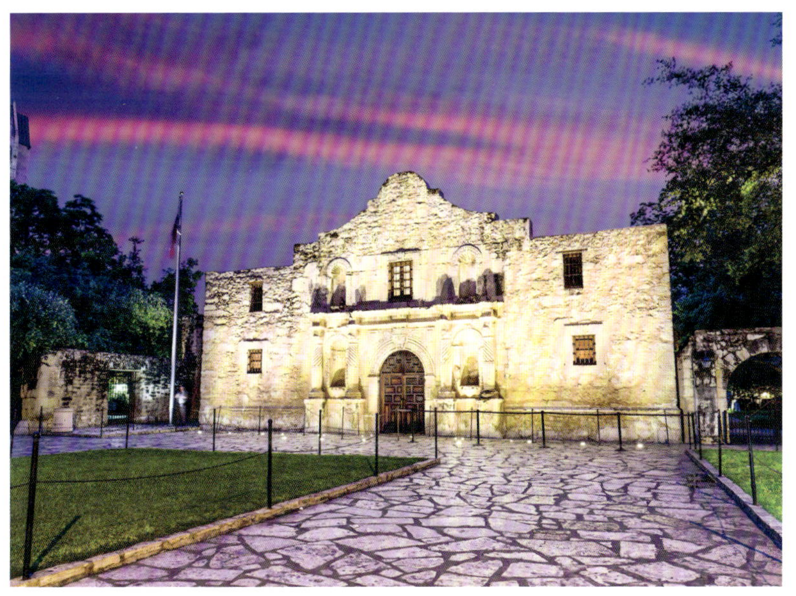

Built as part of a Spanish mission in 1718, the Alamo played a critical role during the Texas Revolution. Though its defenders lost, their defeat served as a rallying cry for later victories.

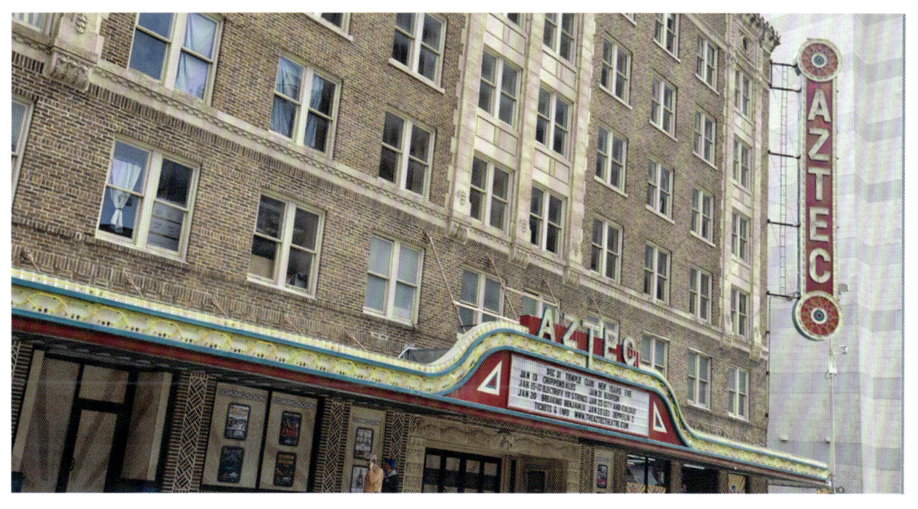

The Aztec Theatre is influenced by Meso-American artwork and architecture.

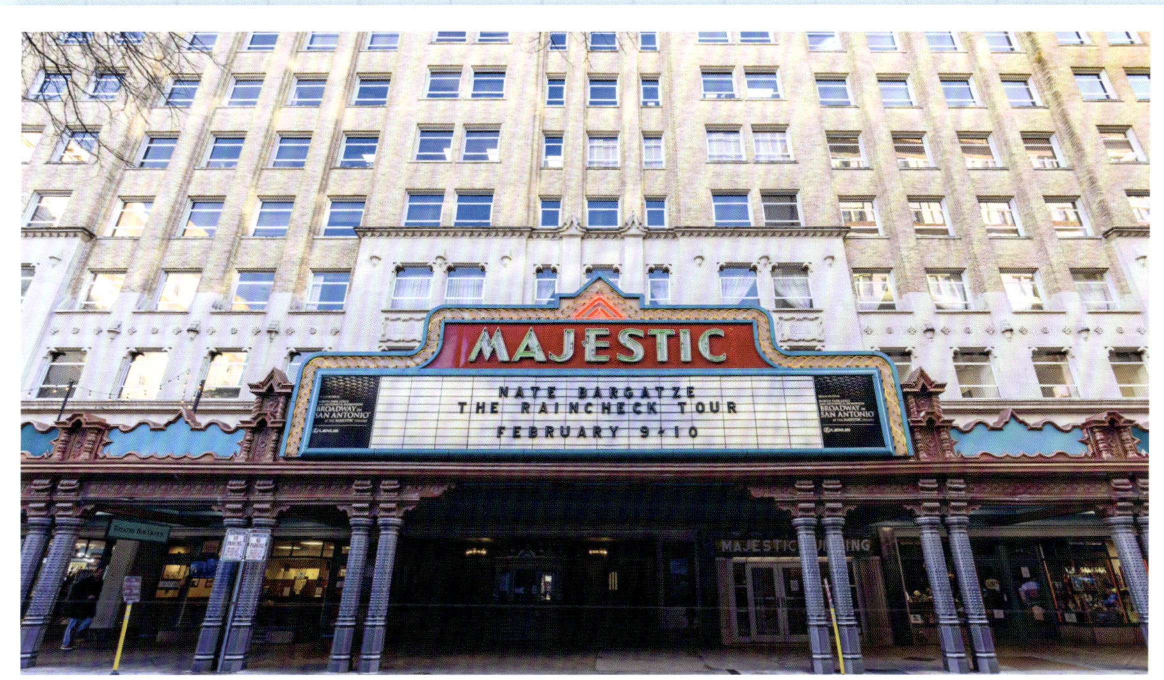

The Majestic Theatre seats more than 2,200.

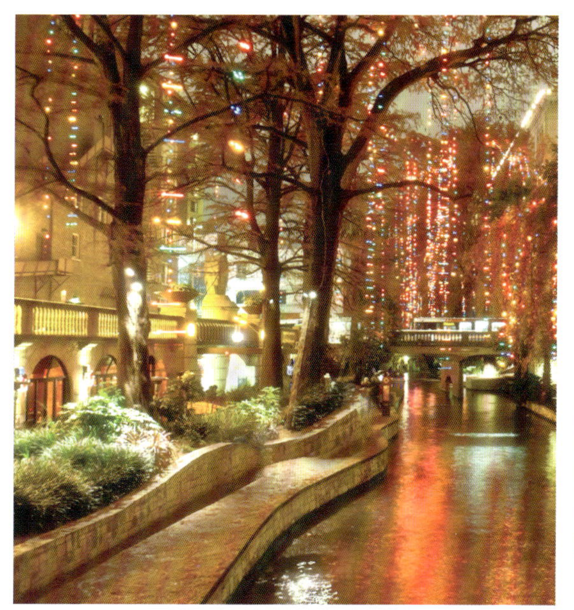

You'll see different decorations at different times of the year. Here, the River Walk is lit with Christmas lights.

Dallas Downtown

Location: Dallas, Texas
Length: About 2.5 miles
Start point: Dallas Museum of Art
End point: The Sixth Floor Museum at Dealey Plaza

This walk through Dallas's downtown area offers cultural opportunities, some fun and quirky public art installations, and a look at various events in Dallas's history.

For art lovers, there are several destinations of interest on the walk. The Dallas Museum of Art features collections from around the world and from both ancient and modern eras. In the immediate vicinity are the Nasher Sculpture Center, which focuses on modern and contemporary sculpture, and the Crow Museum of Asian Art.

From the cluster of art museums, move to a few sites that explore Dallas's frontier history. Pioneer Plaza, a large park, contains a complex bronze sculpture depicting a cattle drive. Artist Robert Summers created the sculpture, which was installed in 1994. The historic Pioneer Park Cemetery, which opened in 1849 and serves as the final resting place for several prominent Dallas politicians, is located adjacent to Pioneer Plaza. Walking towards Dealey Plaza, you'll see a small one-room log cabin on Elm Street. It's a replica of a log cabin build by farmer and trader John Neely Bryan—considered the founder of Dallas—as he settled the area between 1839 and 1841.

Dallas also made history in 1963 when John F. Kennedy was assassinated there. The Sixth Floor Museum can be found in the building that was formerly the home of the Texas School Book Depository, from which Lee Harvey Oswald shot the president. Visitors can walk Dealey Plaza and the Grassy Knoll, and see the John Fitzgerald Kennedy Memorial erected between 1969 and 1970.

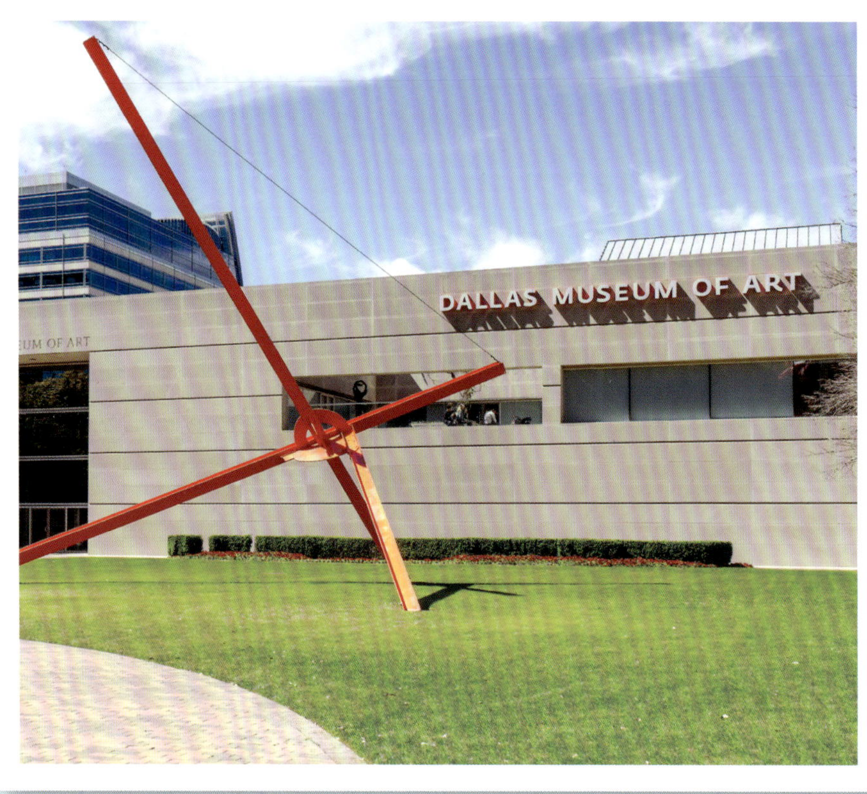

The Dallas Museum of Art traces its origins to the Dallas Art Association that was founded in 1903.

You'll also see art and other sights of interest as you walk from one destination to another. As you walk from the cluster of museums that begins this walk to Pioneer Plaza, take a route that passes by the Thanks-Giving Square, a park with a nondenominational chapel with beautiful stained-glass windows, and the Giant Eyeball, a public sculpture that is exactly what you'd expect from the name. Between Pioneer Plaza and the locations near Dealey Plaza, stop on Young Street to see the Pegasus, a neon sign that was originally erected on top of a hotel in 1934.

Points of Interest

Dallas Museum of Art

Crow Museum of Asian Art

Nasher Sculpture Center

Thanks-Giving Square

Giant Eyeball

Pioneer Plaza

The Pegasus

John Neely Bryan Cabin

John Fitzgerald Kennedy Memorial

Dealey Plaza

The Sixth Floor Museum

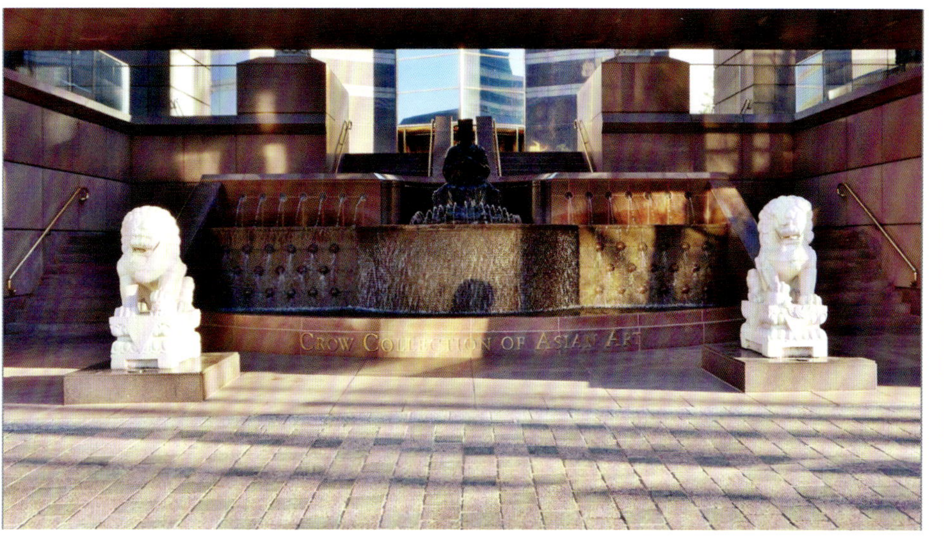

The Crow Museum of Asian Art was founded by collectors Trammell and Margaret Crow.

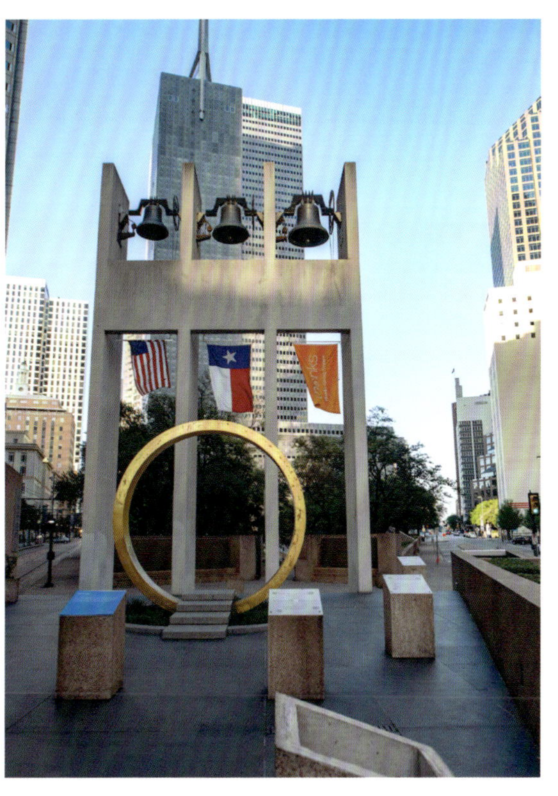

Art at Thanks-Giving Square includes the Ring of Thanks and the Bell Tower.

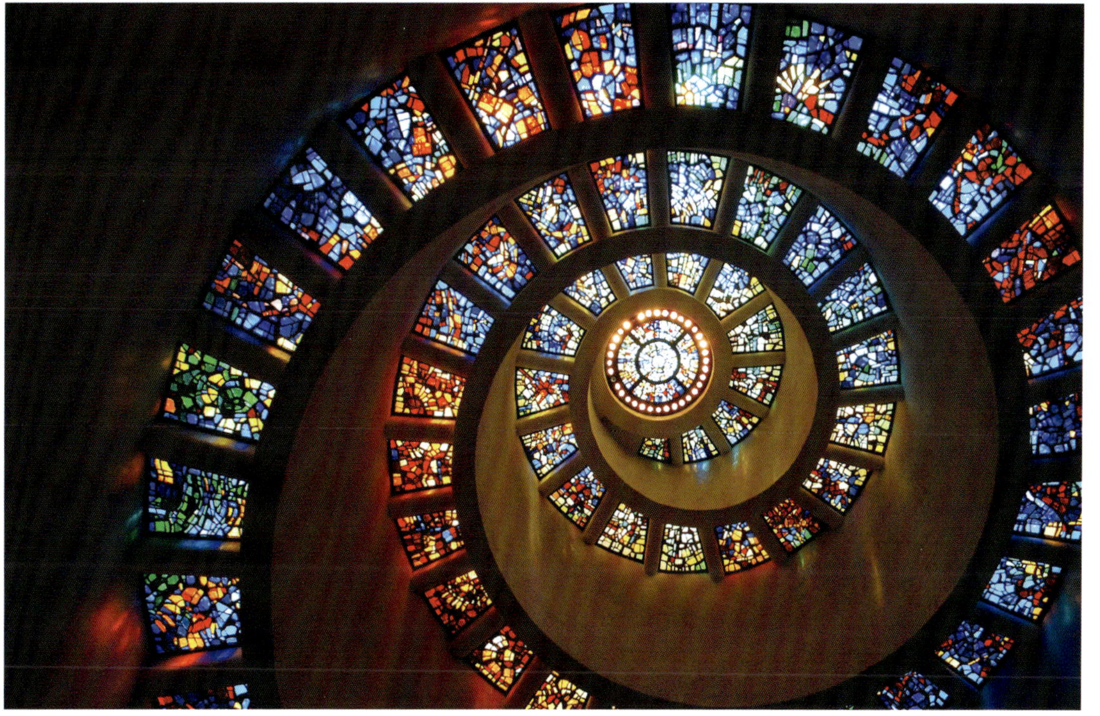

The Chapel in Thanks-Giving Square features the spiral "Glory Window."

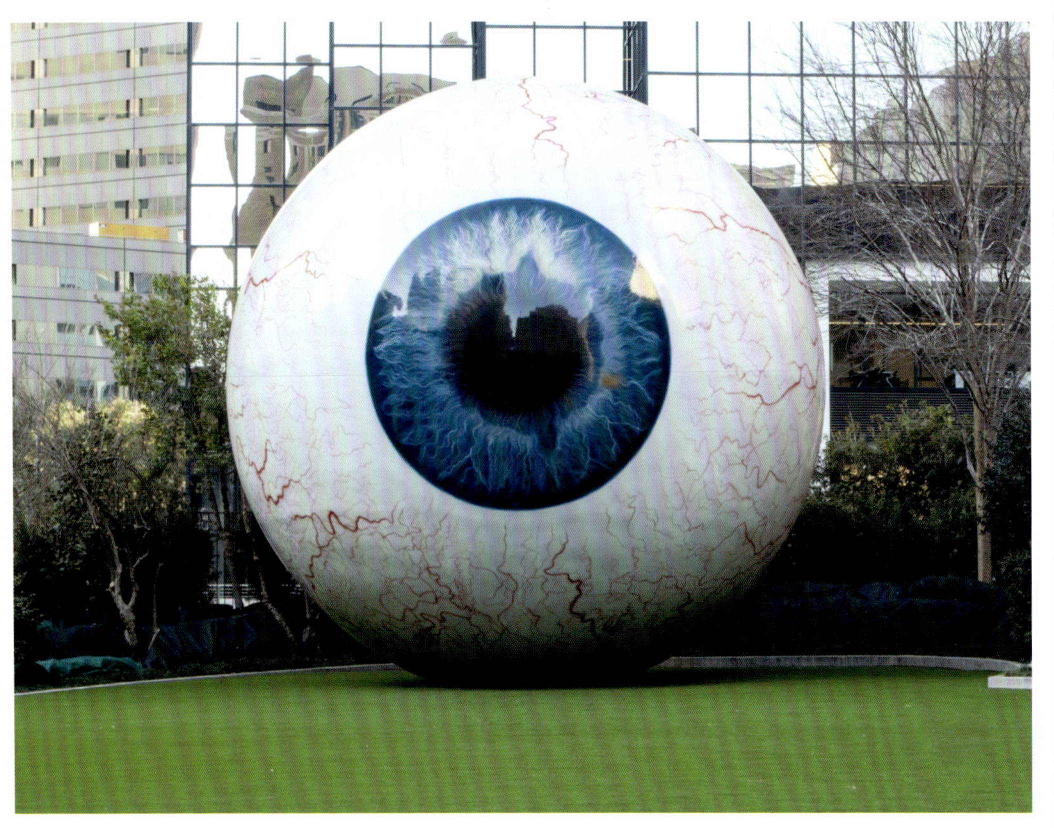

Colloquially known as the Giant Eyeball, the sculpture *Eye* is the work of Tony Tasset.

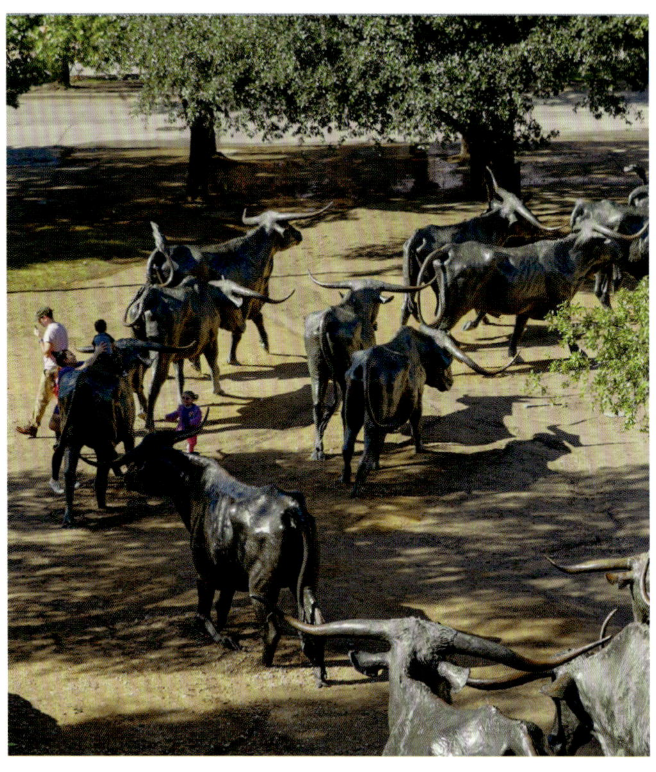

Close to fifty bronze steers form the sculpture of a cattle drive seen at Pioneer Plaza.

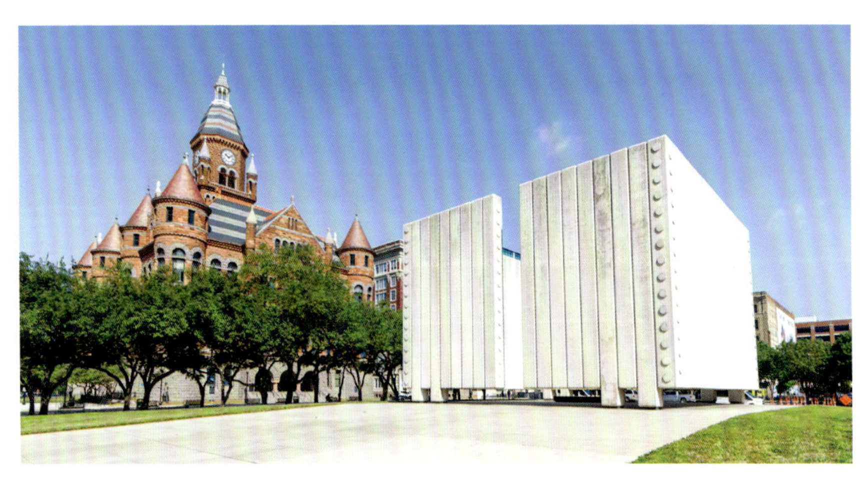

The monument at John Fitzgerald Kennedy Memorial Plaza is intended to be a cenotaph, an empty tomb.

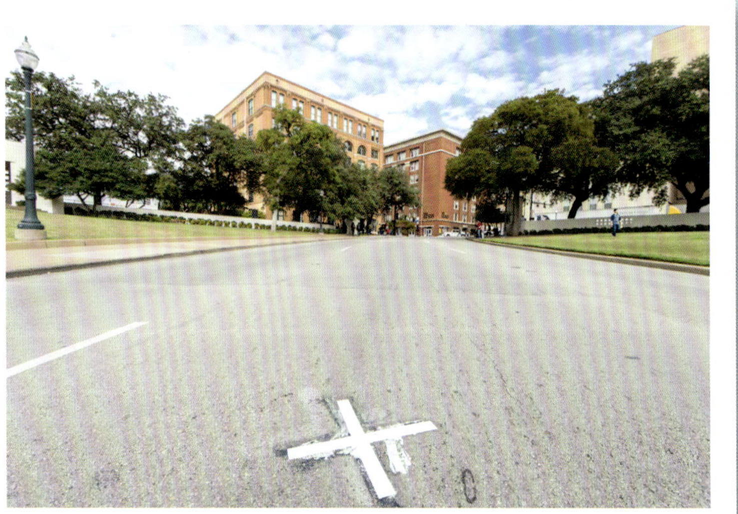

Unnamed people tape an X in the spot where JFK was shot; the tape tends to reappear even after it's been removed.

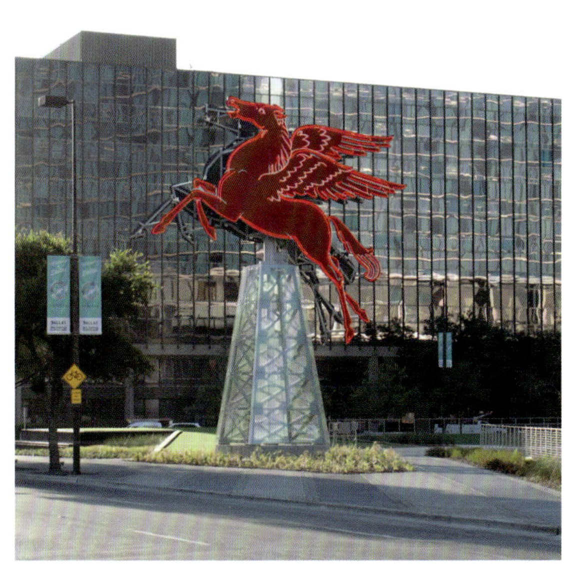

The Pegasus began as a mascot for an oil company, but the "Flying Red Horse" became a symbol for Dallas more generally.

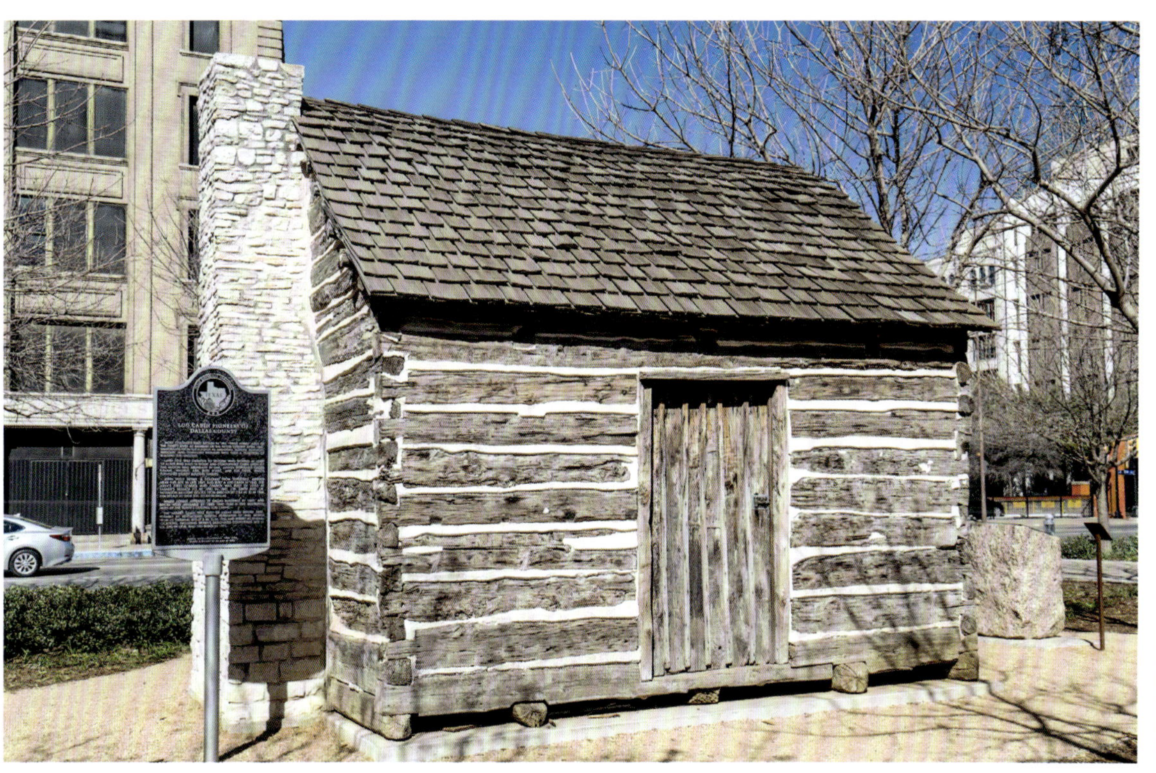

John Neely Bryan was a versatile man who acted as lawyer, farmer, and postmaster at various times in his life.

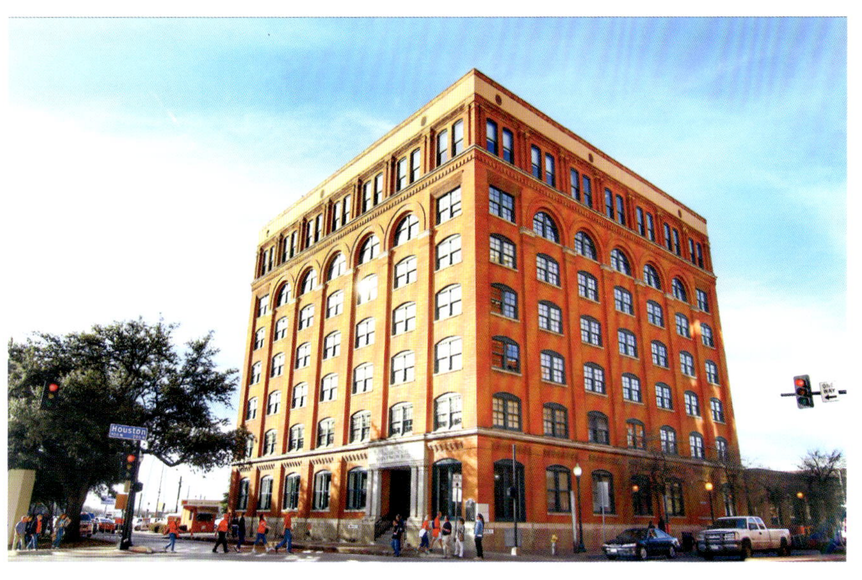

The former Texas School Book Depository building is now owned by and serves as administrative space for the county of Dallas, with the Sixth Floor Museum open to the public.

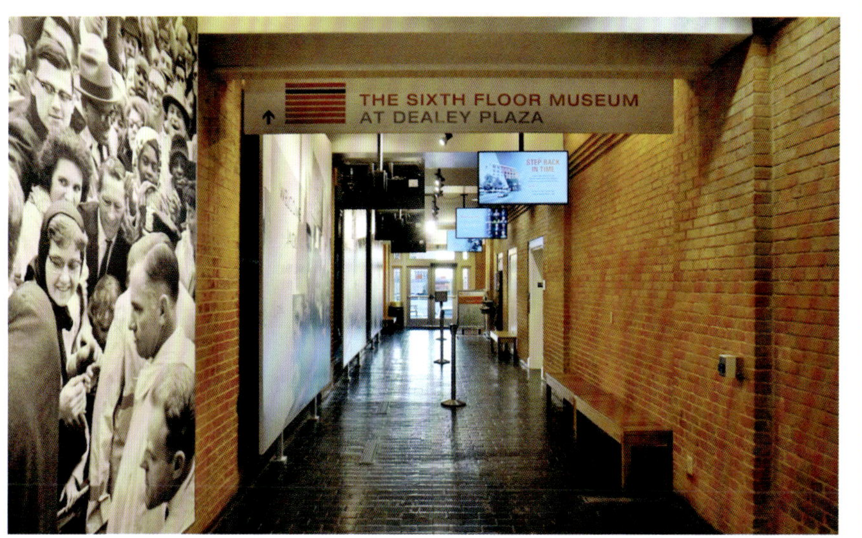

The Sixth Floor Museum

Houston Museum District

Location: Houston, Texas
Length: 1.3 miles
Start point: Museum of Fine Arts
End point: Hermann Park

Points of Interest

Museum of Fine Arts, Houston
Children's Museum Houston
The Health Museum
Hermann Park
Houston Museum of Natural Science
McGovern Centennial Gardens
Japanese Gardens
Hermann Park Railroad
Houston Zoo
Wildlife Carousel

Houston's Museum District includes about twenty museums divided into four zones—a wealth of opportunities for a thriving city, but many more than are manageable in a day! This walk offers some options for a family-friendly itinerary centered around and in Hermann Park, with you deciding which museums sound most appealing. Expect to do more walking than the direct length listed above, as you'll meander through museums and the zoo.

Three museums are found in the Museum District right outside Hermann Park: the Museum of Fine Arts, Houston, which houses about 70,000 works; the Children's Museum Houston, which has tons of play opportunities that teach about the laws of motion, invention, and electricity; and the Health Museum, where visitors can take a walk through a giant model of the human body and perform experiments in a cell lab.

Hermann Park is a huge park—445 acres—with no shortage of things to do. The Houston Museum of Natural Science and the Houston Zoo are actually found in the park, as well as various gardens, the Miller Outdoor Theatre, a golf course, jogging trails, pedal boats, a train ride, a reflection pool, and monuments that memorialize Sam Houston and pioneers. The park was established in the 1910s, with the Zoo added in 1922, and is named after the oilman and philanthropist who donated the land for it upon his death, George Hermann.

When planning your trip, you might want to check first for free days at the museums.

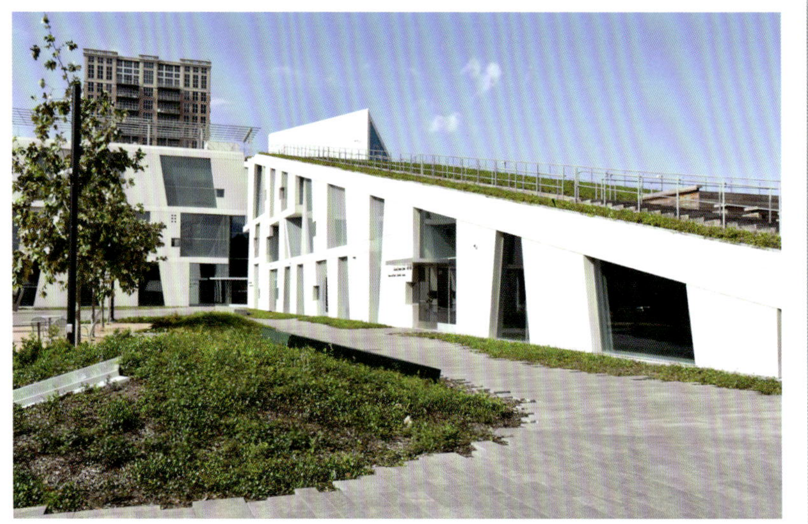

Near the main building of the Museum of Fine Arts, Houston, check out the funky architecture of the Glassell School of Art, the associated teaching school.

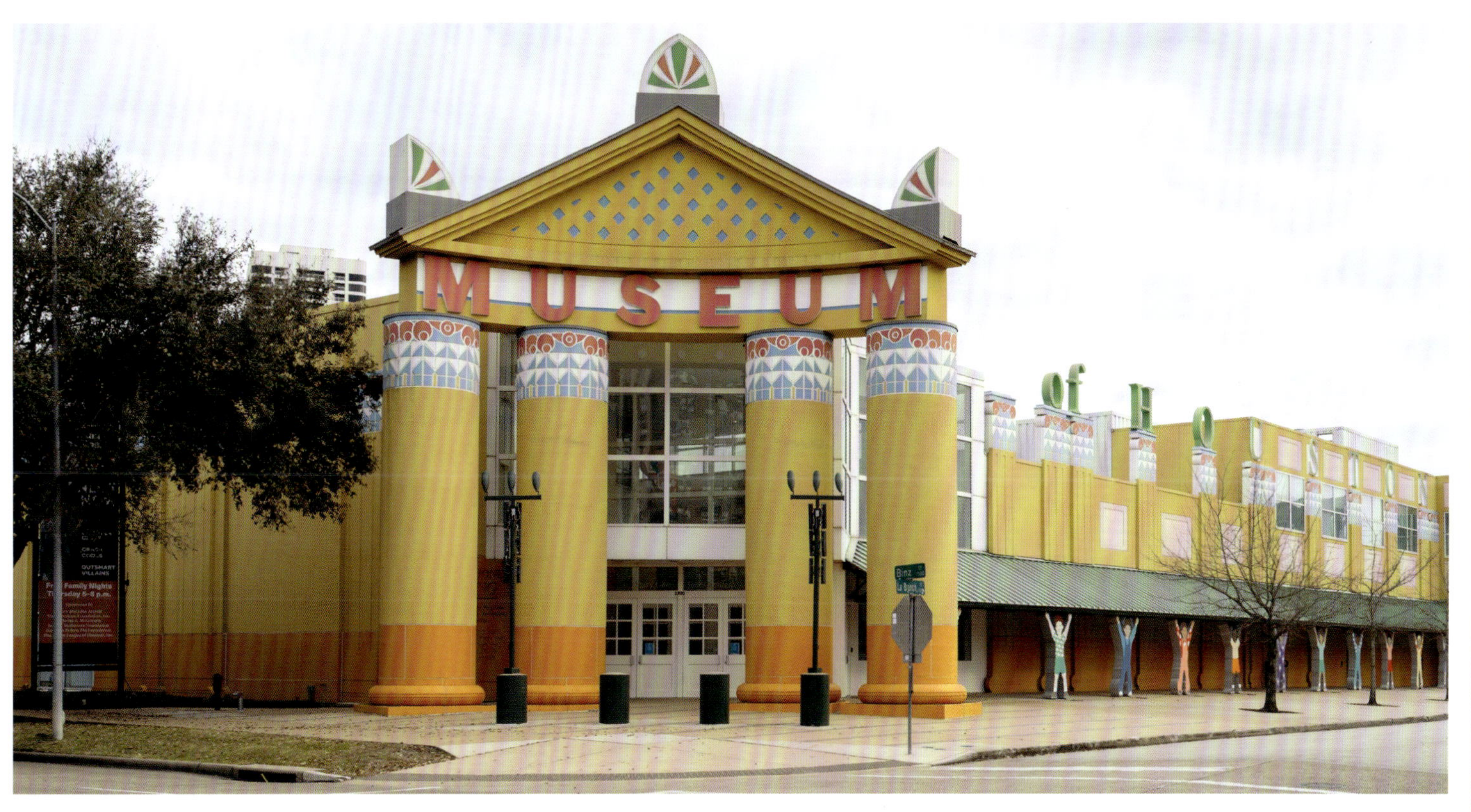

The Children's Museum Houston was established in the 1980s and moved to its current location in 1992.

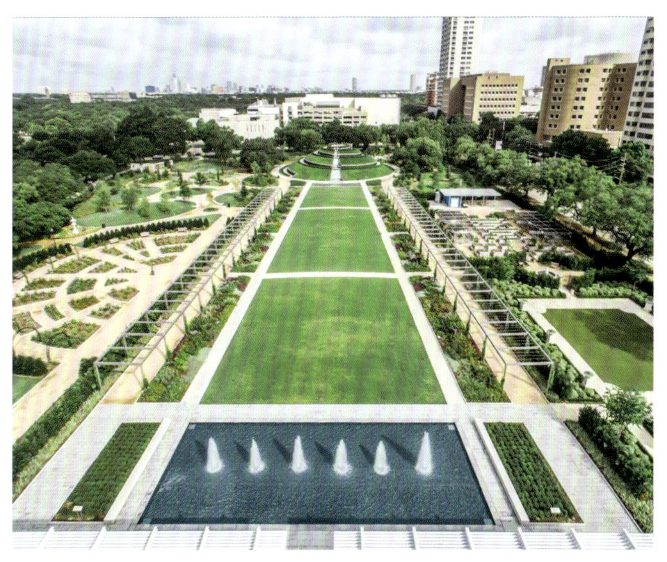

The McGovern Centennial Gardens at Hermann Park cover 15 acres and include a rose garden and a sculpture walk.

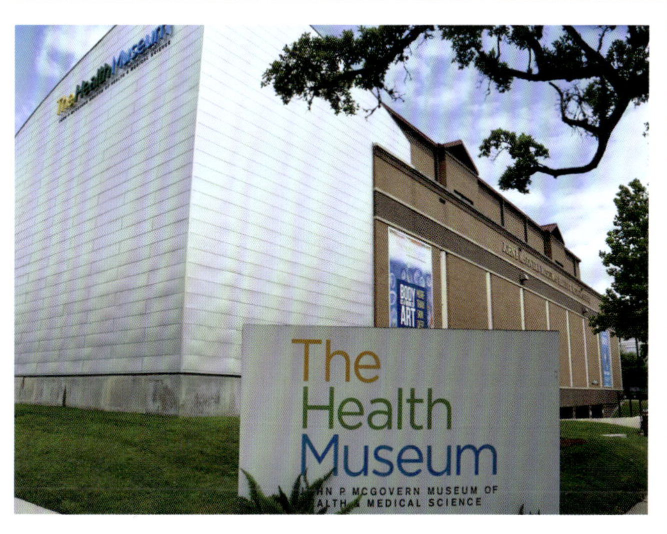

The Health Museum is more formally known as the John P. McGovern Museum of Health and Medicine Science.

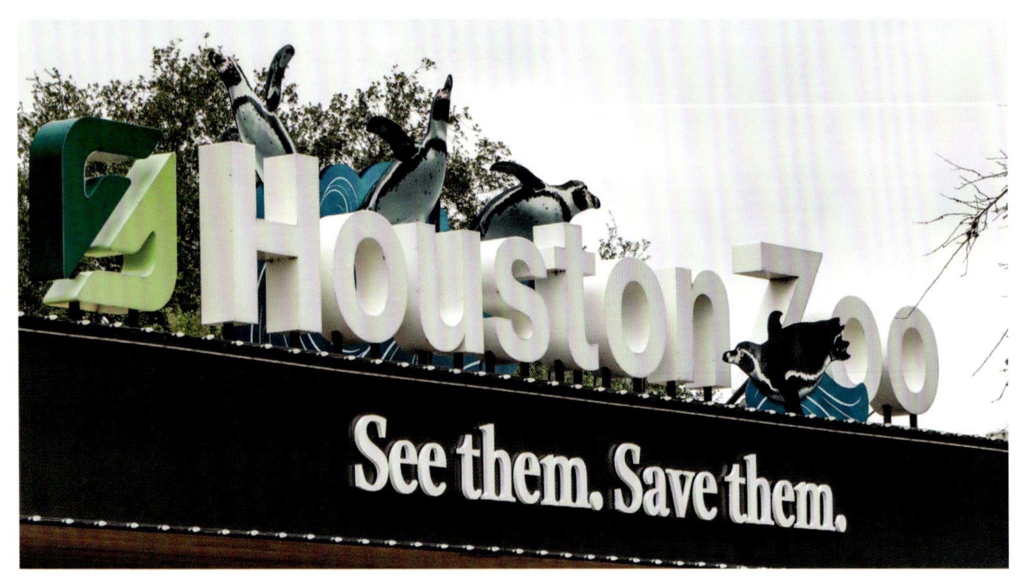

Visitors can see more than 6,000 animals at the Houston Zoo.

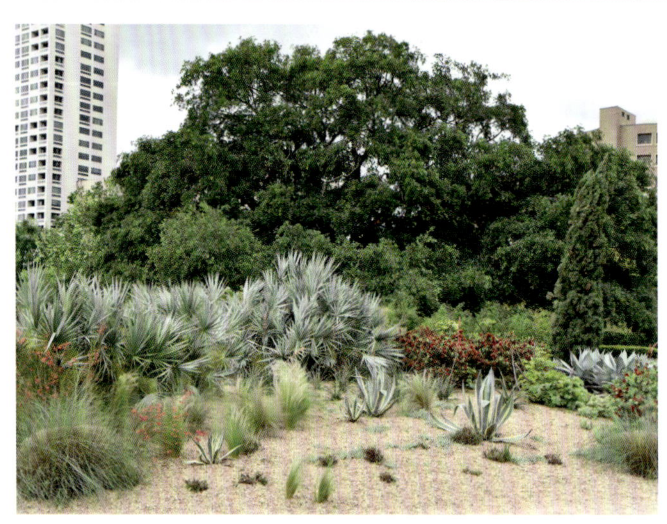

The McGovern Centennial Gardens in Hermann Park feature an Arid Garden.

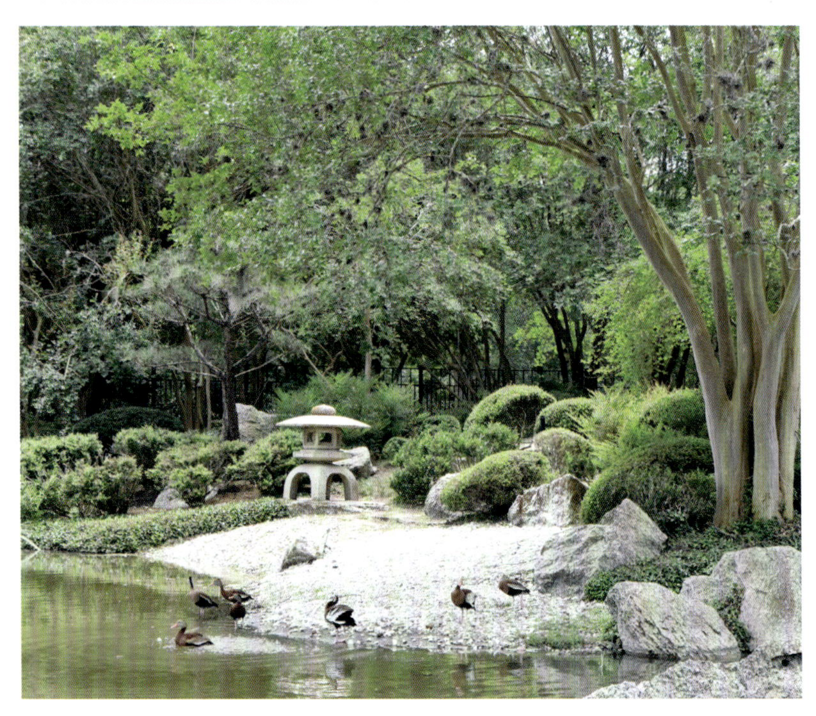

The Japanese Gardens at Hermann Park are a peaceful sight.

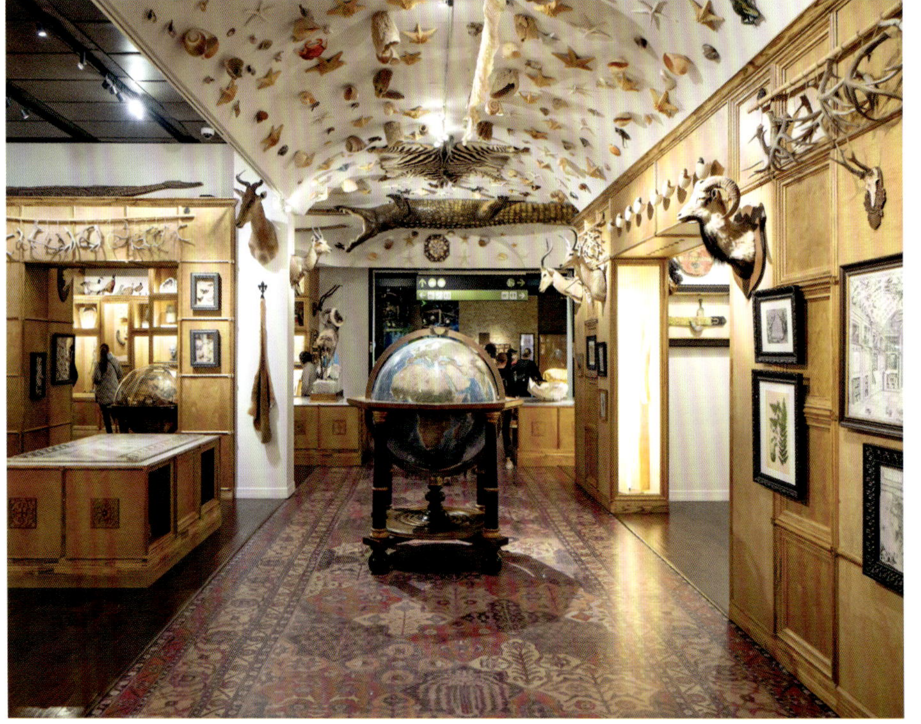

The Houston Museum of Natural Science was established in 1909, and moved to Hermann Park in the 1960s.

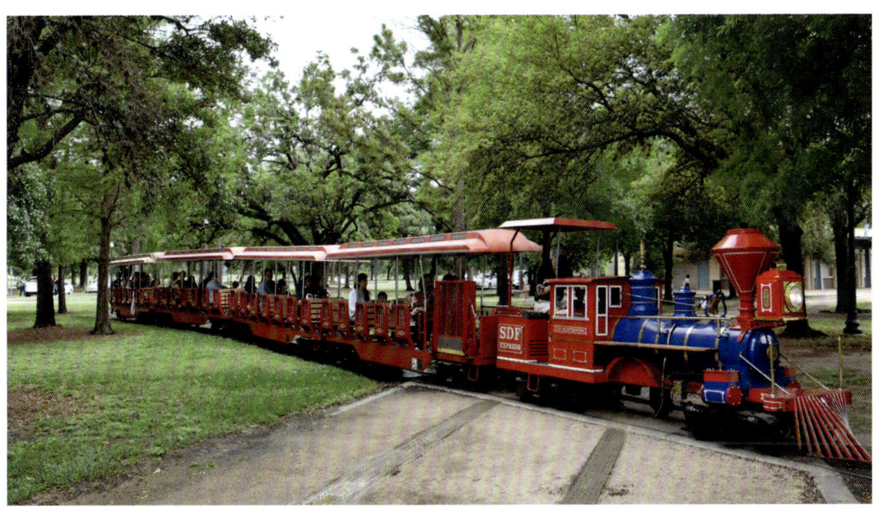

The Hermann Park Railroad runs 2 miles.

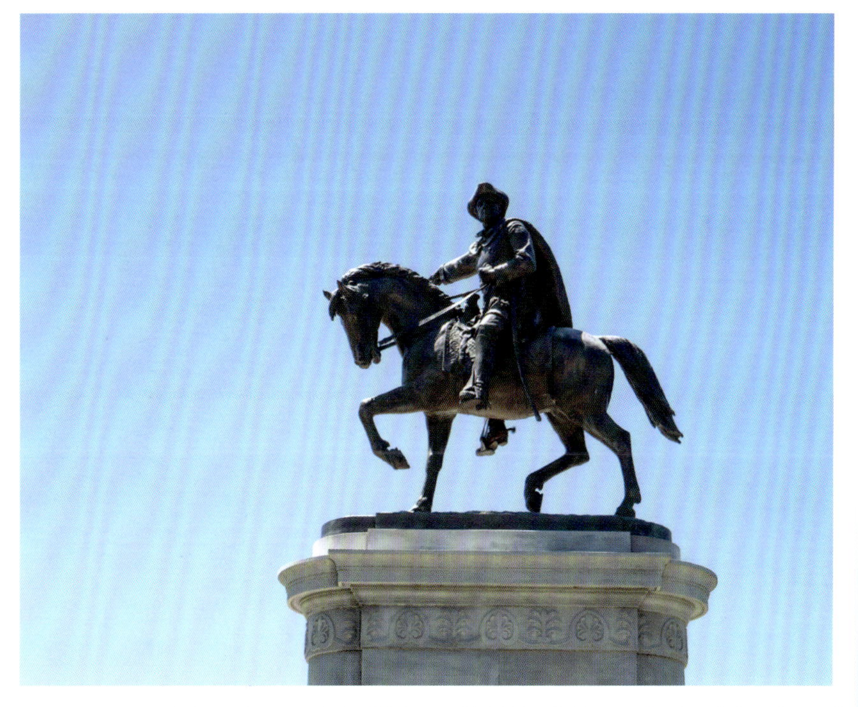

The equestrian statue at Hermann Park honors Sam Houston, the hero of the Texas Revolution and president of the Republic of Texas.

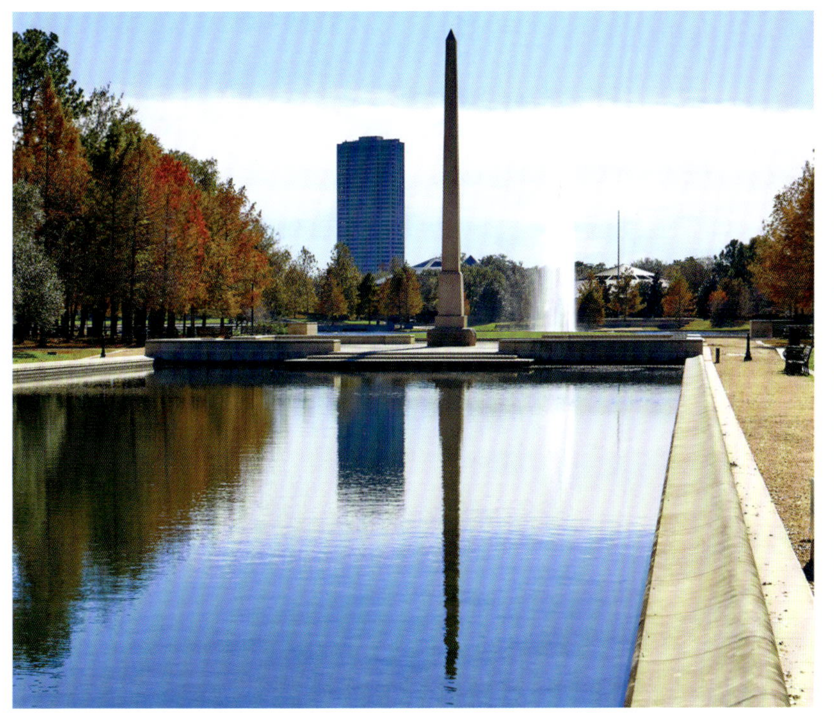

Near a reflecting pool at Hermann Park stands an obelisk from 1936, called *Pioneer Memorial.*

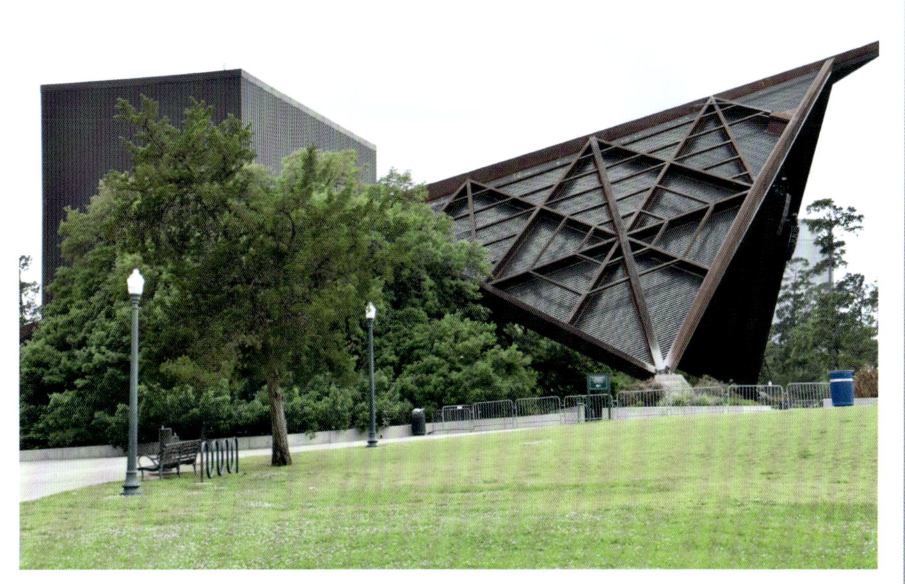

The Miller Outdoor Theatre can seat more than 1,700 people.

Downtown El Paso

Location: El Paso, Texas
Length: 2.1 miles
Start point: Magoffin Home State Historic Site
End point: Pancho Villa Stash House

Get a mix of history, art, and good food with this walk in downtown El Paso. The city has a long, layered history, and its downtown area features a number of historical sites. Start with one of them, the Magoffin Home State Historic Site. An early pioneer family, the Magoffins, build the adobe homestead in 1875, with extensions in the 1880s. From there, stroll west towards San Jacinto Plaza. If you navigate your route through Campbell Street, you'll see Immaculate Conception Church, built in 1893.

San Jacinto Plaza was once the home of a pond of live alligators; though you will not see any real ones today, you may hear references to "Alligator Plaza," and can see a sculpture of them. From the park, take a walk past the historic Plaza Theatre, opened in 1930, on your way to spend some time at the El Paso Museum of Art, the El Paso Museum of History, or both, depending on your interests. The El Paso Museum of Art includes collections of European art, contemporary Southwestern art, and Pre-Columbian art. The El Paso Museum of History focuses on the complex history of the border region.

If you're touring on a Saturday, take a trip to the Downtown Art and Farmers Market between 9 AM and 1 PM to check out artwork and pick up a snack to eat. Otherwise, head directly to the Pancho Villa Stash House, a 1899 home reportedly used by revolutionary Pancho Villa to hide valuables.

Points of Interest

Magoffin Home State Historic Site
Immaculate Conception Church
San Jacinto Plaza
Plaza Theatre
El Paso Museum of Art
El Paso Museum of History
Downtown Art and Farmers Market *(Saturdays)*
Pancho Villa Stash House

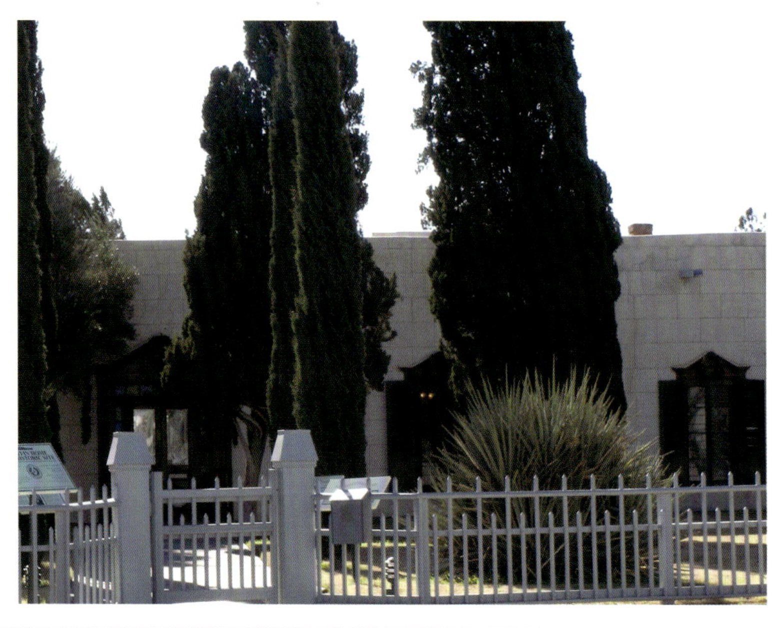

A member of the Magoffin family lived in the Magoffin Homestead until the 1980s. Today the site serves as a house museum.

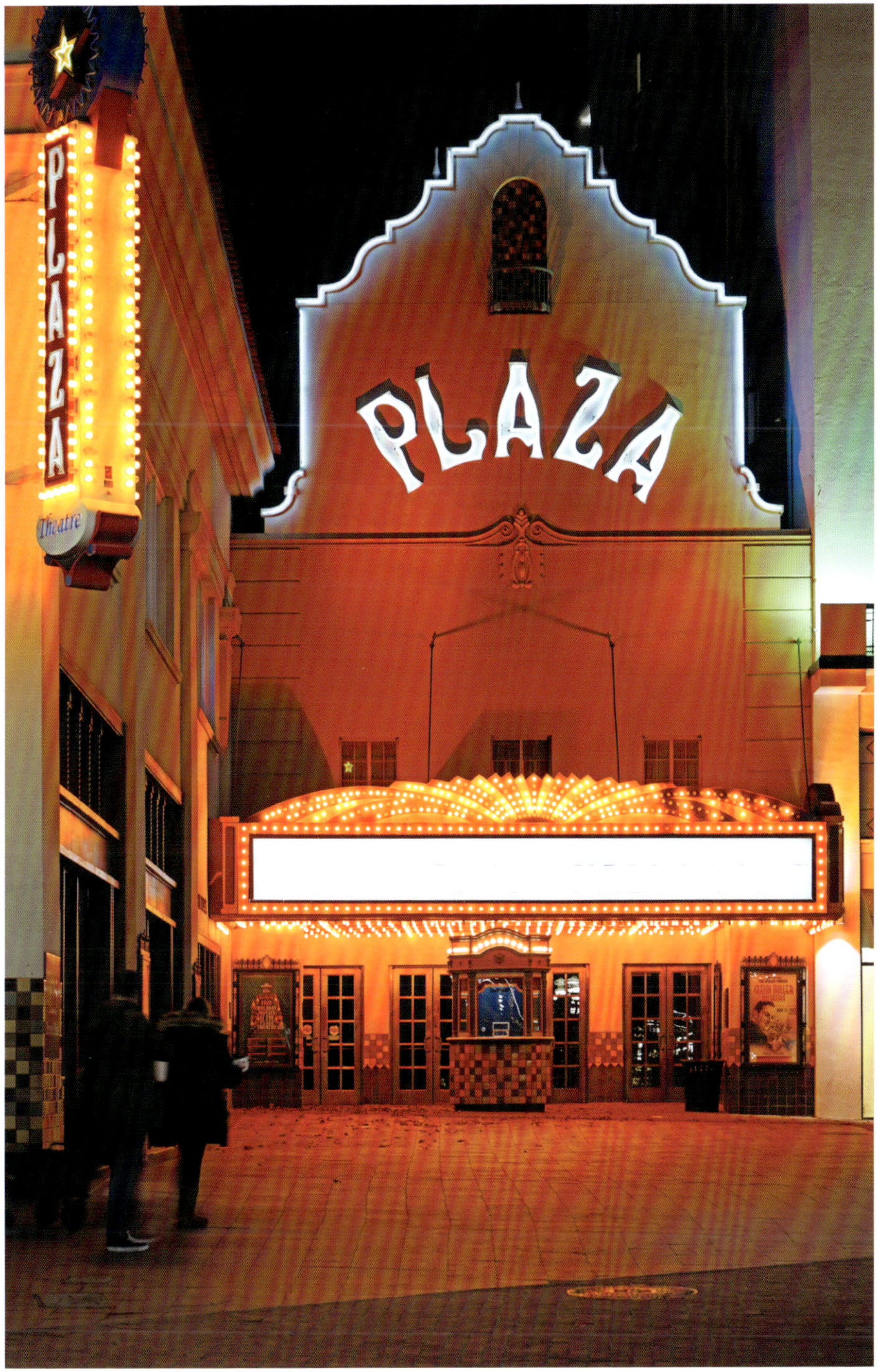

The Plaza Theatre was designed in Spanish Colonial Revival Style by an architect who specialized in movie theaters.

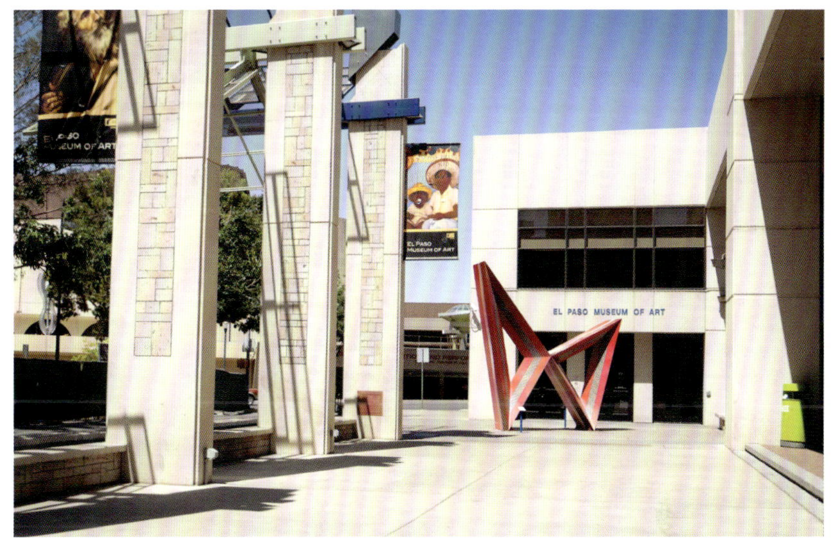

The El Paso Museum of Art offers free admission.

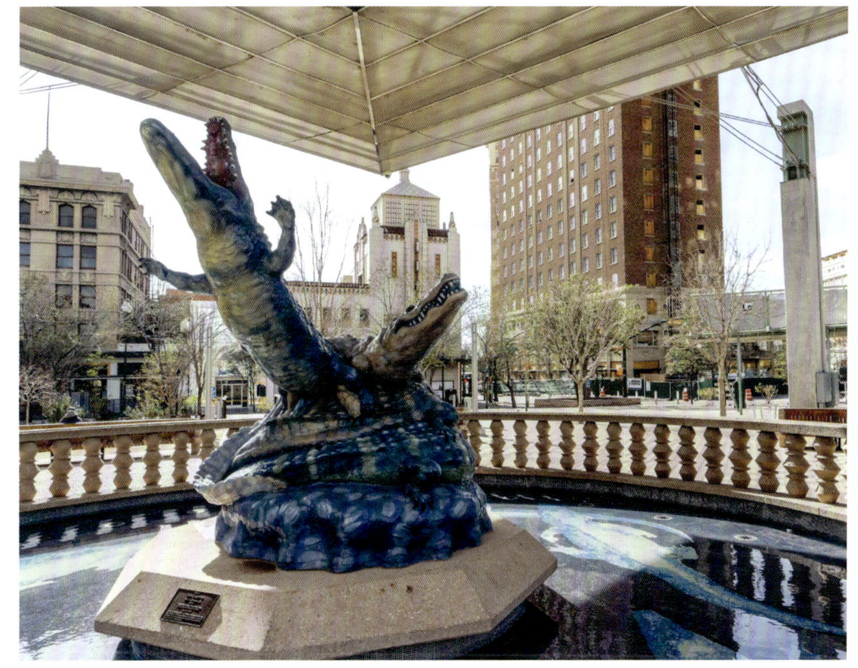

San Jacinto Plaza was once known colloquially as Alligator Plaza.

Ann and Roy Butler Hike and Bike Trail

Location: Austin, Texas
Length: 10-mile loop
Westernmost point: Johnson Creek Greenbelt Trailhead near MoPac Expressway
Easternmost point: Boardwalk Trailhead/South Pleasant Valley Road

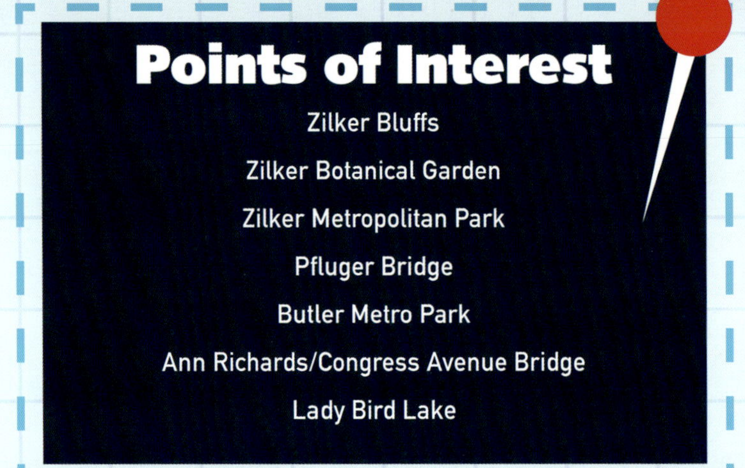

Points of Interest

Zilker Bluffs
Zilker Botanical Garden
Zilker Metropolitan Park
Pfluger Bridge
Butler Metro Park
Ann Richards/Congress Avenue Bridge
Lady Bird Lake

This walk of several hours along a multi-use trail takes you on a loop on the shores of Lady Bird Lake, a reservoir on the Colorado River. In the 1970s, Roy Butler, then mayor of Austin, moved forward some projects to beautify the lake area; former First Lady Lady Bird Johnson was involved in those efforts, and the lake was renamed to honor her after her death.

Along the trail, hikers will see Zilker Park, a 350-acre public park; various beaches and parks; kayaks, canoes, and other boats on the water; overlook points like the Lou Neff Point Gazebo from which the walker can see the downtown area, and more. Parts of the trail can be crowded, so be mindful of other pedestrians and bicyclists to avoid collisions. Restrooms are available at certain points. For those looking for a shorter walk, the Boardwalk on the southeastern portion of the trail provides great views and an attractive walk.

In addition, various cultural attractions are found quite near the trail. On the north side of the waterway, you'll find the Emma S. Barrientos Mexican American Cultural Center (temporarily closed for renovations as of November 2024); the Austin City Hall building; and the Austin Central Library building. On the other shore, you'll find the ZACH Theatre and the Long Center for the Performing Arts.

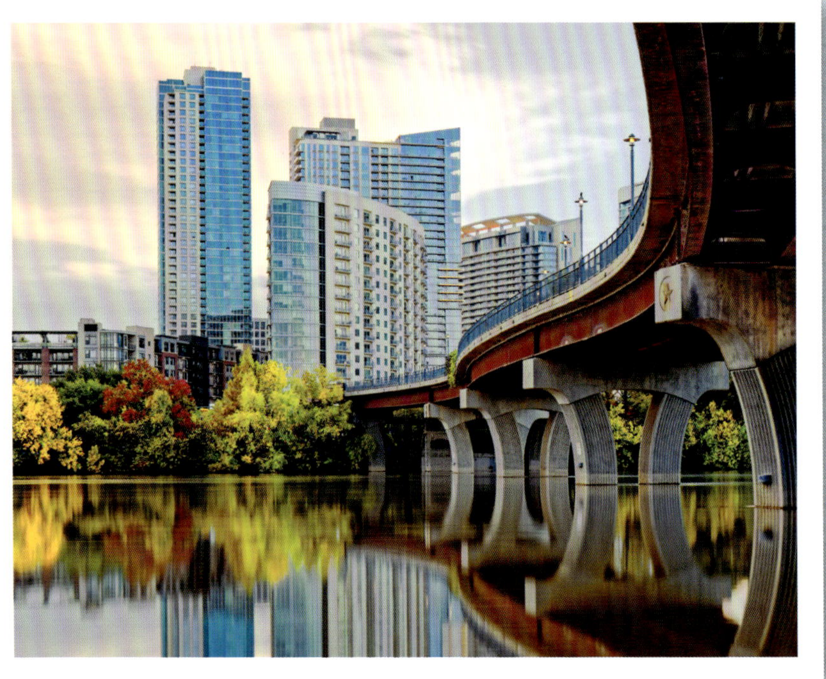

Get a great view of the downtown Austin skyline from the trail.

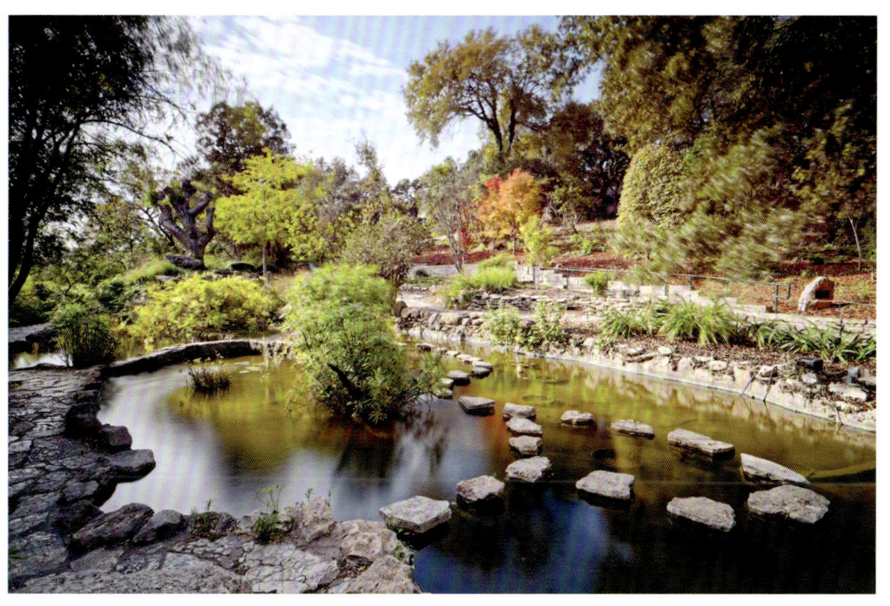

Zilker Park includes the Zilker Botanical Garden *(above),* as well as a theater, a nature and science center, and the Umlauf Sculpture Garden & Museum.

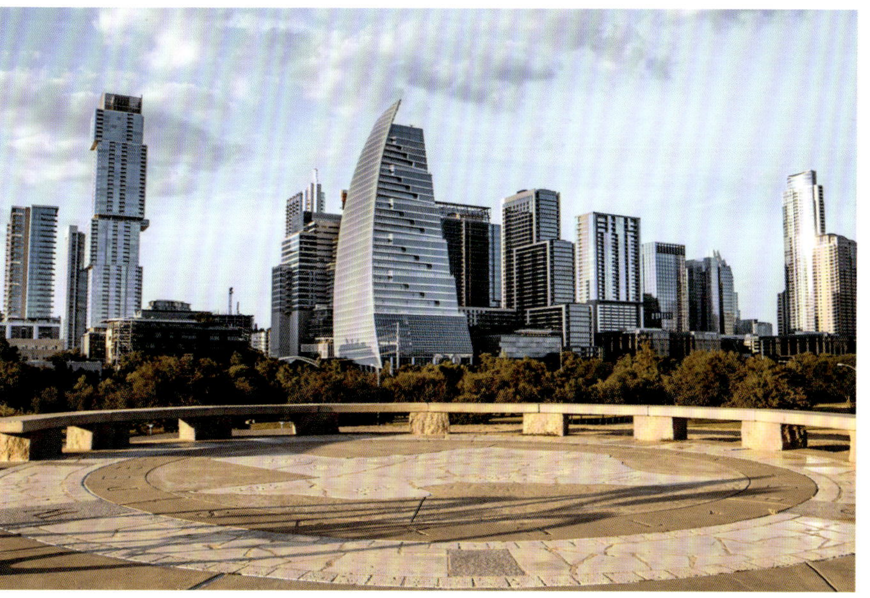

Butler Metro Park features a splash pad, a children's garden, and a summit point with great views. That eye-catching curved office building, Block 185, is a recent addition to the Austin skyline that broke ground in 2019.

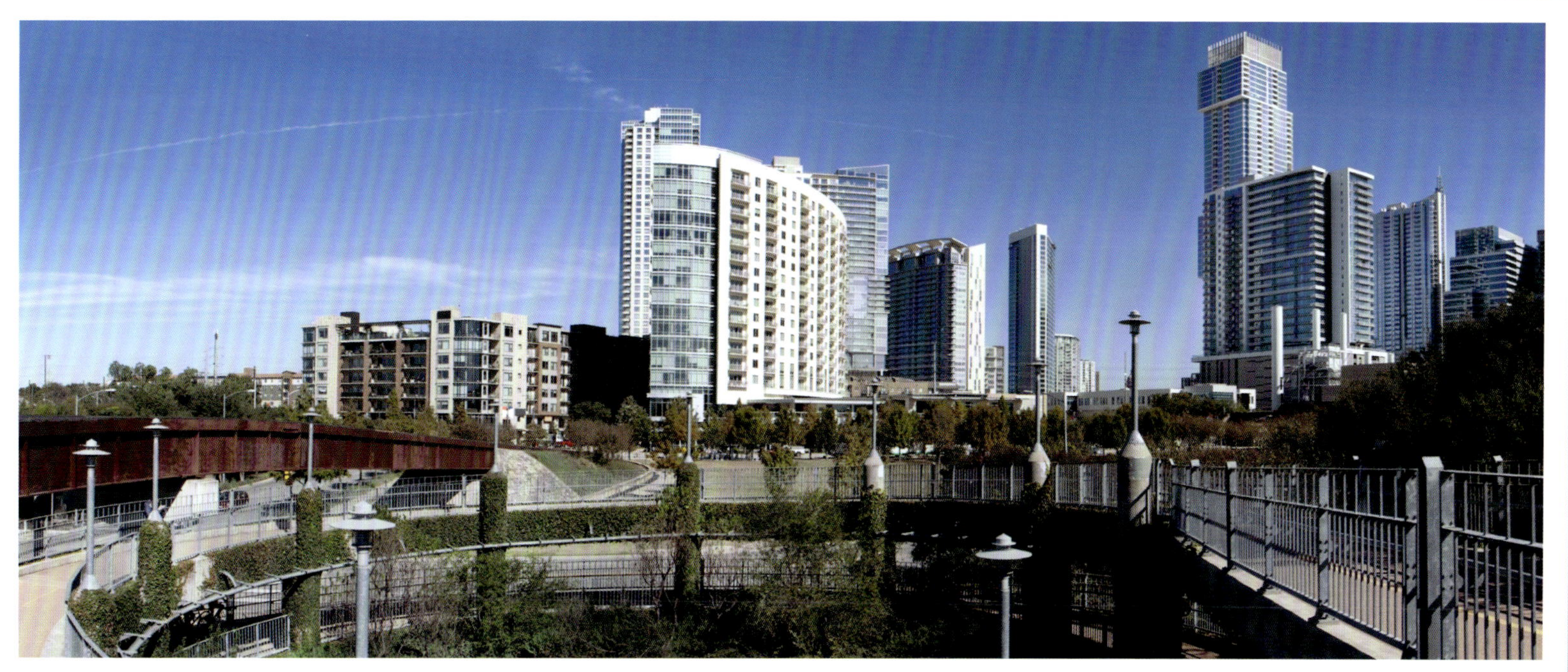

The James D. Pfluger Pedestrian and Bicycle Bridge allows walkers to get from one shore of Lady Bird Lake to the opposite side.

Chicago Riverwalk

Location: Chicago, Illinois
Length: 1.25 miles
Start point: Lake Street
End point: Lake Michigan

The Chicago River flows through the city to connect to the shores of Lake Michigan. The 1.25-mile Chicago Riverwalk was a multi-stage project that provides a landscaped pedestrian pathway along the south edge of the river. At intervals, the walker will see plazas, sculptures, memorials, floating wetland gardens, and some historic buildings. Restrooms are located along the way, too.

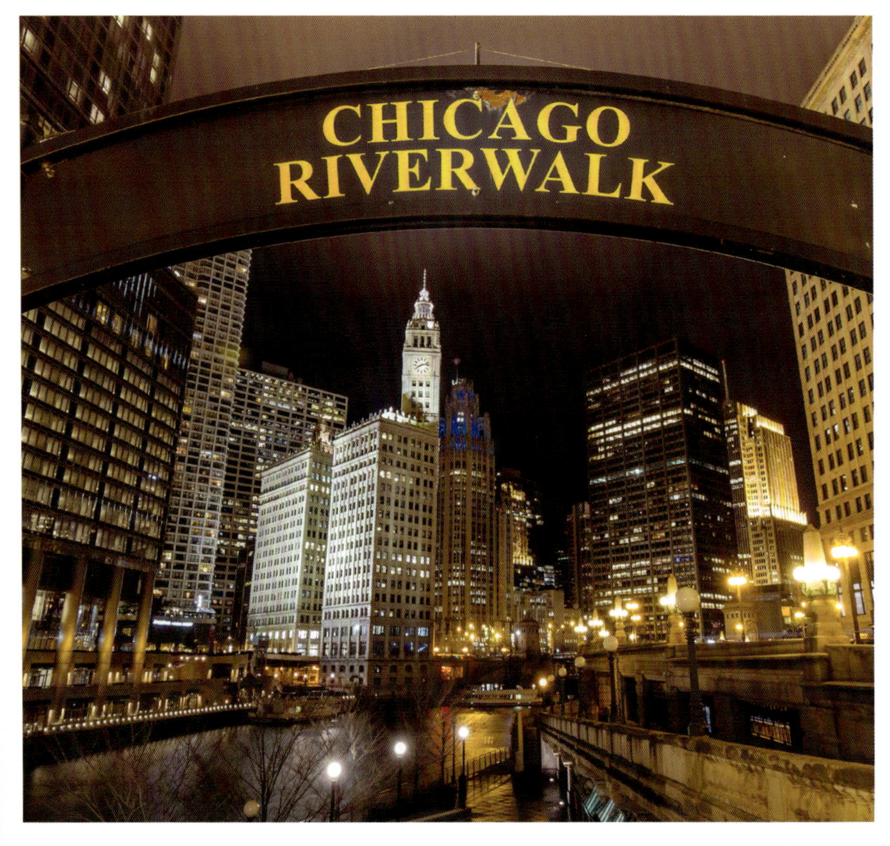

The Riverwalk is open between 6 AM and 11 PM.

Start the walk at its west end, on Lake Street, at the confluence of several branches of the Chicago River, and start walking east to the lake. If you look across the river at N. Orleans Street, you'll see the Merchandise Mart, a historic building created by Marshall Field & Co, with construction beginning in 1928. Between Franklin Street and Wells Street, keep an eye out for the Jetty, a set of floating gardens. At La Salle Street, see the SS *Eastland* Disaster Memorial that commemorates the 1915 event when a passenger ship on the Chicago River sank, killing hundreds. Nearby, the set of terraced streets where you may spot people resting or eating is called the River Theater.

Once you've crossed State Street, you'll see two more memorials: the Vietnam Veterans Memorial and the Heald Square Monument that honors George Washington along with two other Founding Fathers who financially supported the Revolutionary War.

DuSable Bridge, the bridge located at Michigan Street, is a Chicago Landmark that opened in 1920. The McCormick Bridgehouse & Chicago River Museum, open during the summer months, tells the story of the Chicago bridges and lets visitors see inside the place where the bridge tenders operated. At Michigan Street, look across the river for two iconic Chicago buildings: the Wrigley Building and Tribune Tower, both notable for their architecture.

Once you've passed Columbus Avenue, the next memorial is the U.S. Navy Submarine Memorial, before you approach the end of the Riverwalk. The Riverwalk Gateway, an underpass beneath DuSable Lakeshore Drive, is lined with murals by Ellen Lanyon that focus on the history of the river.

Points of Interest

Chicago River

Shops and restaurants

Public artwork and gardens

SS *Eastland* Disaster Memorial

Vietnam Veterans Memorial

Heald Square Monument

McCormick Bridgehouse & Chicago River Museum

Wrigley Building

DuSable Bridge

Tribune Tower

U.S. Navy Submarine Memorial

Lake Michigan

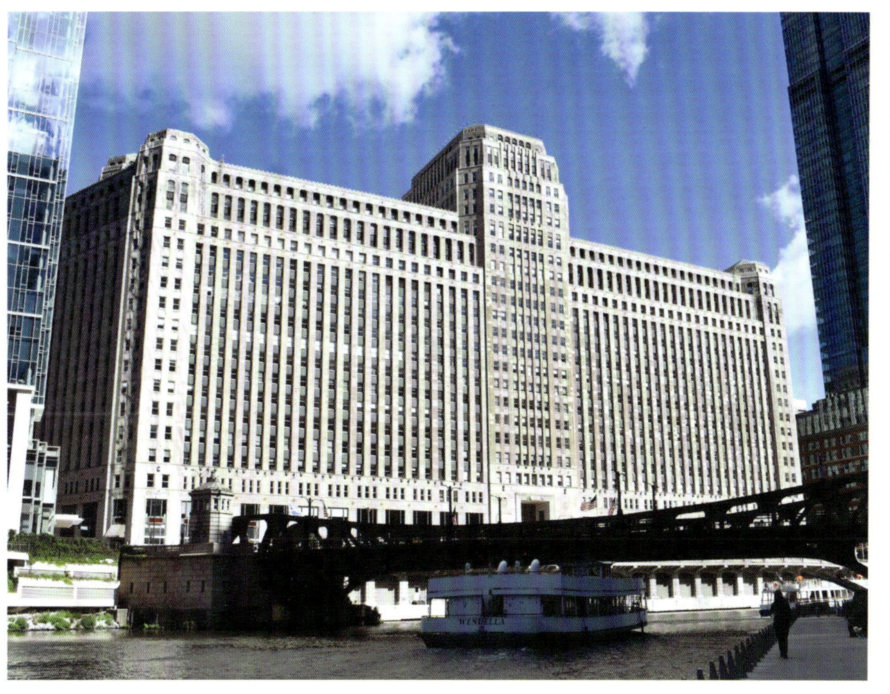

The Merchandise Mart, a massive building in Art Deco style, opened in 1930.

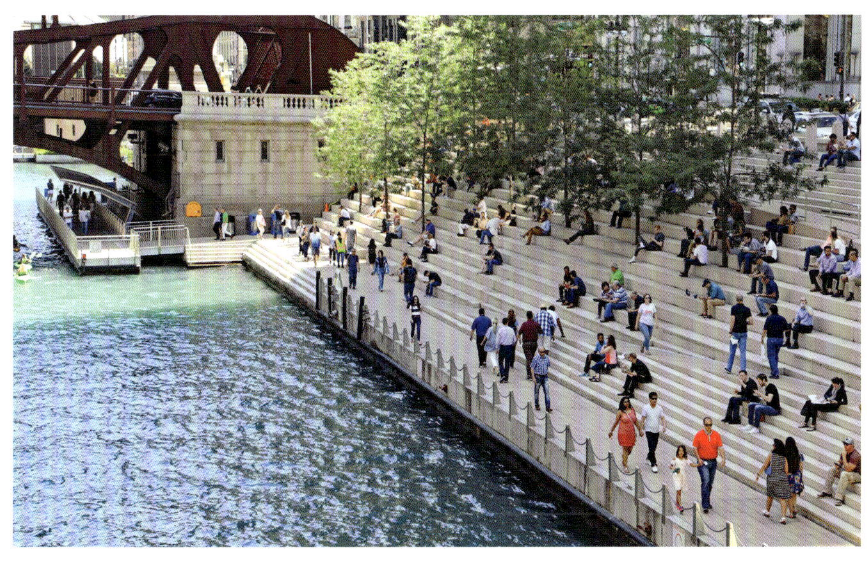

Chicago's Riverwalk is a popular route, so expect to see plenty of people and boat tours.

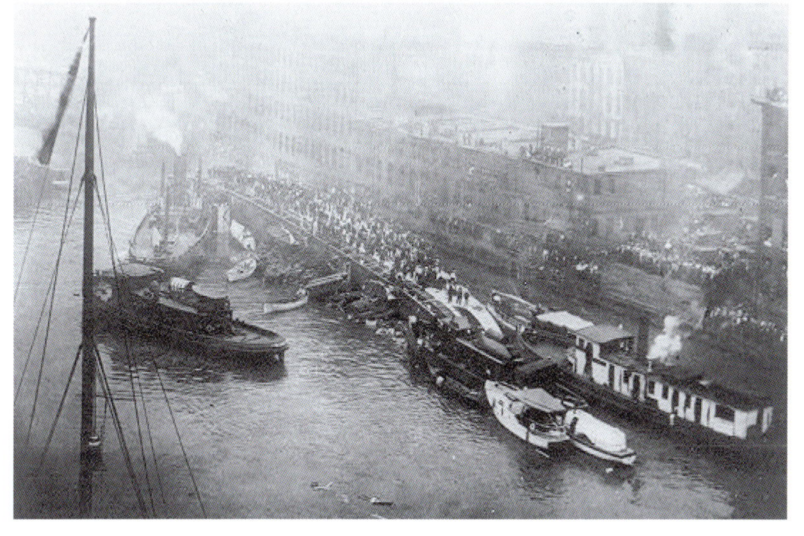

It's a disaster that haunts Chicago history: the 1915 overturning of the SS *Eastland* while it was on the Chicago River. More than 800 people died.

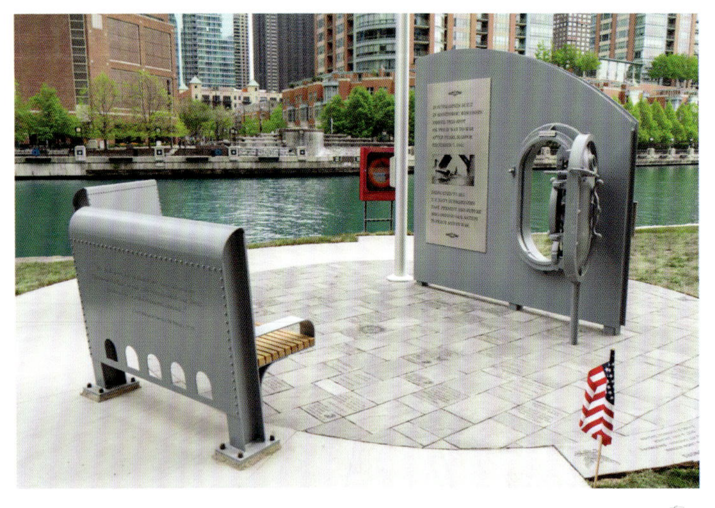

In 2019, a new monument joined the Riverwalk, dedicated to World War II submariners.

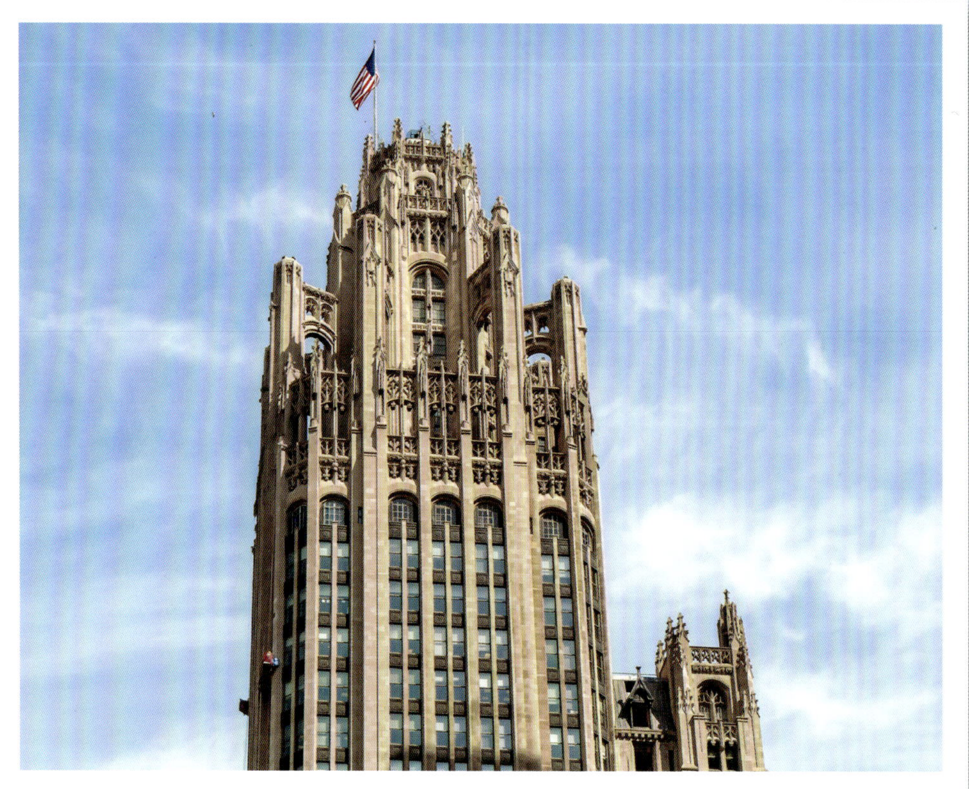

The Tribune Tower was built in neo-gothic style between 1923 and 1925.

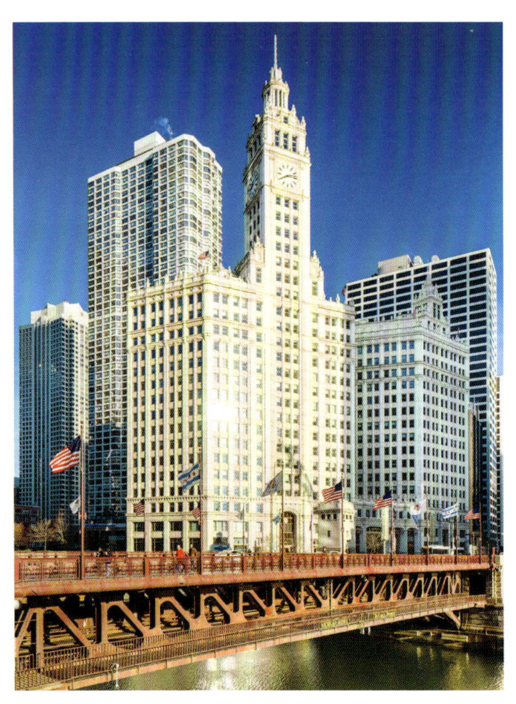

Seen past DuSable Bridge is the Wrigley Building, built between 1920 and 1921. For many years, the building was the headquarters of the chewing gum company owned by the wealthy Wrigley family.

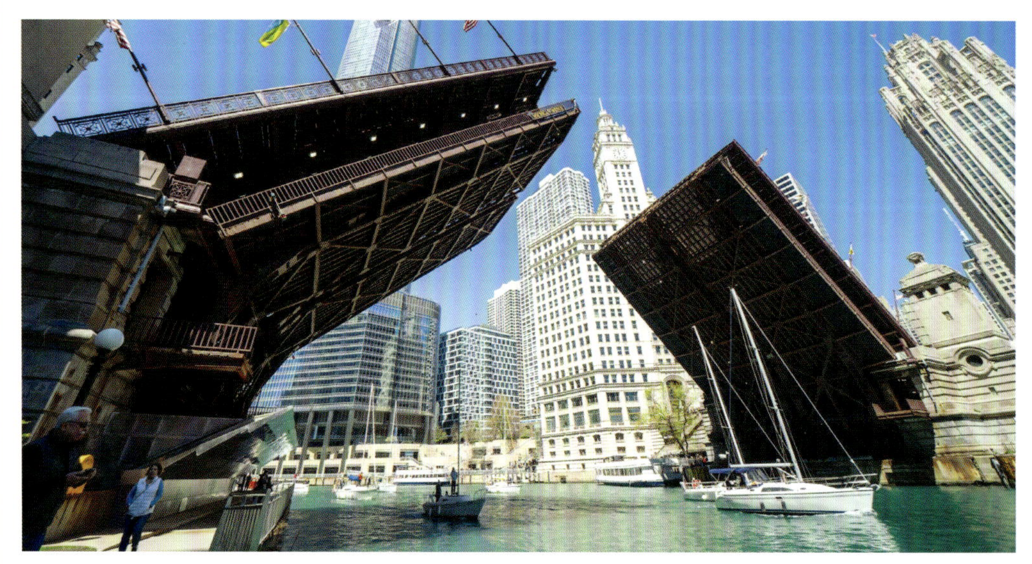

DuSable Bridge has two levels, one for pedestrians and one for cars.

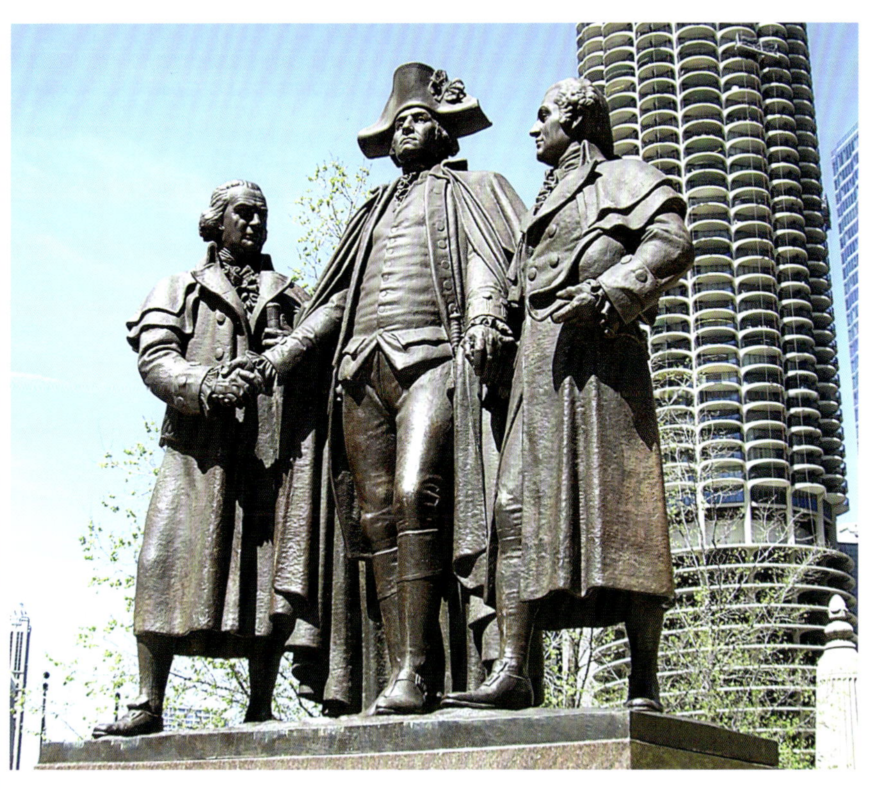

The Heald Square Monument that honors General Washington, crafted during the 1930s, was the work of sculptor Lorado Taft.

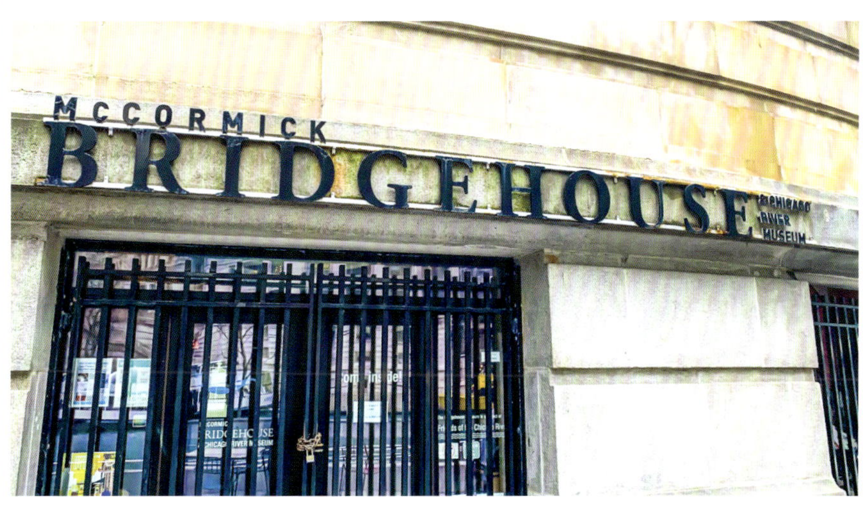

If walkers visit the McCormick Bridgehouse at the right time, they might get an unusual viewpoint of the DuSable Bridge being raised and lowered.

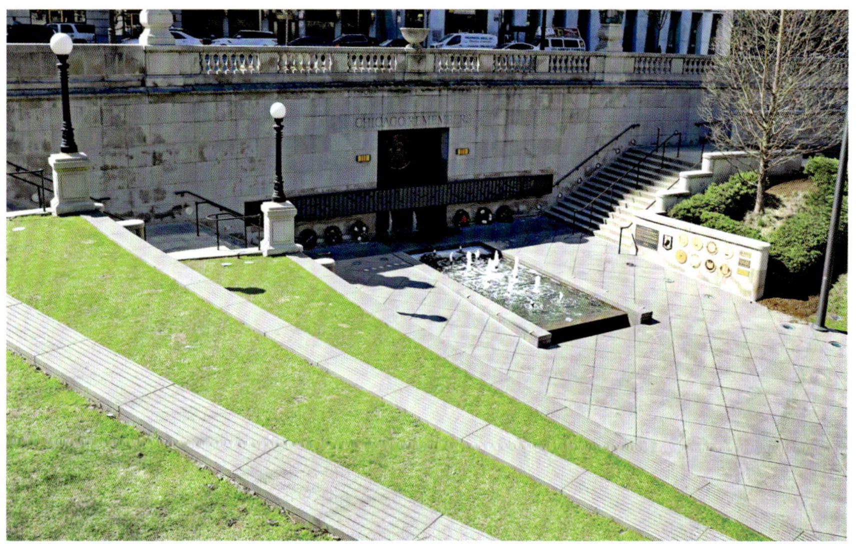

The Vietnam Veterans Memorial

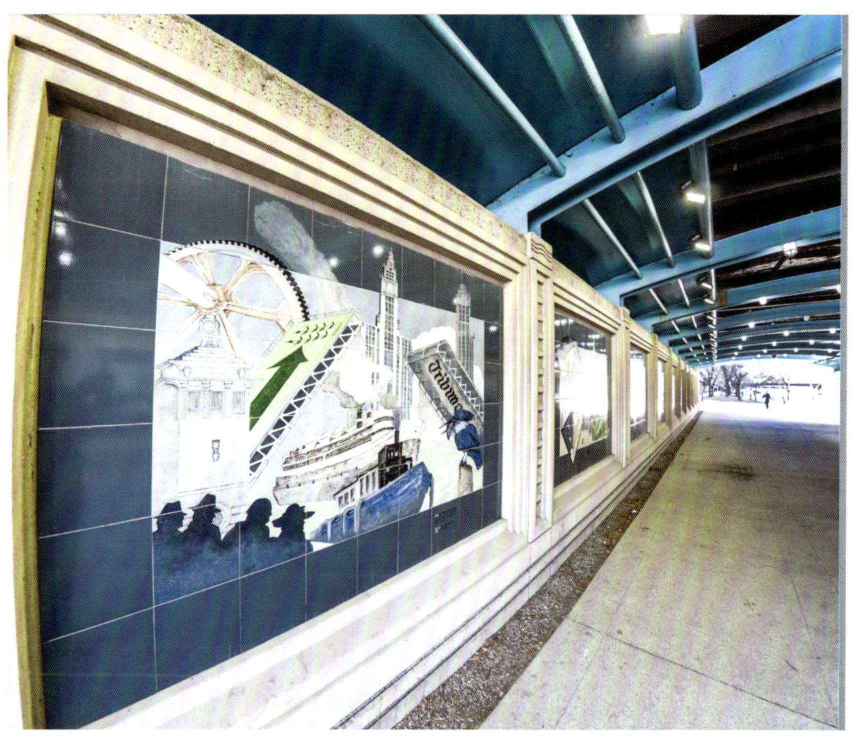

Ellen Lanyon's Riverwalk Gateway murals can be seen at the east end of the Riverwalk.

Lincoln Park

Location: Chicago, Illinois
Length: Variable. Lincoln Park runs 7 miles. This walk highlights a section of about 2 miles between North Avenue and Diversey Parkway.
Start point: North Avenue and Clark Street
End point: Diversey Parkway

In Chicago, Lincoln Park can refer to both a neighborhood and Lincoln Park itself, a huge urban park of more than 1,200 acres adjacent to Lake Michigan. For dedicated hiking or biking with a great view of Lake Michigan, you might hike the Lincoln Park section of the larger Chicago Lakefront Trail that extends 18.5 miles along the shoreline and passes through Lincoln Park, Grant Park, Burnham Park, and Jackson Park.

This walk passes through a shorter stretch of Lincoln Park that's packed with sculptures, a couple of museums, and Lincoln Park Zoo. The straight-line distance is about two miles but expect to walk more as you go through the zoo and wander the park paths.

Start with the Chicago History Museum on Clark Street for a quick tour through local history and a chance to see an "L" car from 1893. If you want to see Lake Michigan up close, head east once you've left the museum and hike out to the North Avenue Beach Pier, crossing DuSable Lakeshore Drive. Back on the west side of DuSable Lakeshore Drive, heading north, keep an eye out for monuments to Benjamin Franklin, Giuseppe Garibaldi, and Ulysses S. Grant. As you approach the South Pond, you'll also start to see the structures of the Lincoln Park Zoo, along with the charming Carlson Cottage.

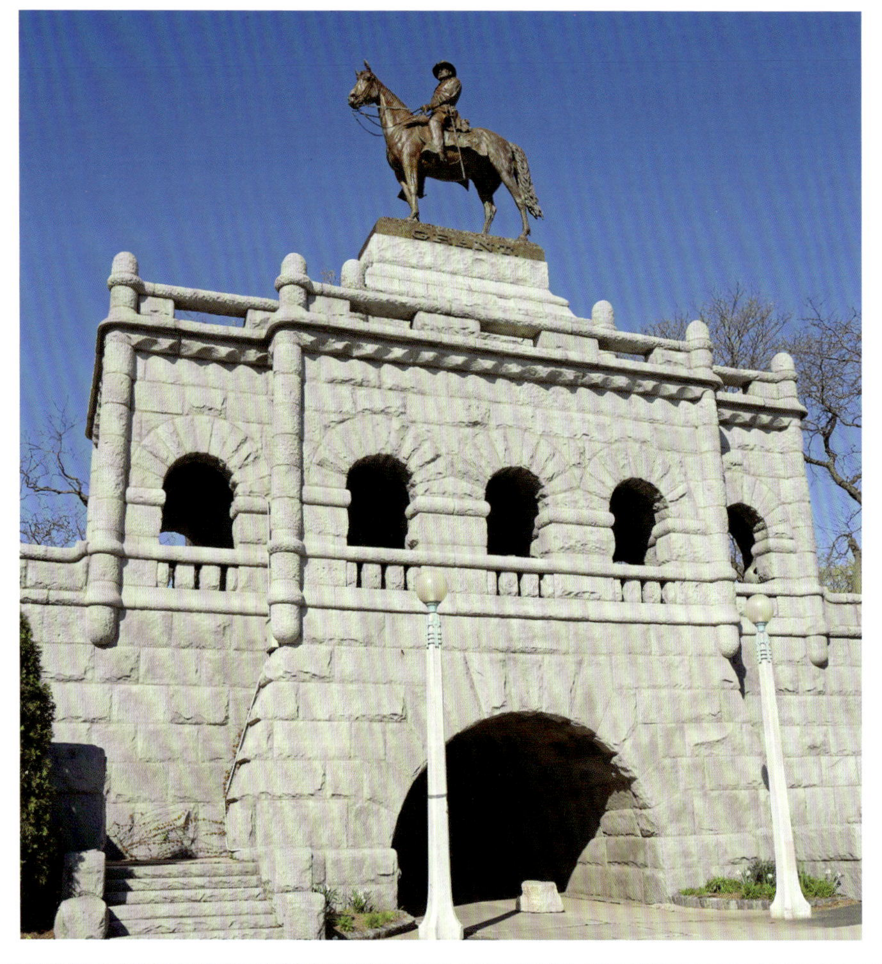

The Ulysses S. Grant Monument was created between 1885 and 1891.

Heading further north towards Fullerton Avenue, you'll find the Lincoln Park Conservatory and the beautifully landscaped Alfred Caldwell Lily Pool. Past Fullerton, the Peggy Notebaert Nature Museum is a kid-friendly museum that includes a butterfly house.

Points of Interest

- Chicago History Museum
- North Avenue Beach Pier
- Lincoln Monument and Gardens
- Ulysses S. Grant Monument
- Lincoln Park Cultural Center
- Lincoln Park Zoo
- Lincoln Park Conservatory
- Alfred Caldwell Lily Pool
- Peggy Notebaert Nature Museum
- North Pond Nature Sanctuary

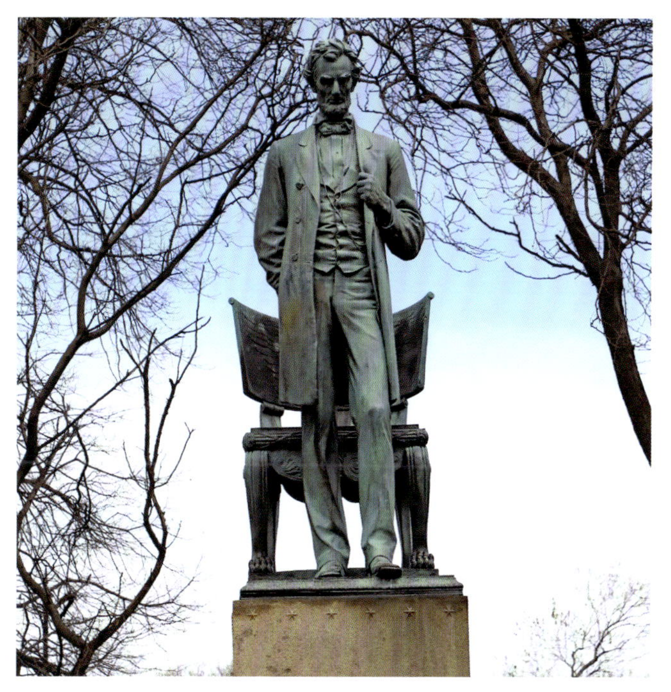

A statue of Abraham Lincoln looks out over the park, not far from the Chicago History Museum. Sculptor Augustus Saint-Gaudens created both this sculpture, *Abraham Lincoln: the Man*, and a seated sculpture of Lincoln called *Abraham Lincoln: the Head of State,* that is found in Chicago's Grant Park.

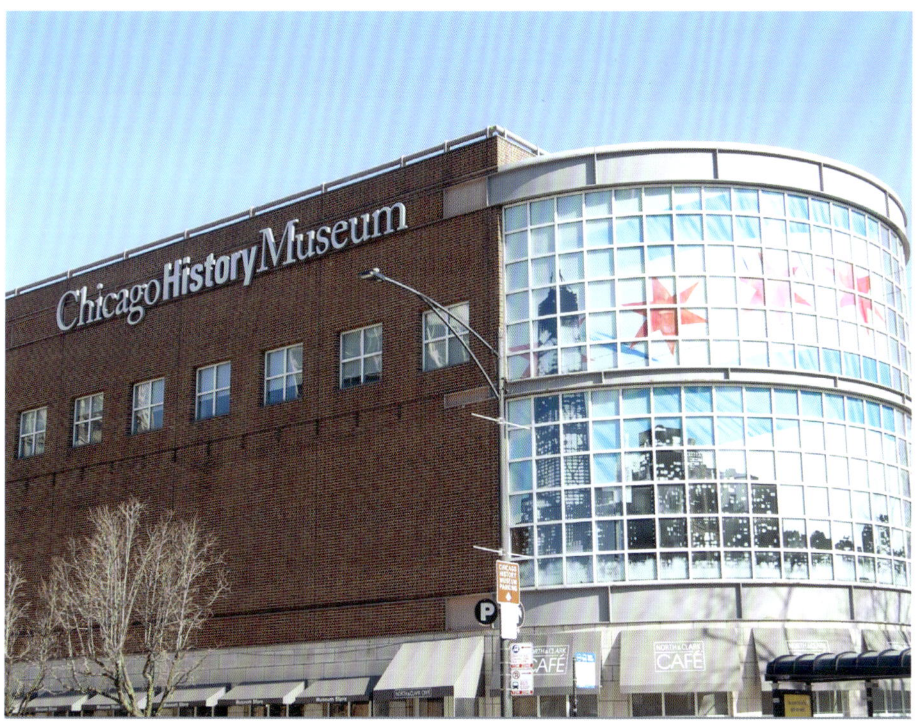

The Chicago Historical Society moved to its current location in 1932, into a Works Progress Administration building.

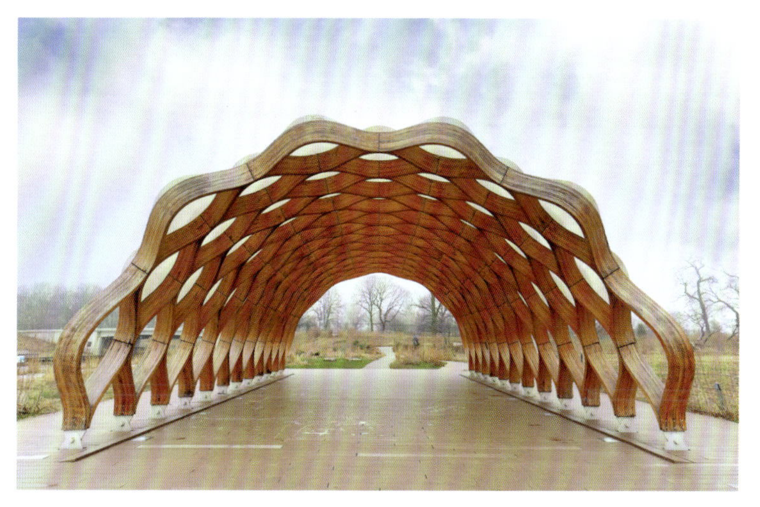

Not far from the monument to Grant, walk through the *Honeycomb* sculpture in the Lincoln Park Zoo.

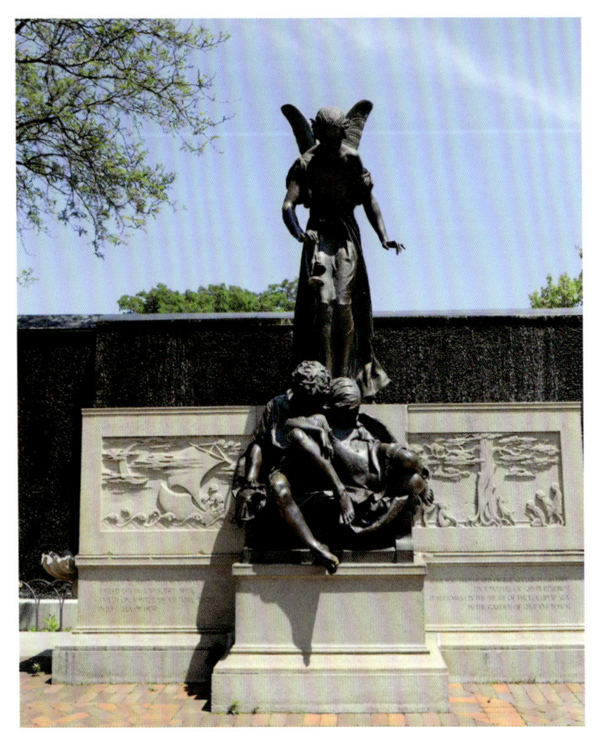

The sculpture *Dream Lady* is also known as the *Eugene Field Memorial*, named after the poet Eugene Field who wrote the bedtime poem "Wynken, Blinken, and Nod."

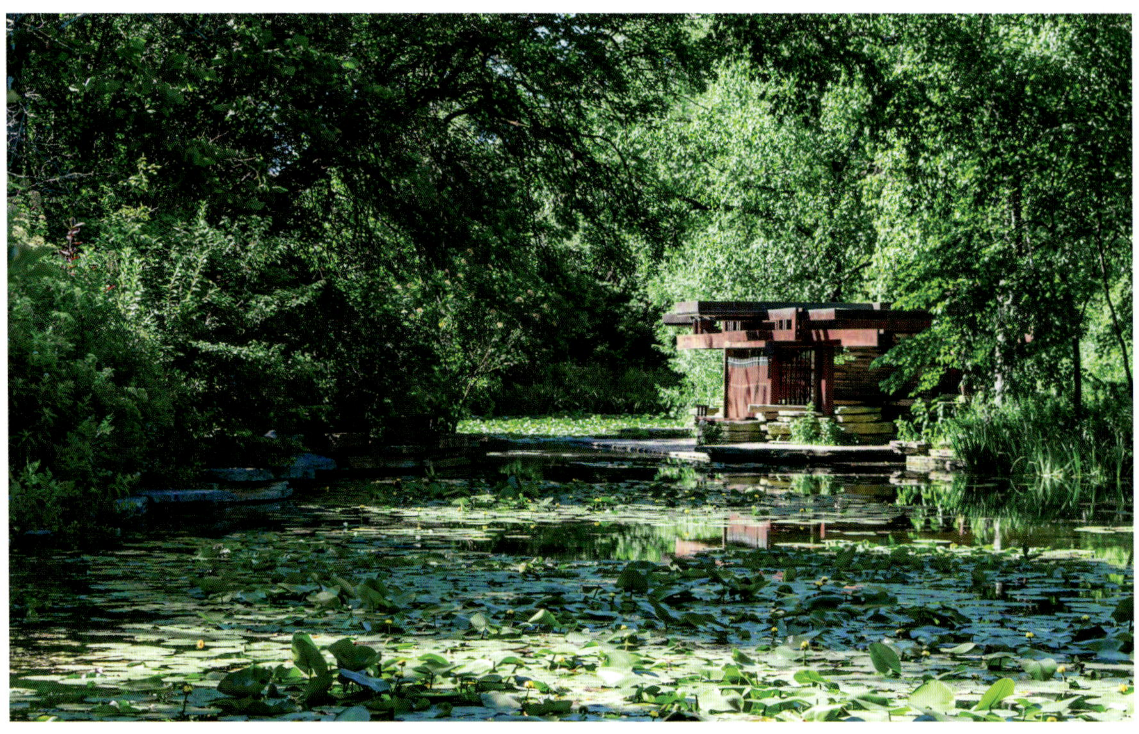

The Alfred Caldwell Lily Pool is named after the landscape architect who created it. Caldwell's mentor, Jens Jensen, is known for another Chicago treasure, the Garfield Park Conservatory.

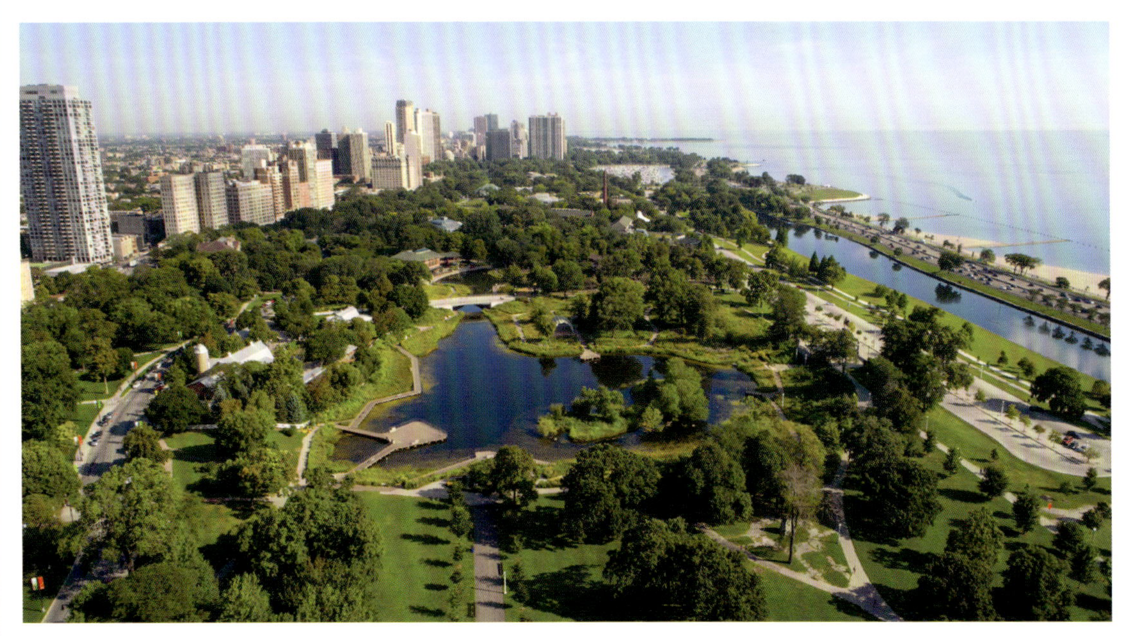

Lincoln Park sees about 20 million visitors each year.

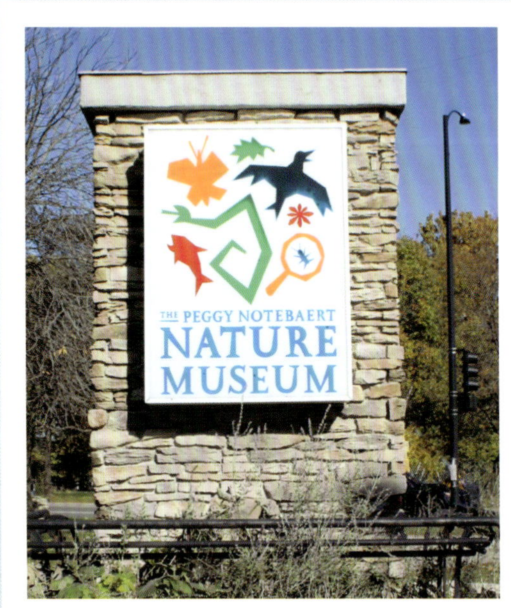

The Chicago Academy of Sciences created the Peggy Notebaert Nature Museum.

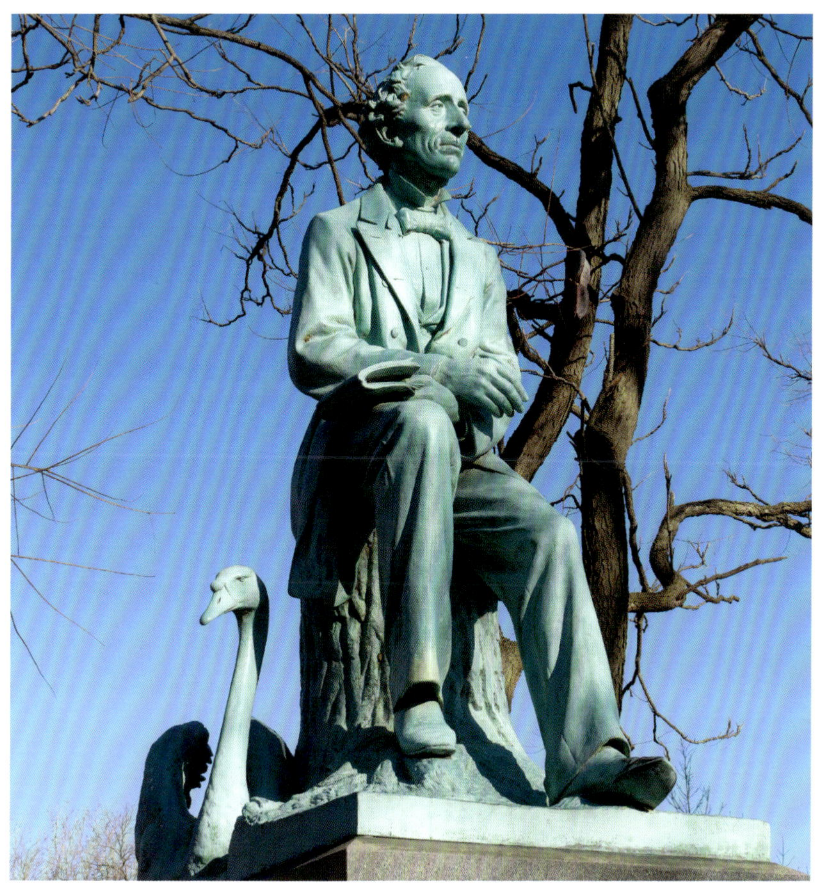

As you move through the Zoo, keep an eye out for the 1896 Hans Christian Andersen Monument near Stockton Drive.

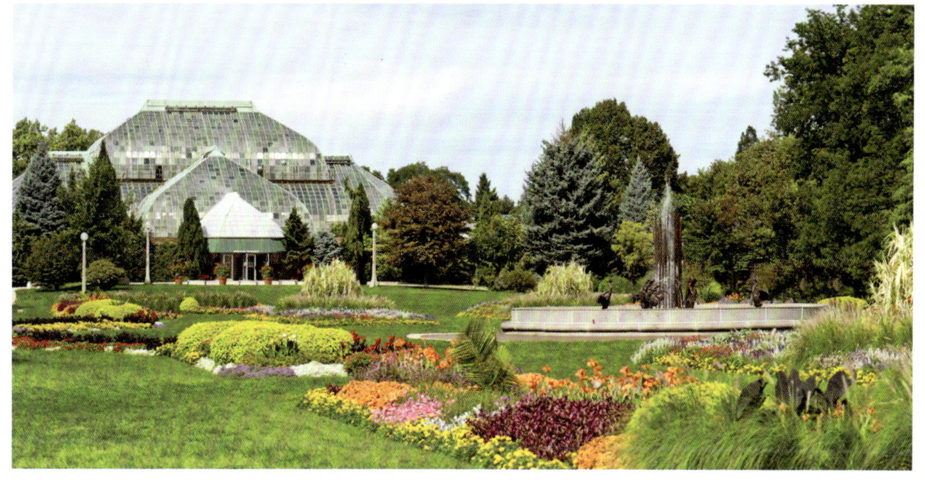

While both the Lincoln Park Zoo and Lincoln Park Conservatory are free, the Lincoln Park Conservatory currently requires timed reservations.

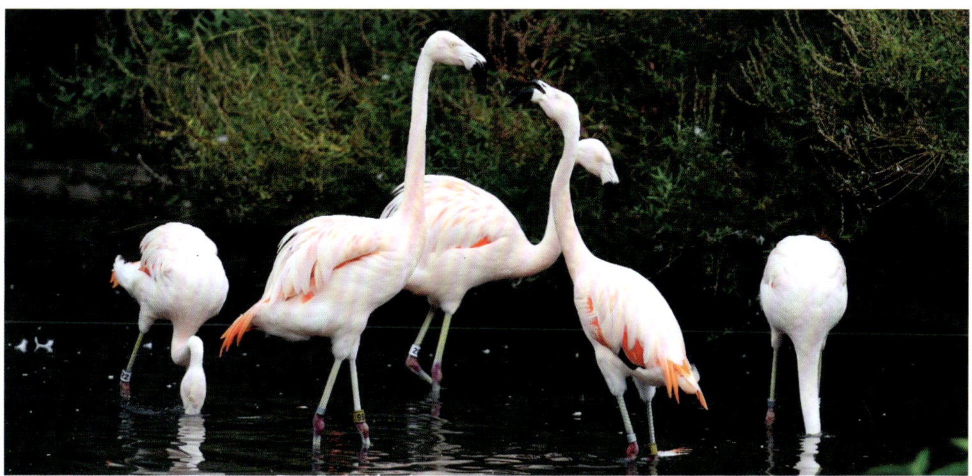

The Chilean Flamingo Pond at the Lincoln Park Zoo

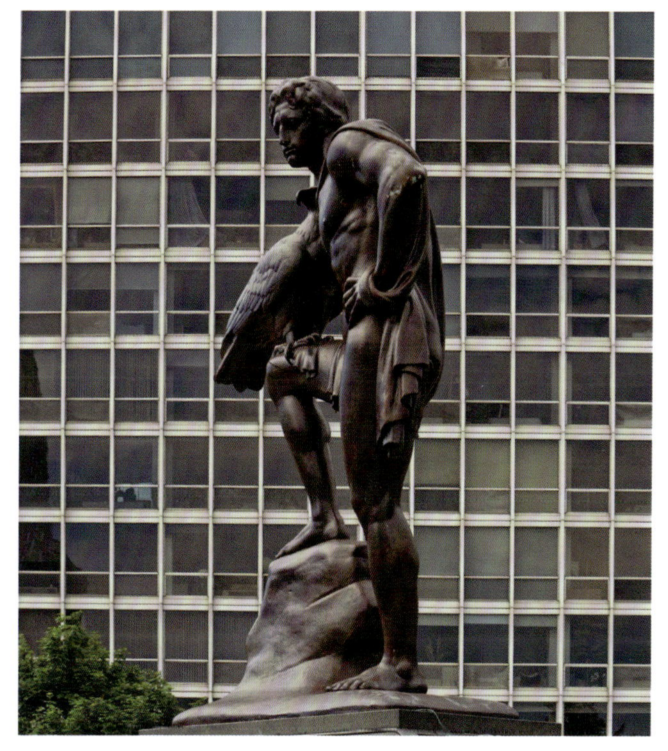

If you see the statue of Johann Wolfgang von Goethe, you're almost at Diversey Parkway! Wrap up your walk, or continue north to see sports fields, a dog park, the AIDS Garden Chicago, an archery range, and a bird sanctuary.

White River State Park and Canal Walk

Location: Indianapolis, Indiana
Length: 3-mile loop
Start point: White River State Park
Northernmost point: 11th Street

Points of Interest

White River State Park
Indiana State Museum
Eiteljorg Museum of American Indians and Western Art
Indianapolis Zoo
NCAA Hall of Champions
Military Park
White River Gardens
Indiana Historical Society
USS *Indianapolis* CA 35 Memorial

The Indiana Central Canal was originally conceived as a larger, more ambitious project so people could ship goods from state to state. Work began in 1836, but stopped in 1839 due to lack of money. Today, walkers, bikers, and pedal boat operators can all appreciate Indianapolis's Canal Walk for a pretty walk with great views in downtown Indianapolis.

Start your day in White River State Park, a 267-acre urban park that's home to many of the attractions listed in the Points of Interest box and where one end of the canal walk is found. For those who love art, the Eiteljorg Museum features collections of artwork made by indigenous North Americans, as well as Western-themed art. History buffs can visit the Indiana State Museum for exhibits on the area's history going back to prehistoric times. Sports fans might appreciate the NCAA Hall of Champions. Military Park and the adjacent Medal of Honor Memorial honor veterans and their sacrifices.

As walkers stroll along the Canal Walk after leaving White River State Park, they might want to stop at the Indiana Historical Society, an interactive museum found on the west bank near Ohio Street. Also on the west side of the river, within a quarter mile of the canal, walkers might check out two sites found on Indiana Street: the Kurt Vonnegut Museum and Library that honors the writer, and the Madam Walker Legacy Center, a historic landmark building from 1927 that was world headquarters for the company owned by the African American entrepreneur Madam C. J. Walker. At the east side of the Canal Walk, near Walnut Street, the USS *Indianapolis* CA 35 Memorial honors the crew who perished in 1945 when the USS *Indianapolis* sank; the veterans who survived pushed for the memorial.

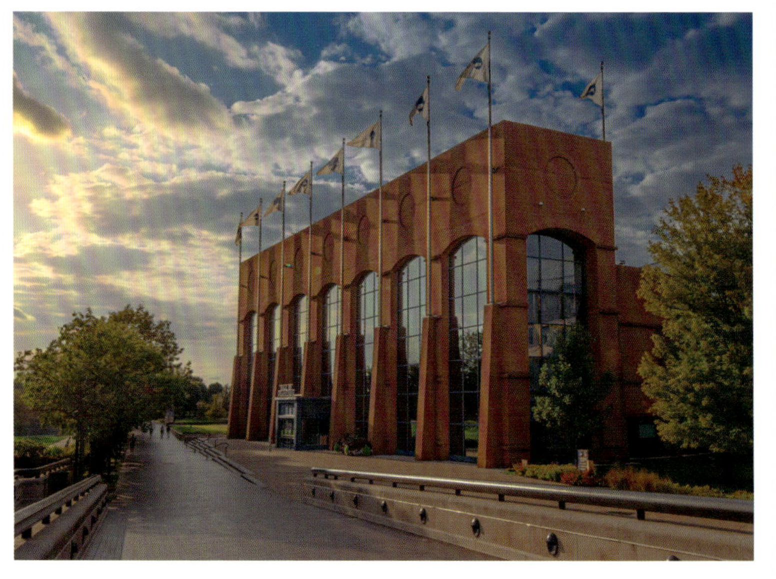

The NCAA Hall of Champions in White River State Park

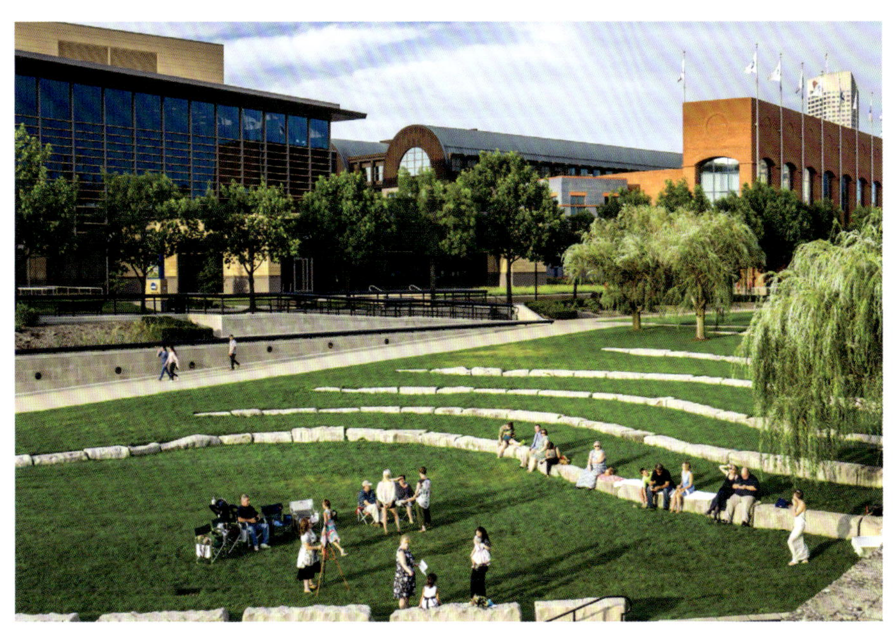

White River State Park offers a number of cultural and recreational options.

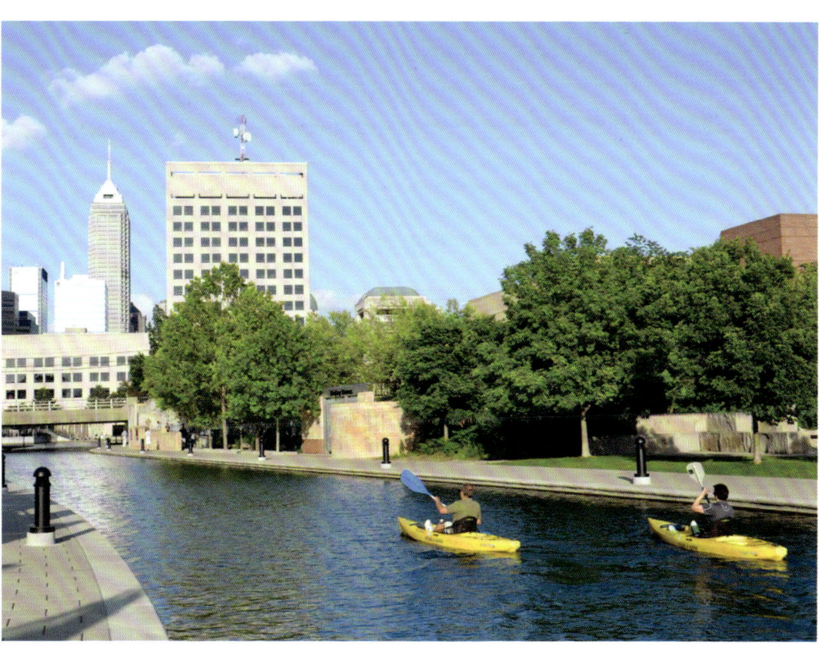

Expect to see walkers, joggers, and boaters along the Canal Walk.

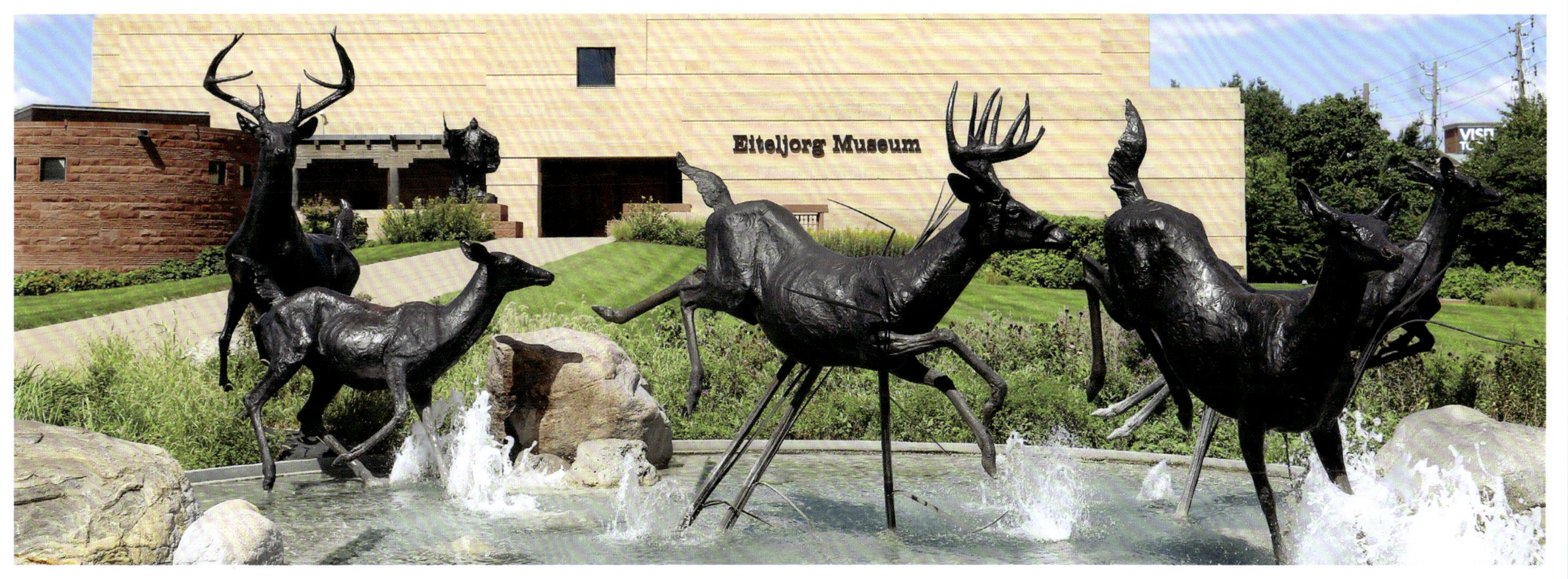

The Eiteljorg Museum includes artwork by Georgia O'Keeffe, Frederic Remington, and other artists associated with the American West, as well as Native American artwork.

Woodward Avenue

Location: Detroit, Michigan
Length: 1 mile (Woodward only); ~1.6 with nearby sites
Start point: The Majestic Theatre
End point: Variable

Woodward Avenue, dubbed "Detroit's Main Street," runs north through the city. This mile-long stretch takes you through the Cultural Center Historic District, where you can see fascinating architecture and visit a number of museums.

Start at the historic Majestic Theatre at 4140 Woodward Avenue, built in 1915, for a glimpse into Detroit's architectural history. As you stroll north, keep an eye out for the Whitney building at 4421. The 1894 mansion, once home to a lumber baron, now operates as a restaurant. Moving from historic to modern, continue down the street to the site of a former auto dealership that's now the home to the Museum of Contemporary Art Detroit. For more art, check out the Detroit Artists Market at 4719 Woodward, a gallery that's been running since 1930.

As you approach Warren Avenue, you'll see Woodward | Warren Park on one side; Wayne State University also has campus buildings in the vicinity. Opposite from the park, the Cathedral Church of St. Paul dates to 1907; Henry Ford's funeral services were held there. Continuing north past Warren and then Farnsworth, you'll see the Main Building of the Detroit Public Library, the Detroit Institute of Arts, and the Detroit Historical Museum in short succession.

Optionally, if you go east on Farnsworth, you can add a few additional sites to your route. The Horace H. Rackham Educational Memorial Building is a historic building that dates to 1941. Two museums are found a little further away: the family-friendly Michigan Science Center and the Charles H. Wright Museum of African American History, which includes the Tuskegee Airmen National Historical Museum.

Points of Interest

On Woodward Avenue

The Majestic Theatre
The Whitney
Museum of Contemporary Art
Detroit Artists Market
The Cathedral Church of St. Paul
Detroit Main Library
Detroit Institute of Arts
Detroit Historical Museum

Nearby

Horace H. Rackham Educational Memorial Building
Michigan Science Center
Charles. H. Wright Museum of African American History

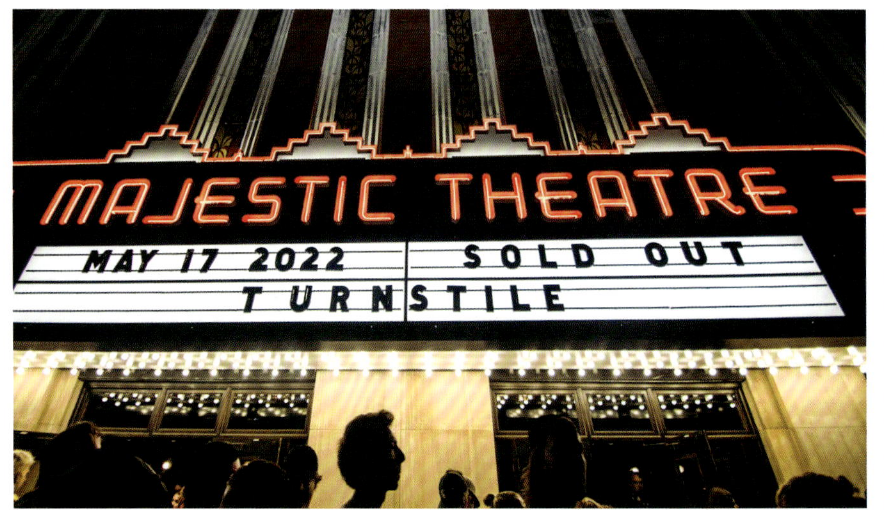

While the building is older, the Art Deco facade of the Majestic Theatre dates to 1934.

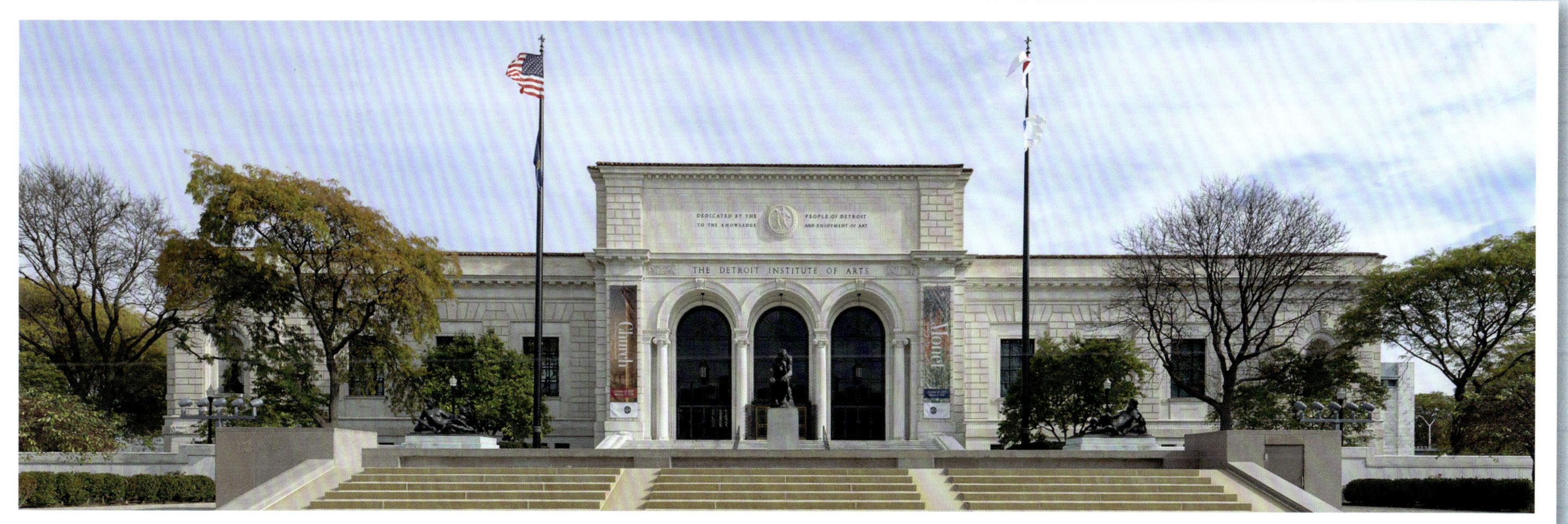

The Detroit Institute of Arts building dates to 1927 and contains one hundred galleries with collections from around the world.

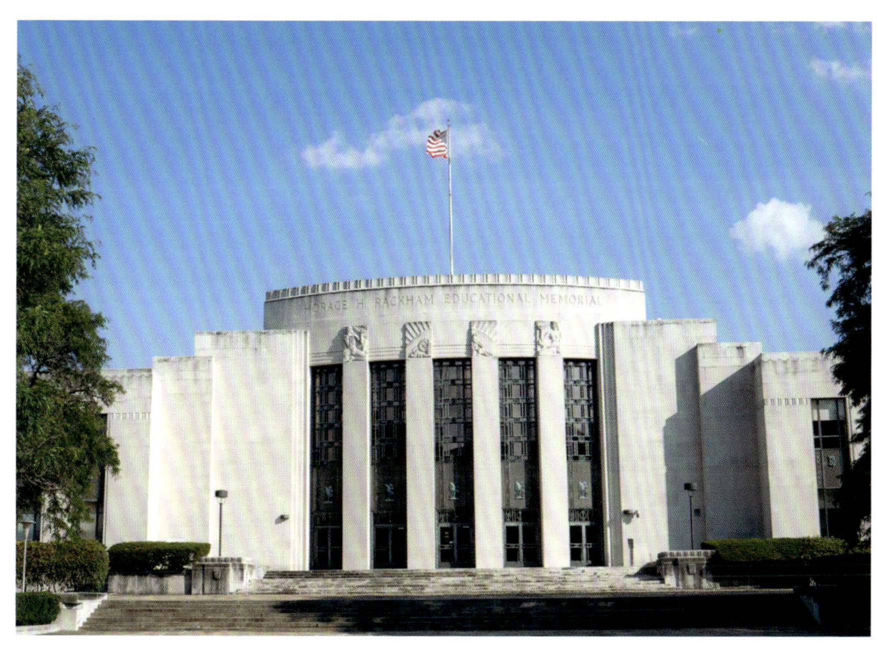

The Horace H. Rackham Educational Memorial Building was once the headquarters for the Engineering Society of Detroit.

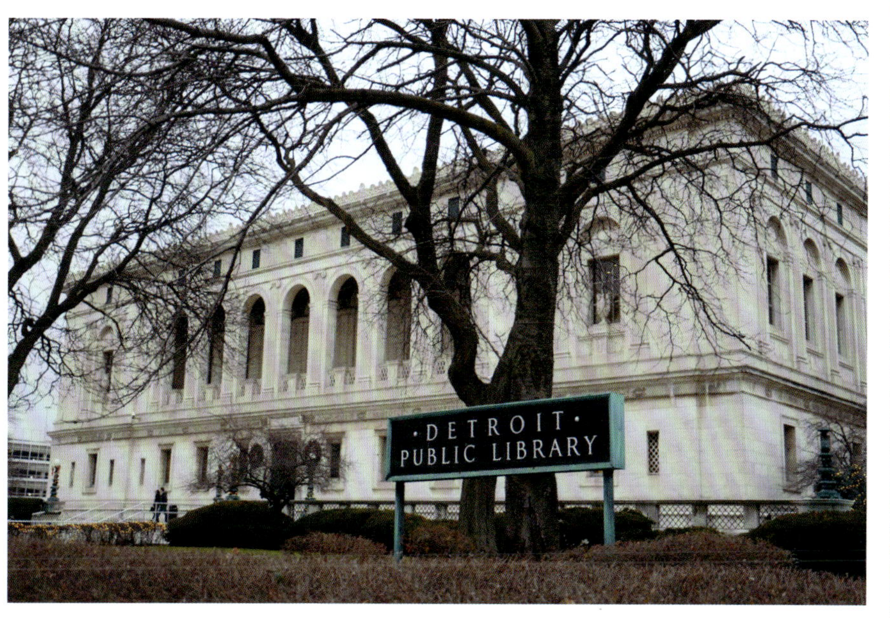

The Main Library building of the Detroit Public Library opened in 1921, with additional wings added in the 1960s. The style is Italian Renaissance.

Scioto Trail

Location: Columbus, Ohio
Length: 5.6 miles
Start point: Berliner Sports Park
End point: North Bank Park/Olentangy Trail

Ohio's capital Columbus runs along the Scioto River, the name coming from a Wyandot word for "deer." The Scioto Trail runs for more than five miles along the Scioto River, before connecting to the Olentangy Trail that continues north for 13 miles. One especially busy section is the "Scioto Mile" that runs through the downtown Columbus area, where you can stroll through a number of fantastic public parks with different pieces of public art, fountains, gardens, and recreational opportunities. Each park has their own highlights and charms; at McFerson Commons, for example, you'll see an 1893 arch that was once part of Columbus Union Train Station, while Bicentennial Park features the Scioto Mile Fountain, and Genoa Park has both an amphitheater and several pieces of public art.

Along with the parks found all along the Scioto Trail, there are a few places where you may want to stop for a more in-depth visit on the Scioto Mile. On the west side of the river, the Center of Science and Industry (COSI) features interactive exhibits on space, gadgets, life, and dinosaurs. A third of a mile away is the National Veterans Memorial and Museum, which shares the stories of individual veterans.

On the east side of the river, the Priscilla R. Tyson Cultural Arts Center features art and historical artifacts, as well as offering art classes. The building, a former armory, dates to 1861. The Ohio Judicial Center, the home of the state's Supreme Court, and its City Hall building are also interesting architecturally.

Points of Interest

Berliner Sports Park
Scioto Audubon Metro Park
Dodge Park
Priscilla R. Tyson Cultural Arts Center
Bicentennial Park
Genoa Park
Center of Science and Industry (COSI)
National Veterans Memorial and Museum
Ohio Judicial Center
Promenade
City Hall building
Battelle Riverfront Park
McFerson Commons
North Bank Park
Olentangy River

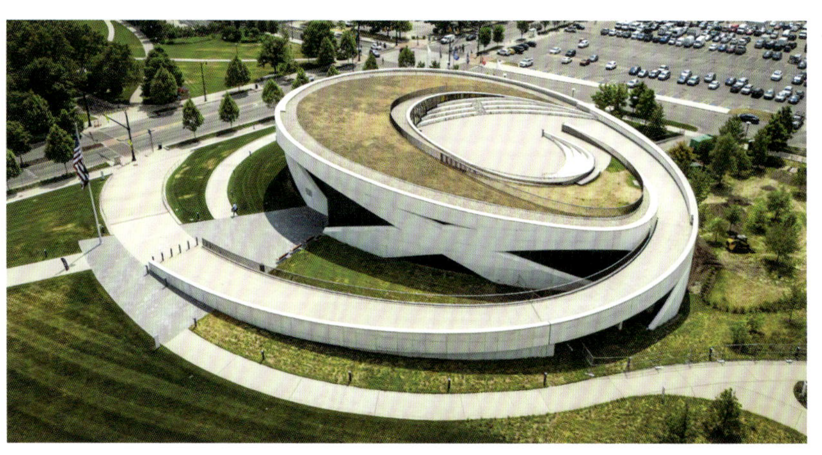

Unlike traditional military museums, the National Veterans Memorial and Museum focuses on the lives of individual veterans.

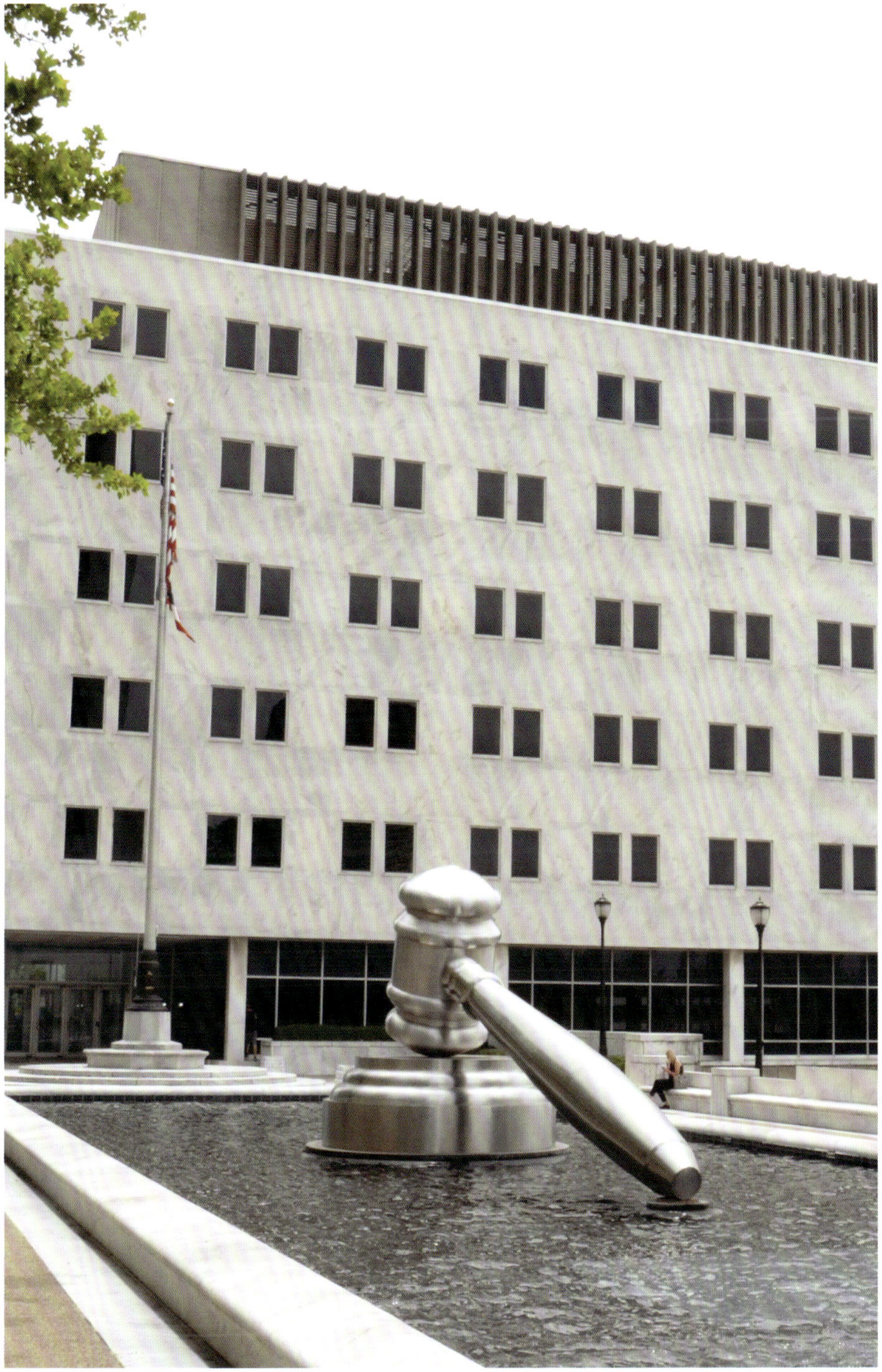

You'll know you've reached the Ohio Judicial Center when you see the 2008 Andrew Scott sculpture *Gavel.*

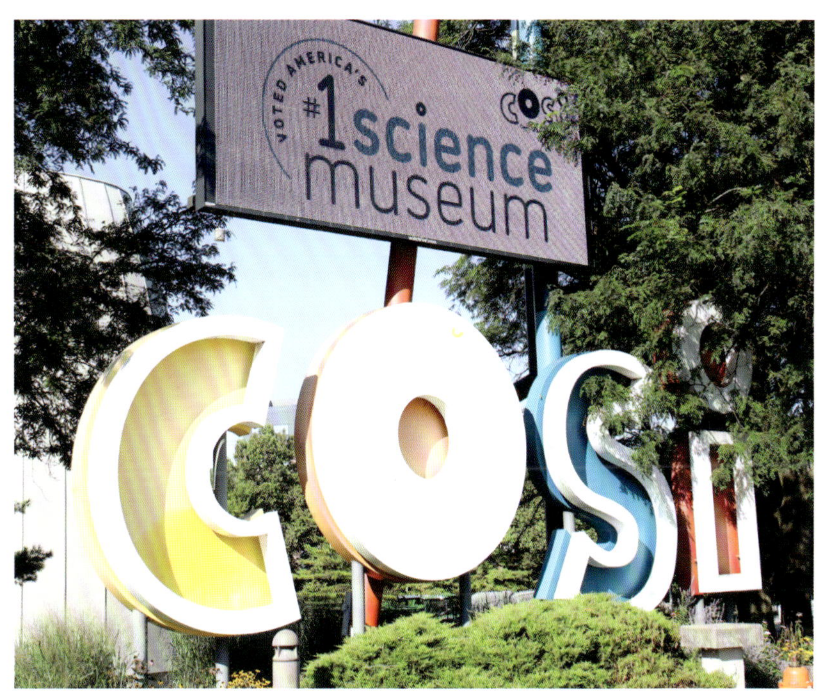

COSI moved to its current home near Genoa Park in 1999.

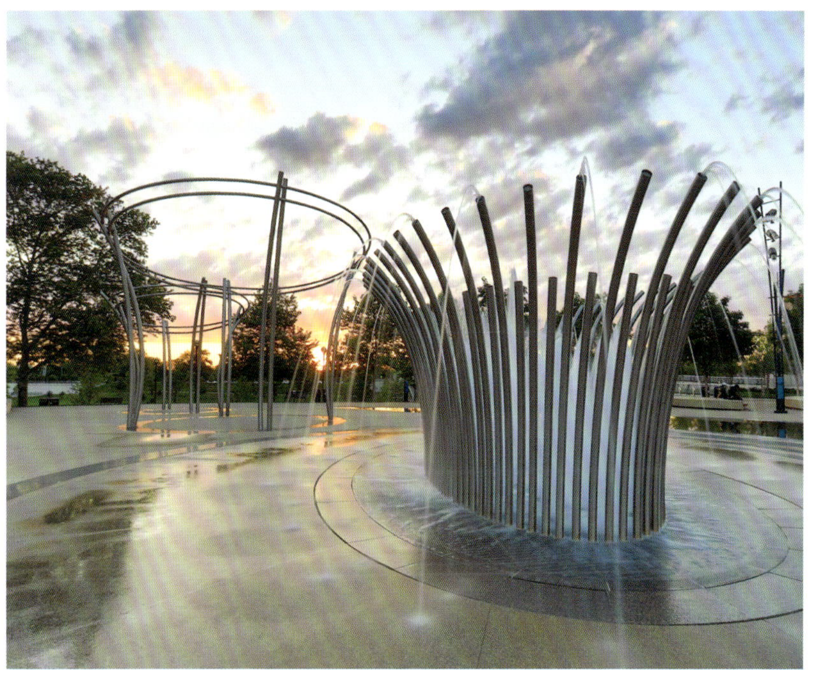

Bicentennial Park is home to a restaurant, the Scioto Mile Fountain, and a performing arts pavilion.

Downtown Madison

Location: Madison, Wisconsin
Length: About 1.1 miles
Start point: Madison Museum of Contemporary Art
End point: Lake Monona

This walk features a mix of attractions that include art, architecture from various eras, a veterans museum, and the State Capitol building. You'll start on State Street, a pedestrian street full of shops, restaurants, museums, and theaters, with the Madison Museum of Contemporary Art. It has been housed since 2006 in an equally modern building, designed by César Pelli. Moving east on State Street toward the State Capitol building, you'll see the 1926–27 Orpheum Theatre that began life as a vaudeville venue, along with the 2004 state-of-the-art Overture Center for the Arts.

Approaching the Capitol grounds, you'll find the Wisconsin Veterans Museum, as well as the *Forward* statue. The *Forward* statue was originally created in 1893, representing Wisconsin's state motto, "Forward." A replica, which is what you'll currently see, was placed on the grounds in 1996. The State Capitol building itself dates to 1917; Daniel Chester French, who designed the statue of Lincoln in Washington, D.C.'s, Lincoln Memorial, also designed the "Golden Lady" that tops its dome.

From the State Capitol grounds, swing north. Madison Children's Museum is nearby for those with kids, and very close to that is another historic theater from 1906, the Bartell Theatre. From there it's a quick walk to the 1903 Robert Lamp House, an early work designed by famous Midwestern architect—and periodic Wisconsin resident—Frank Lloyd Wright for a friend of his.

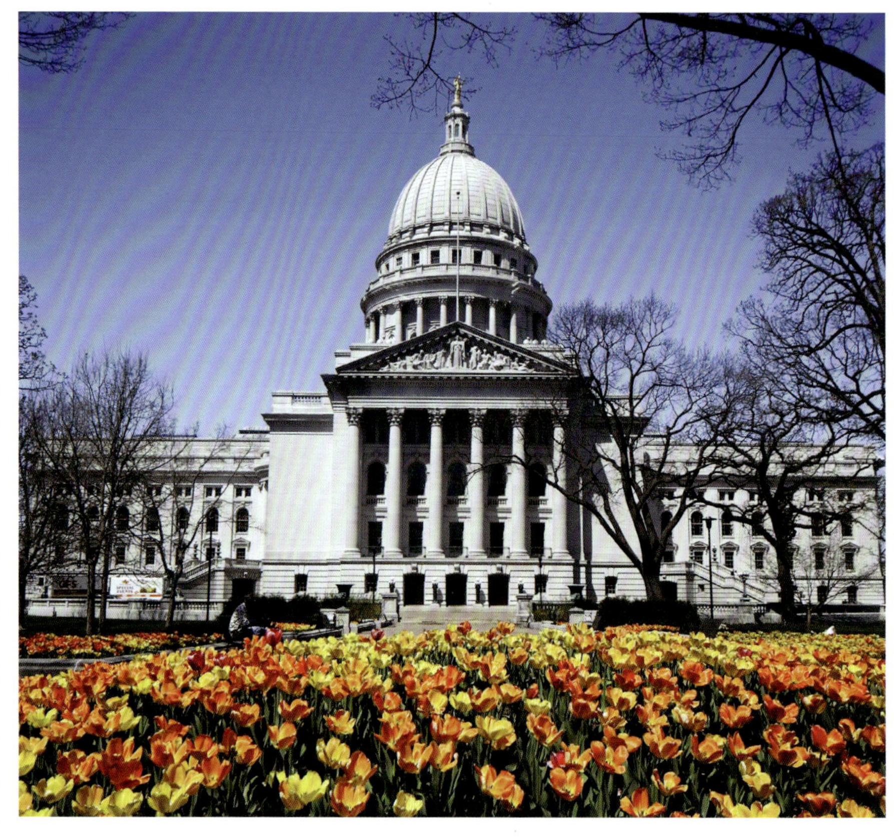

Building ordinances ensure that the State Capitol building remains the tallest in the city.

One more theater is on the list as you make your way south toward the shores of Lake Monona: the Majestic Theatre opened in 1906 as a vaudeville venue. From there, move to the Monona Terrace Community and Convention Center, based on a Frank Lloyd Wright design from the late 1938s, although it wasn't built until the 1990s, long after his death. From the rooftop terrace, you can get a great view of the State Capitol building. From there, you may want to meander along the shores of Lake Monona via the 13-mile Monona Lake Loop.

Points of Interest

Madison Museum of Contemporary Art

Theaters on State Street

Wisconsin Veterans Museum

Wisconsin State Capitol

Madison Children's Museum

Bartell Theatre

Robert Lamp House

Majestic Theatre

Monona Terrace Community and Convention Center

Lake Monona

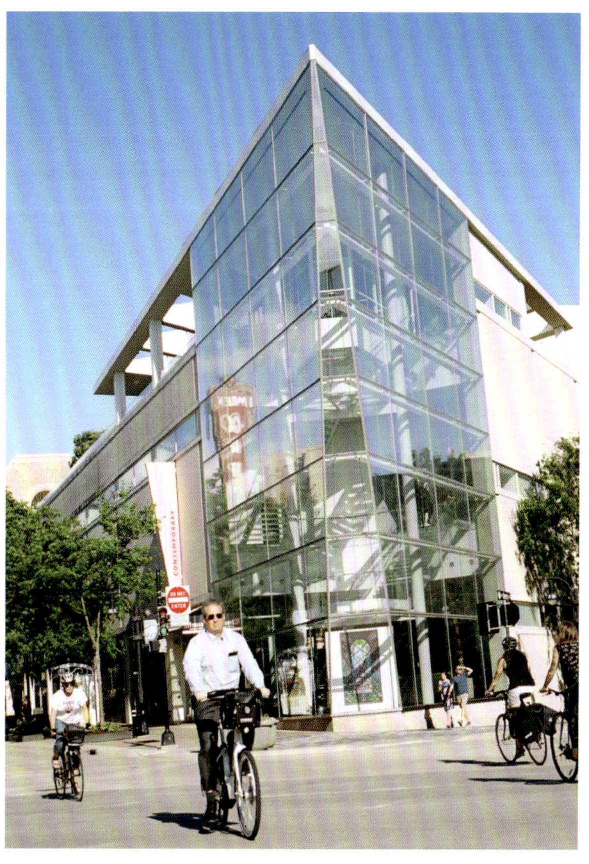

The Madison Museum of Contemporary Art has about 6,000 objects in its permanent collections, including works by Frida Kahlo, Andy Warhol, and Alexander Calder.

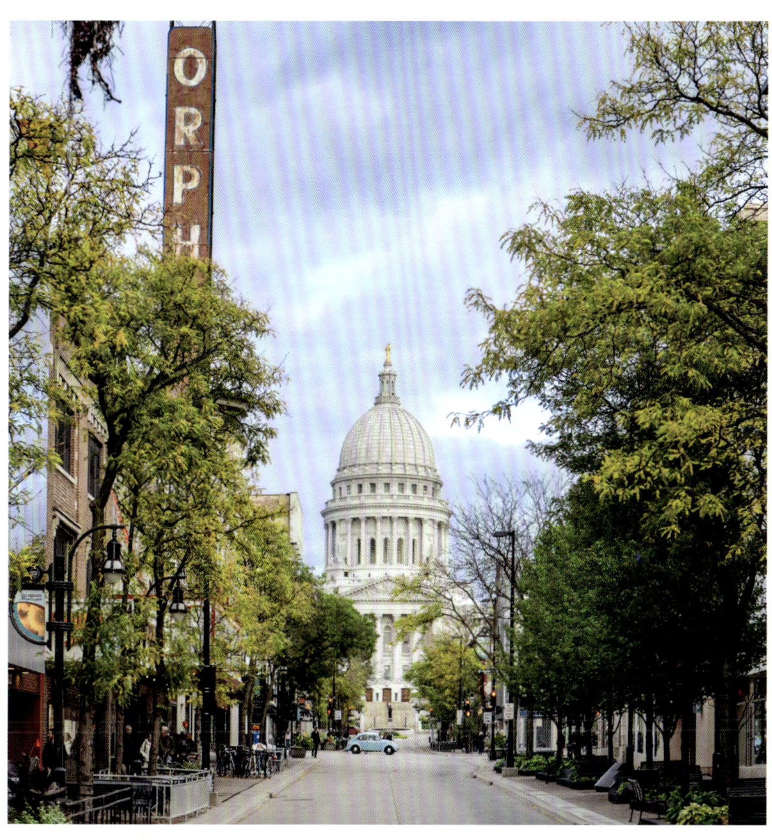

A view of State Street, with the Orpheum Theatre sign in the foreground and the Capitol building in the background.

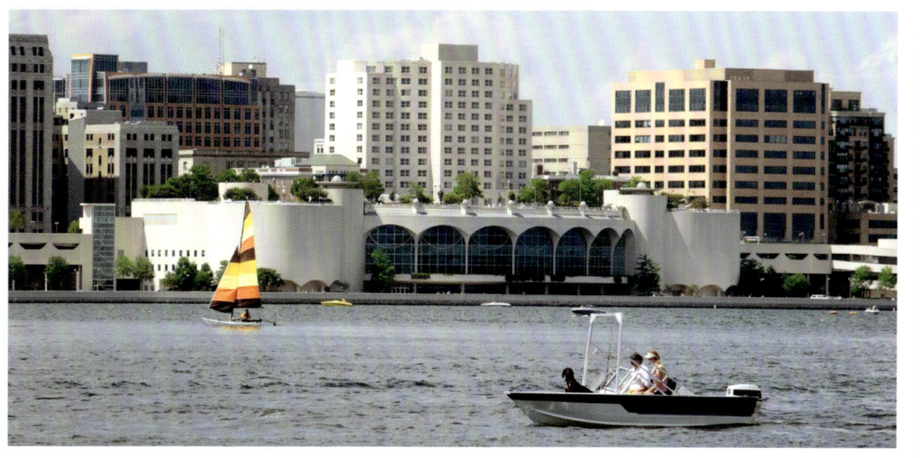

The Monona Terrace Community and Convention Center serves as an events venue, as well as offering tours and a gift shop with merchandise inspired by Frank Lloyd Wright's designs.

Downtown Minneapolis

Location: Minneapolis, Minnesota
Length: About 1.6 miles; 2.2 miles with City Hall
Start point: Walker Art Center
End point: Foshay Tower or City Hall

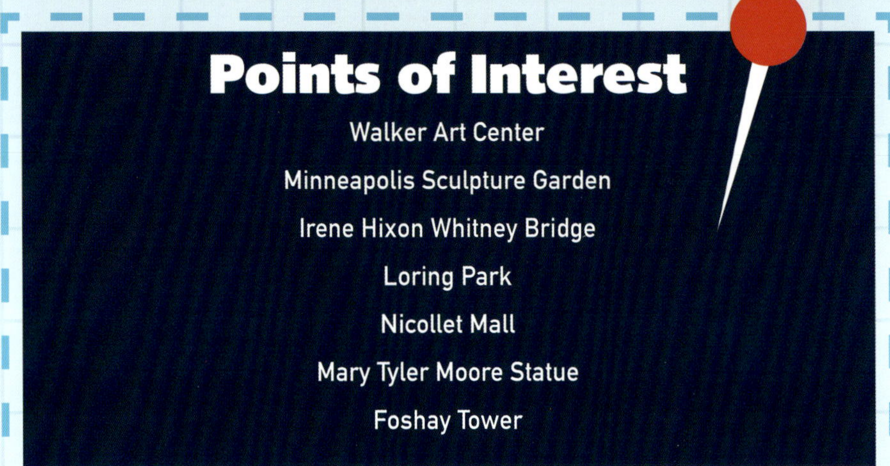

Points of Interest

Walker Art Center
Minneapolis Sculpture Garden
Irene Hixon Whitney Bridge
Loring Park
Nicollet Mall
Mary Tyler Moore Statue
Foshay Tower

This walk combines quirky artwork, natural beauty, shopping, and a bit of television history. The straight-line distances come to a couple of miles, but expect to walk more as you tour the museum and sculpture garden and wind through Loring Park.

Start with the artwork: The Walker Art Center features contemporary art, and is adjacent to the Minneapolis Sculpture Garden that lets you see about forty permanent installations. Once you've had your fill, use the Irene Hixon Whitney Bridge to cross Hennepin Avenue and I-94. The pedestrian bridge is itself an architectural work of art, and features the words of a poem by John Ashbery.

Amble through Loring Park, keeping an eye out for the Berger Fountain, and then take the Loring Greenway that extends past the park and connects to Nicollet Mall. On Nicollet Mall, you'll find plenty of places to shop and dine. Between Twelfth Street and Eleventh Street, check out Peavey Plaza, home of the Orchestra Hall building and some lovely fountains. At Seventh Street, you'll find a statue of Mary Tyler Moore, honoring the fact that the scene in the opening credits of *The Mary Tyler Moore Show* where the heroine tosses her cap was filmed on Nicollet Mall.

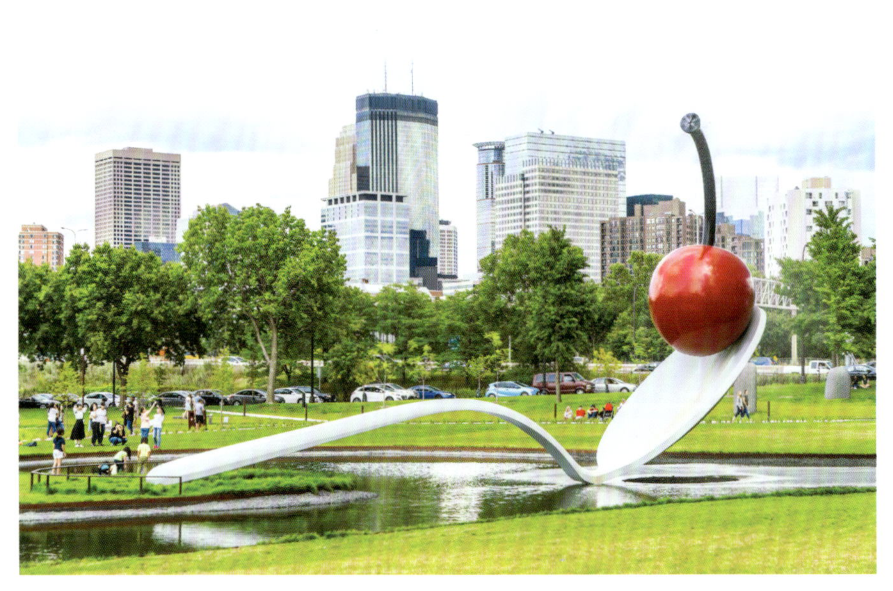

Spoonbridge and Cherry, the work of Claes Oldenburg and Coosje van Bruggen, was commissioned for the opening of the Minneapolis Sculpture Garden.

From there, one street to the east on Marquette, between Ninth Street and Eighth Street, you'll see the 1929 Art Deco Foshay Tower, which now houses a hotel. That can serve as one ending point to your walk—you may want to check if the Observation Deck is open for a great view of the city—but if you're up for a slightly longer walk, head northeast to find the Minneapolis City Hall building on South Fifth Street between Third Avenue and Fourth Avenue. The historic building was constructed between 1888 and 1909.

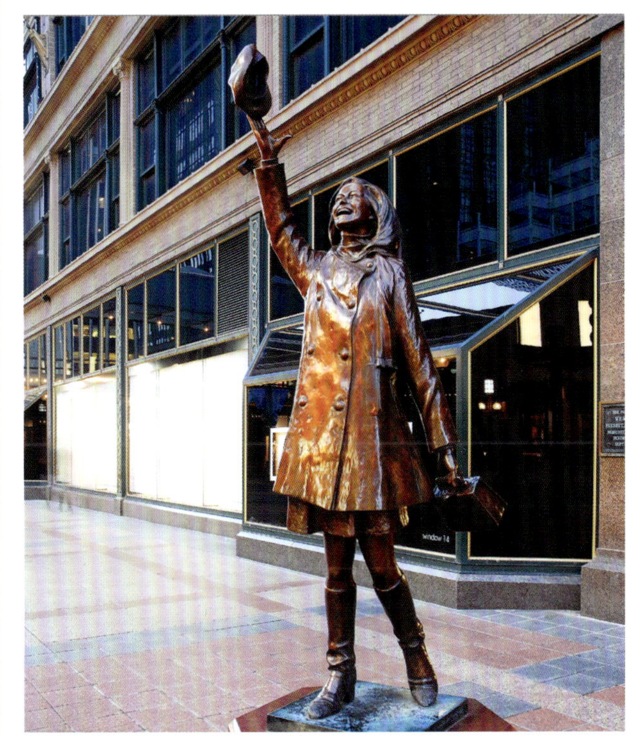

The Mary Tyler Moore Show was set in Minneapolis. Mary's apartment in the show was also based on a real Minneapolis location.

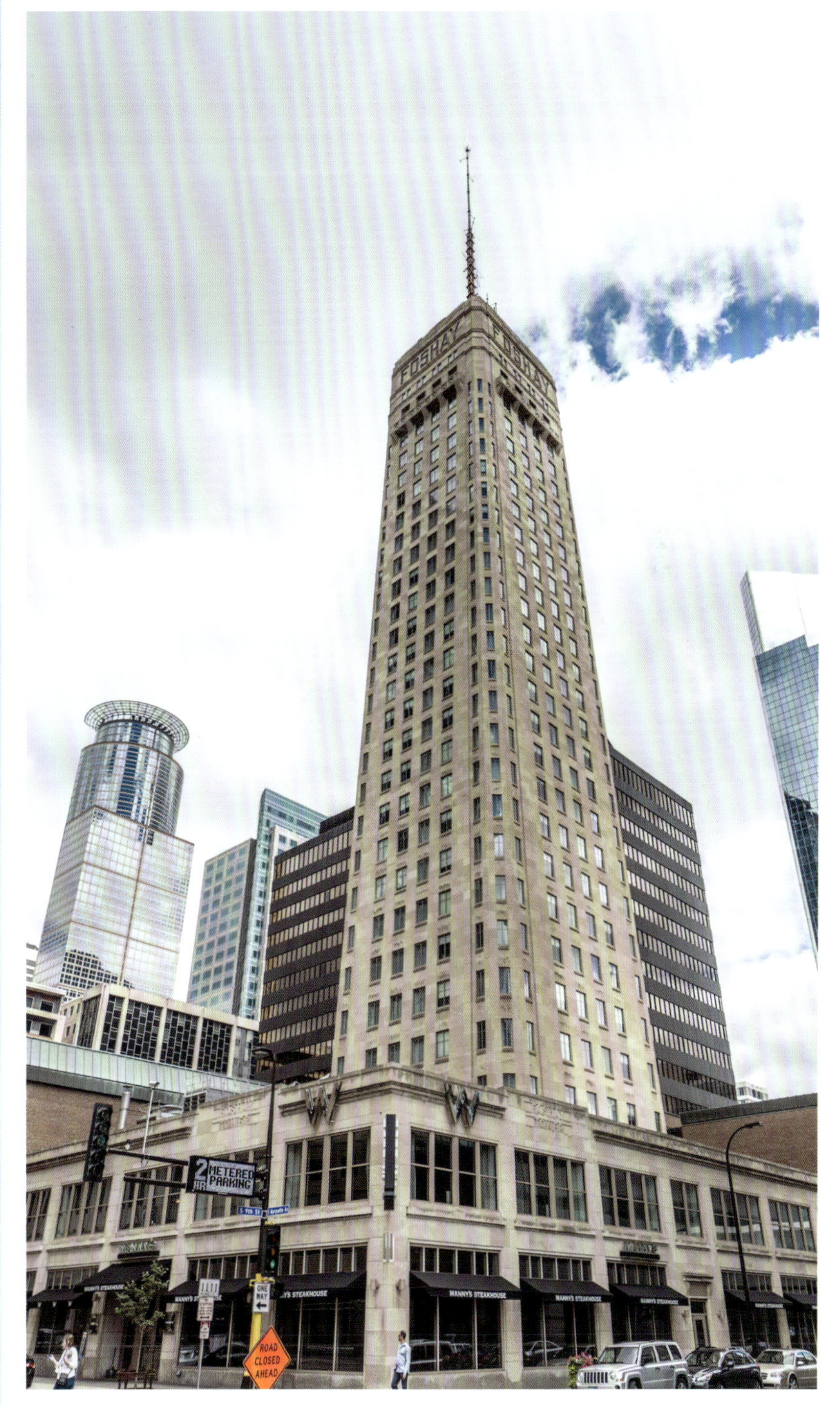

The Foshay Tower's builder, Wilbur Foshay, was a wealthy businessman who lost much of his wealth very shortly after the building's 1929 opening, when the Great Depression began, and later went to prison for a pyramid scheme.

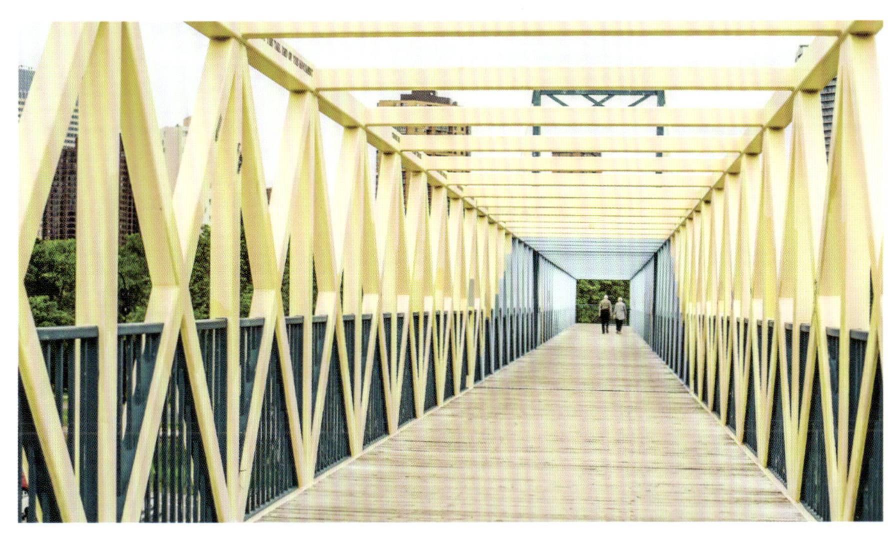

The Irene Hixon Whitney Bridge connects the sculpture garden to Loring Park.

Arkansas River Path

Location: Wichita, Kansas
Length: About 10 miles
Start point: West 21st Street North near I-235
End point: Galena Street and Washington Street

The Arkansas River Path, or Arkansas River Trail, is a multi-use trail for walkers, runners, and bikers that runs along the Arkansas River. For the most part the trail runs along the west side of the river, but there is a stretch of a few miles where you can hike on either side. As you hike, you'll see a number of parks and bridges, and pass along one section where the Arkansas River runs parallel to the aptly-named Museum Boulevard.

On Museum Boulevard, the Old Cowtown Museum is an open-air museum that includes more than fifty buildings that depict life in Wichita between 1865 and 1880. The Empire House Theater is part of that campus; if you stop by at the right time, you may be able to see the Empire House Players put on a period melodrama. Also on Museum Boulevard, the Wichita Art Museum focuses on the work of American artists, including works by Mary Cassatt and Edward Hopper.

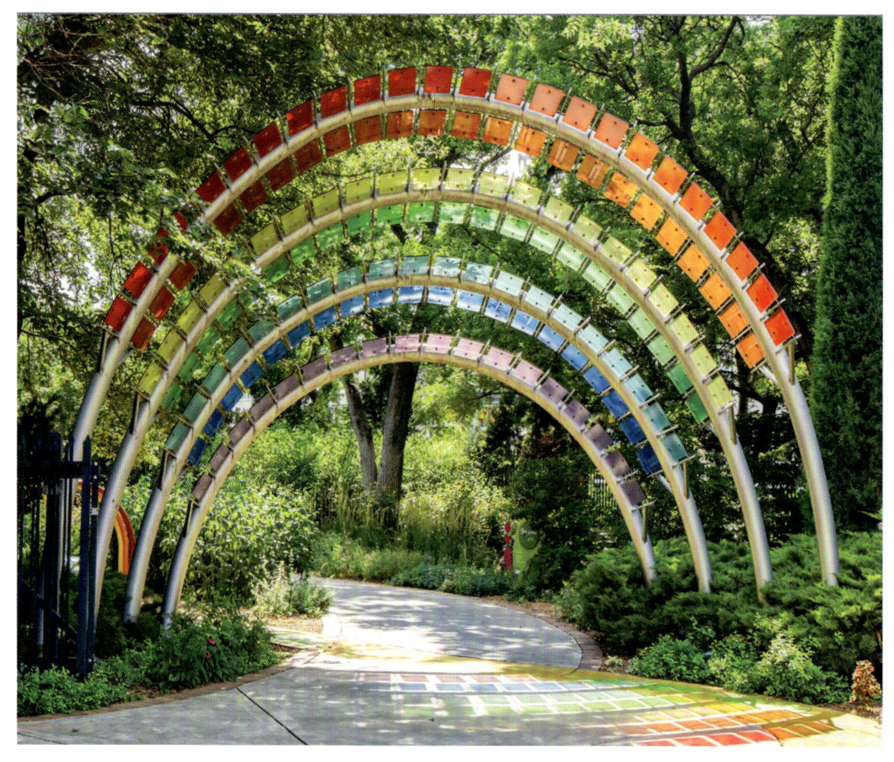

Botanica offers beautiful views as you amble its paths.

A little further north from the river, past the Old Cowtown Museum, you'll find more than 17 acres of botanical gardens, including a butterfly garden. If you continue moving east along the path, staying closer to the river, you'll find the Mid-America All-Indian Museum, which has more than 3,000 pieces in its collection of works by American Indian artists.

One of the founders of the Mid-America All-Indian Museum, whose work you'll see there, was Blackbear Bosin. The child of a Kiowa father and Comanche mother, he became a Wichita resident and was the sculptor of the *Keeper of the Plains* statue that is found not far from the museum, at the point where the Arkansas and Little Arkansas Rivers meet. If you stay on the same side of the river after seeing the statue, you'll find Veterans Memorial Park; if you cross to the other bank, you'll see Exploration Place, a family-friendly science museum.

Points of Interest

Old Cowtown Museum

Empire House Theater

Wichita Art Museum

Botanica, the Wichita Gardens

Mid-America All-Indian Museum

Keeper of the Plains

Veterans Memorial Park

Exploration Place

Lincoln Street Bridge

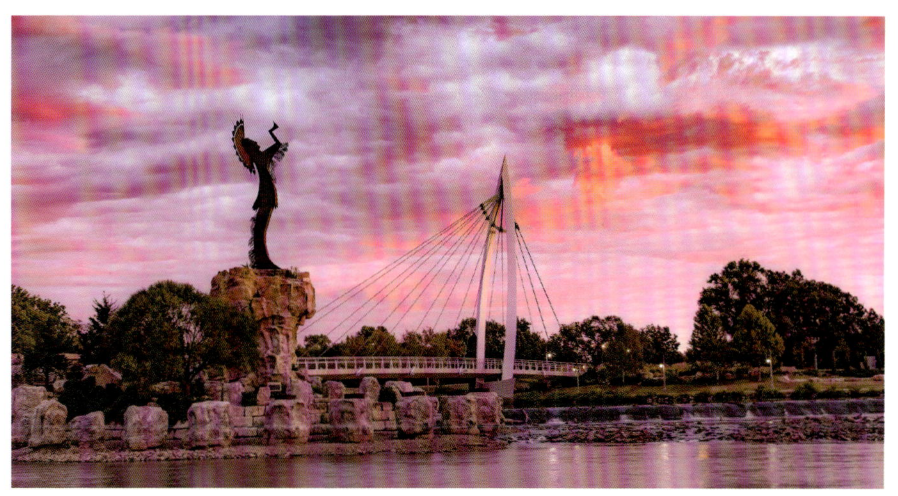

A pedestrian bridge crosses the river near the *Keeper of the Plains* statue. The 1974 statue stands 44 feet tall.

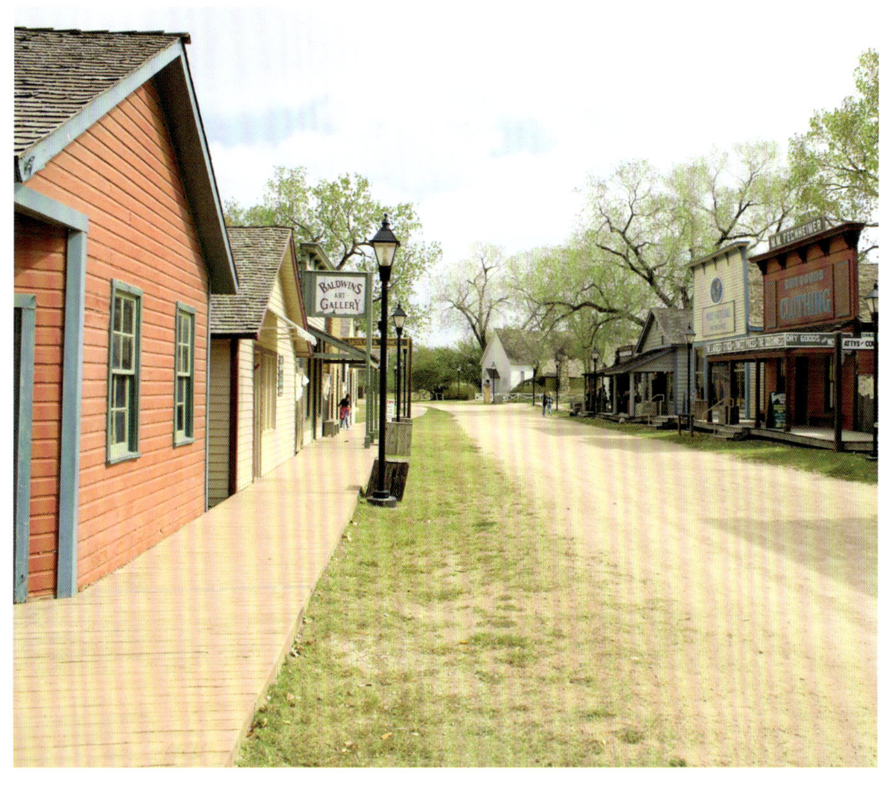

Step into the past at the Old Cowtown Museum that explores Wichita's history.

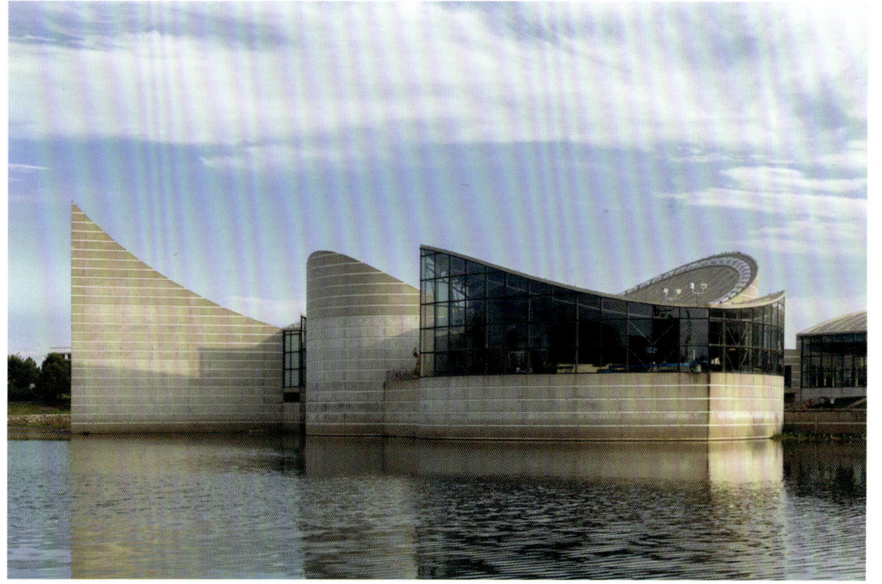

The Exploration Center is seen here from Veterans Memorial Park across the river.

Gateway Mall and Gateway Arch

Location: St. Louis, Missouri
Length: About 1.5 miles
Start point: Union Station
End point: Mississippi River

Walk between Union Station and the Mississippi River through the Gateway Mall, a series of parks filled with public art between Chestnut Street and Market Street.

Start in Union Station itself: The former train station (1894–1978) transitioned in 1985 to host a set of other attractions. Along with various food options, Union Station includes an aquarium, a mirror maze, a carousel, a ropes course, a mini-golf course, and the St. Louis Wheel.

From there, head towards the Mississippi through a series of green spaces. Aloe Plaza features *The Meeting of the Waters*, a Carl Milles sculpture that opened in 1940, depicting the symbolic meeting of the Mississippi and Missouri Rivers. As you walk further down, once you cross 14th Street, you'll see the Soldiers Memorial Military Museum, which opened in the 1930s to honor World War I veterans. As you pass 13th Street, you'll see a complex of government buildings on your right, including the St. Louis City Hall building, built between 1890 and 1904.

When you've passed Eleventh Street, you'll start to encounter sculptures! Richard Serra's *Twain* is found between Eleventh and Tenth Streets, and then the landscape comes alive with the Citygarden Sculpture Park between Tenth and Eighth Streets.

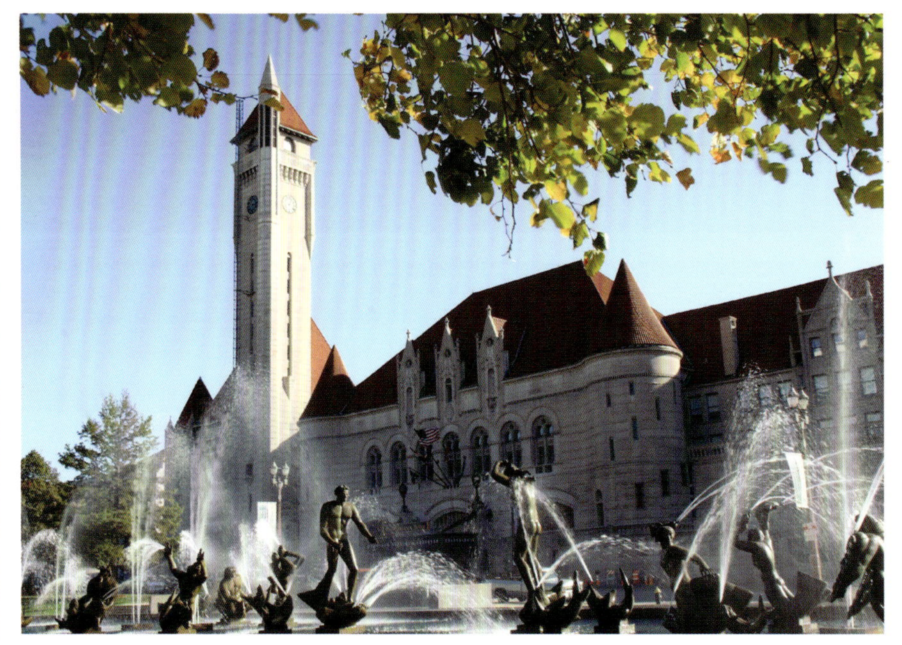

The *Meeting of the Waters*, with Union Station in the background

Between Broadway and Fourth Street, you'll find one part of Gateway Arch National Park, the Old Courthouse building that was the site of the infamous Dred Scott case of 1857. As of November 2024, the Old Courthouse was closed to visitors for a period of renovation, with an anticipated reopening in summer 2025. Together, the courthouse, the Gateway Arch, and the museum at the Gateway Arch, form Gateway Arch National Park. At the museum, visitors can find out more about the Lewis and Clark expedition and westward expansion.

Wrap up your day by taking a tram ride up the iconic St. Louis symbol, the Gateway Arch, and strolling the grounds to see more of the Mississippi River!

Points of Interest

Union Station
Aloe Plaza
Memorial Plaza
Soldiers Memorial Military Museum
Poelker Park
Citygarden Sculpture Park
Kiener Plaza Park
Old Courthouse
Gateway Arch Museum
Gateway Arch

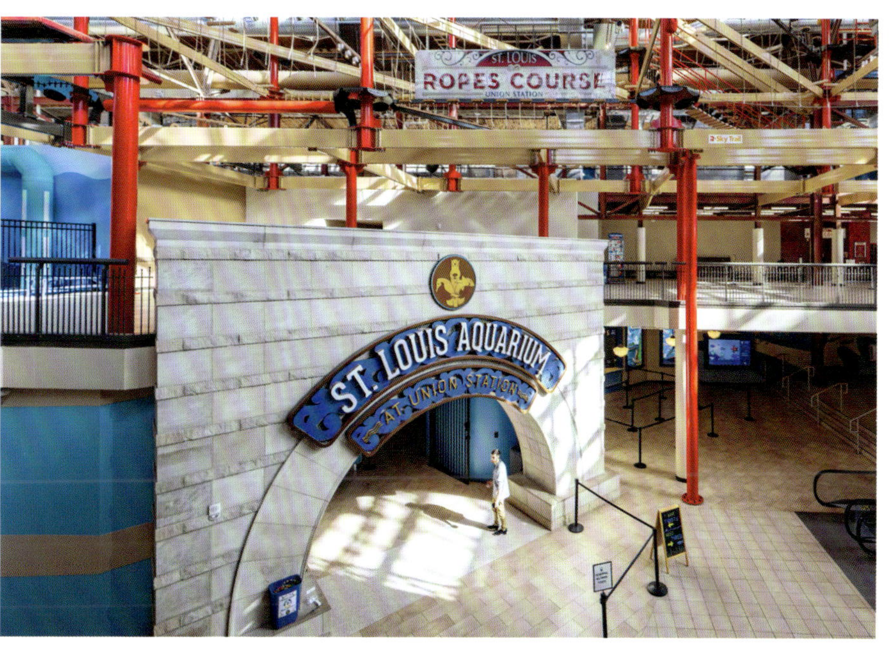

There is no shortage of things to do inside St. Louis's Union Station. If you have a few days in St. Louis, you could spend a whole day there, and then do this walk on the following day!

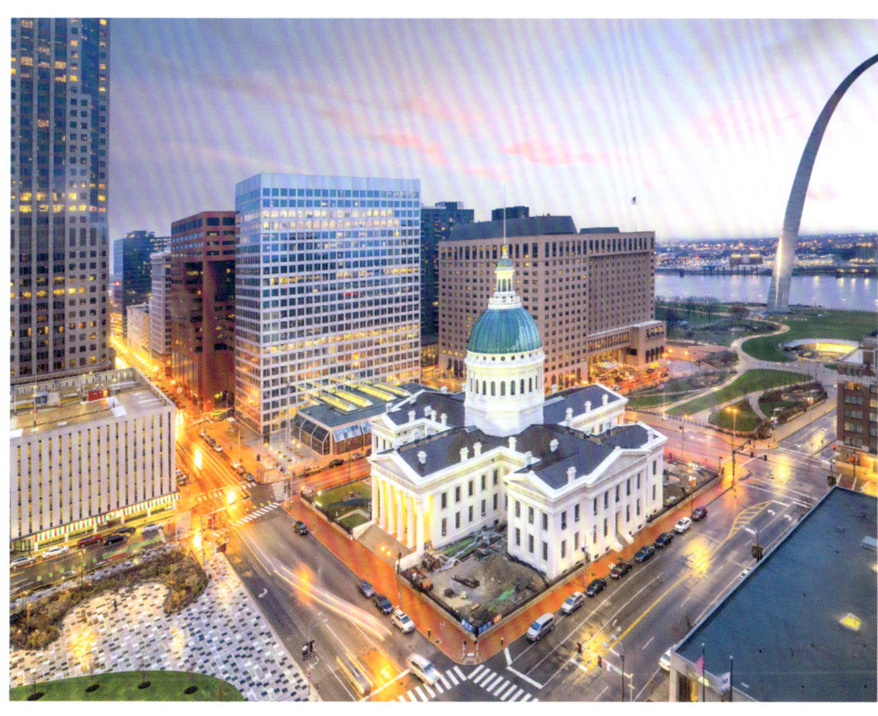

The Old Courthouse, with the Arch seen to the right. The Arch opened to the public in 1967.

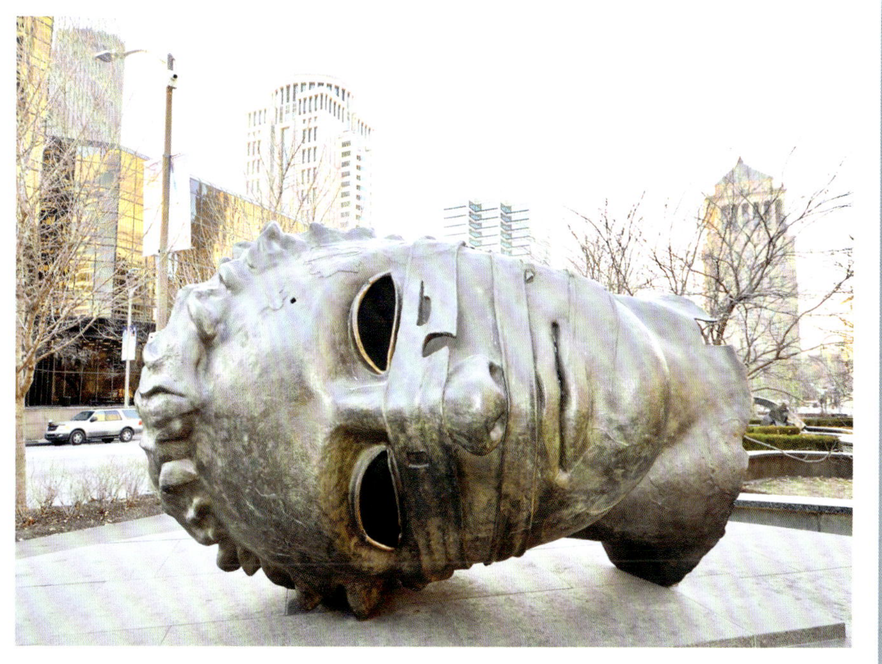

Citygarden Sculpture Park opened in 2009. *Eros Bendato* is the work of Igor Mitoraj.

Downtown Lincoln

Location: Lincoln, Nebraska
Length: Variable, minimum 1 mile
Start point: Nebraska History Museum
End point: Haymarket District

Points of Interest

Nebraska History Museum
Lincoln Children's Museum
Great Plains Art Museum
Sheldon Museum of Art
Haymarket District
Bill Harris Iron Horse Park

This tour of downtown Lincoln starts off in an area dominated by the University of Nebraska campus, packed full of museums, theaters, and performing arts centers, before moving west to the historic Haymarket District, featuring a number of shops and restaurants.

The Nebraska History Museum offers a long view of history in the area, going back 13,000 years. The Lincoln Children's Museum is right around the corner, with three floors full of interactive exhibits. It's on P Street; if you move west on P Street to your next destination, you'll see the 1929 Rococo Theatre building along the way at 13th Street.

The Great Plains Art Museum, operated by the University of Nebraska-Lincoln, is free and focuses on works by Great Plains artists, including Jackson Pollock and Grant Wood. The Sheldon Museum of Art nearby features a broad span of American art; its collections also include the University of Nebraska collection. In the same area, walkers might see the Lied Center for the Performing Arts, operated by the University of Nebraska-Lincoln.

Moving west, once walkers cross Ninth Street, they'll find themselves in the Haymarket District. Lincoln, then called Lancaster, was founded in 1856. In the town's early decades, Haymarket Square was established as a place for goods and livestock to be sold. Wander the area bounded by Seventh and Ninth Streets running north-south, and N and R Streets running east-west, to see shops and restaurants in historic buildings from Lincoln's past. At Bill Harris Iron Horse Park, see an original steam locomotive.

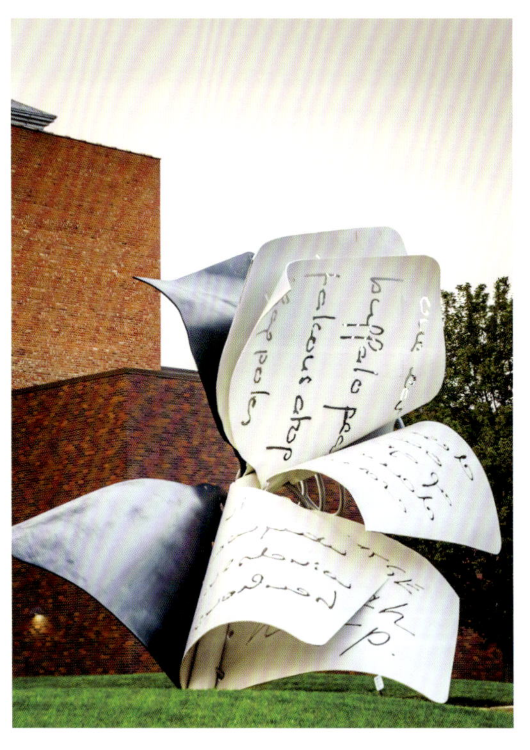

Claes Oldenburg's *Torn Notebook*, part of the Sheldon Museum of Art's collections, is near the museum in Madden Garden.

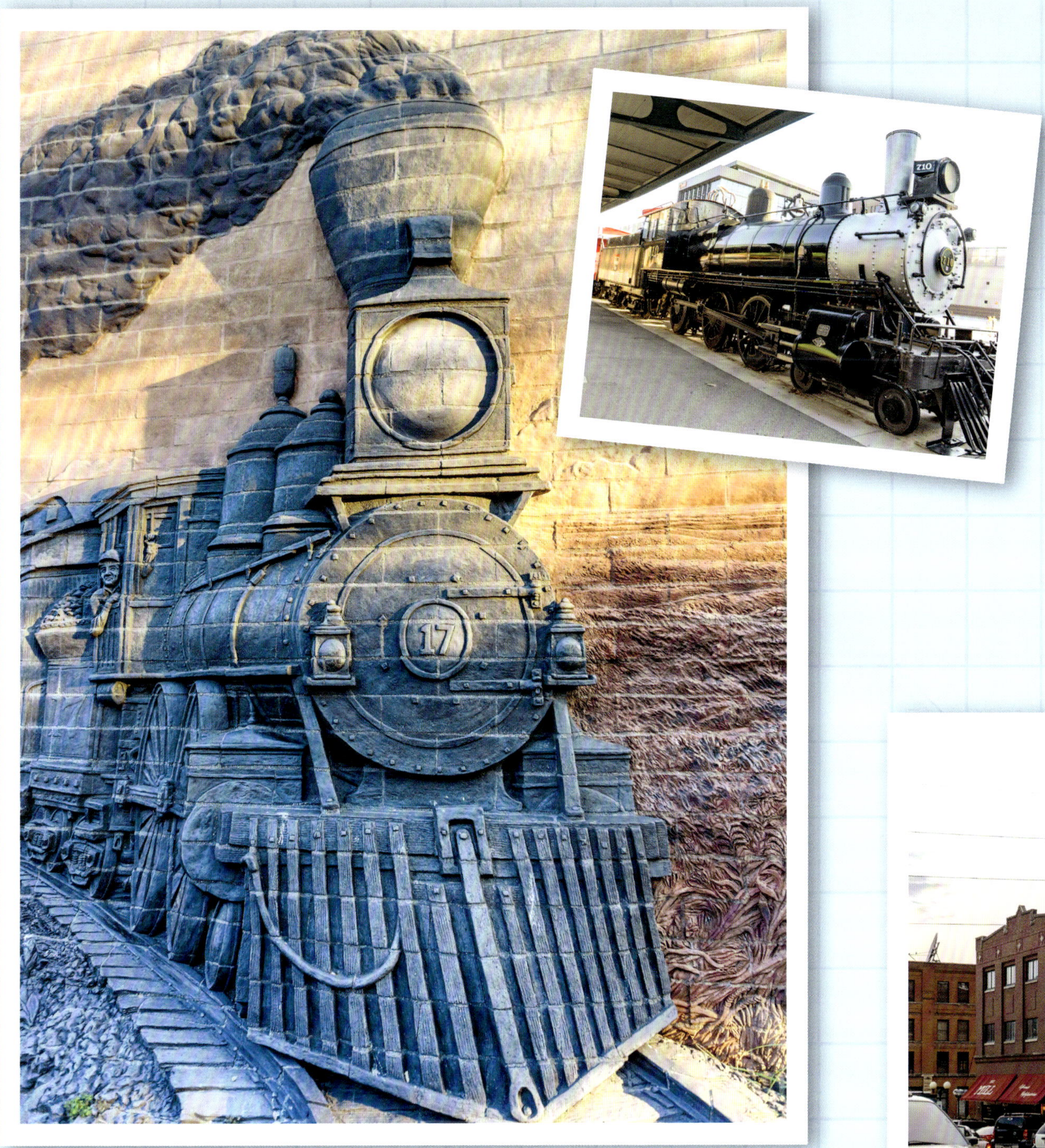

At Bill Harris Iron Horse Park in the Haymarket District, visitors can see both a restored steam train and artwork of one.

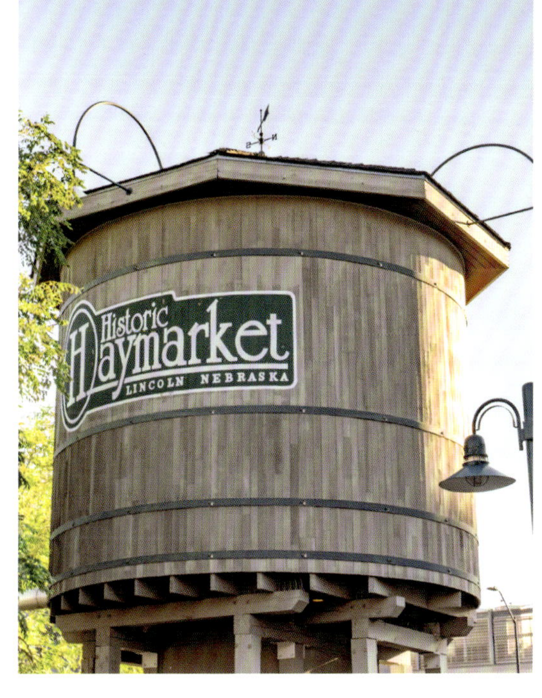

An old railroad water tower announces the presence of the Historic Haymarket District.

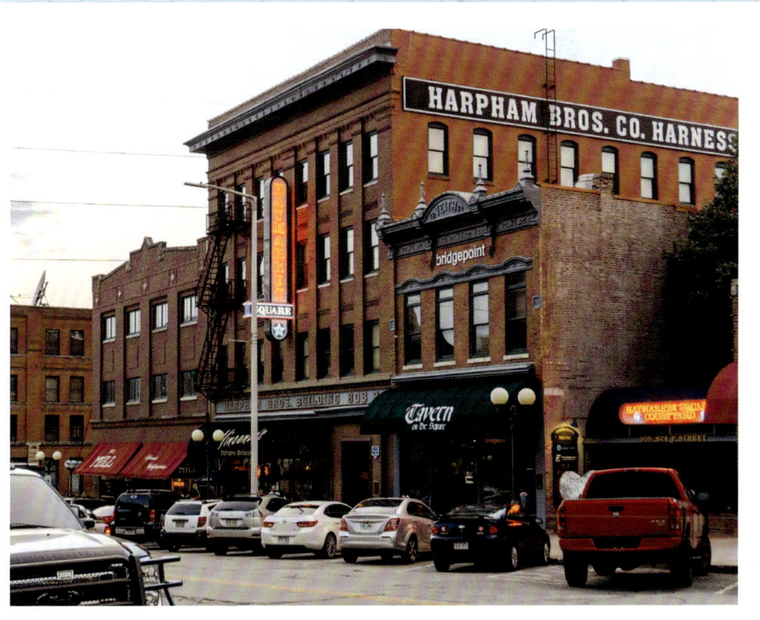

The Harpham Brothers building on P Street, a former warehouse for a harness and saddle company, dates to 1903.

16th Street Mall

Location: Denver, Colorado
Length: 1.25 miles
Start point: Broadway
End point: Wewatta Street

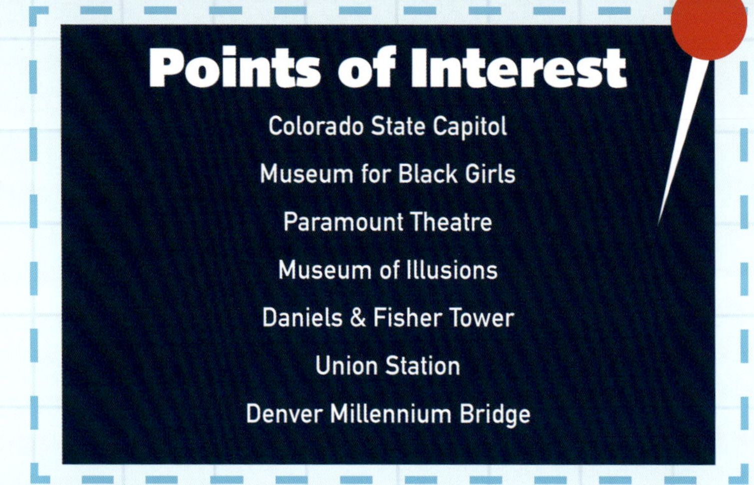

Points of Interest

Colorado State Capitol
Museum for Black Girls
Paramount Theatre
Museum of Illusions
Daniels & Fisher Tower
Union Station
Denver Millennium Bridge

Illustrious architect I.M. Pei and his firm designed the pedestrian mall that runs along 16th Street, full of shops and restaurants. The architecture is tied to Denver's location, with the sidewalks having a pattern meant to evoke the scales of a western diamondback rattlesnake. The mall is an easy walk, but you can also hop on the free MallRide shuttle buses that run between Broadway and Wewatta Street if you only want to walk one way and take an easier route back to your starting point.

One end of the 16th Street Mall is found at Broadway. On the other side of Broadway and Colfax Avenue, you'll find Civic Center Park and the grounds of the State Capitol building, so you might want to have a quick walk around those before heading up 16th Street. While the attraction of the 16th Street Mall will generally be the shopping, there are some points of interest along the way. As you approach Glenarm Place, you might want to check out the pop-up museum, the Museum for Black Girls. On Glenarm Place, the Art Deco Paramount Theatre building opened in 1930.

Between Champa Street and Curtis Street, you'll find the Museum of Illusions–Denver, which features a number of illusion rooms that test your perception. The museum notes that most visitors take about 45 minutes to an hour to explore. Back in the real world, past Arapahoe Street, spot the Daniels & Fisher Tower, a clock tower dating to about 1910. Guided tours up to its observation deck are available.

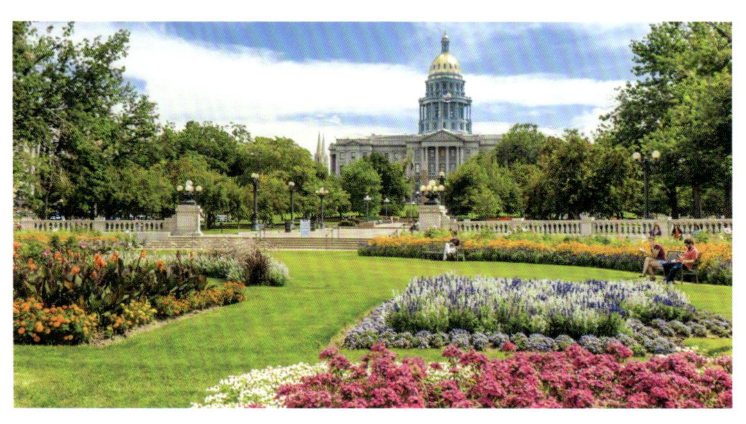

If you'd like, take a walk around the Colorado State Capitol building before heading to the 16th Street Mall.

As you approach the end of the 16th Street Mall, you'll be near Union Station at 17th and Wynkoop Streets. Parts of the current building date to 1914. The Denver Millennium Bridge then connects the 16th Street Mall to an area of parks near the South Platte River.

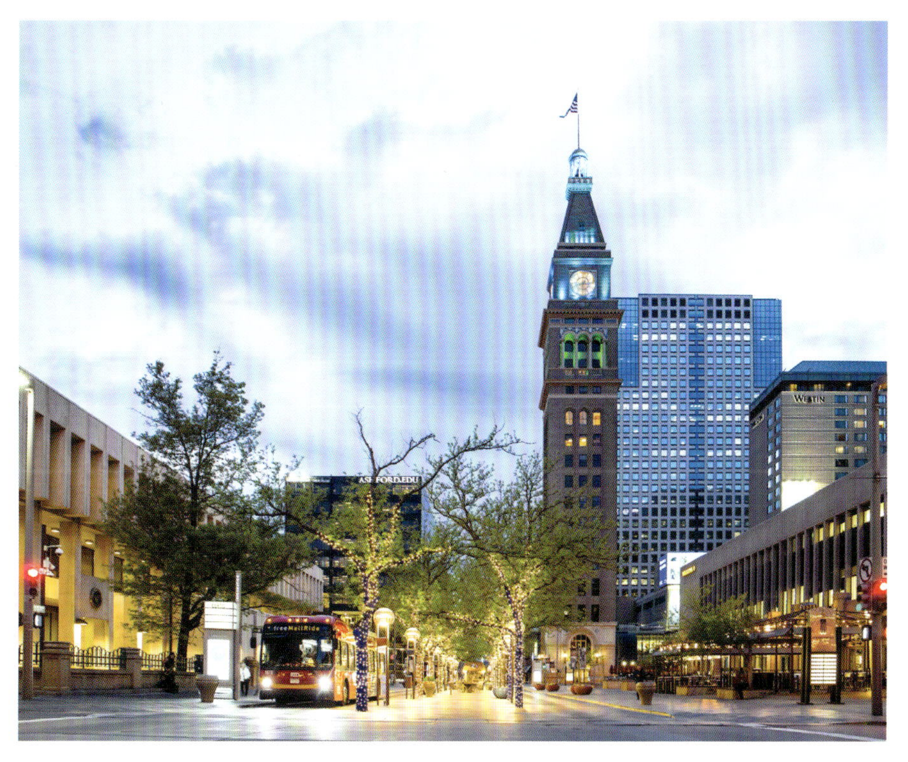

The Daniels & Fisher Tower was part of a building owned by the Daniels & Fisher department store.

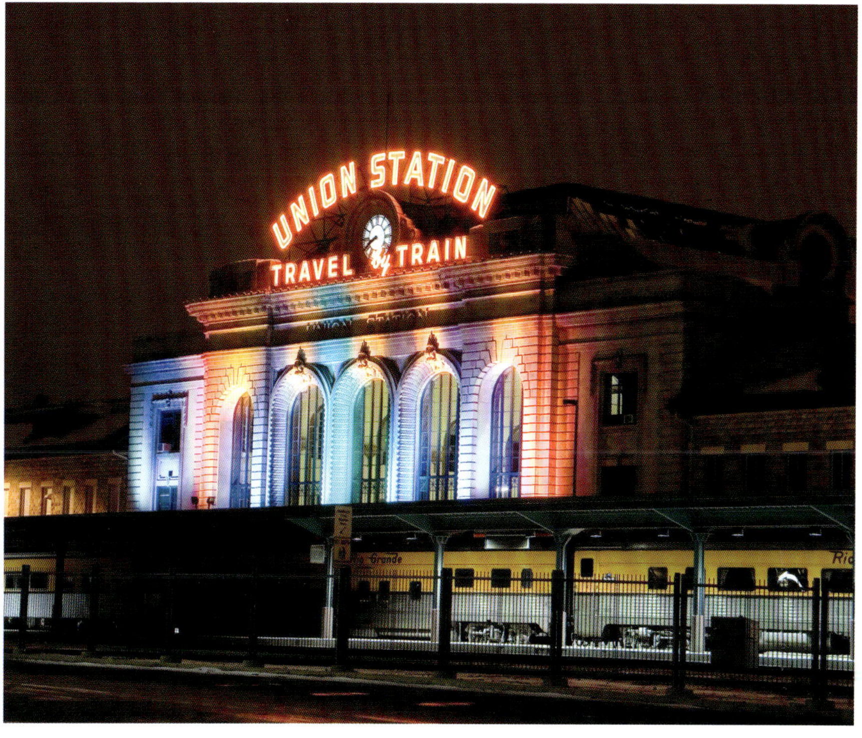

Denver's Union Station building is lit up during the month of December.

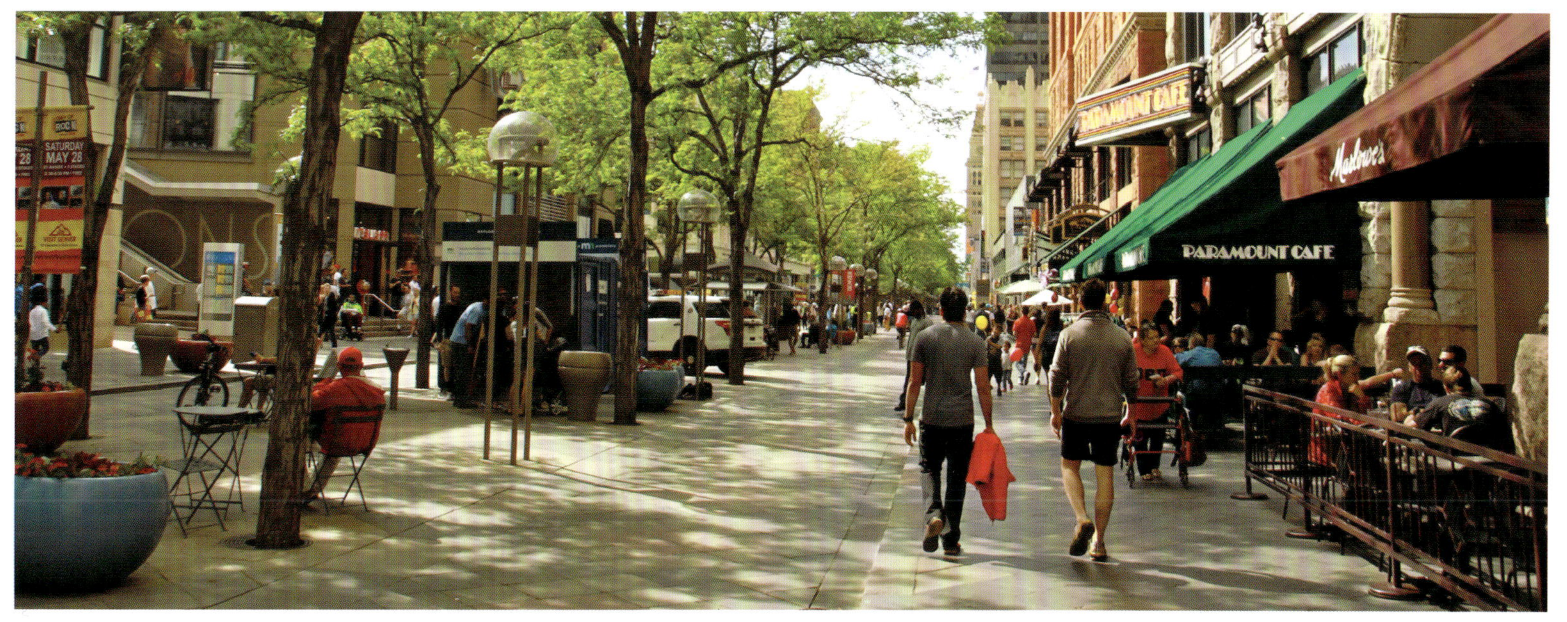

The 16th Street Mall is lined with shops and restaurants both large and small.

Downtown Phoenix

Location: Phoenix, Arizona
Length: About 2.5 miles
Start point: Arizona State Capitol
End point: Children's Museum of Phoenix

Points of Interest

Arizona State Capitol
Wesley Bolin Memorial Plaza
Phoenix City Hall
Orpheum Theatre Phoenix
Hotel San Carlos
Herberger Theater Center
Phoenix Convention Center
St. Mary's Basilica
Heritage and Science Park
Children's Museum of Phoenix

Downtown Phoenix has a lot to offer, with a mix of architecture from different eras and fun, family-friendly museums. Start your walk on the grounds of the Arizona State Capitol building. The oldest part of the original capitol building, which dates to 1901, now hosts a museum. Across the street, you'll see Wesley Bolin Memorial Plaza, named after a former governor of the state. There, you can see dozens of memorials and monuments, including the Bill of Rights monument, the World War I Memorial, the Korean War Memorial, the Vietnam Veterans Memorial, the Desert Storm Memorial, the Navajo Codetalkers memorial, and the mast and other parts from the USS *Arizona*.

Moving east on Washington Street, you'll pass a number of government buildings, eventually encountering the current Phoenix City Hall, completed in 1994, at 200 W. Washington Street. A short distance away, at 125 W. Washington Street, you could see the Old City Hall building, now a county courthouse, that dates to the late 1920s. A block north on Adams Street, the 1929 Orpheum Theatre also goes back to that era, as does the 1928 Hotel San Carlos that's another street north and a few streets east of the Orpheum.

From the Hotel San Carlos, keep heading east on Monroe Street. Past Second Street, you'll find some newer cultural institutions: the Herberger Theater Center on one side and the Phoenix Convention Center, including Symphony Hall, on the other. At Third Street, you'll find another historical building, St. Mary's Basilica, which was built between 1902 and 1914. It's particularly known for its stained glass.

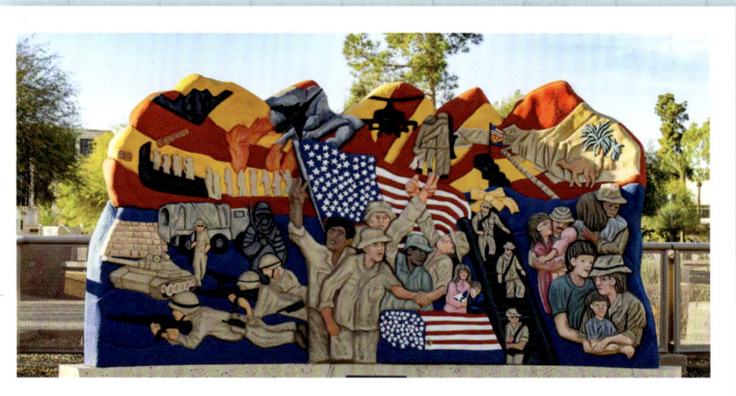

At Wesley Bolin Memorial Plaza, visitors can see memorials to those who fought for the United States in various wars and conflicts.

From there, keep heading east on Monroe Street to the Heritage and Science Park, which features both the Rosson House Museum from the Victorian era and the Arizona Science Center. Just across the street, you'll find the Children's Museum of Phoenix for a fun time for the under-10 crowd.

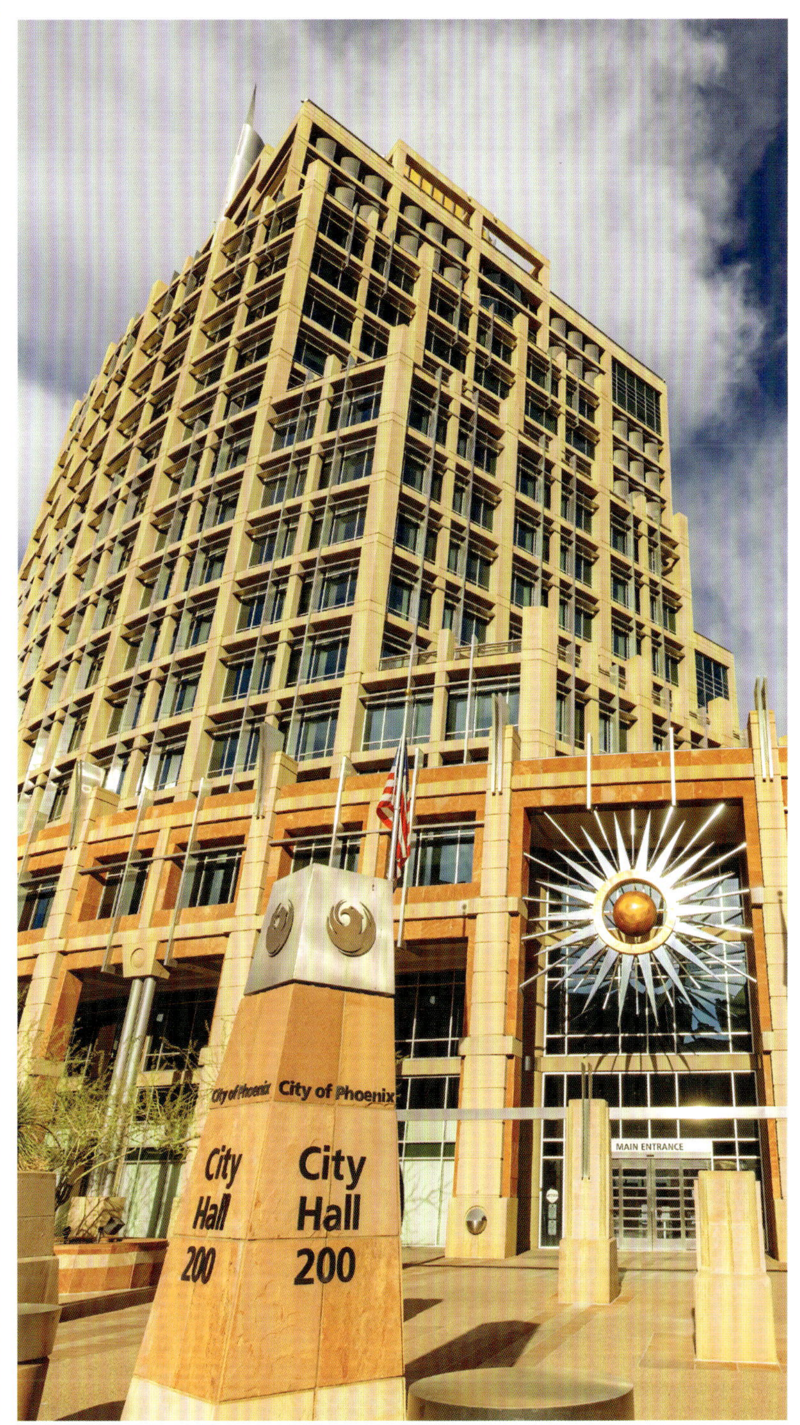

The current Phoenix City Hall building was constructed between 1992 and 1994.

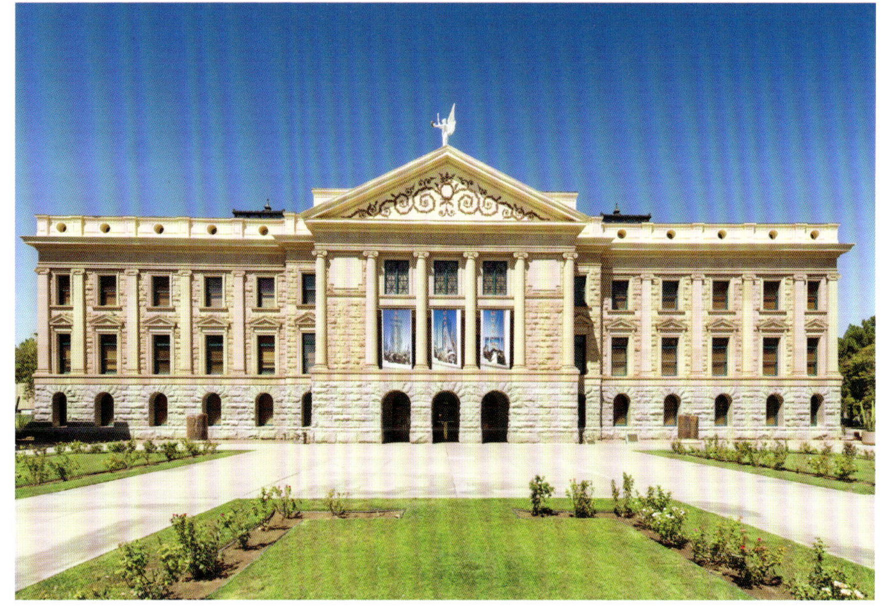

The oldest building on the Capitol grounds, now home to the Arizona State Capitol Museum, was built between 1899 and 1901. Among other artifacts, visitors can see ones related to the USS *Arizona* that was sunk at Pearl Harbor.

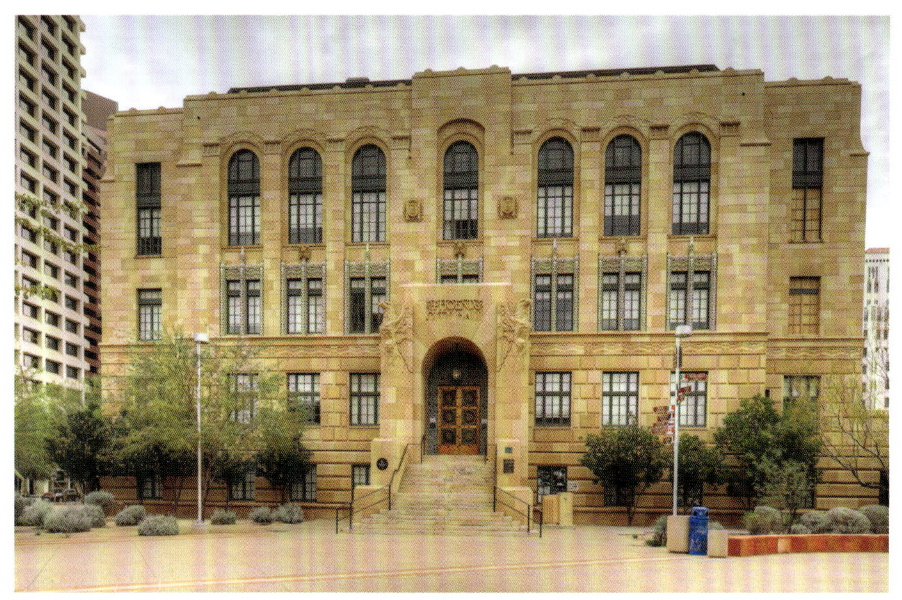

Now the Maricopa County Courthouse, the former City Hall building has elements of Spanish Colonial Revival architecture.

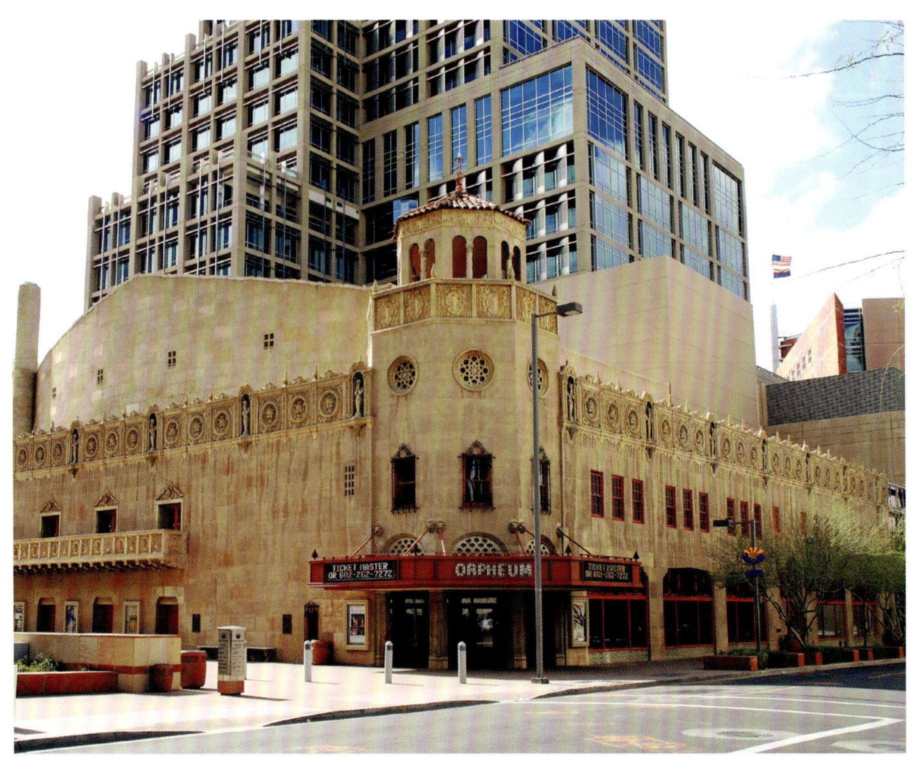

Like so many historical theaters, the Orpheum began life as a vaudeville theater, later falling into a state of disrepair before a revival.

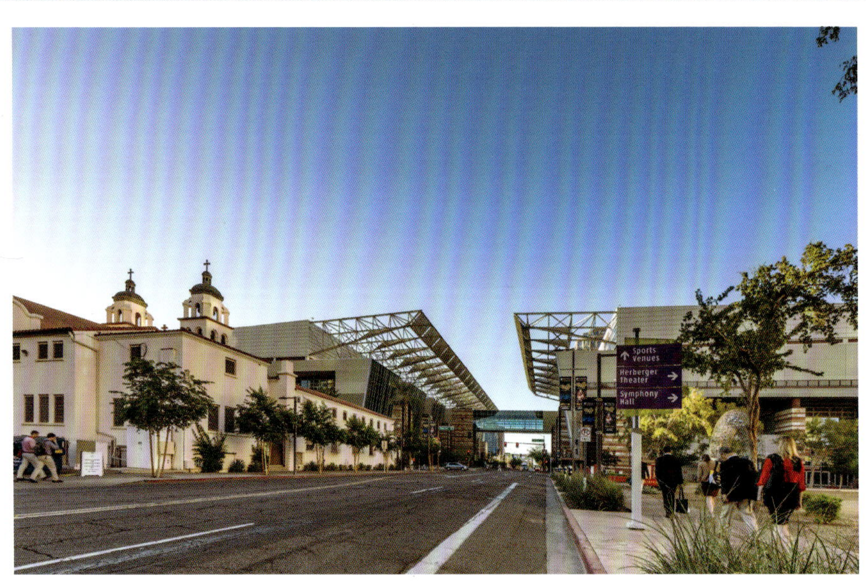

The Phoenix Convention Center includes several buildings on its campus.

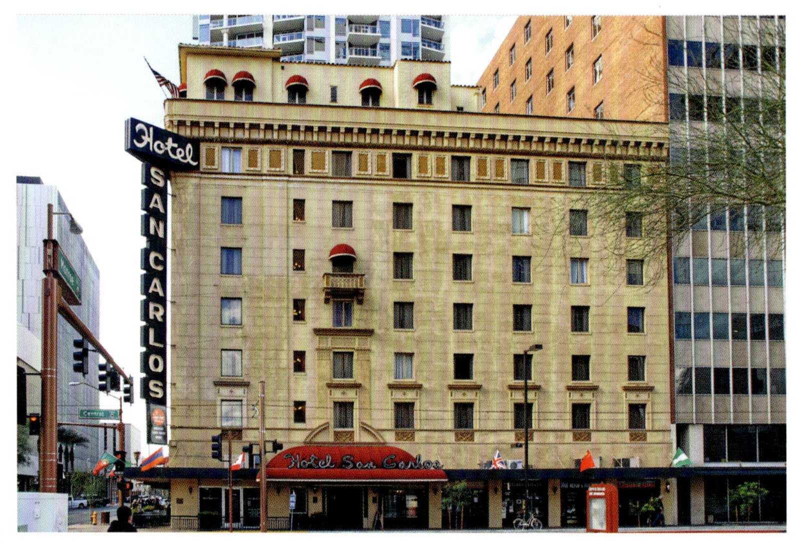

The Hotel San Carlos is reportedly haunted.

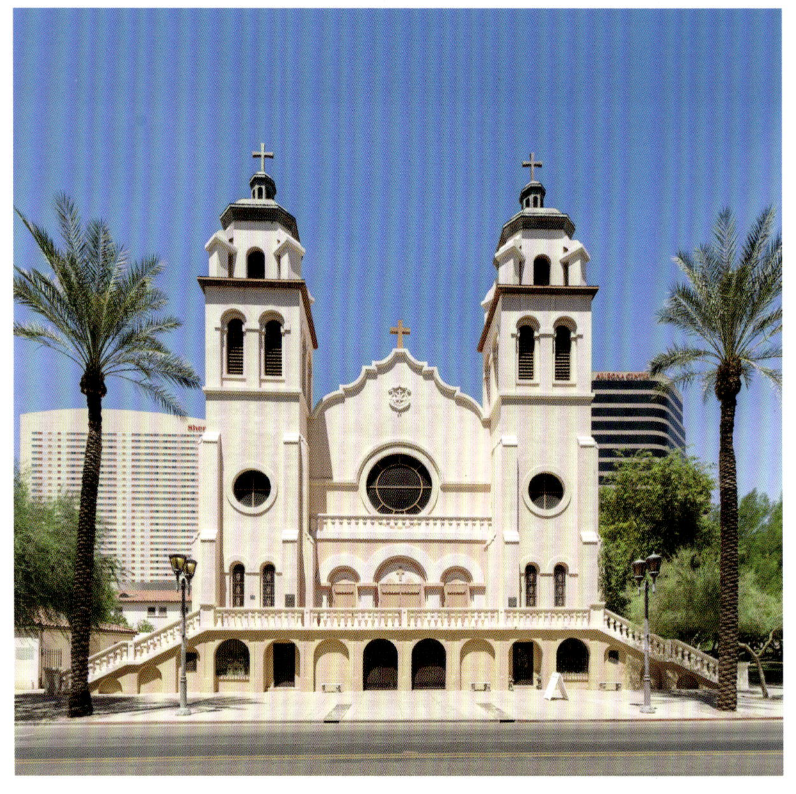

The architecture of St. Mary's Basilica has elements of both Mission Revival and Spanish Colonial Revival styles.

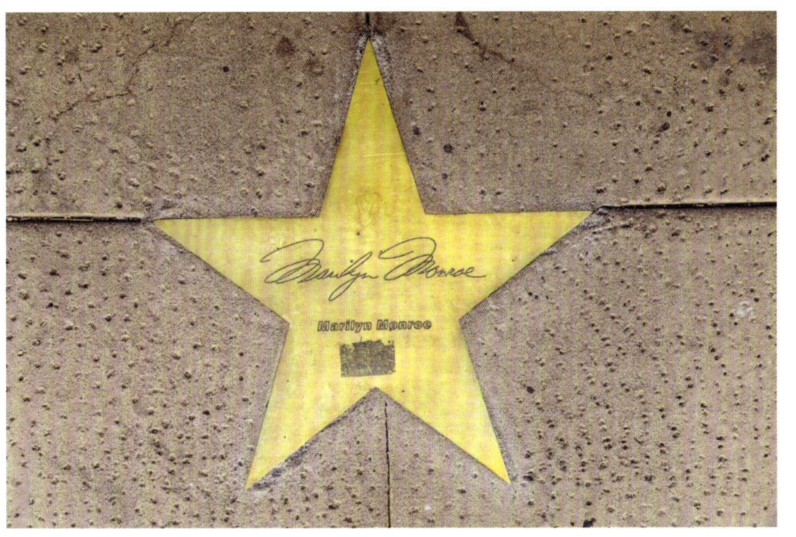

A number of Hollywood actors like Marilyn Monroe and Clark Gable stayed at the Hotel San Carlos, which features a "Star Walk" honoring its famous clientele.

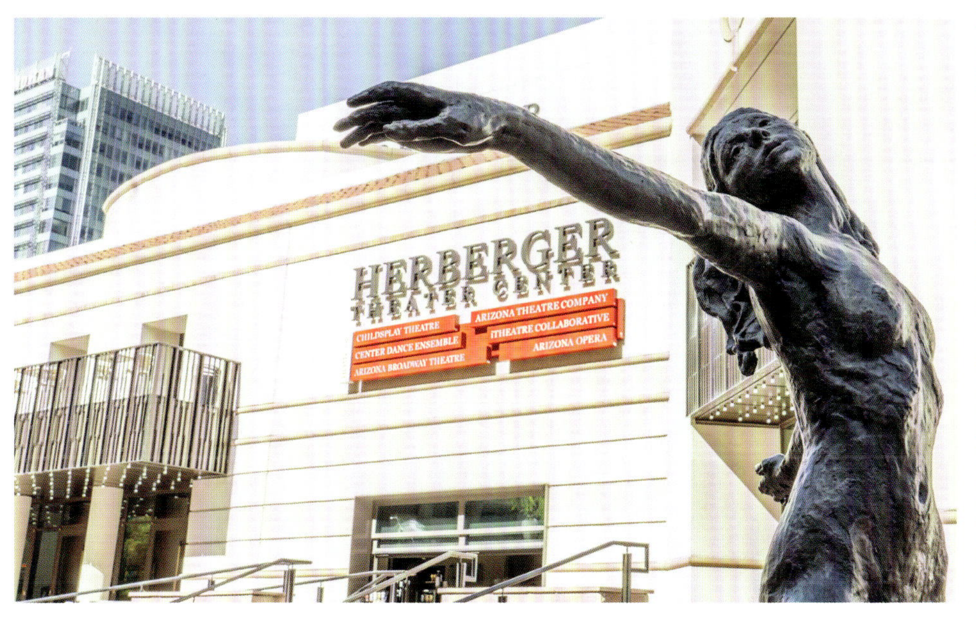

The Herberger Theater Center opened in 1989.

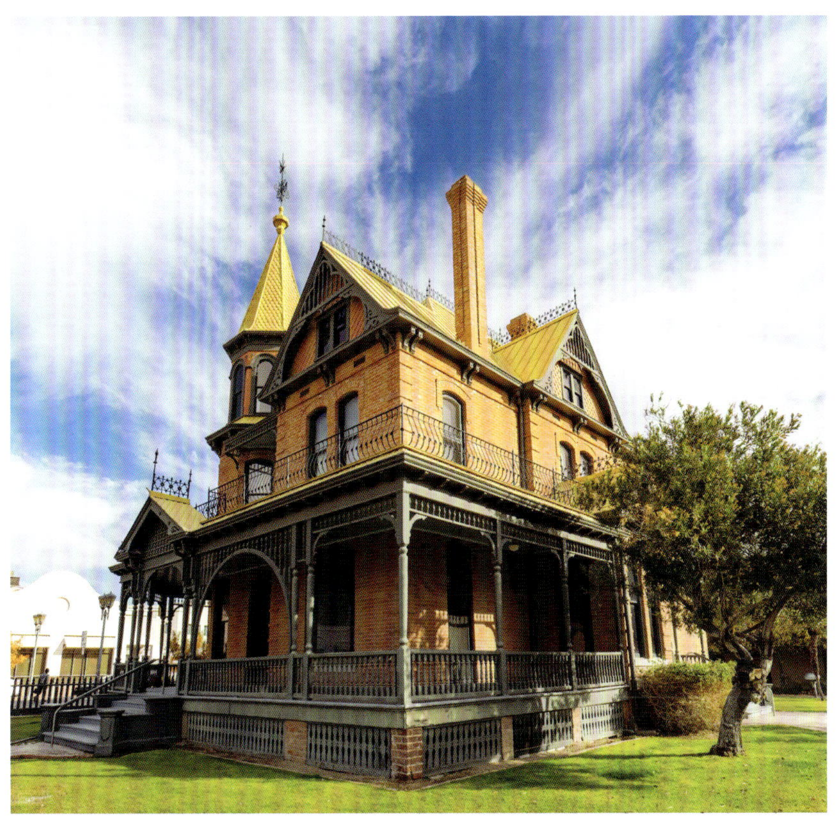

Rosson House, part of Heritage and Science Park along with the Arizona Science Center, was built between 1894 and 1895.

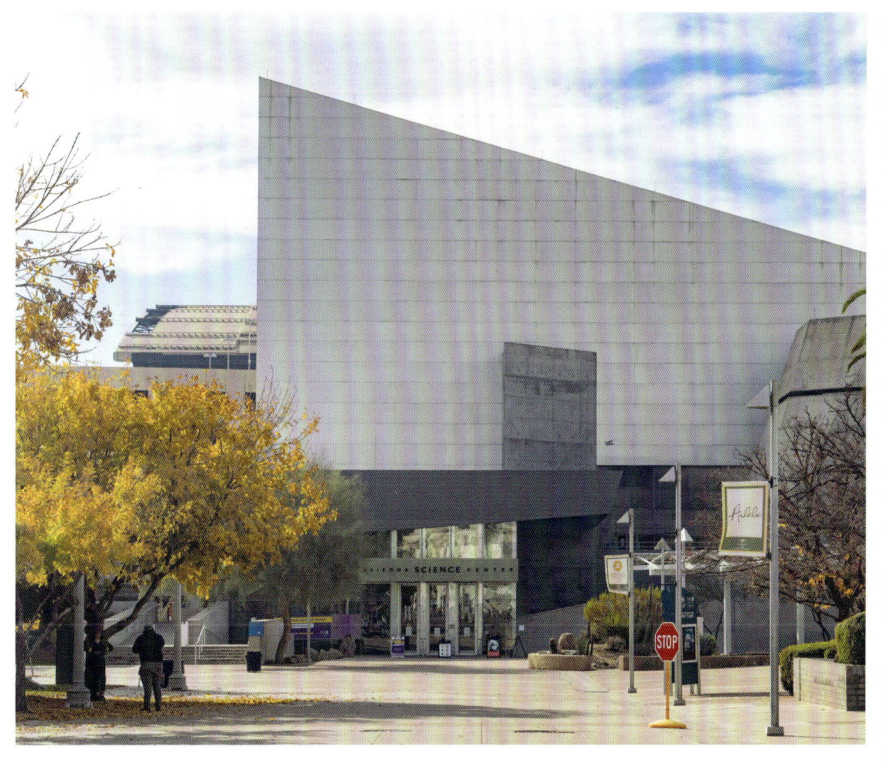

The Arizona Science Center moved to its current location in 1997.

Downtown Santa Fe

Location: Santa Fe, New Mexico
Length: About 2 miles
Start point: Georgia O'Keeffe Museum
End point: Canyon Road between Paseo de Peralta and Palace Avenue

New Mexico's state capital was founded in 1610, and its architecture reflects its centuries of history. The city is also known as an art haven, with artists working in a variety of mediums and styles, so it's appropriate that this walk starts with the Georgia O'Keeffe museum and finishes with a stroll down Canyon Road, a half-mile full of studios and galleries.

Born in Wisconsin, O'Keeffe began spending time in the southwest as an adult, and eventually moved to New Mexico. The Santa Fe branch of the Georgia O'Keeffe Museum includes pieces of her work from throughout her career. From there, head to the Santa Fe Plaza, a city square that was originally laid out during Spanish colonial times. A number of other points of interest are clustered on or near the Plaza, including the 1610 Palace of the Governors, the New Mexico History Museum, and the New Mexico Museum of Art.

Moving east along Palace Avenue from the Plaza, you'll find the IAIA Museum of Contemporary Native Arts at Cathedral Place, along with the cathedral that gave the road its name: the Cathedral Basilica of St. Francis of Assisi. The current building dates to the 1880s and was built on the site of an earlier church. Outside, those who wish to do so can stroll through a prayer garden that features sculptures of the Stations of the Cross.

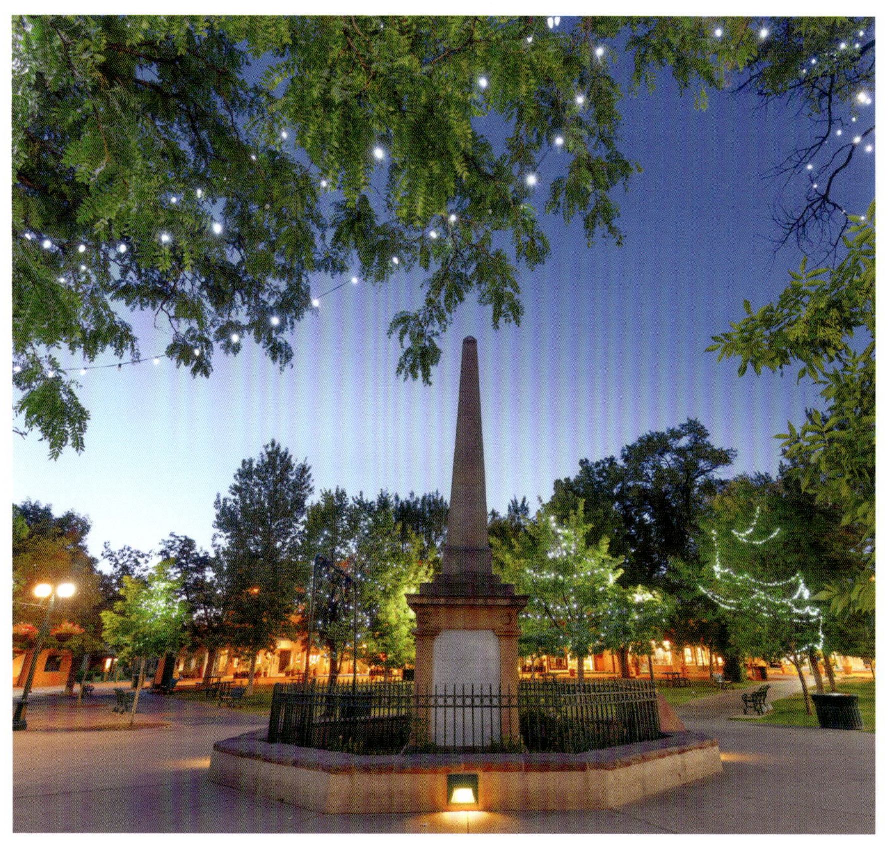

Santa Fe Plaza

Not far away is a nondenominational chapel, the Loretto Chapel, in an 1878 building. From Loretto Chapel, walk south down Old Santa Fe Trail until you reach De Vargas Street, where you'll see the San Miguel Chapel that dates to 1610—by some claims, the oldest church in the contiguous United States. Across the street is an adobe house that may be the oldest in Santa Fe, although its actual age is unknown. Continuing east on De Vargas, you'll encounter Canyon Road, packed with art galleries, restaurants, and shops.

Points of Interest

Georgia O'Keeffe Museum

Santa Fe Plaza

New Mexico Museum of Art

Palace of the Governors

New Mexico History Museum

IAIA Museum of Contemporary Native Arts

The Cathedral Basilica of St. Francis of Assisi

Loretto Chapel

De Vargas Street House

San Miguel Chapel

Canyon Road

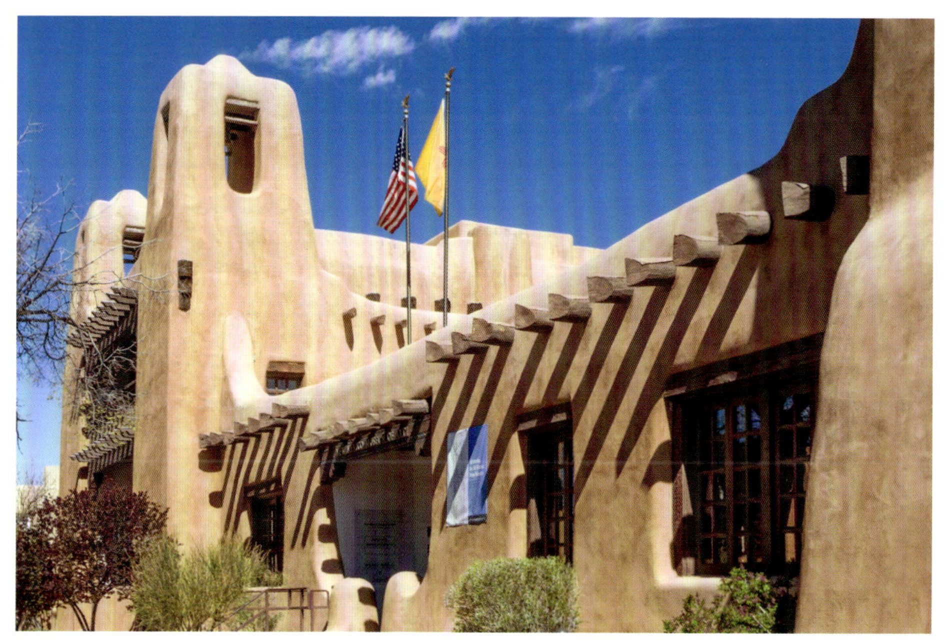

The New Mexico Museum of Art has extensive collections of more than 20,000 pieces of art. Its building dates to 1917.

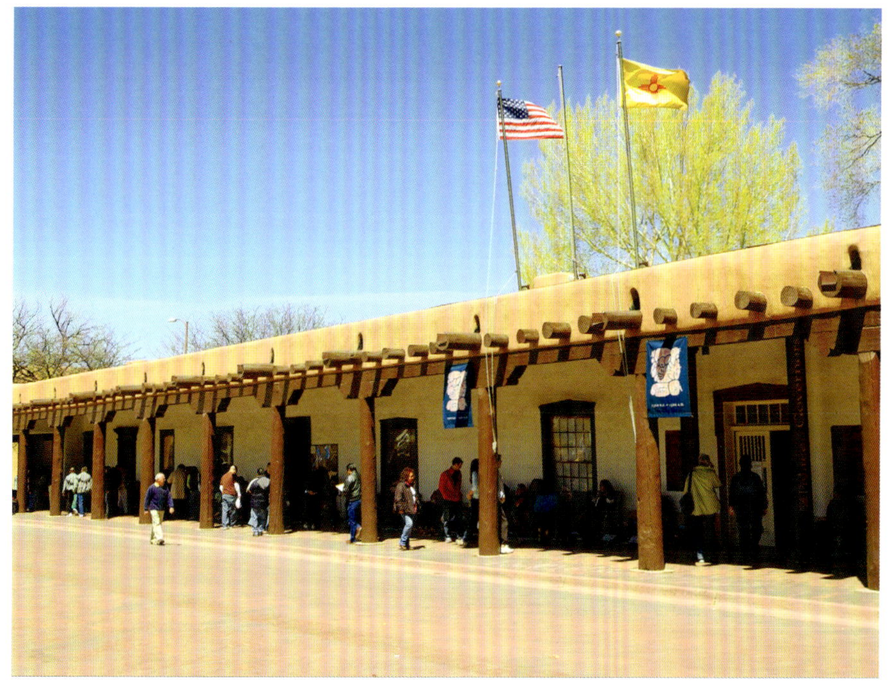

Vendors sell jewelry and artwork in front of the Palace of the Governors.

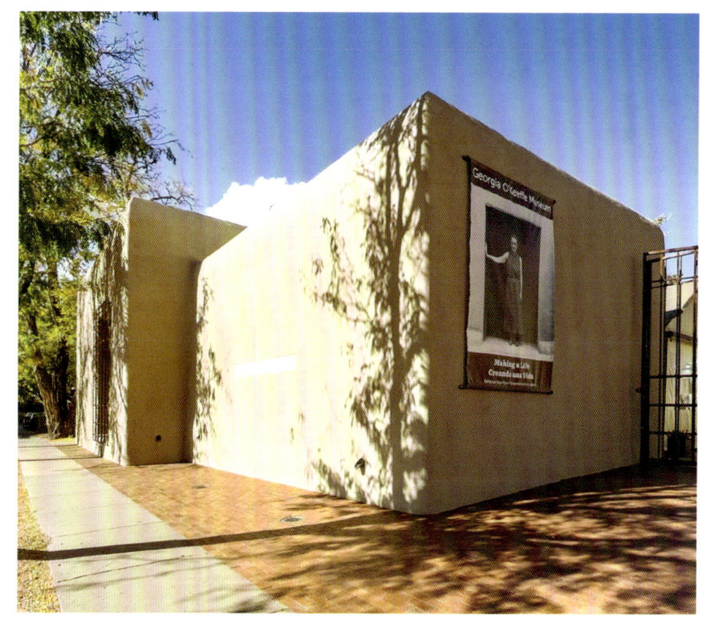

The Georgia O'Keeffe Museum is split between two locations where the artist lived: Abiquiu and Santa Fe.

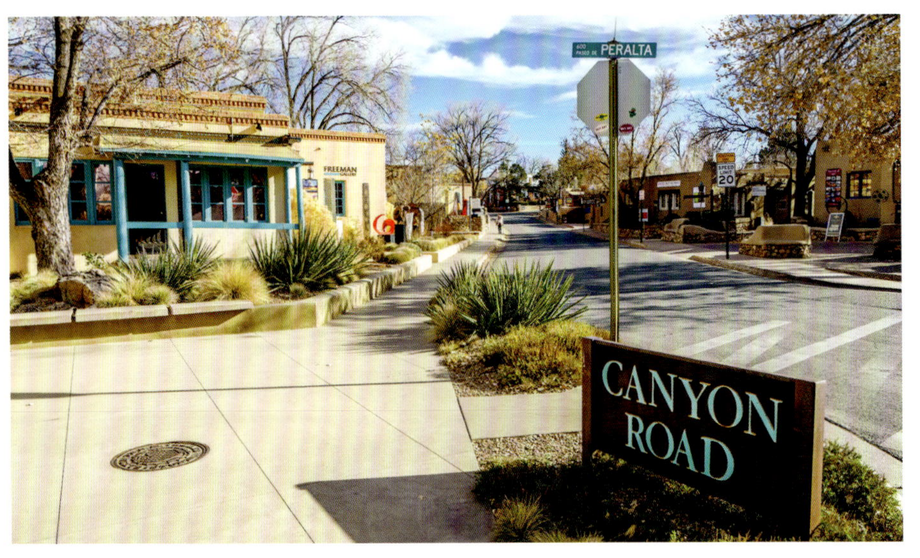

Browse pottery, sculptures, jewelry, and paintings on Canyon Road.

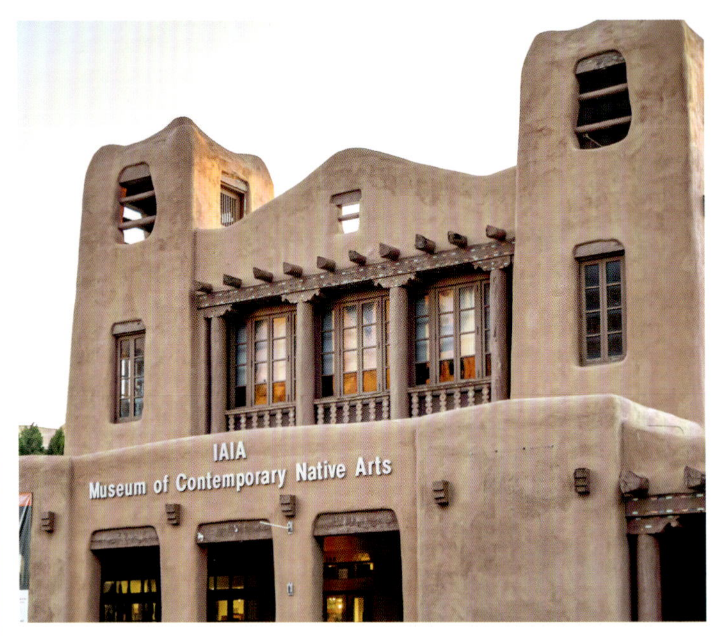

The Institute of American Indian Arts, a college, runs the Museum of Contemporary Native Arts to showcase contemporary work.

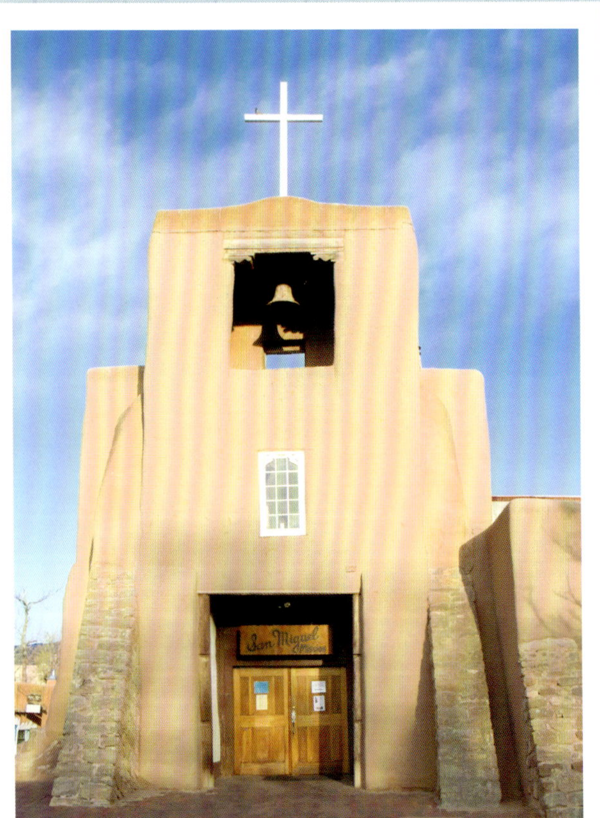

San Miguel, a mission church, was originally built in 1610 and renovated over time.

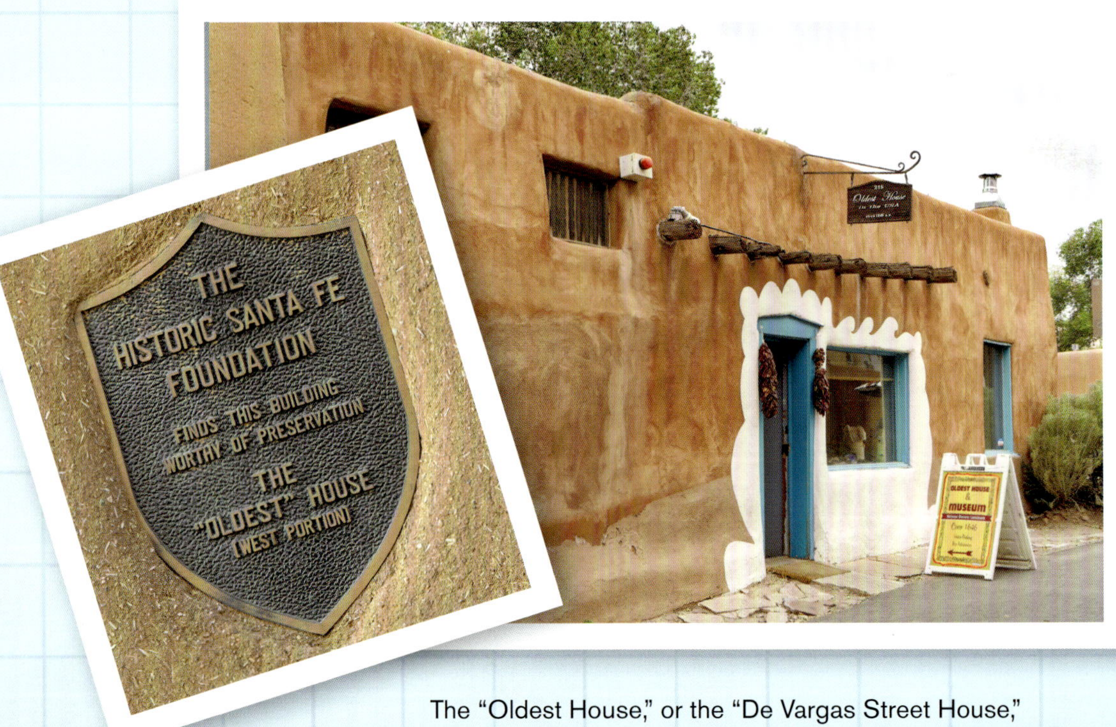

The "Oldest House," or the "De Vargas Street House," reportedly rests on a Pueblo foundation from about 1200.

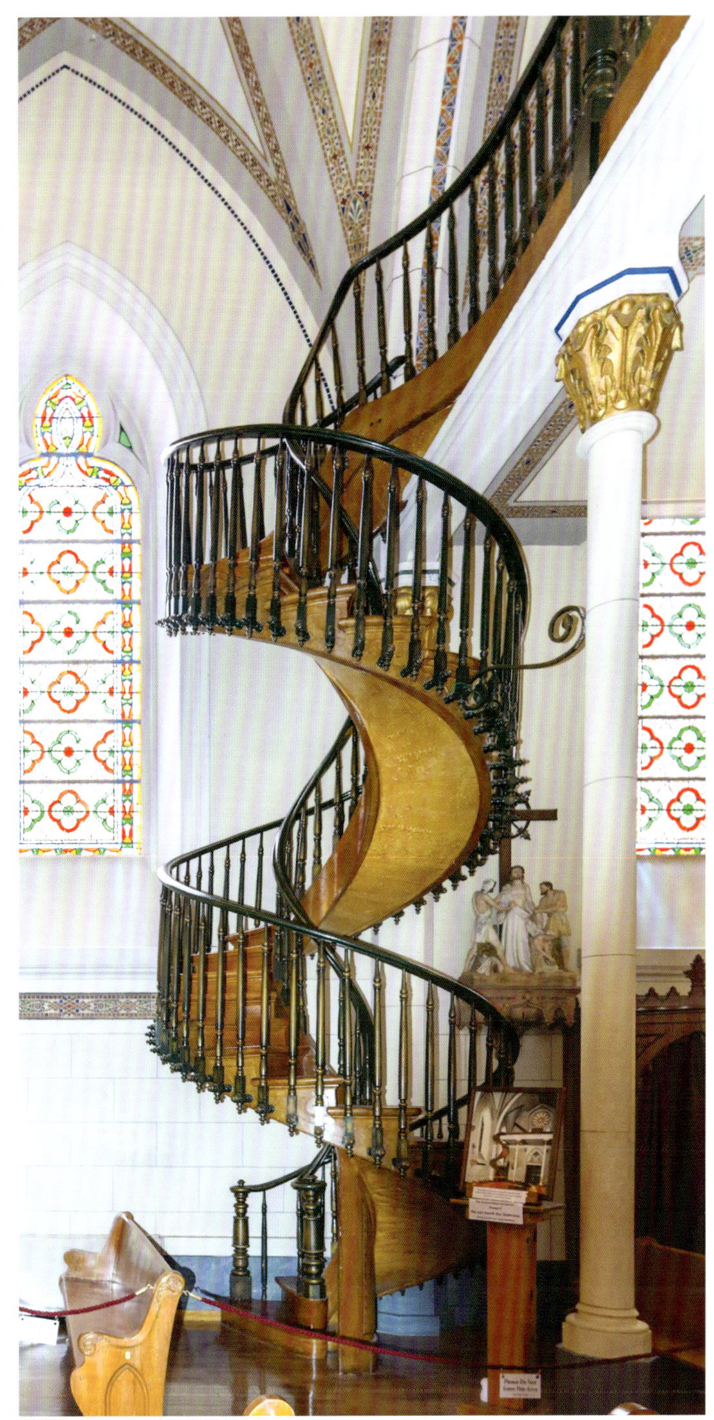

Inside the Loretto Chapel is an elaborate wooden spiral staircase that does not use any central pole. It's been dubbed the "Miraculous Staircase" for the mystery of its building.

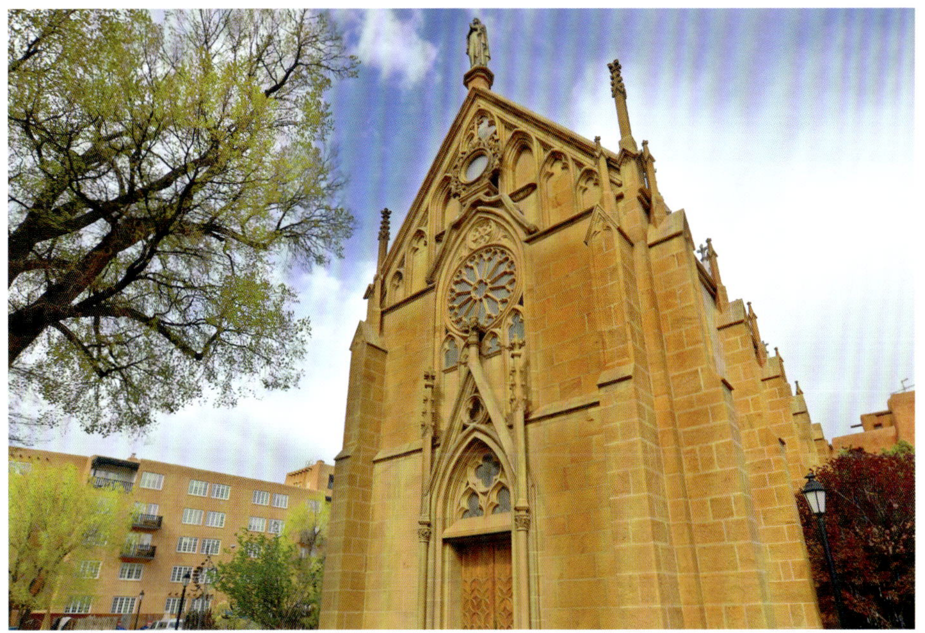

Once a Catholic church but now a nondenominational chapel, the Gothic Revival Loretto Chapel offers tours and is used as a space for events and weddings.

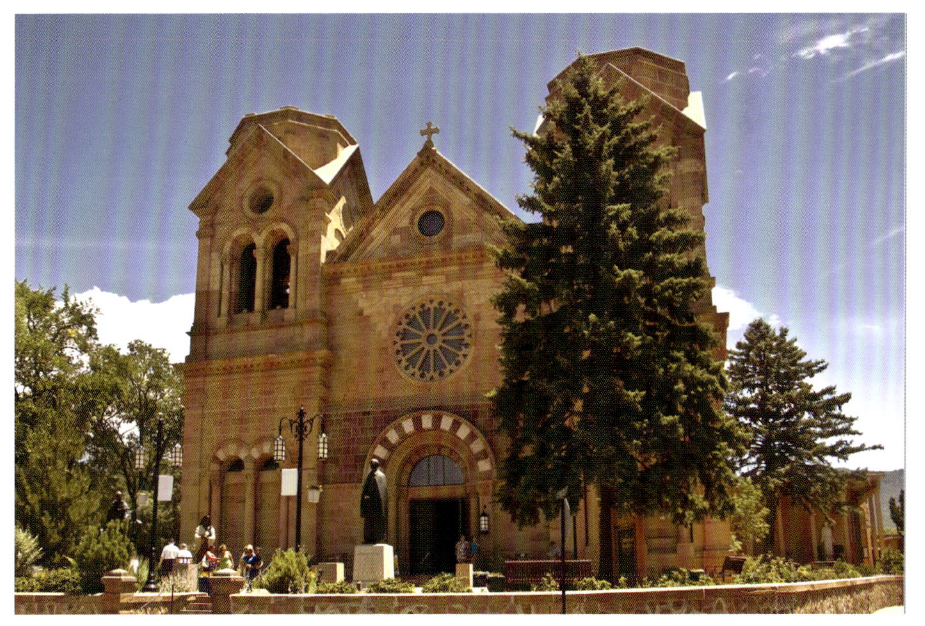

The Cathedral Basilica of St. Francis of Assisi was designed in Romanesque Revival style.

Plaza to Plaza Walk

Location: Albuquerque, New Mexico
Length: About 1.3 miles
Start point: Civic Plaza
End point: Old Town Plaza

A marked trail in the city of Albuquerque takes walkers from a modern public plaza to a much older one, offering an insider's glimpse at the city and its long history. A map and guide with explanatory text for each location are available through visitalbuquerque.org.

The walk features buildings in a mix of eras and architectural styles. The Luciano Duran House is a very old house built sometime before 1850, while the William Lyon House and the Trumbull-Hesselden House both date to the 1880s. The W. E. Mauger House and the Kate Nichols Chaves House both come from the early 1900s, the latter the work of an early woman architect, Kate Nichols. The Stamm House, in Arts and Crafts style, was built in 1912.

However, there are also examples of more modern architecture. The Lew Wallace School, built in 1934, began as a project of the Works Progress Administration during the Depression, while the Office Complex that's the second stop on the route is done in mid-century modernist architecture. A sculpture midway through the route by Federico Armijo, as well as the "Las Mesas" bus stop, were both projects of the city's "1% for Arts" program in 1983.

The walk is bracketed by two plazas. Old Town Plaza was built by the Spanish in 1706, with the San Felipe de Neri Church that is located on the plaza dating to 1793. In close vicinity to the plaza, you'll find a visitor center, plenty of shops, the Albuquerque Museum, and—if you dare—the Rattlesnake Museum.

Points of Interest

Civic Plaza
Office Complex
Lew Wallace School
W. E. Mauger House
Fourth Ward Historic District
William Lyon House
Whitmer-McKinnon House
Kate Nichols Chaves House
Trumbull-Hesselden House
Stamm House
Mary Fox Park
JJ Megs House
Federico Armijo Sculpture
Course of Acequia Madre de Albuquerque
Adobe House at 1803 Lomas NW
"Las Mesas" Bus Stop
Luciano Duran House
House at 1913 Lomas NW
San Felipe School Playground
Bottger House
Cristobel, Armijo House, San Felipe & South Plaza
Old Town Plaza

At Civic Plaza, you'll find City Hall and the Al Hurricane Pavilion, named after the musician who fostered the New Mexico style of music, while nearby is the Albuquerque Convention Center.

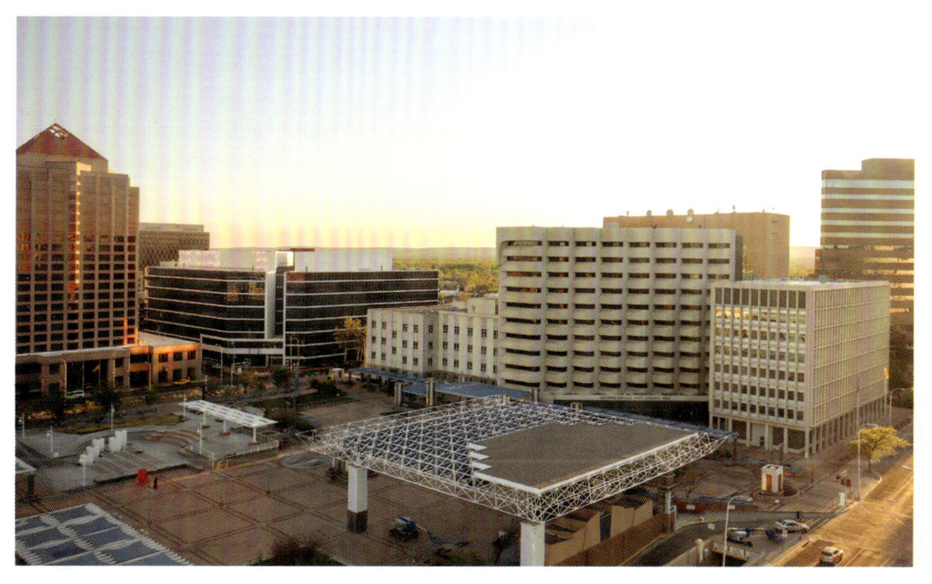

This photograph shows Albuquerque's Civic Plaza, with the open-air Al Hurricane Pavilion and stage in the foreground.

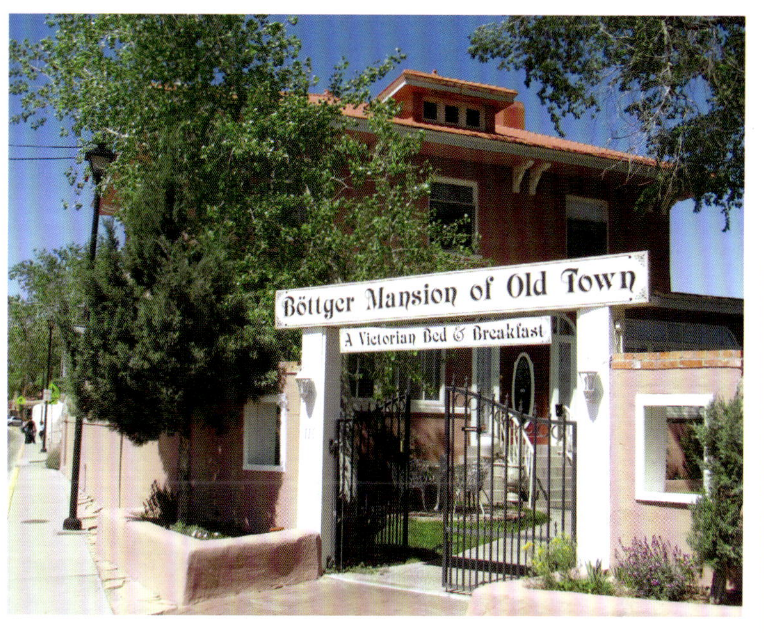

The Charles A. Bottger House, now a bed and breakfast, was built between 1910 and 1912.

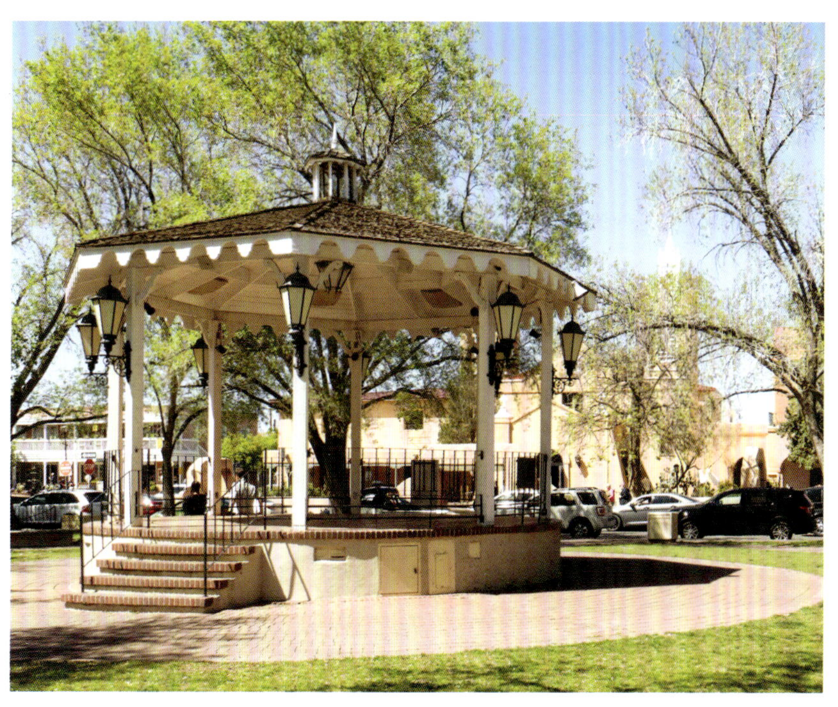

Take a picture at the gazebo in Old Town Plaza!

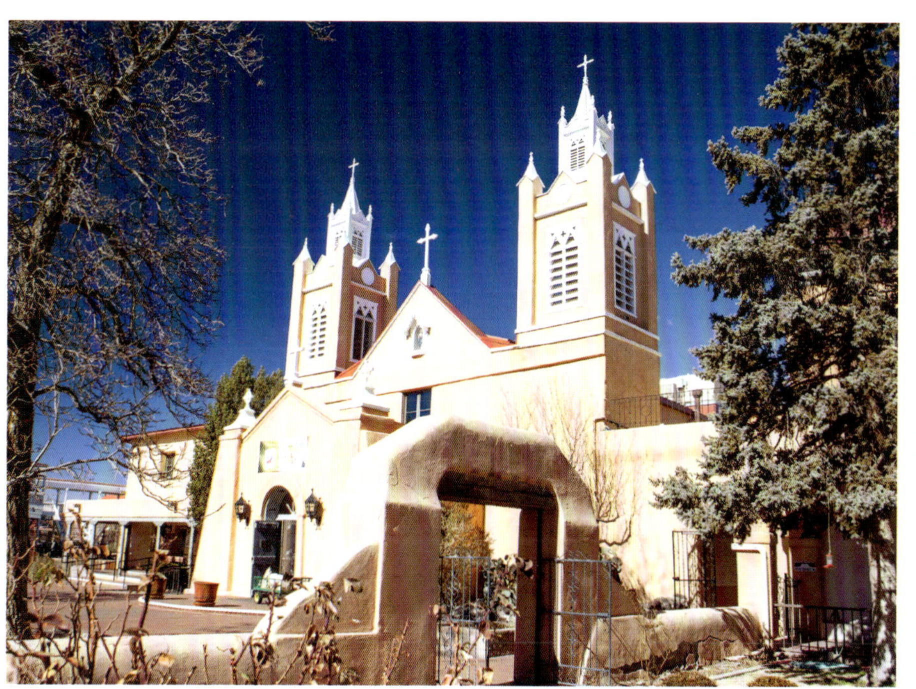

San Felipe de Neri church was built in 1793, although some later renovations added Gothic Revival elements. The church's associated buildings–a rectory, convent, and school–were built mainly between the 1870s and 1890s.

The Las Vegas Strip

Location: Near Las Vegas, Nevada
Length: 4.2 miles
Start point: Sahara Avenue
End point: Russell Road

El Rancho Vegas, the first full-service casino and hotel in Las Vegas, Nevada, opened April 3, 1941, on Highway 91. Its success led to the massive development of the Las Vegas Strip, a 4.2-mile portion of Las Vegas Boulevard filled with hotels, casinos, restaurants, entertainment venues, high-rise living quarters, and fancy resorts. Today the Strip—it's technically just south of the Las Vegas city limits, in the unincorporated towns of Paradise and Winchester—attracts tourists worldwide and serves as the region's economic lifeline.

A leisurely amble along the Strip offers plenty of sights to see and things to do—and lots of shopping opportunities. The hotels along the Strip provide any number of attractions, from the Mandalay Bay's Shark Reef Aquarium to the Bellagio's Botanical Gardens to performances at the Colosseum, a performing arts theater at Caesars Palace. There's even a roller coaster at New York-New York Hotel & Casino, and an indoor theme park at Circus Circus.

Walking the Strip in the summer months is not recommended because of the intense heat, especially during the day. Even in cooler months, remember to bring water with you. A daytime walk will generally be more family-friendly and less crowded; an evening walk offers great views of the city lit up, and also has more of a party atmosphere. Some of the hotels are connected by internal walkways, so you can opt to do parts of your walk inside: For example, you can get from Mandalay Bay to the Luxor to Excalibur without leaving air-conditioned comfort.

Points of Interest

Various hotels, casinos, performing arts venues, shops, and restaurants
Las Vegas Convention Center
Siegfried & Roy Monument
The Rat Pack Memorial Plaque
Fountains at the Bellagio
Eiffel Tower and Arc de Triomphe at Paris Las Vegas
Miracle Mile Shops
ARTE Museum Las Vegas
Replica Statue of Liberty at New York-New York

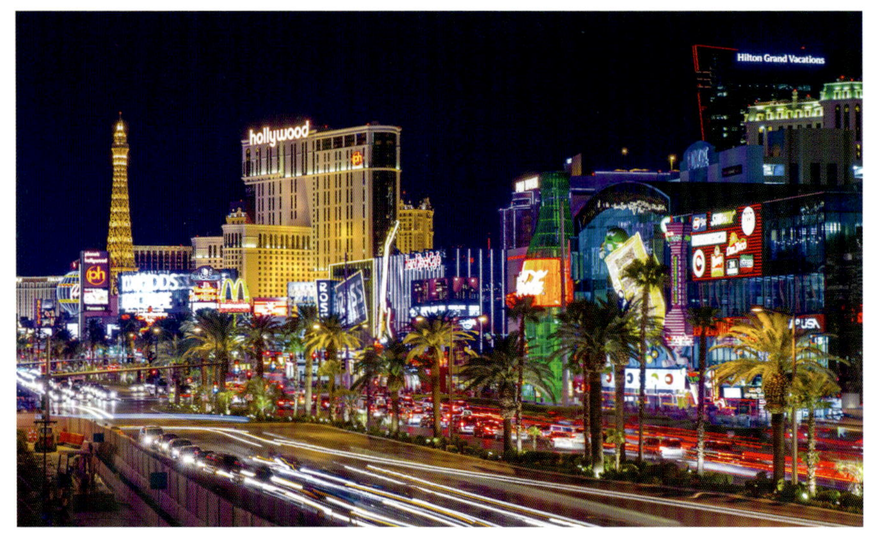

At night, the Strip lights up in neon colors.

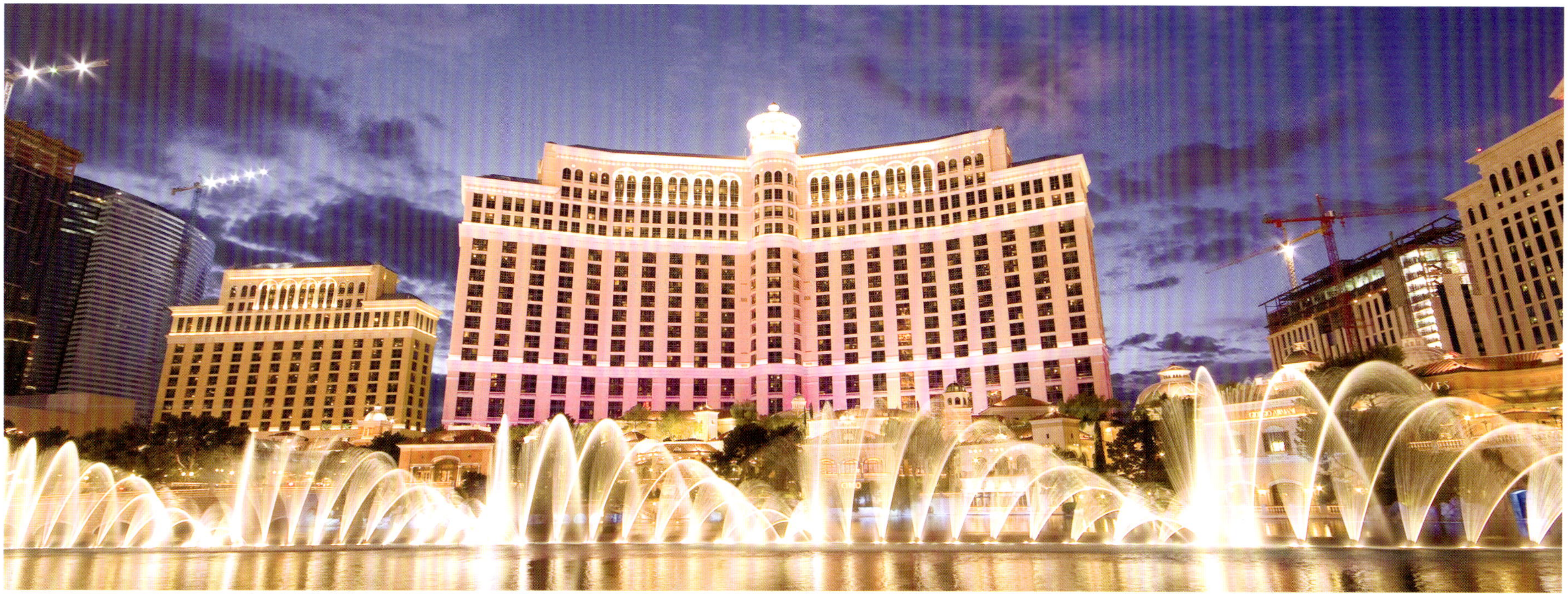

The choreographed show of music, lights, and water of the Fountains of Bellagio is a Vegas must-see. The free show is scheduled regularly during afternoons and evenings.

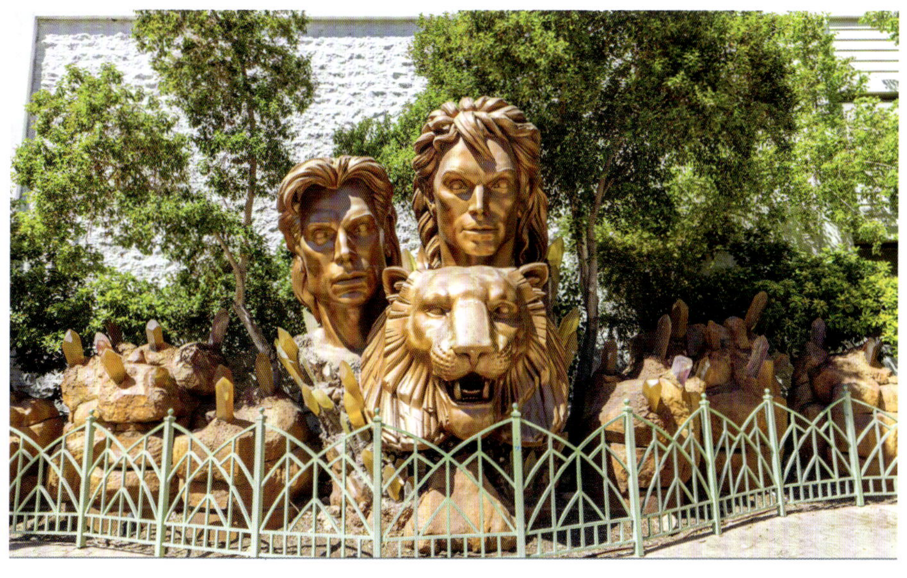

A monument to the entertainers Siegfried and Roy is found near the Mirage Casino.

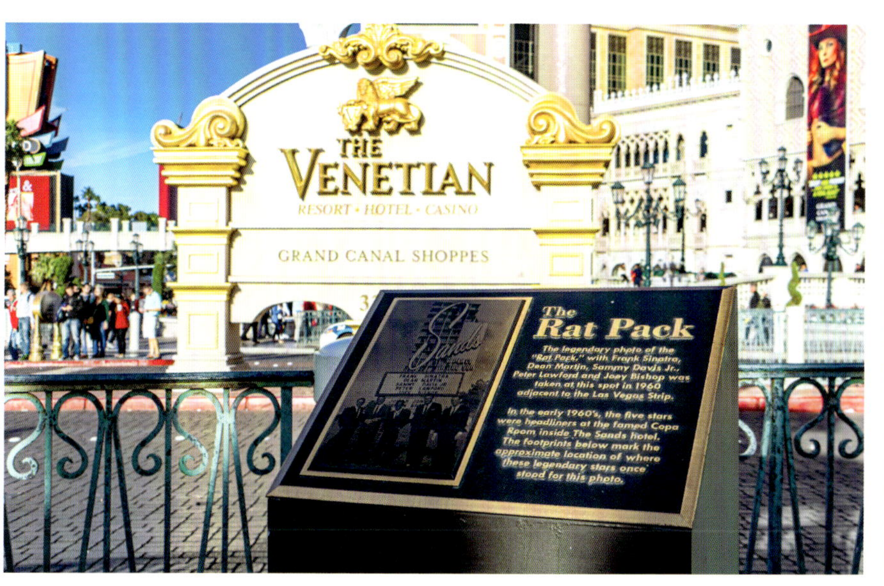

The singers of the Rat Pack all put on shows in Las Vegas in the 1960s and starred in the original 1960 version of *Ocean's 11*.

Seattle Center to Pike Place

Location: Seattle, Washington
Length: About 2 miles
Start point: Seattle Center
End point: Pike Place Market

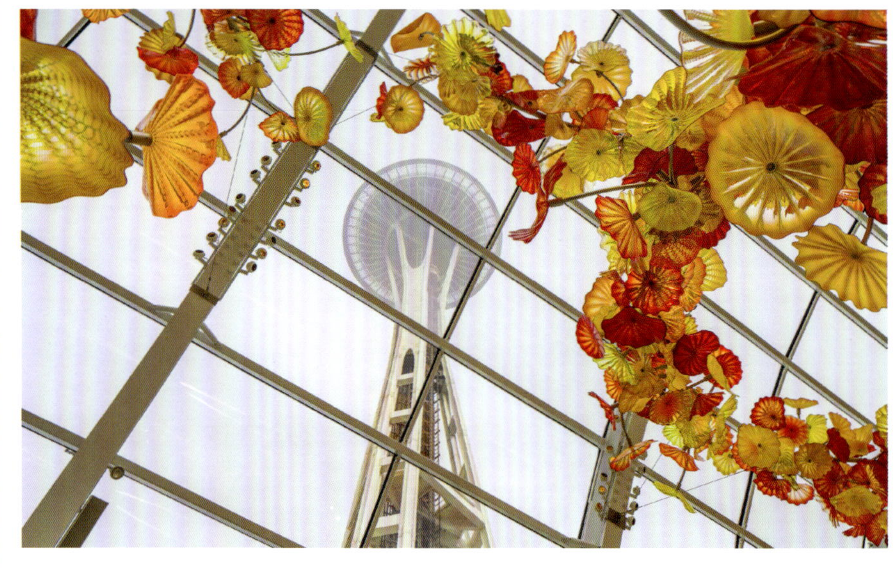

Glassblowing artist Dale Chihuly was born in Tacoma and has deep roots in the state of Washington.

In 1962, Seattle hosted the Century 21 Exposition—the World's Fair—and built the iconic tower of the Space Needle, a monorail, and a number of other buildings in the process. The former fairgrounds are now the home of the Seattle Center, a space with many event venues and museums for all ages. Several of the buildings can trace their roots to or even before that World's Fair. The Washington State Coliseum, built for the Fair, has been renovated over the decades into today's Climate Pledge Arena. The Civic Auditorium that was remodeled for the Fair into the Seattle Opera House has become McCaw Hall.

Along with the Space Needle, the Seattle Center is a cultural powerhouse with a number of different event venues and theaters, including the stages of the Seattle Repertory Theatre; the Cornish Playhouse; and the SIFF Film Center. For interactive learning, families can check out the Pacific Science Center and the Seattle Children's Museum, and the Artists at Play Playground for sheer fun. For those who appreciate visual art, there's the Chihuly Garden and Glass exhibit and the Museum of Pop Culture (MoPOP).

Scattered throughout the campus, there are gardens, plazas, sculptures, and water features. The International Fountain, for example, was a carryover from the World's Fair that was redone in the 1990s. The Kobe Bell Meditation Garden is based around a bell that was a gift from Seattle's sister city in Japan for the World's Fair.

You could spend several days just exploring the various attractions of the Seattle Center. For a manageable one-day itinerary and a good walk, go up the Space Needle, check out one of the museums, and spend some time wandering the grounds before eating lunch at the food court in the Armory building. Then head towards Puget Sound until you reach Olympic Sculpture Park. The Seattle Art Museum opened this free outdoor sculpture museum in 2007, and it's a beautiful place to explore, plus you can get great waterfront views.

The last stop on the walk is the Pike Place Market, another Seattle staple that's been open since 1907. As well as the famous fish market, visitors can find many kinds of foods and crafts. Plan your day so that you arrive in advance of 5 PM, when many of the shops close, although restaurants may be open later.

Points of Interest

- McCaw Hall
- SIFF Film Center
- Climate Pledge Arena
- International Fountain
- Artists at Play Playground
- Museum of Pop Culture
- Seattle Children's Museum
- Chihuly Garden and Glass
- Seattle Children's Theatre
- Pacific Science Center
- Space Needle
- Olympic Sculpture Park
- Puget Sound
- Pike Place Market

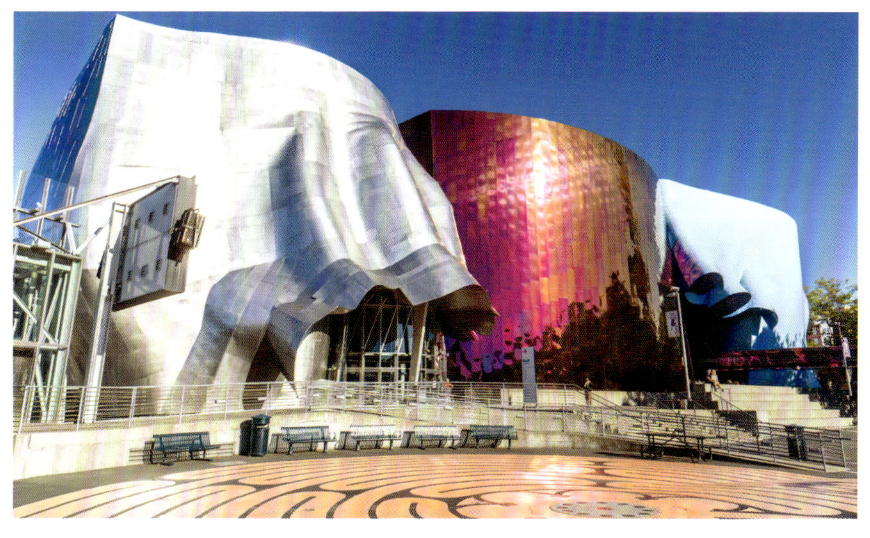

Frank Gehry designed the building that houses the Museum of Pop Culture.

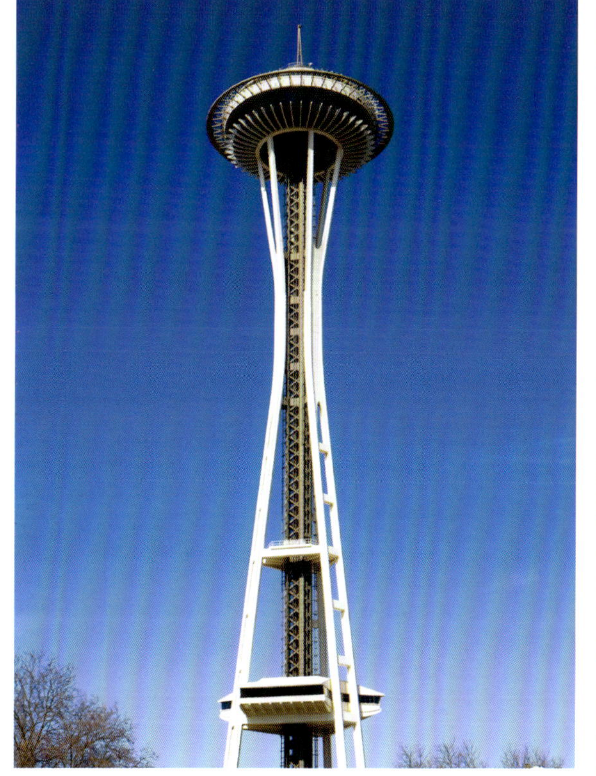

The Cold War Space Race was in full swing at the time of the 1962 World's Fair, which helped inspire the design of the flying saucer-shaped Space Needle.

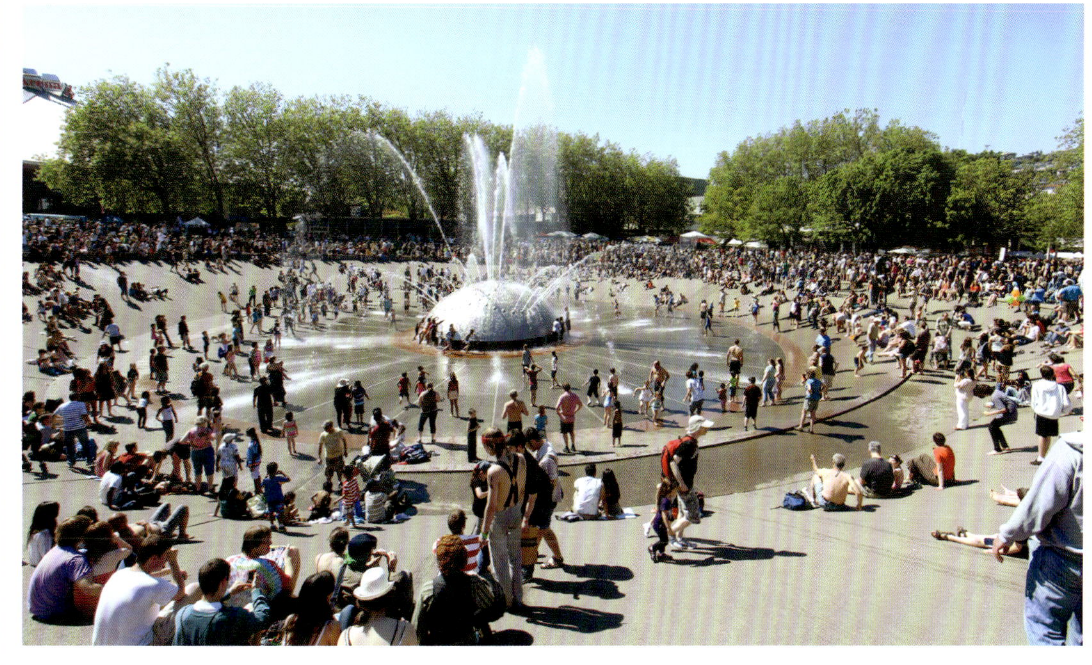

Expect crowds at the Seattle Center and the International Fountain.

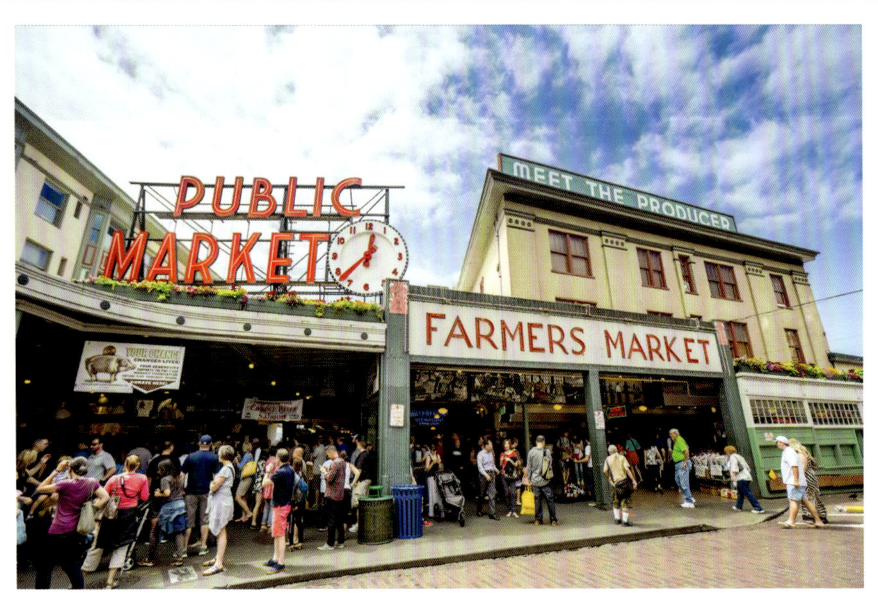

As well as buying fresh produce at the Farmer's Market at Pike Place Market, visitors can browse for crafts and other goods.

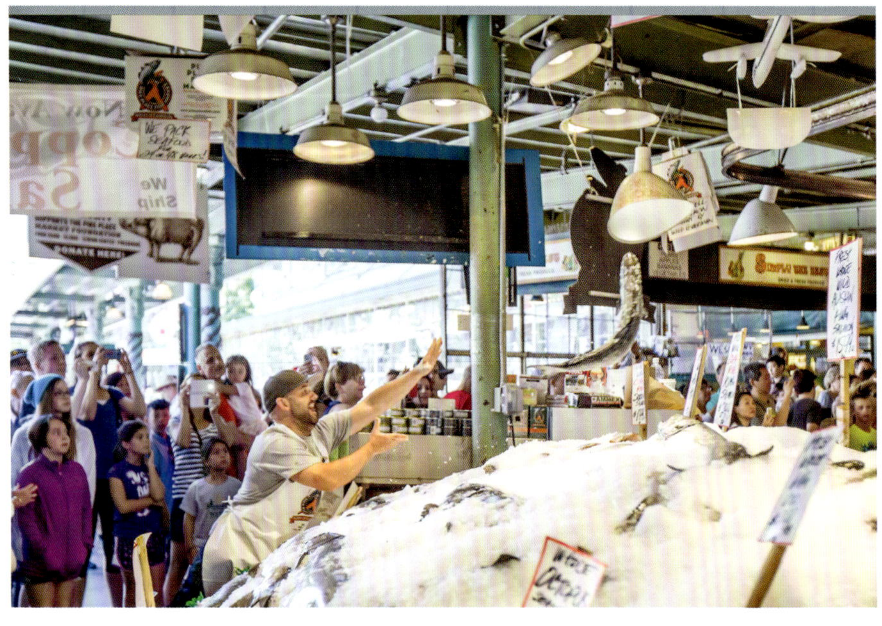

At the Pike Place Fish Market, the throwing of fish has become a tradition and a tourist favorite.

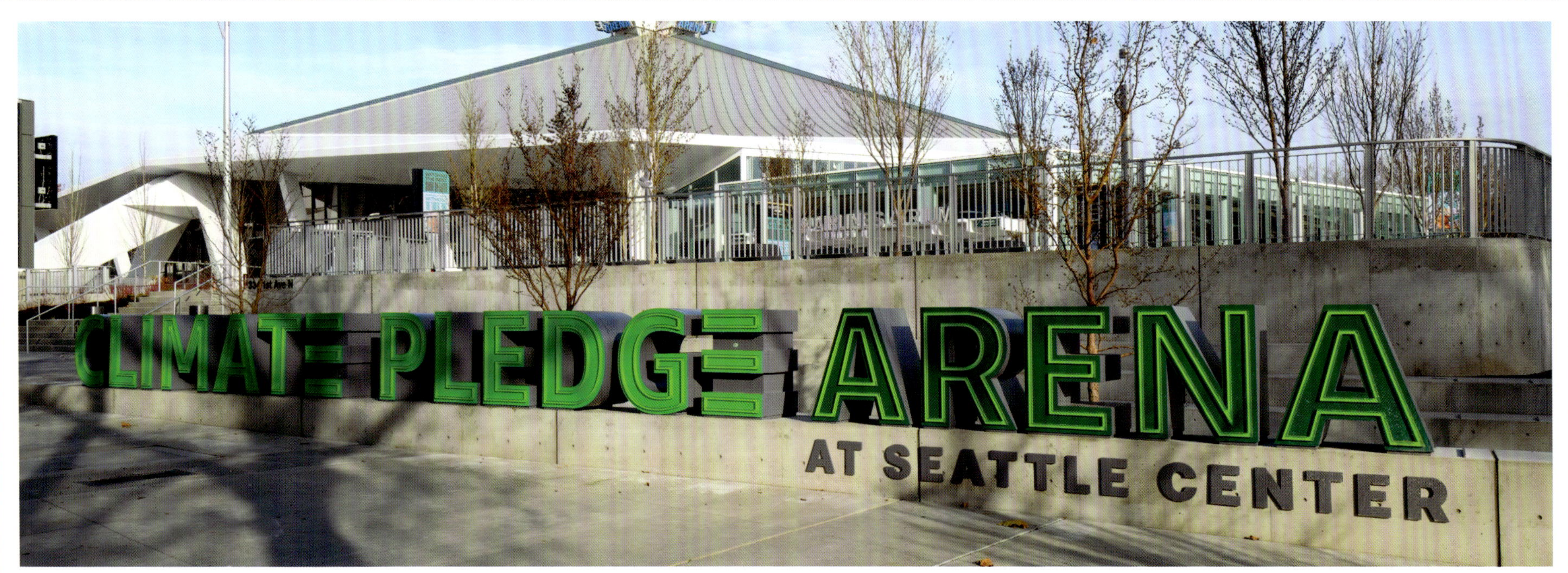

Hockey fan? The Seattle Kraken play from Climate Pledge Arena.

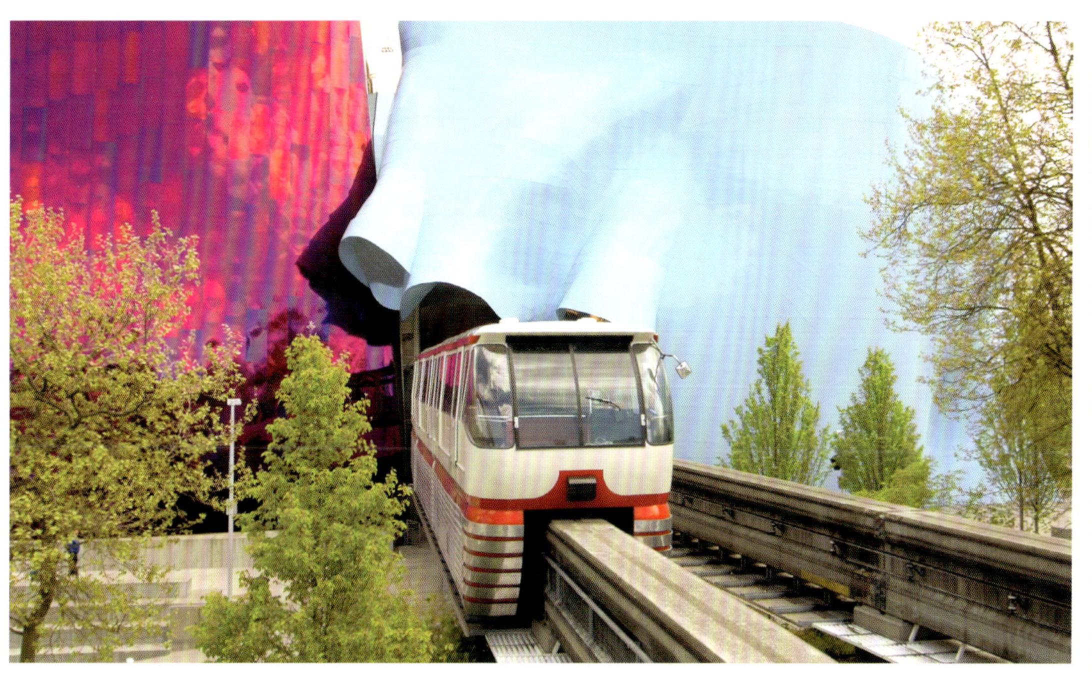

The monorail built for the Seattle World's Fair runs through the Museum of Pop Culture.

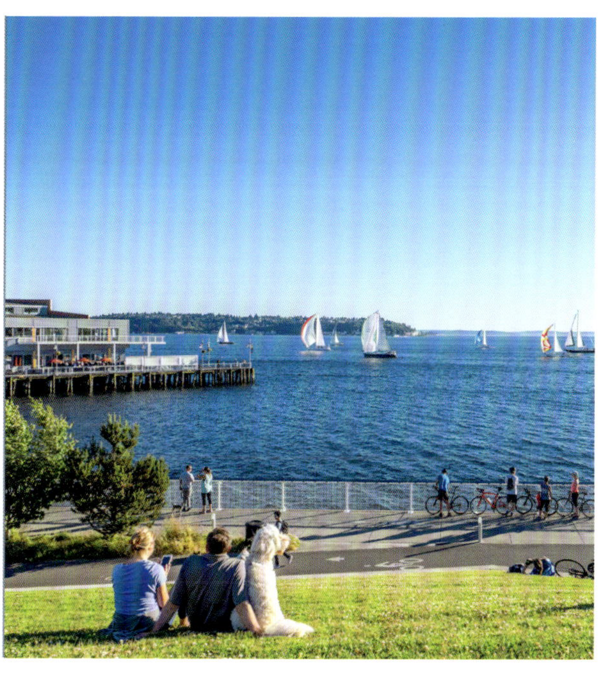

Olympic Sculpture Park is close to the waterfront of Puget Sound.

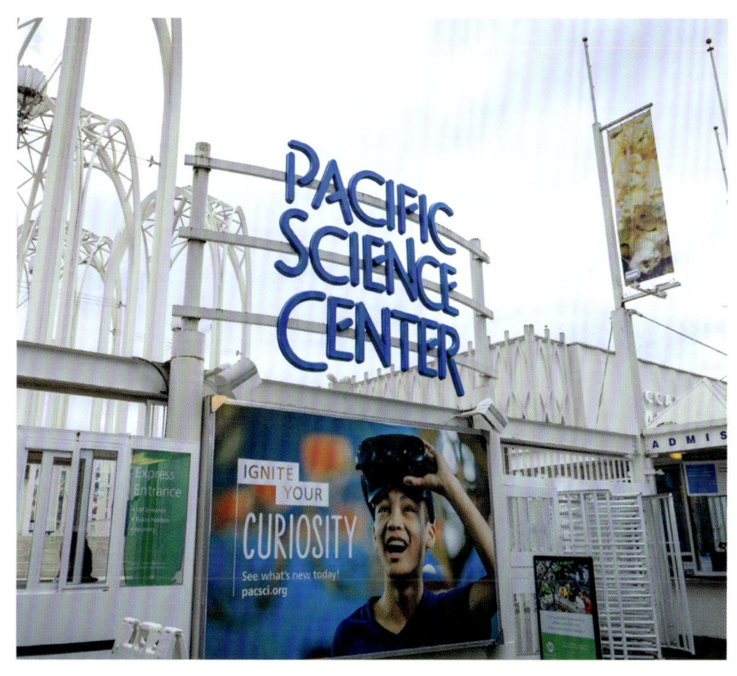

Sights at the Pacific Science Center include a planetarium, two IMAX theaters, and a Laser Dome show.

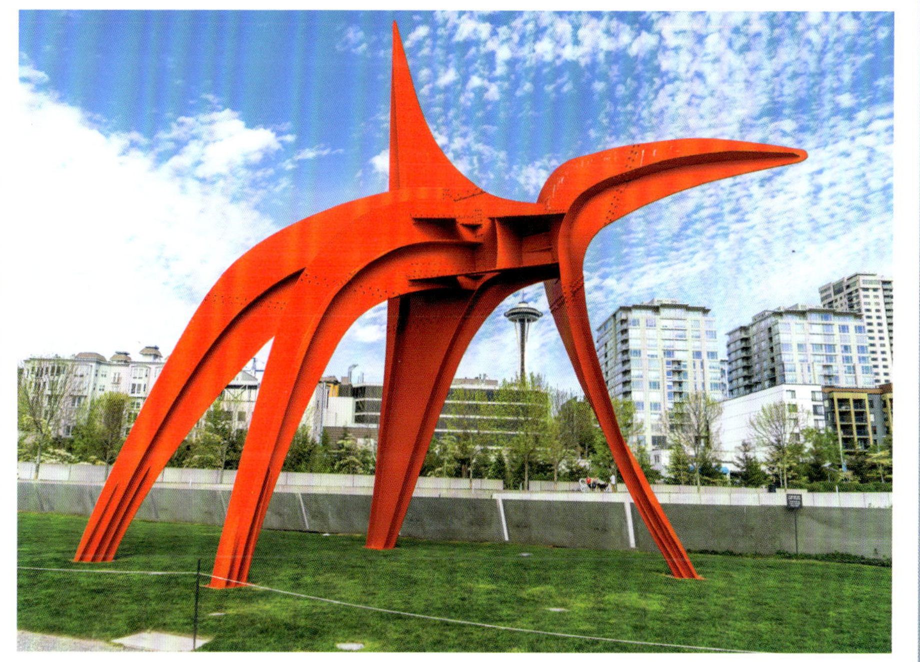

Alexander Calder's *Eagle* at Olympic Sculpture Park

Washington Park

Location: Portland, Oregon
Length: Variable; the park is 400 acres and offers 15 miles of trails
Northern boundary: Burnside Road
Southern boundary: I-26

Points of Interest

Oregon Holocaust Memorial
Secret Garden
Washington Park Amphitheater
Portland Japanese Garden
International Rose Test Garden
Redwood Observation Deck
Hoyt Arboretum
Vietnam Veterans of Oregon Memorial
Oregon Zoo
World Forestry Center Discovery Museum

As far back as the 1870s, parts of what is now Washington Park were set aside by the city of Portland as "City Park." Trails and gardens were added over the next few decades, and the area became known as Washington Park in 1909.

Today, the large urban park is a place where you can spend the day wandering, sometimes up hills of fairly steep elevation. If you tire at any point, a free shuttle loops around the park's major destinations.

Two large gardens, the Portland Japanese Garden and the International Rose Test Garden, are both found in the same general area in the northeastern section of the park. The Portland Japanese Garden features several smaller, peaceful spaces, like the Strolling Pond Garden, the Sand and Stone Garden, and the Tea Garden. The International Rose Test Garden contains more than 10,000 rose bushes, with peak blooming season in the summer months. Moving towards the middle of the park, the Hoyt Arboretum is the place to see conifers and offers trails at multiple levels of hiking difficulty, along with a Bamboo Forest. The Oregon Zoo is found in the southernmost part of the park, near the World Forestry Center Discovery Museum.

Along with the larger attractions listed at top right, you'll also come across various monuments and pieces of public art, like the 1904 Chief Multnomah memorial statue; an 1891 fountain called the Chiming Fountain; and the 1908 Lewis and Clark Memorial Column.

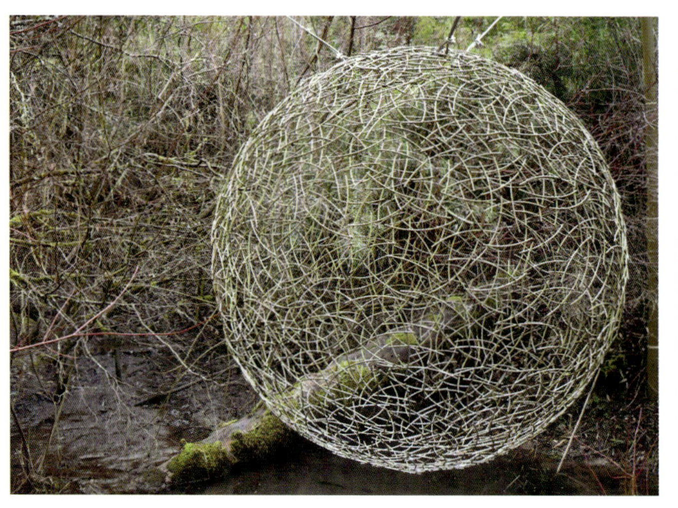

The 2016 sculpture *Basket of Air* by Ivan McClean can be found in the Bamboo Forest at Hoyt Arboretum, and is just one piece of art that can be spotted at Washington Park.

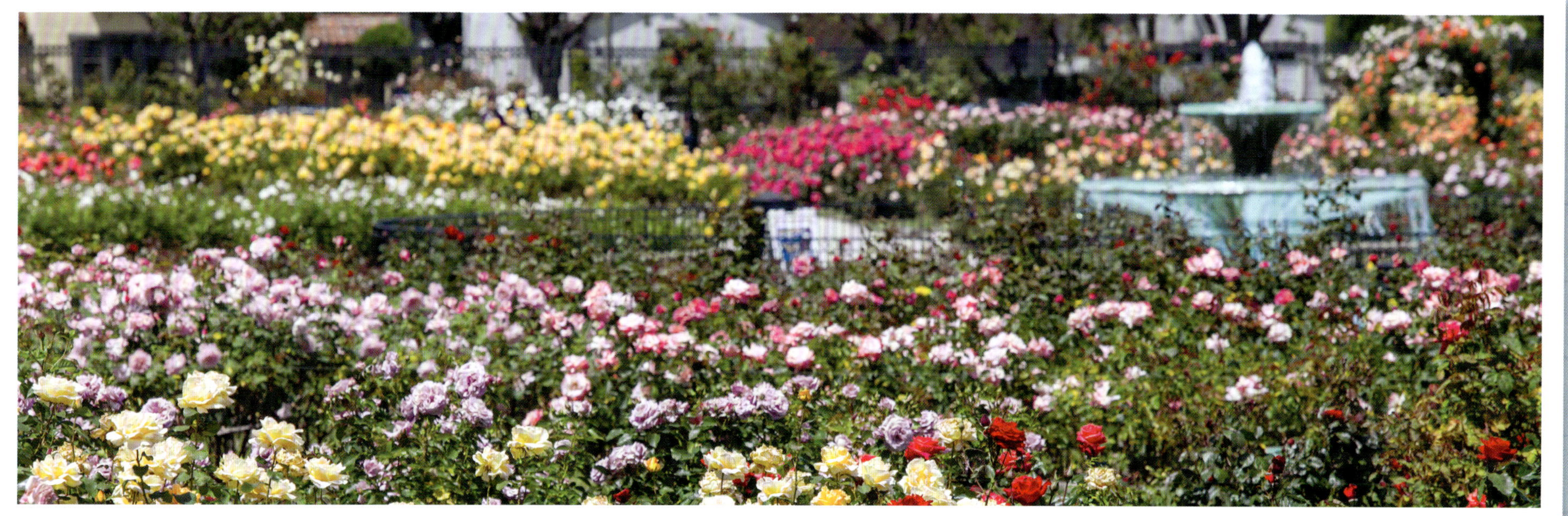

More than 600 varieties of roses are cultivated at the International Rose Test Garden.

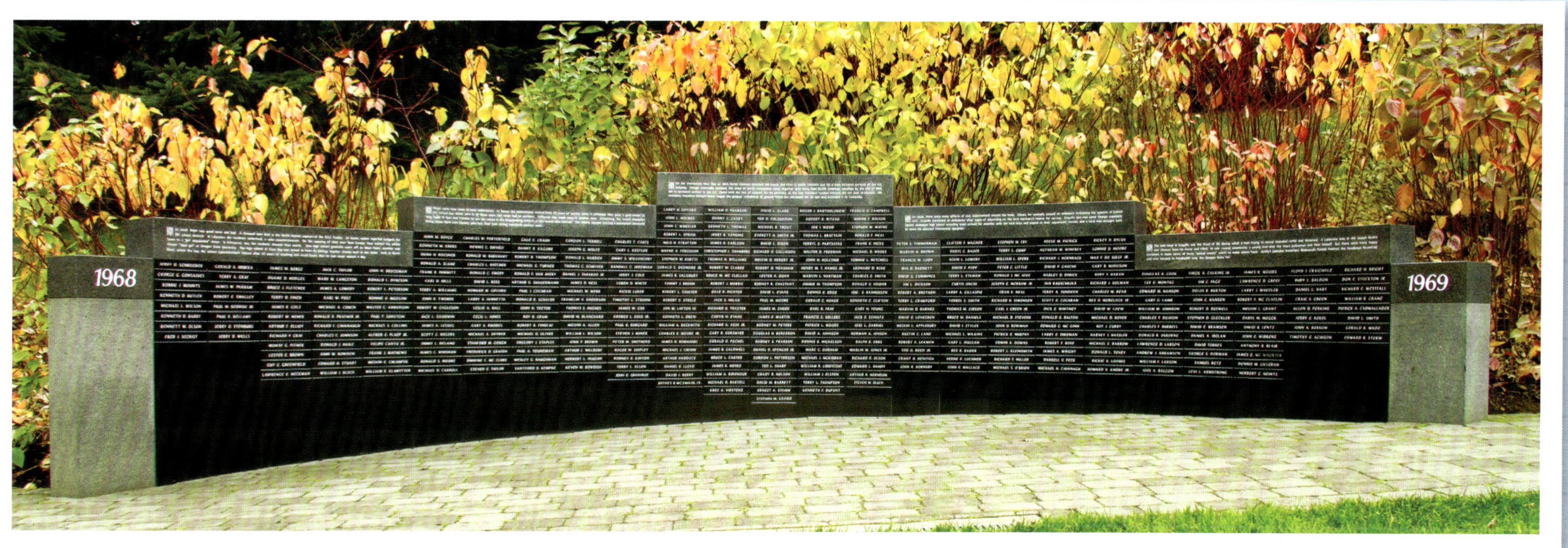

The Oregon Vietnam Veterans Memorial was installed in 1987. The 8-acre space includes an amphitheater and the Garden of Solace, as well as this wall listing the names of Oregonians who died or went missing in action.

Golden Gate Park

Location: San Francisco, California
Length: Distance from western to eastern boundary is more than 3 miles
Eastern boundary: Stanyan Street
Western boundary: Great Highway (on the Pacific Ocean)

A part of San Francisco since 1870, Golden Gate Park is a sprawling urban park of more than 1,000 acres. The park has numerous trails running through its various parts, and the car-free JFK Promenade stretches through much of the park—although certain sections do still have vehicle traffic, and walkers do need to keep a sharp eye out for bicyclists and skaters.

On its eastern edge, the park abuts the Haight-Ashbury neighborhood, for those visitors who want to start their walk by rambling through those quirky streets. On its western edge, the park gets quite close to the Pacific Ocean, so you can finish your walk with views of the shorelines. Along the way, as well as the attractions listed here, you'll see sculptures, picnic areas, soccer and polo fields, gardens, playgrounds, meadows, a golf course, and scenic lakes.

For a shorter walk, explore only the eastern half of the park, which features the museums and botanical garden. The park also provides a free shuttle through many of the most popular destinations in its eastern half, so you can walk in one direction and then take the shuttle back to your origin point.

Golden Gate Park includes the M. H. de Young Memorial Museum, which includes collections from around the world of contemporary art, textiles, and costumes. The California Academy of Sciences, by contrast, focuses on natural history and even includes a planetarium.

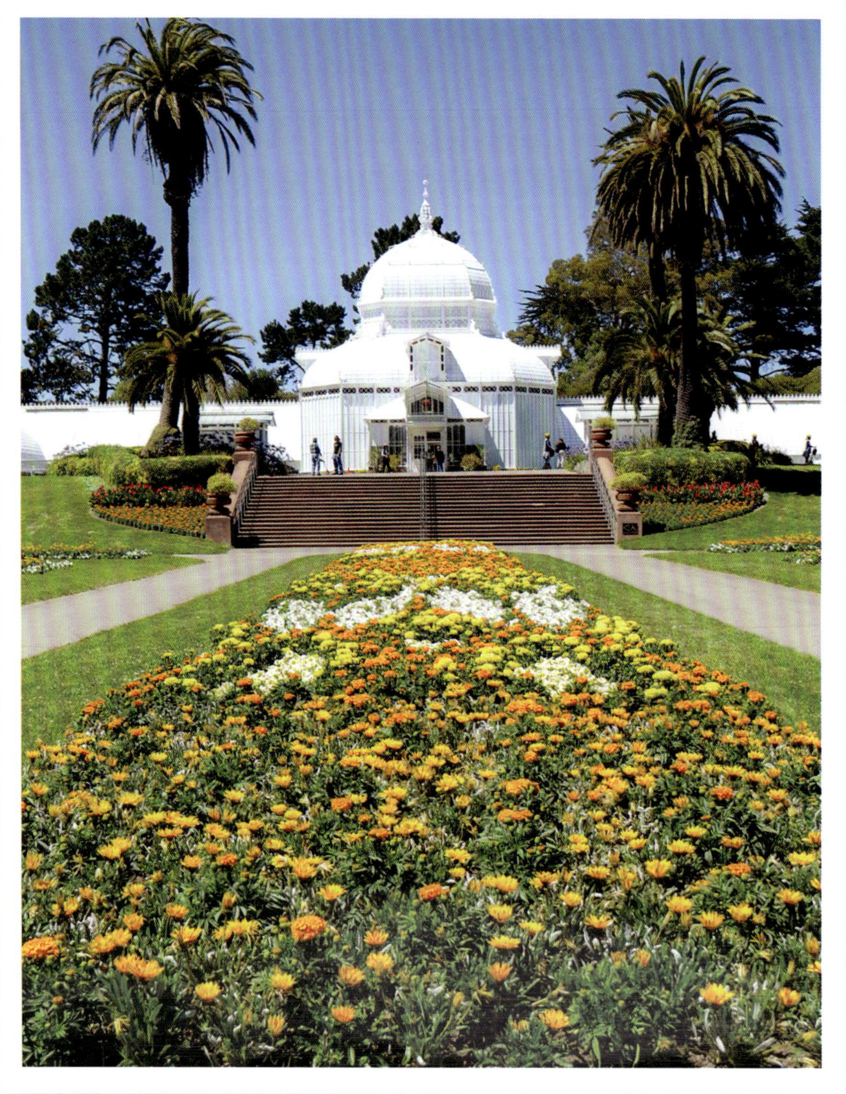

The Conservatory of Flowers dates to 1879, not long after the park's opening.

For eating options, there's a café at the Blue Heron Lake Boathouse toward the center of the park, and the Beach Chalet Brewery and Restaurant on its western edge.

Points of Interest

McLaren Lodge

Kezar Stadium

Conservatory of Flowers

National AIDS Memorial Grove

Shakespeare Garden

M. H. de Young Memorial Museum

California Academy of Sciences

San Francisco Botanical Garden

Japanese Tea Garden

Strawberry Hill

Queen Wilhelmina Garden

Bison Paddock

Windmills

Beach Chalet

Pacific Ocean

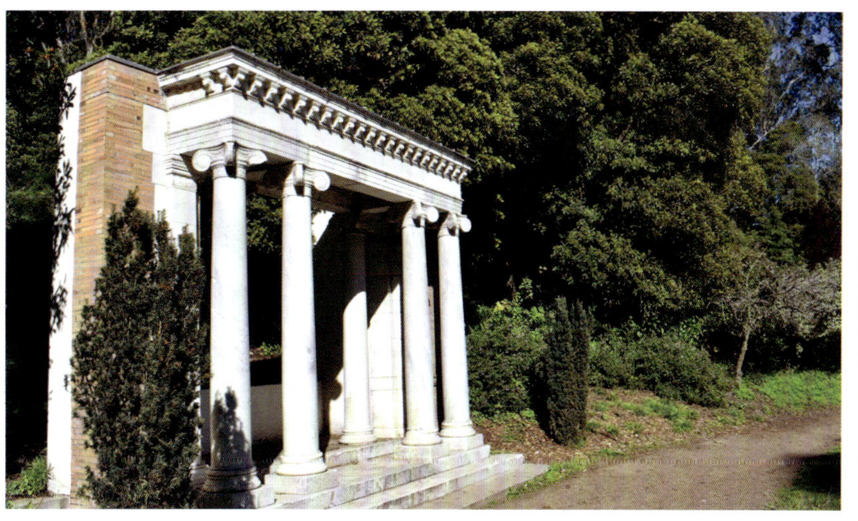

The Portals of the Past are a memorial to the 1906 San Francisco Earthquake. They're the remains of a Nob Hill Mansion—after the earthquake, the entranceway to the mansion remained upright.

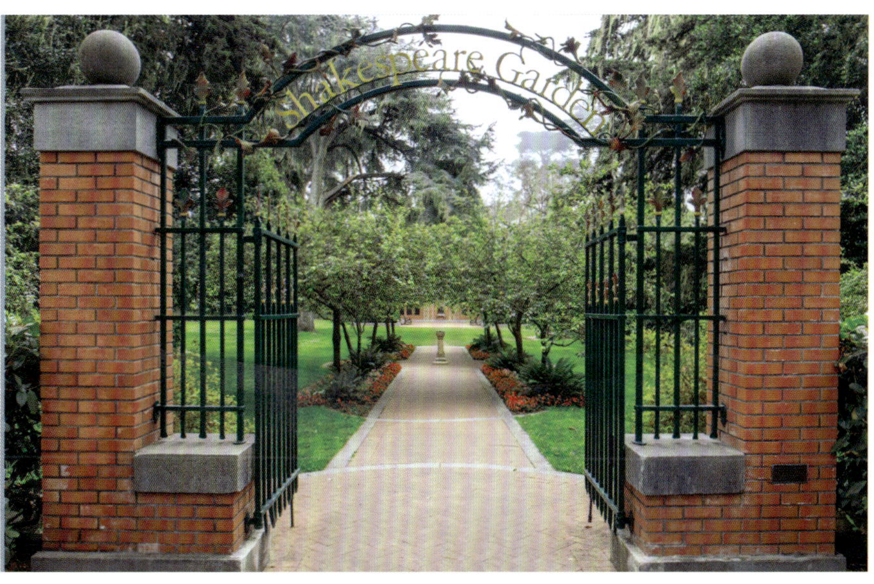

The Shakespeare Garden is a popular destination for weddings.

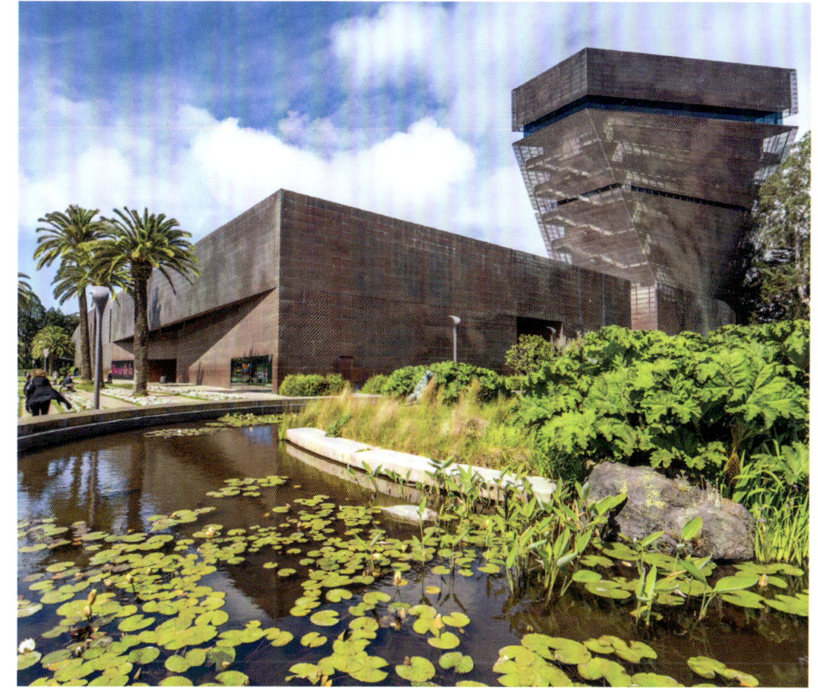

While the de Young Museum was first begun in 1895, its current building dates to 2005. The Hamon Observation Tower provides a way to see the park from above.

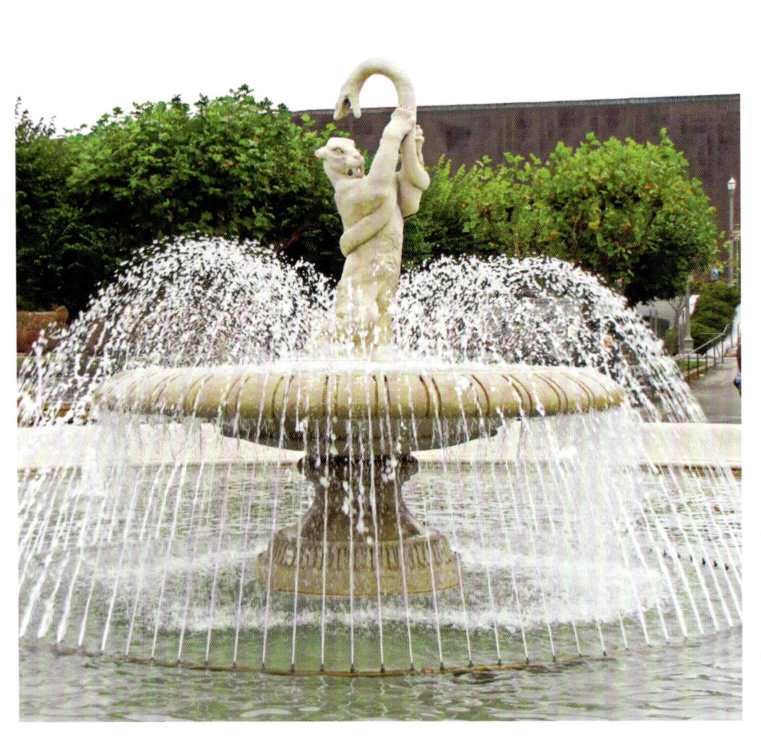

The Rideout Fountain was erected in 1924.

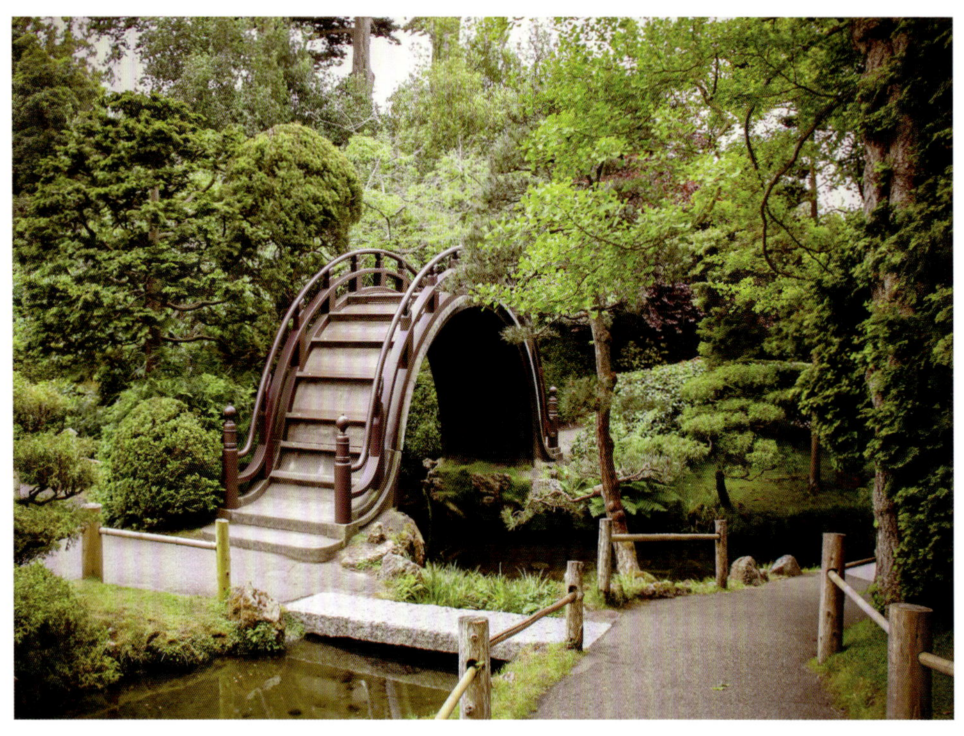

The Japanese Tea Garden was originally created for an 1894 exposition.

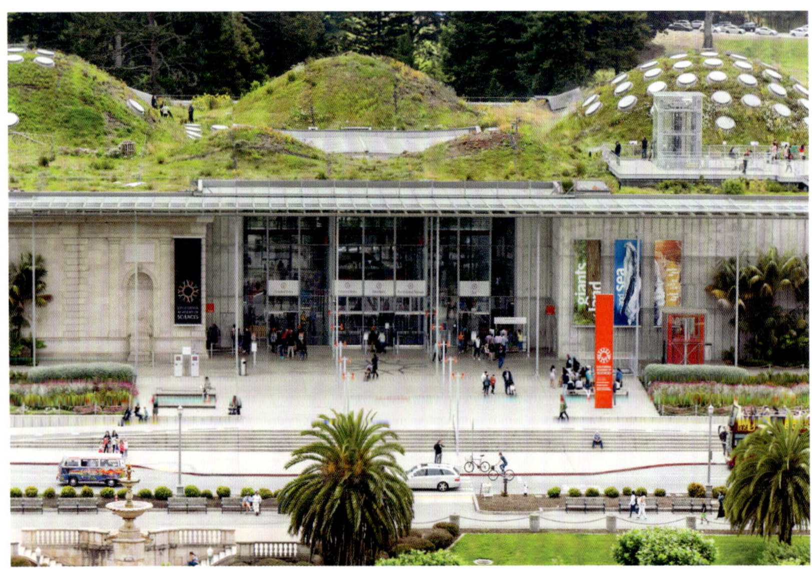

Along with being a museum, the California Academy of Sciences acts as a research institute. Its current building was constructed in 2008.

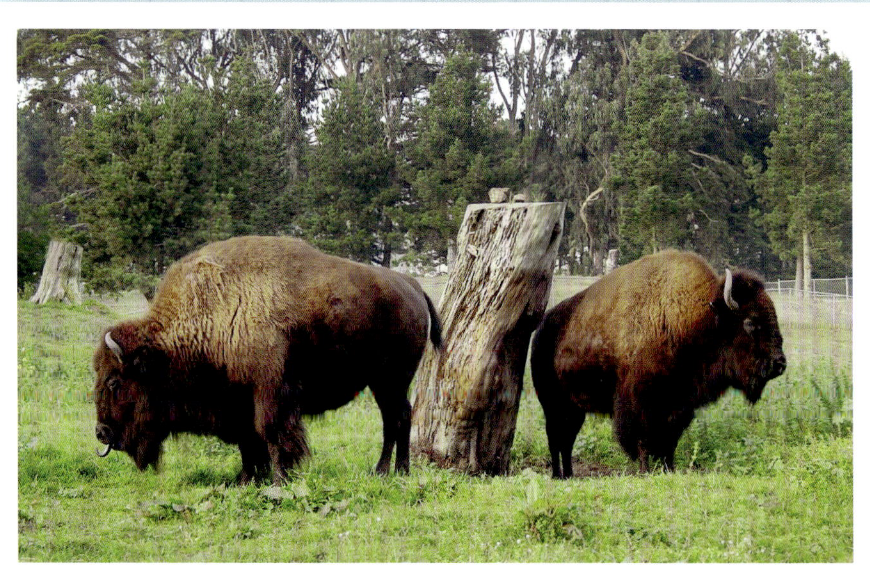

There's been a herd of bison in the park since 1891. The Bison Paddock is found in the park's western side.

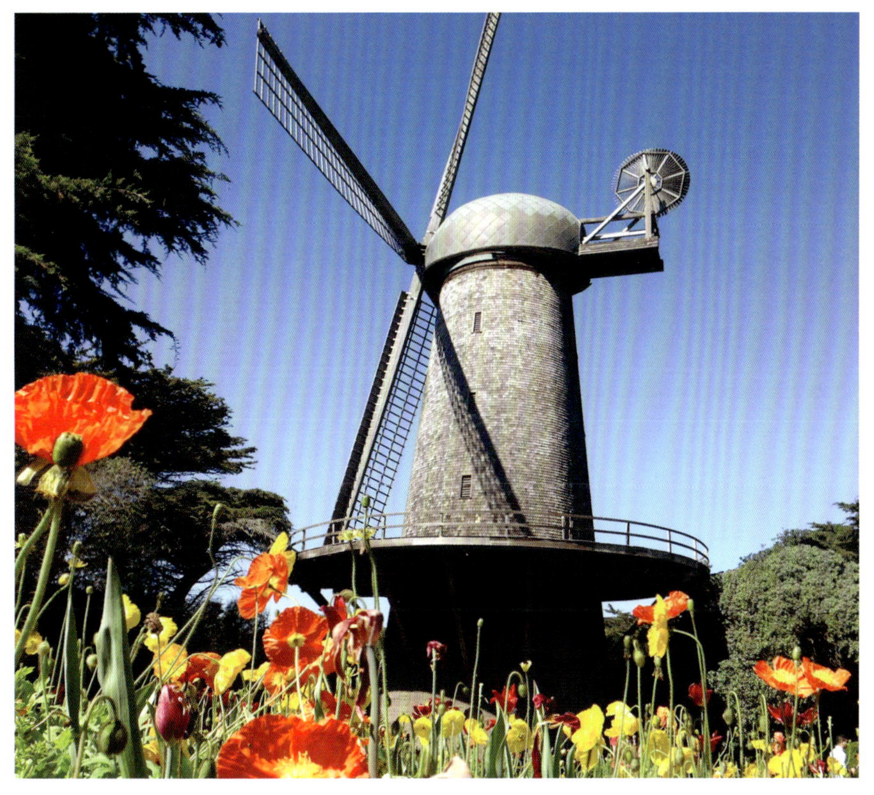

In the western part of the park, spot two wooden windmills that were originally built in the 1900s.

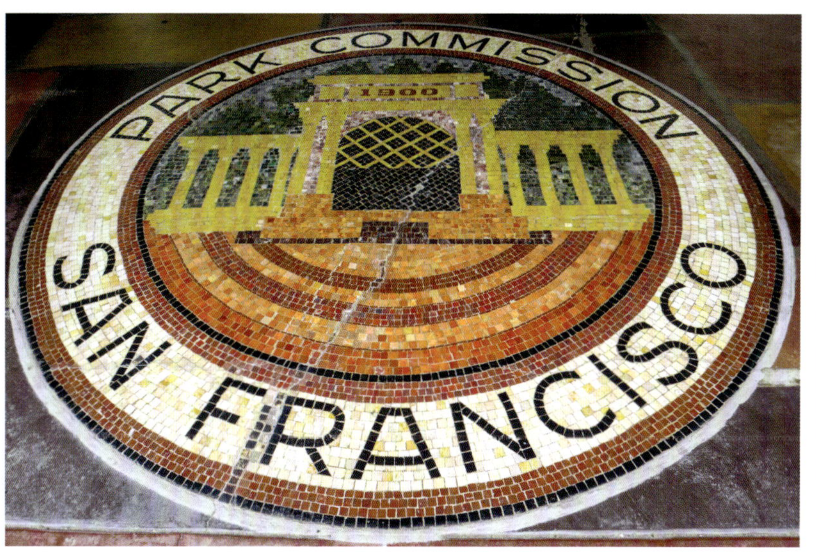

The Beach Chalet restaurant is located in a historic 1925 building. Murals were added as part of a WPA project in the 1930s.

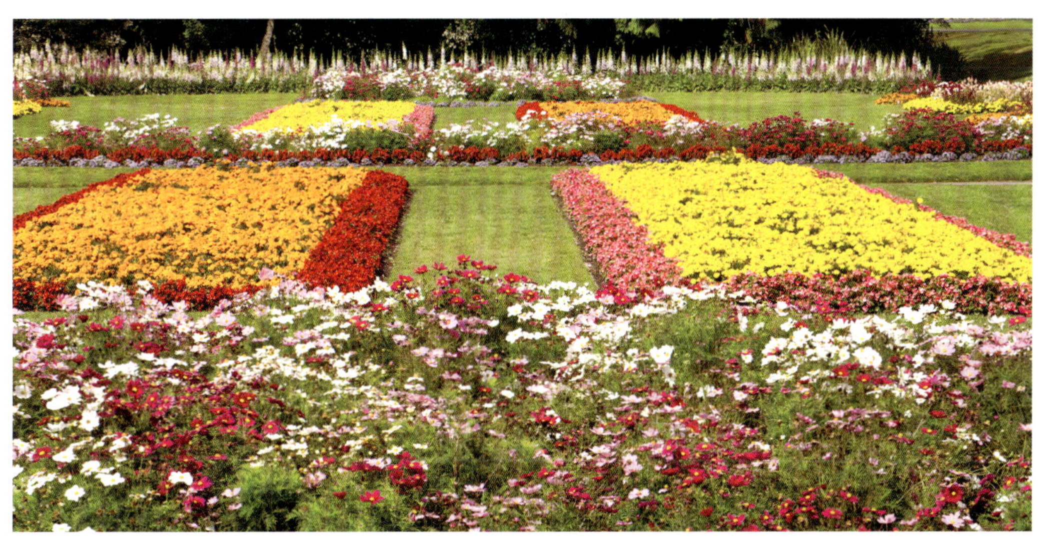

The San Francisco Botanical Garden features plants from various climates around the world.

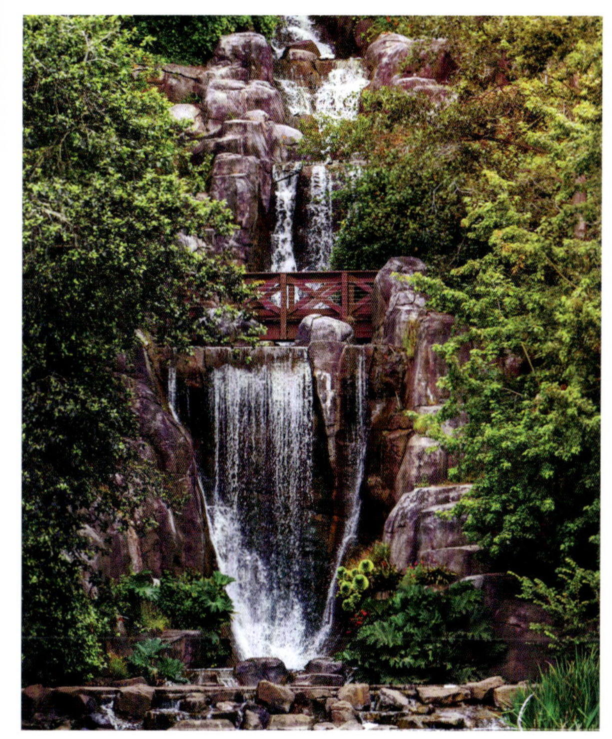

Strawberry Hill, an island found in one of the park's lakes, has a small waterfall.

Griffith Park

Location: Los Angeles, California

Length: Variable

Visitor Center to Griffith Park Observatory: About 3.5 miles

Visitor Center to Griffith Park and Southern Railroad: About 1.1 miles

Visitor Center to Los Angeles Zoo: About 2 miles

Visitor Center to Autry Museum: About 2 miles

Griffith Observatory to Bronson Caves: About 3 miles

Griffith Park covers an area of more than 4,310 acres—more than 6.5 square miles. Along with the attractions listed here, the park features extensive trails, including some fairly strenuous ones in the Santa Monica Mountain Range. The famous Hollywood Sign is located on Mount Lee in Griffith Park. While the Hollywood Sign itself is fenced in, the park offers several trails that can give you good viewpoints of it. Trails that get you close to the back side of the Hollywood Sign exist, but access is sometimes shut down or discouraged since it takes hikers through residential areas.

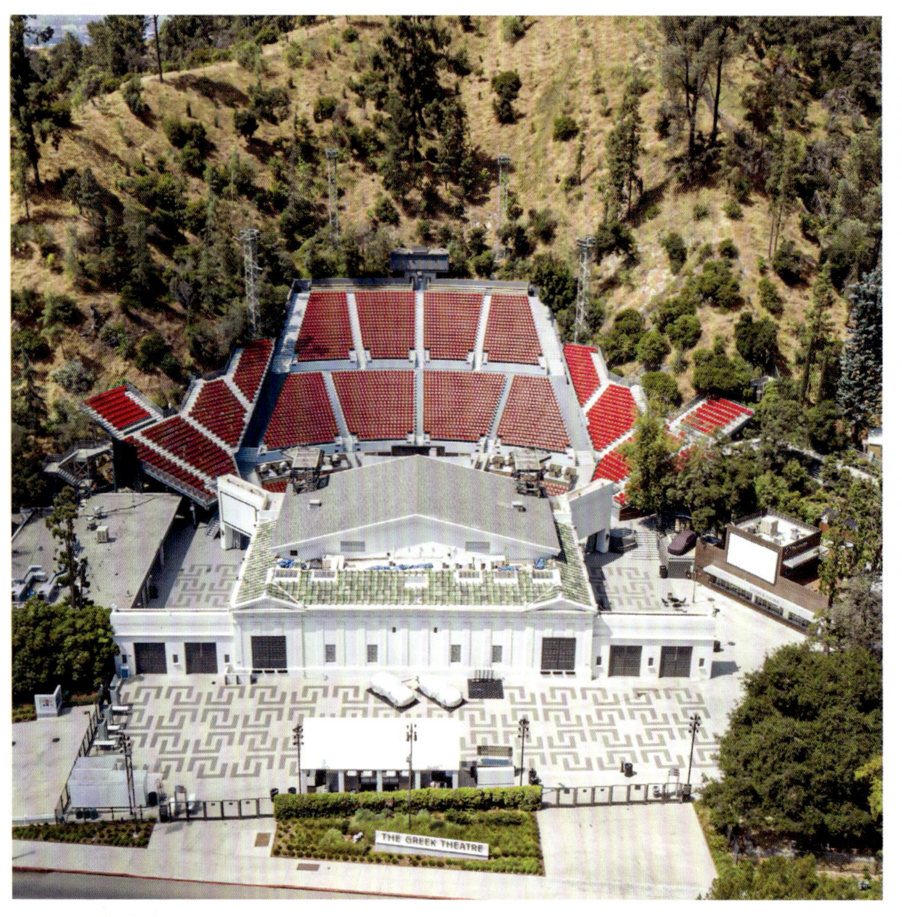

The Greek Theatre was built between 1928 and 1930, and has hosted a number of famous musicians.

You probably won't be able to visit all the park's attractions in one walking day, but you might want to visit two or three and hike between them to get good views of the park. One popular attraction is the Griffith Observatory, built as a WPA project between 1933 and 1935. The observatory offers good views of the Hollywood Sign, as well as exhibits on astronomy and a Tesla coil.

For families, the Los Angeles Zoo and Botanical Gardens are found at Griffith Park, and there's also Travel Town, a railway museum, and the Griffith Park Southern Railroad train ride that takes riders through a mile of the park. For adults or slightly older kids, the Autry Museum of the American West features a collection of more than 500,000 artifacts, including Native American artwork.

Along with the Hollywood Sign, movie buffs will probably appreciate the Bronson Caves, which have been the filming location for many movies and TV shows.

Points of Interest

Los Angeles Zoo

Griffith Observatory

Autry Museum of the American West

Southern Railroad

Hollywood Sign

Bronson Caves

Travel Town

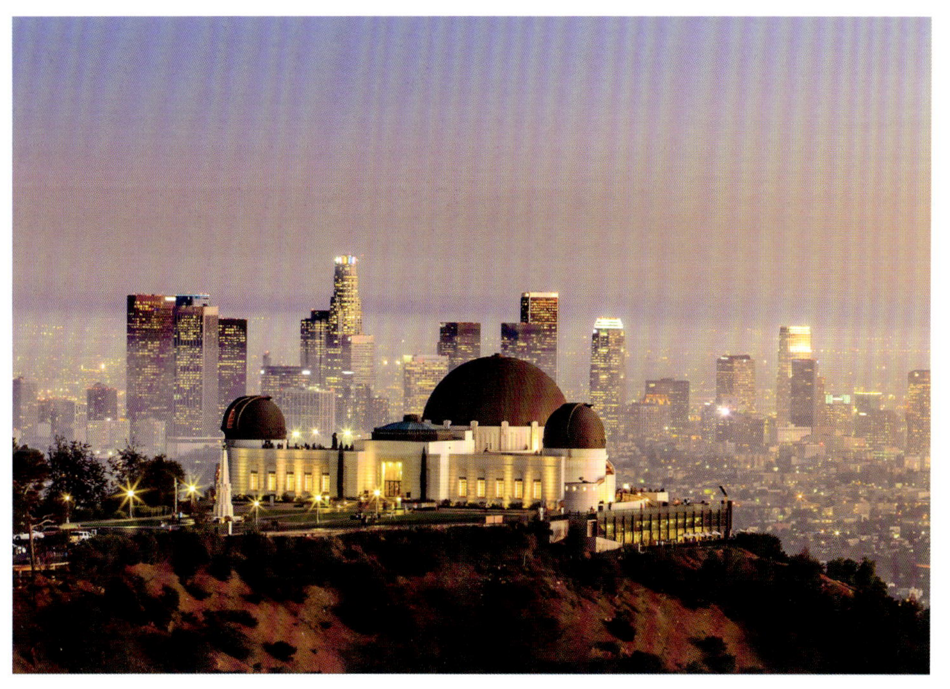

The Griffith Observatory has featured in many movies, including the 1955 James Dean film *Rebel Without a Cause*, and more recently, 2016's *La La Land*.

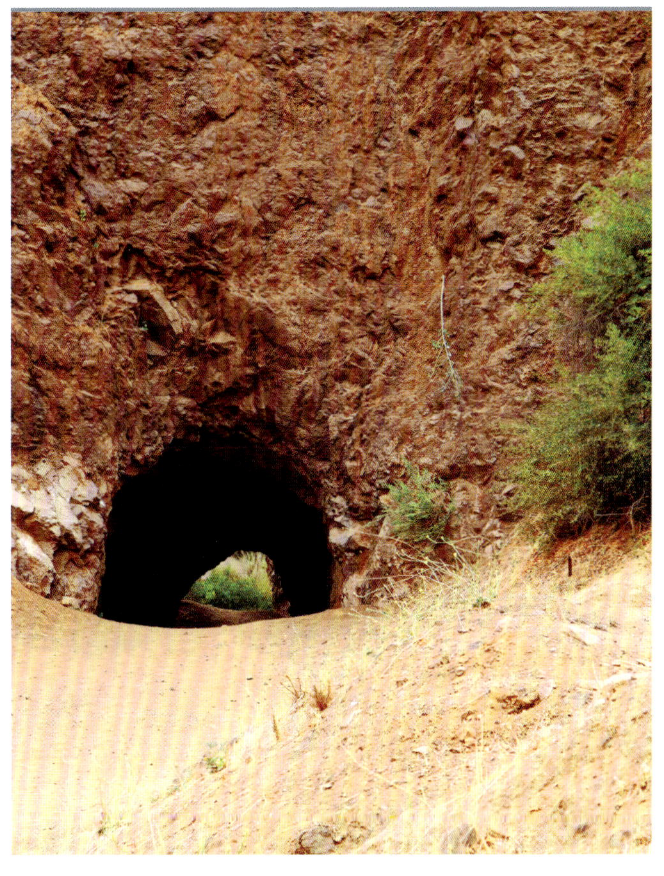

It's the entrance to the Batcave! The 1960s *Batman* television show used Bronson Caves as a filming location.

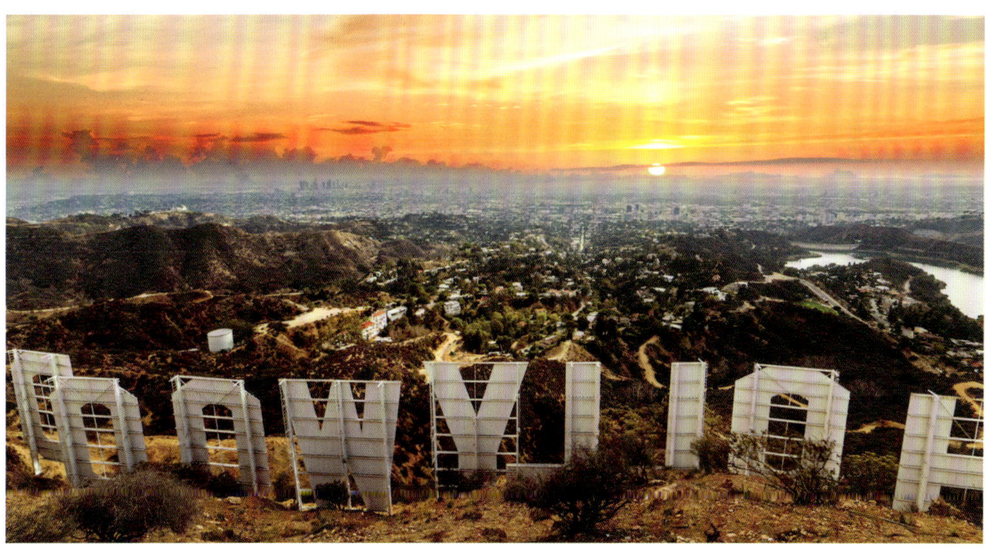

The Hollywood Sign, seen here from Griffith Park, was originally erected in 1923.

A Taste of LA

Location: Los Angeles, California
Length: 2.7-mile loop
Start and end point: Los Angeles City Hall

This walk in downtown Los Angeles takes you counterclockwise in a rough oval and features a mix of both historic and very modern architecture. Start at Los Angeles City Hall, an Art Deco building from the 1920s found on Spring Street; its observation deck is open to the public if you'd like to start your walk with a bird's-eye view of the neighborhood. Across the street from City Hall, wander through the Gloria Molina Grand Park to see its fountains, until you reach the end of the park at Grand Avenue.

On Grand Avenue, you'll see the Walt Disney Concert Hall, designed by Frank Gehry; The Broad, a contemporary art museum housed in a 2015 building designed by Diller Scofidio + Renfro; and the Museum of Contemporary Art, Los Angeles.

Moving east, swing over to the Angels Flight Railway, a very short funicular railway originally built in 1901. Continuing east, you'll see a cluster of locations on Broadway: the Grand Central Market, where people have been able to pick up food and snacks since 1917; the Million Dollar Theater, which also dates to 1917; and the 1893 Bradbury Building, notable for its inside atrium.

From there, moving further east to Central Avenue takes you to the Japanese American National Museum, where you can see history exhibits and artifacts; the Museum of Contemporary Art also has a satellite location, the Geffen Contemporary, nearby.

Take First Street as you head back towards City Hall. You'll see a number of city and county buildings, as well as the former Los Angeles Times building from 1935, before finishing the loop back at City Hall.

Points of Interest

- Los Angeles City Hall
- Gloria Molina Grand Park
- Walt Disney Concert Hall
- The Broad
- Museum of Contemporary Art
- Angels Flight Railway
- Grand Central Market
- Bradbury Building
- Japanese American National Museum
- The Geffen Contemporary at MOCA
- Los Angeles Times Building

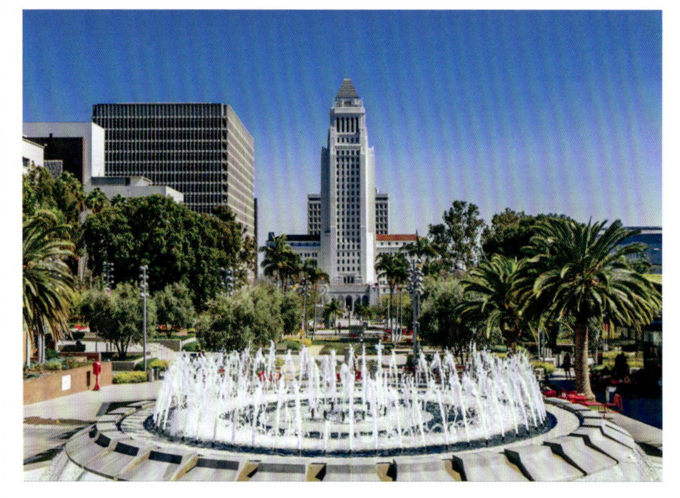

Los Angeles City Hall is seen here from Gloria Molina Grand Park. The park was designed in 2012 as part of a larger revitalization project in the area.

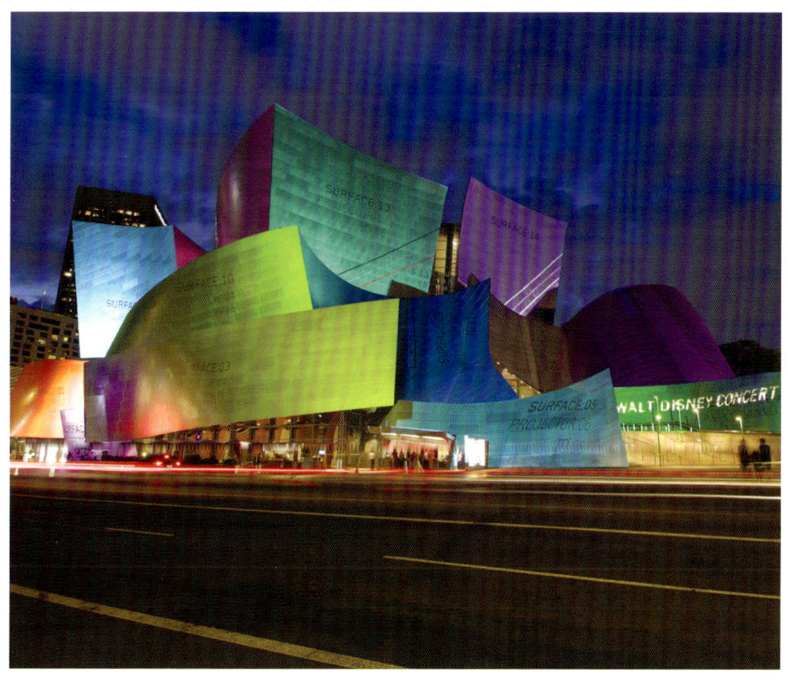

The Walt Disney Concert Hall, the home of the Los Angeles Philharmonic Orchestra, was designed by Frank Gehry and opened in 2003.

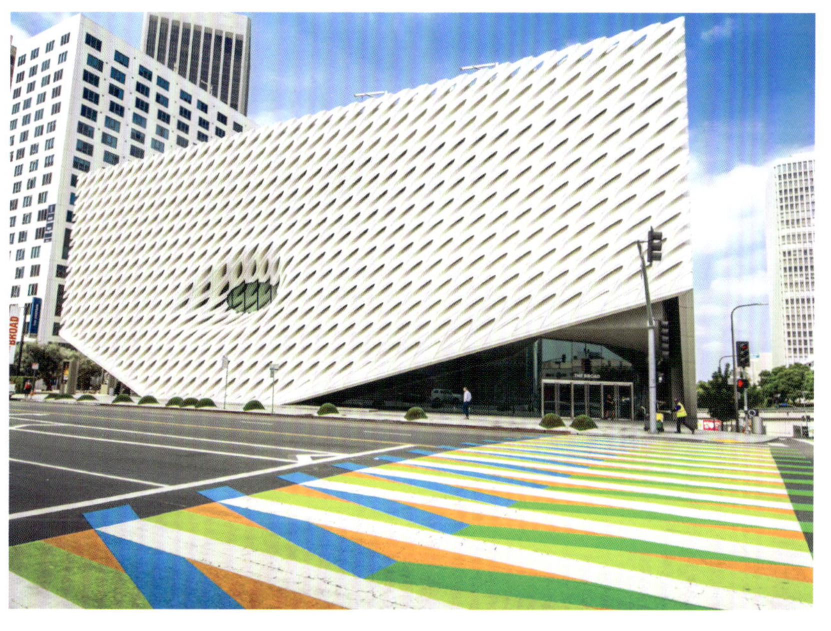

Many of The Broad's exhibitions are free, so it's easy to pop in for a short visit.

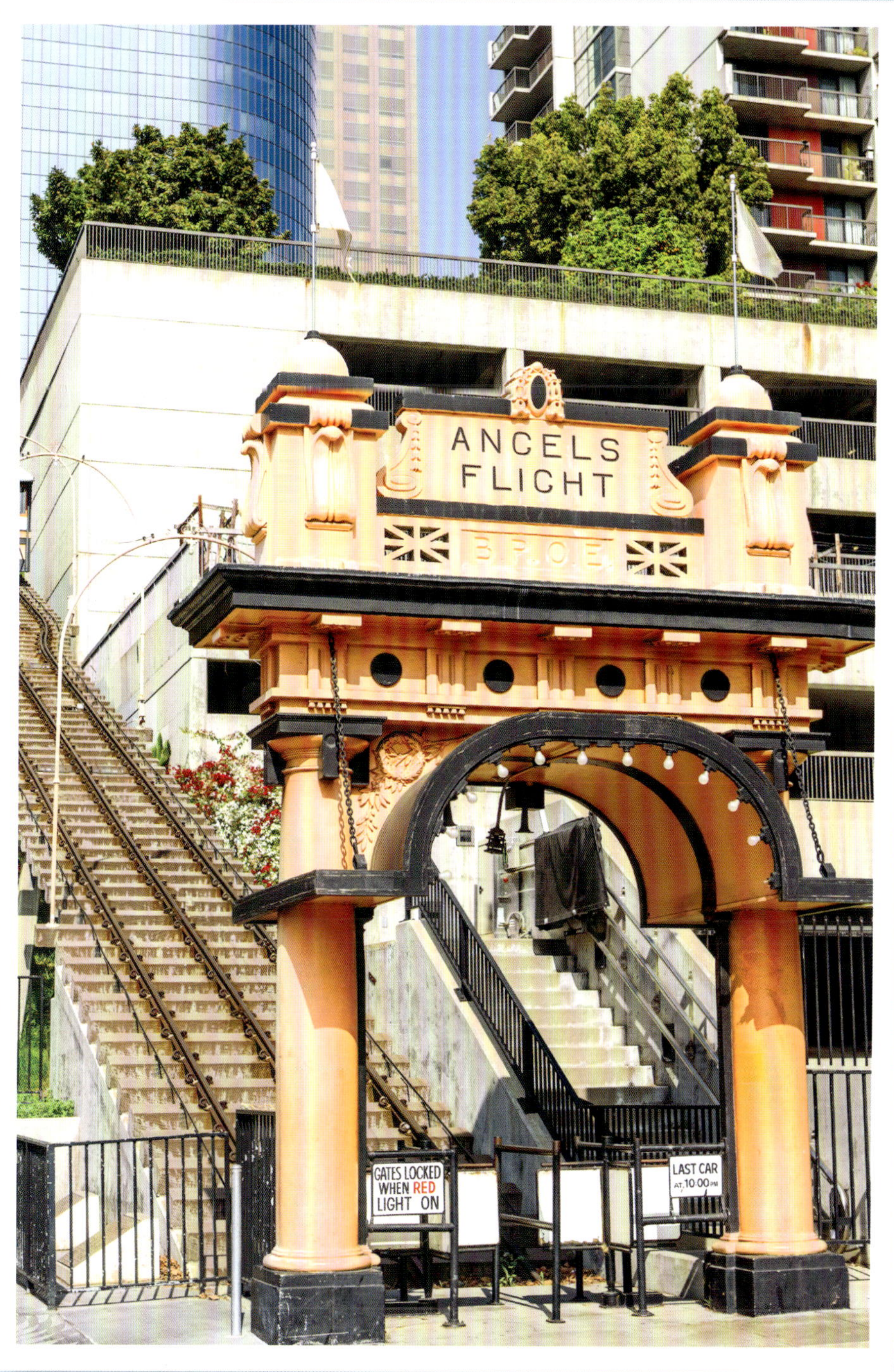

Angels Flight bills itself as "the world's shortest railway." Its stations are found on One California Plaza on Grand Avenue and Hill Street near the Grand Central Market.

El Prado Complex at Balboa Park

Location: San Diego, California
Length: Balboa Park is 1,200 acres; suggested itinerary is about 1.5 miles
Start point: Cabrillo Bridge
End point: San Diego Natural History Museum

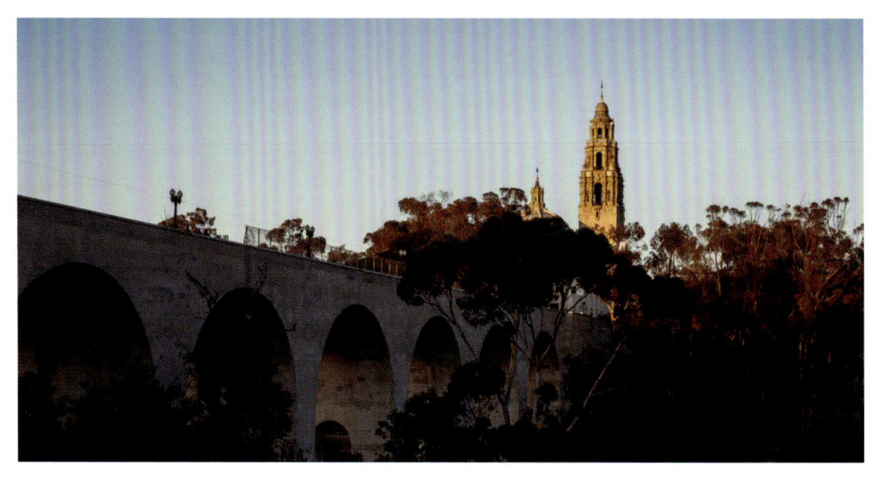

The Cabrillo Bridge was built between 1912 and 1914. Renovations for safety and stability took place in 2014.

San Diego's Balboa Park, established in the 1860s, covers 1,200 acres and contains the famed San Diego Zoo, many museums, various gardens, trails, a golf course and disc golf course, dog parks, a swimming pool, ballparks, and more.

In short, there's no lack of things to do in Balboa Park—the challenge is narrowing down your choices! In this walk, we focus on the buildings and structures of the El Prado Complex, a set of historic buildings primarily designed in the Spanish Colonial Revival style. Most were created in 1915–1916 when Balboa Park hosted the Panama-California Exposition or are replicas of temporary buildings created for those events; some were later reused in 1935–1936 when Balboa Park hosted the California International Exposition.

The western edge of the park is bordered by Sixth Avenue running north-south. The east-west Laurel Street becomes El Prado as you enter the park. Walking along, you'll cross the Cabrillo Canyon and Cabrillo Parkway on the 1914 Cabrillo Bridge before reaching a cluster of historic buildings created for the Panama-California Exposition. The California Quadrangle includes the California Building, the California Tower, Evernham Hall, and the St. Francis Chapel. Today, those buildings host the Museum of Us, an anthropology museum.

Moving east, walkers can amble through the Alcazar Garden before heading to the Spreckels Organ Pavilion, an open-air pavilion. (At this point, for a longer walk, head down Pan-American Road to see a set of small buildings created in the 1930s as "International Cottages". If you walk down far enough, you'll pass the Comic-Con Museum and the San Diego Automotive Museum to reach the San Diego Air & Space Museum, housed in a historic building from the 1935–1936 Exposition.)

Returning to El Prado from the Spreckels Organ Pavilion, you'll see the Plaza de Panama, bordered by the reconstructed House of Charm, now home to the Mingei International Museum; the reconstructed House of Hospitality that appropriately houses Balboa Park's Visitors Center; and the San Diego Museum of Art, built in 1926.

Moving further east, you'll see the Botanical Building and its Lily Pond, along with two buildings that are also reconstructions of former exposition buildings: the Casa del Prado and the Casa de Balboa that now houses the San Diego Model Railroad Museum. A bit north and east, the San Diego Natural History Museum was a later addition to Balboa Park, dating to 1933. For a longer walk, proceed north to discover the Spanish Village Art Center, full of shops and galleries, in buildings created for the 1935–1936 Exposition.

Points of Interest

- Cabrillo Bridge
- Plaza de California
- Alcazar Garden
- Spreckels Organ Pavilion
- Plaza de Panama
- House of Charm *(Mingei International Museum)*
- House of Hospitality
- San Diego Museum of Art
- Botanical Building
- Casa del Prado
- Casa de Balboa
- San Diego Natural History Museum

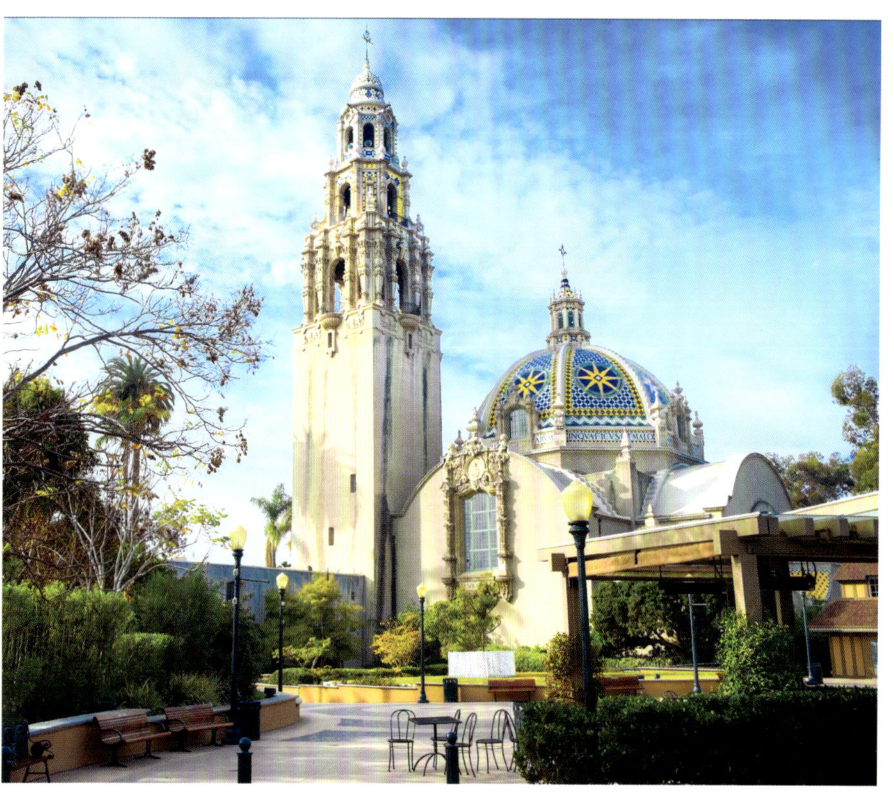

The California Building and Tower. The Tower includes a carillon that can play songs.

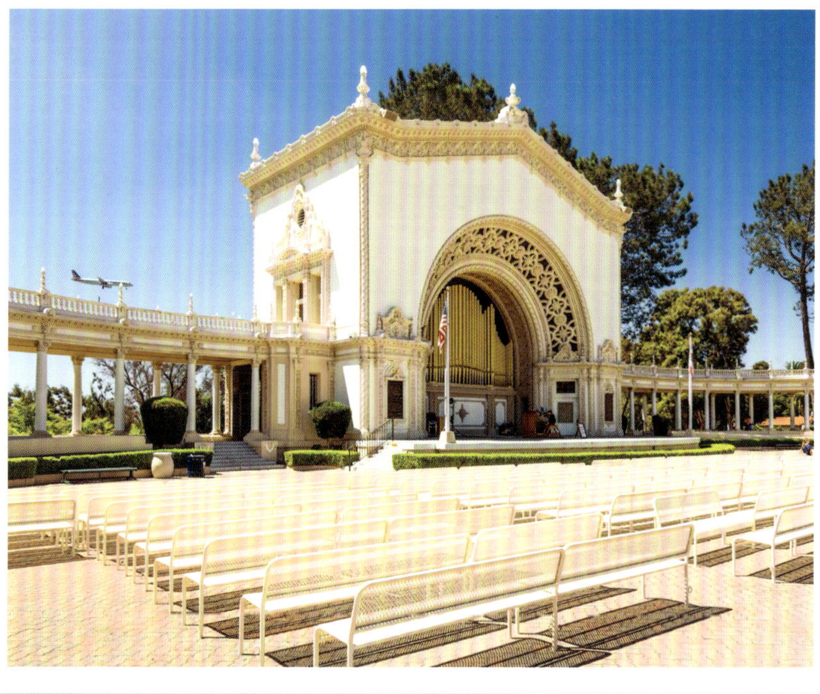

After a period of disrepair, Spreckels Organ Pavilion and its large pipe organ were restored during the 1980s.

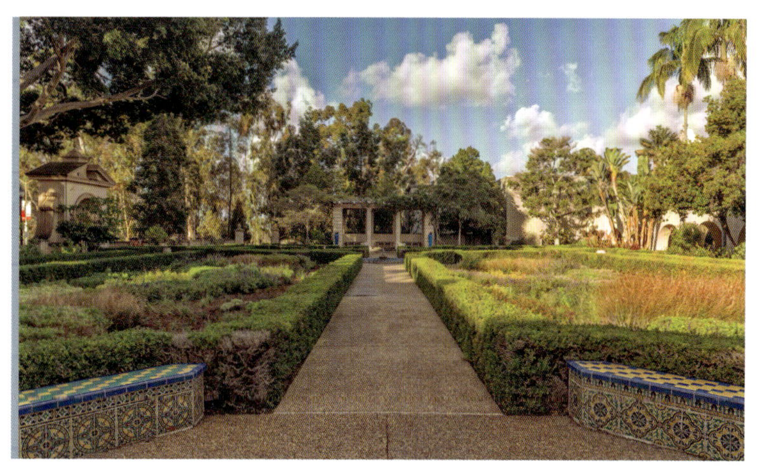

The Alcazar Garden was inspired by the gardens of Seville's Alcazar Castle.

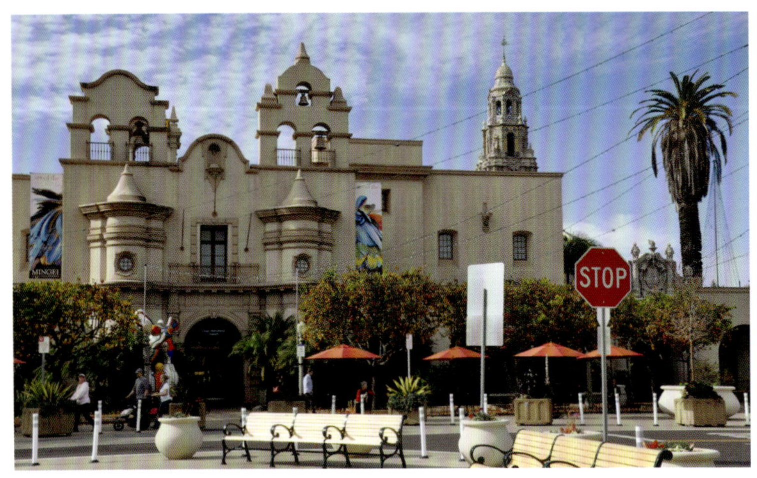

The House of Charm served several uses during the two Expositions, but wasn't intended as a permanent structure. The rebuilt House of Charm opened in 1996 and now hosts the Mingei International Museum that displays folk art.

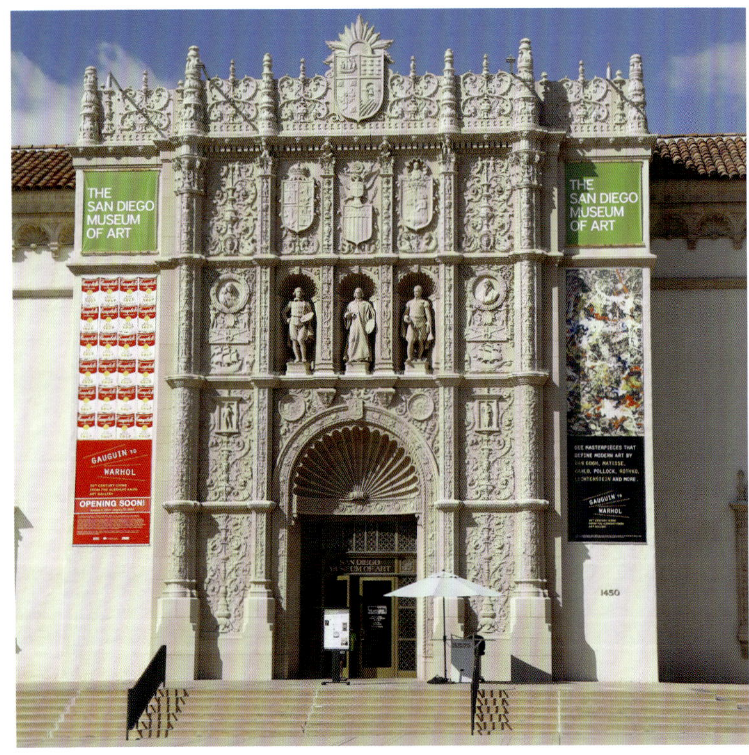

The San Diego Museum of Art, built in 1926 on the site of a temporary structure that had been torn down, was meant to mimic the style of the 1915–1916 buildings.

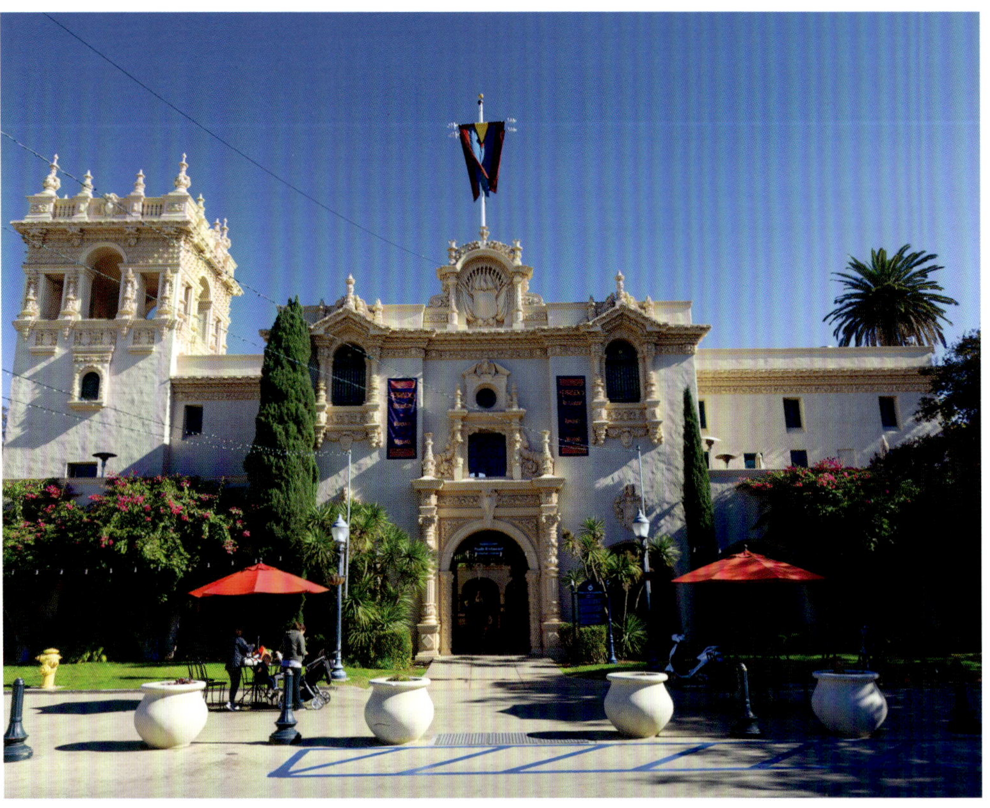

Most Visitors Centers aren't as fancy as the House of Hospitality, a reconstructed building based on the Foreign Arts building from the 1915 Exposition.

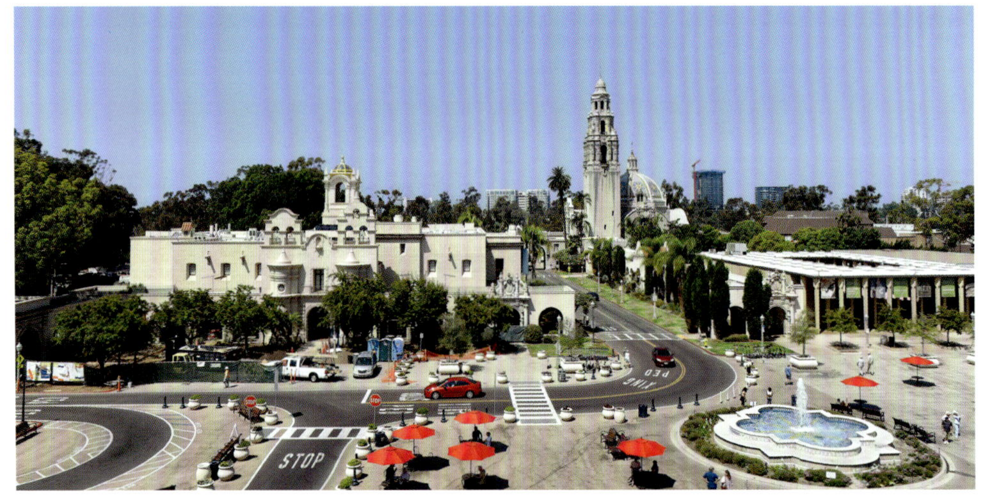

The Plaza de Panama, with the Mingei International Museum in the center and the California Quadrangle in the background

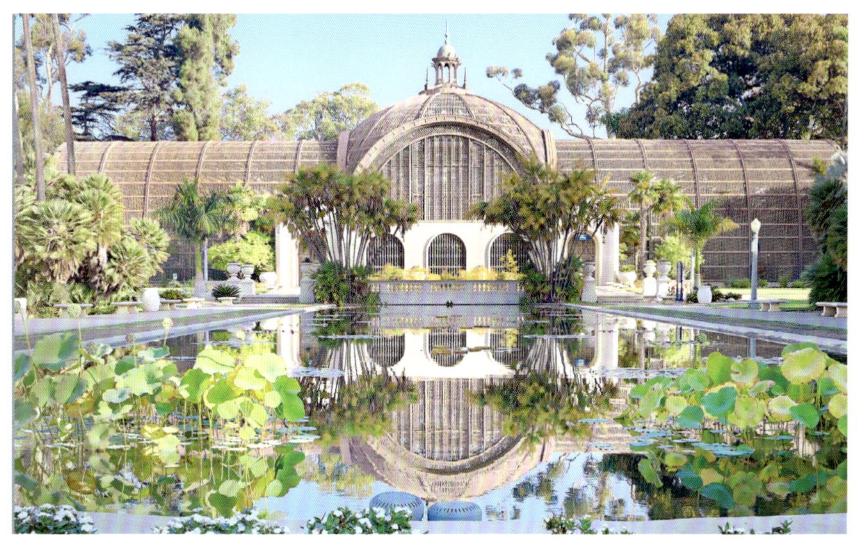

The Botanical Building is home to more than 2,000 plants. As of November 2024, this facility is closed for renovations.

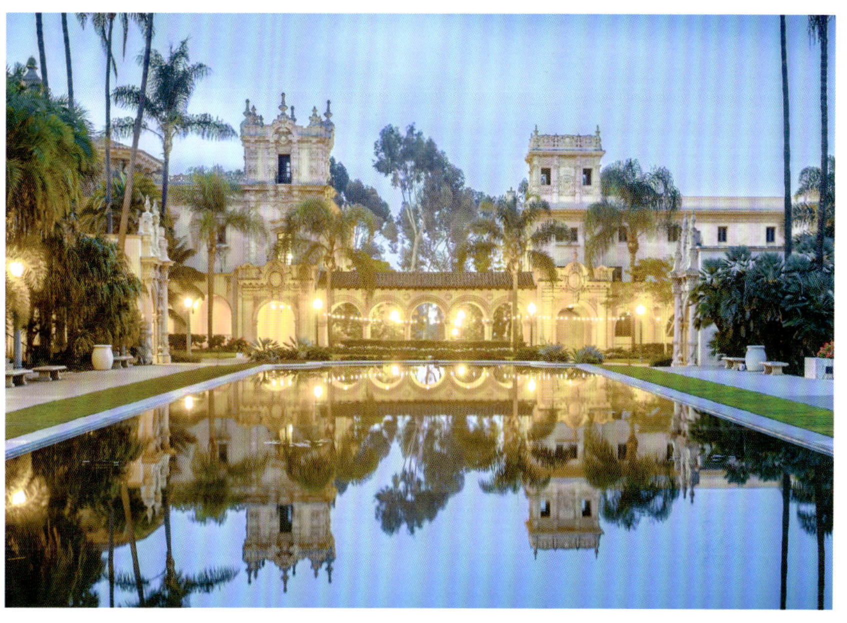

The Casa de Balboa is a reconstruction of an earlier building.

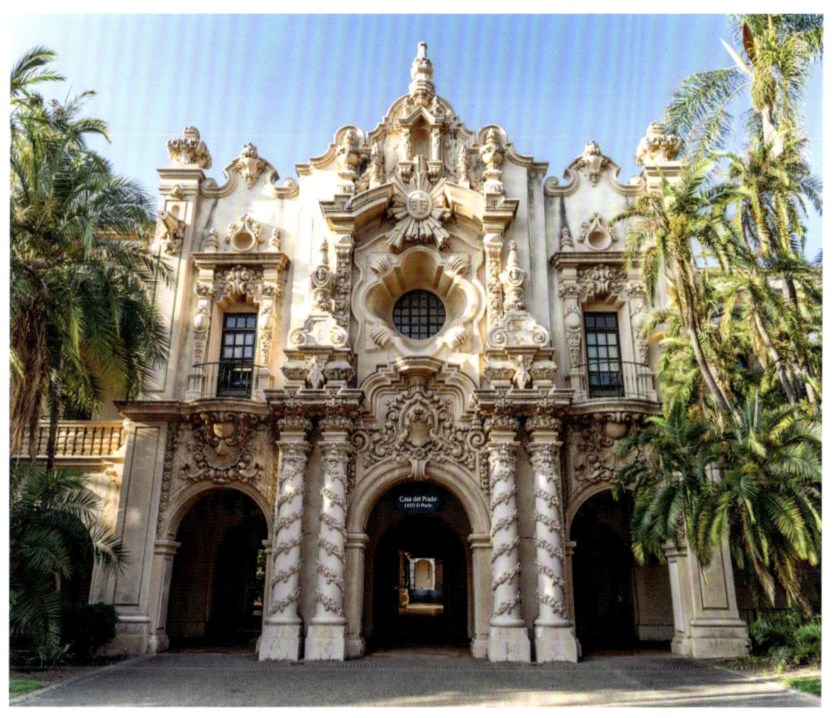

The Casa del Prado is home to a number of youth organizations like the San Diego Youth Symphony and the San Diego Junior Theatre.

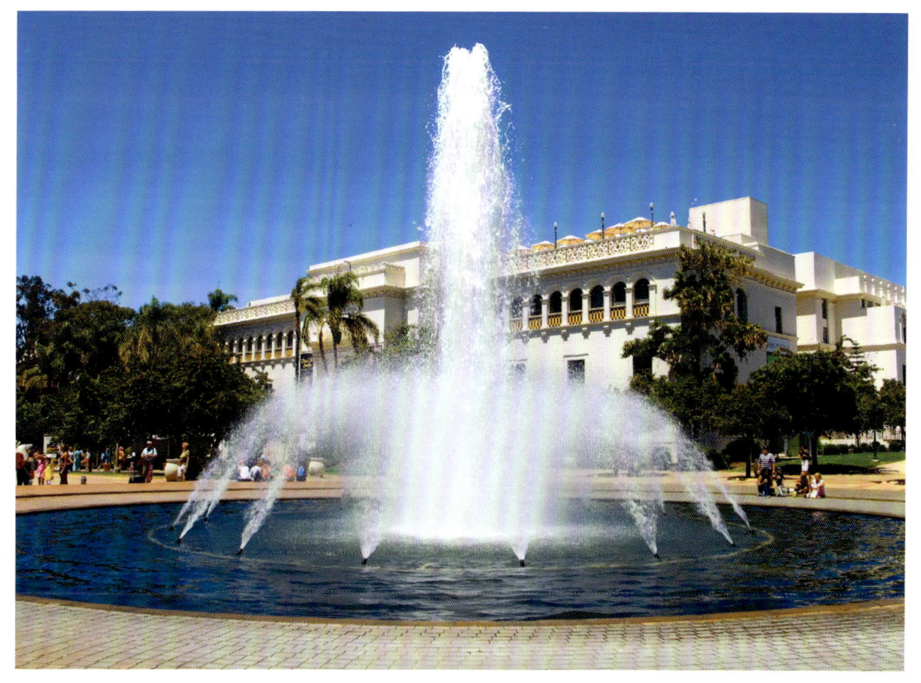

San Diego's Natural History Museum was built in 1933, but expanded in 2001 to a larger and more modern facility.

Around the State Capitol

Location: Honolulu, Hawaii
Length: About 1.8 miles
Start point: Washington Place
End point: Sky Gate

The buildings clustered around Hawaii's State Capitol building are a reminder of the state's history, from the time it was an independent kingdom, to the overthrow of the monarchy, to its days as a republic, to its transition to a United States territory, to its eventual statehood in 1959. Many of the sites on this walk are considered part of the Hawaii Capital Historic District.

Begin this walk at Washington Place. This 1846 building was the home of Queen Lili'uokalani before her monarchy; later, in 1893, the final queen of Hawaii was arrested there. She lived at Washington Place under house arrest until her 1917 death. The building then served for a time as the governor's mansion, but has become a museum.

Across the street, you'll find the Hawaii State Capitol building, which dates to 1969. The state house grounds include several monuments, such as the 1944 Eternal Flame Memorial that commemorates Pearl Harbor and Hawaiian service members. From the current State Capitol building, go to 'Iolani Palace and the nearby barracks; the palace was built on the site of an earlier palace and was the royal residence before the overthrow of the monarchy. It later became the capitol building of the short-lived republic and then the territorial and state capitol.

Across King Street from the palace, Ali'iolani Hale was built in the 1870s at the instigation of King Kamehameha V. Today it serves as the home for Hawaii's State Supreme Court. In front of the building, visitors will see a statue of Kamehameha I, who formed the Kingdom of Hawaii. Nearby, the Kapuaiwa Building, which dates to 1884, and the

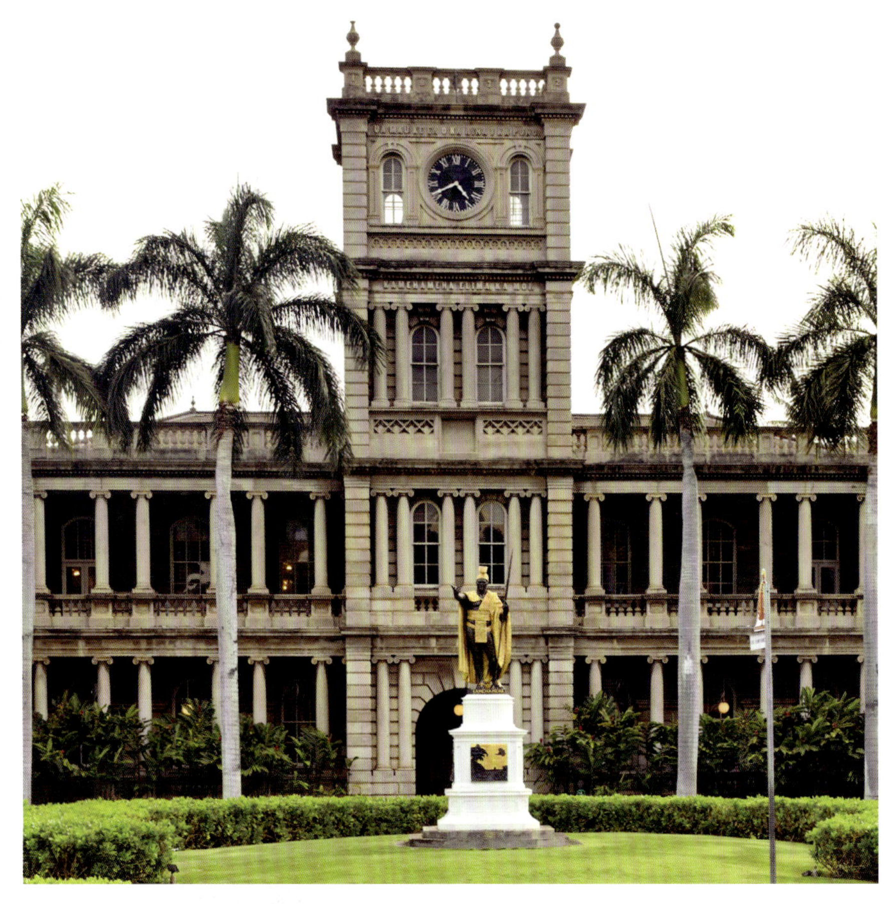

The King Kamehameha statue in front of Ali'iolani Hale

King Kalakaua Building, are both government buildings that form part of the Hawaii Capital Historic District.

Close by, the Kawaiaha'o Church is notable both for its architecture—the building is made of coral—and its history, as it was once frequented by the royal family. From there, walkers can go along King Street past the Honolulu City Hall building to see Isamu Noguchi's sculpture, *Sky Gate*, an outdoor sculpture from 1977.

Points of Interest

Washington Place

Eternal Flame Memorial

Hawaii State Capitol

ʻIolani Palace

ʻIolani Barracks

King Kamehameha Statue

Aliʻiolani Hale

Kawaiahaʻo Church

Sky Gate

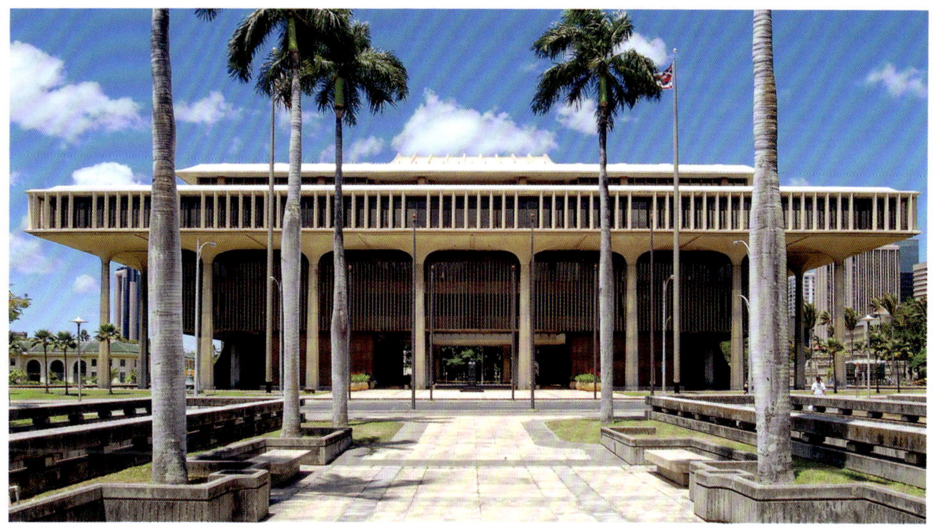

The Hawaiian State Capitol was designed to use Hawaiian motifs, with a reflecting pool meant to symbolize the ocean and sets of eight columns to symbolize the islands of Hawaii.

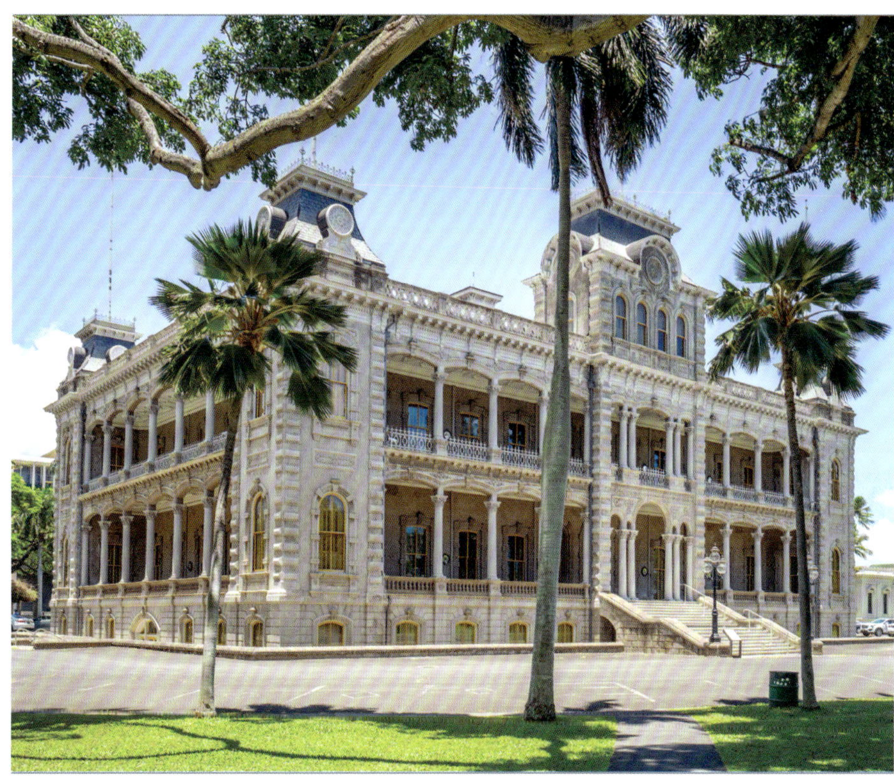

As far back as 1845, members of the Kamehameha Dynasty used buildings on the site where ʻIolani Palace currently stands as a royal residence. The current building was constructed between 1879 and 1882.

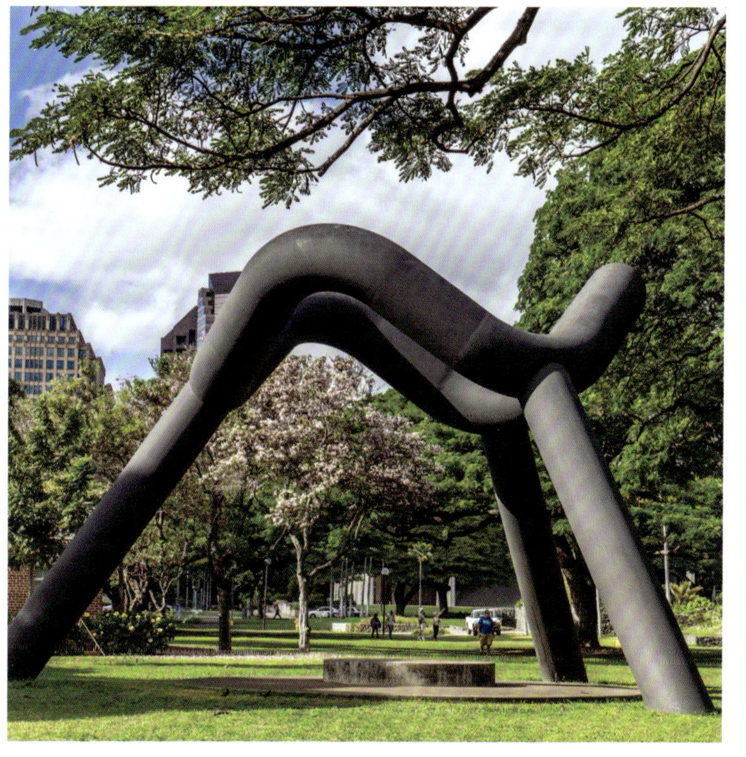

Isamu Noguchi's scultpure *Sky Gate*

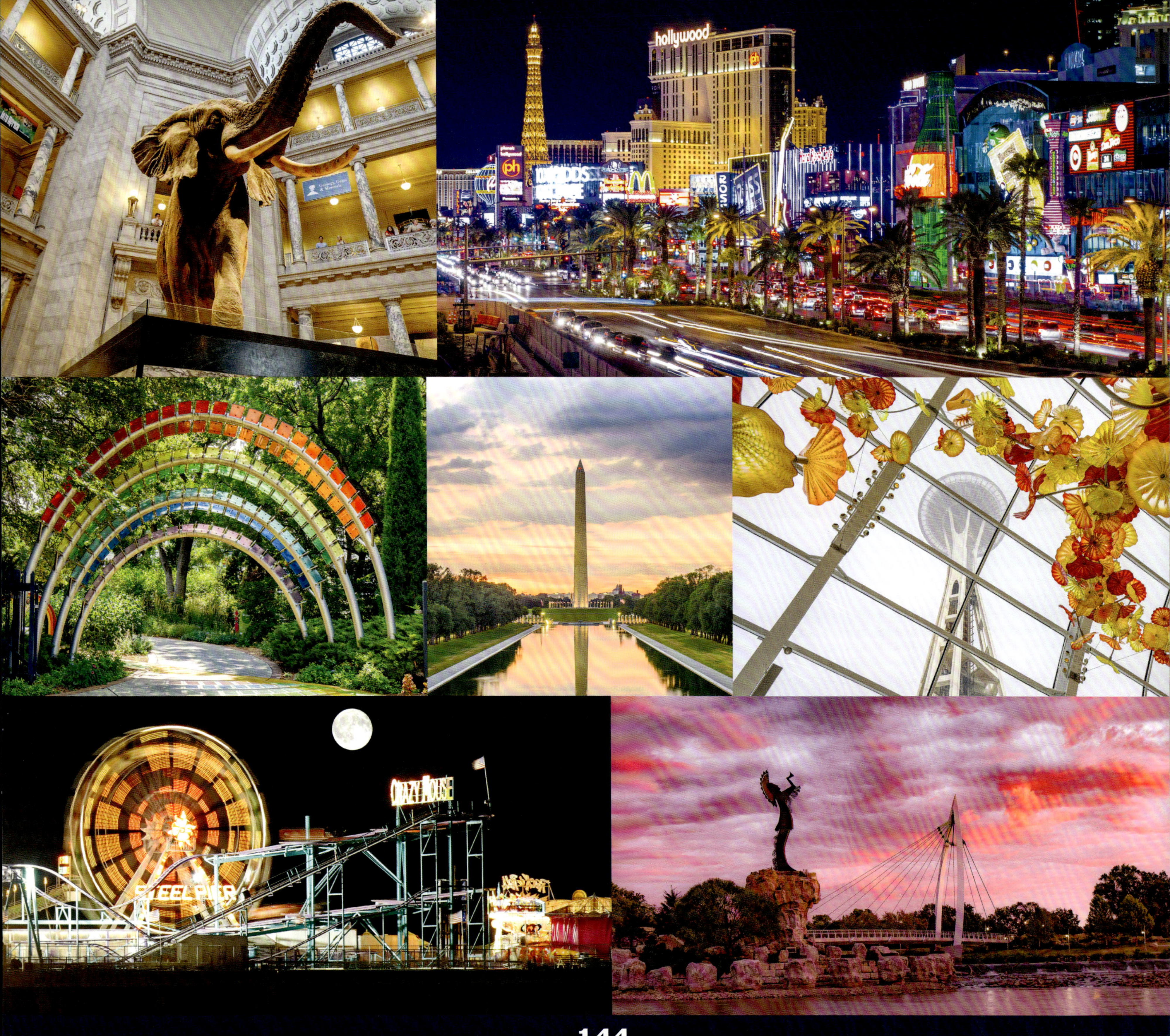
hollywood
CRAZY HOUSE
STEEL PIER